Prelude

to

Bonanza

THE DISCOVERY
AND
EXPLORATION
OF THE
YUKON

ALLEN A. WRIGHT

1976

 GRAY'S PUBLISHING LTD., SIDNEY, BRITISH COLUMBIA, CANADA

Canadian Cataloguing in Publication Data

Wright, Allen A., 1916-
    Prelude to bonanza

    Includes bibliography and index.
    ISBN 0-88826-062-8

    1. Yukon Territory — Discovery and
exploration.   2. Yukon Territory — History.
I. Title.
FC4021.W75   971.9'1   C76-016034-1
F1093.W75

Designed and printed in Canada by
MORRISS PRINTING COMPANY LTD.
Victoria, British Columbia

To the late W. D. MacBride

A MAN WHO ALWAYS BELIEVED THAT
THE YUKON HAD A FUTURE, BUT WHO
NEVER FORGOT THAT IT ALSO HAD A PAST, AND
WHO LABOURED VALIANTLY TO PRESERVE IT.
THE MACBRIDE MUSEUM IN WHITEHORSE IS HIS FITTING MEMORIAL.

The publisher wishes to acknowledge the assistance of THE CANADA COUNCIL and to extend particular thanks to the following Patrons, who have all aided in the publication of this book.

CASSIAR ASBESTOS CORPORATION LIMITED
VANCOUVER, B.C.

CYPRUS ANVIL MINING CORPORATION
VANCOUVER, B.C.

EPEC CONSULTING WESTERN LTD.
WHITEHORSE, YUKON

GENERAL ENTERPRISES LIMITED
WHITEHORSE, YUKON

GOVERNMENT OF THE YUKON TERRITORY

IMPERIAL OIL LIMITED
CALGARY, ALBERTA

THE ROYAL BANK OF CANADA
VANCOUVER, B.C.

TRANS NORTH TURBO AIR LTD.
WHITEHORSE, YUKON

UNITED KENO HILL MINES LIMITED
VANCOUVER, B.C.

WHITE PASS & YUKON ROUTE
VANCOUVER, B.C.

THE YUKON ELECTRICAL COMPANY LIMITED
WHITEHORSE, YUKON

Foreword

Prelude to Bonanza

BEING AWARE OF OUR HISTORY ALLOWS US TO HAVE A BETTER understanding of where we are today and where we are capable of going tomorrow.

Yukon's history is often referred to as "short but exciting." It is true that Yukon has only existed as a distinct political entity since 1898, but that certainly doesn't mean we shouldn't bother with what happened before. In fact, the exploration and commercial activity in the latter part of the 18th century and through the 19th century determined such crucial elements of our present way of life in Yukon as the dominance of the English language and our territorial status within the Canadian confederation.

Allen Wright's *Prelude to Bonanza* provides an entertaining and informative commentary on this important period. Going over old diaries, official reports and other records must have been a painstaking task, but from these sources we can gain insight into the personalities of the pioneers—their motives, their attitudes and their experiences are revealed to us first hand. Robert Campbell's journal and reports to the Hudson's Bay Company, for instance, give us a striking picture of this strong-willed and determined man who was so influential in the development of the region.

It is pleasing for me to see this story being told, and I hope it will encourage further study by historians and stimulate a greater interest by the public in that period.

JAMES SMITH

April 2, 1976   *Commissioner of the Yukon Territory, 1966-1976*

Prologue

Prelude to Bonanza

IN 1898, WHEN THE STAMPEDERS BOUND FOR THE KLONDIKE BEGAN pouring through the mountain passes, the country into which they were entering was, contrary to popular opinion, neither unpopulated nor unknown. On that August day in 1896 when George Washington Carmack and his Indian companions found, on a remote tributary of a remote salmon stream, the richest concentration of placer gold that the world has ever known, there were already over a thousand miners exploring the river bars and creeks of the Yukon basin. At the mouth of the Fortymile River, and at Circle City, downstream on American soil, small settlements had been established, and tiny river steamers struggled upstream from St. Michael's each year with goods and supplies for these tenuous communities, and for trading posts elsewhere on the river. Missionaries had been a long time in the district, and an outpost of the North-West Mounted Police had been established near Fortymile, in time for the force to control the influx of gold seekers that were soon to come. Scientific explorers and surveyors, dispatched by learned societies and government agencies, had begun the investigation and mapping of the rugged terrain. The fur traders, Russian and British, had preceded most of the others into the country by fifty years or more: they had been the first to sight the coast, and the first to venture into the interior and build forts. The Yukon basin before the Klondike find was not an empty land.

This book is the history of this pre-Klondike era, as recorded in the journals, letters, reports, and books of the first Europeans to penetrate the American northwest. It is a distillation of their accounts of pioneer journeys, of their descriptions of the terrain, of their impressions of the natives with whom they came in contact, and of whatever else was grist for their mills. They wrote with uneven literary skills and with varying degrees of prejudice, but they wrote at first hand, and often with considerable flair and freshness. For this reason, therefore, their own words are used generously in the telling of their story.

The genesis of the book was simple curiosity. In 1958, as a technical officer with the Department of Public Works of Canada, I came to the Yukon — not for the first time — to investigate the feasibility of certain proposed road routes that would link the skimpy existing highway system to isolated areas of the territory that possessed resource potential. In the lonely country into which I travelled in the course of this work there were no people, often sketchy maps, but a surprisingly large number of place-names for such an empty land. Curiosity impelled me to search for the origins of some of them, and I soon discovered that most that I looked into had been bestowed by the traders, miners, and explorers who had passed through the country before the stampeders came. Further research led me to the little-appreciated fact that the pre-Klondike Yukon had an interesting and robust history in its own right, which has been largely overshadowed by the madness of the gold rush and its quixotic tales. This book is an attempt to move the story of that earlier period out of obscurity and into the light of day.

There is, however, another history of the region that predates the advent of the white men by several thousand years. It is found in the record, unwritten and as yet little known, of the comings and goings of the native tribes and cultures of the Yukon valley, from the first migrations of people over the land bridge from Asia, to the emergence of a hunting and fishing economy dominated by the well-established trading rights of the Tlingit Indians of the coast. This too is part of the pre-Klondike story, but its events are still being pieced together by the patient probings of archeologists and anthropologists. The treatment of this aspect of the Yukon's past, therefore, is not attempted in this book. It is left in the province of the specialists to whom for the moment it rightfully belongs.

A.A.W.

Contents

Map Section following page 58

CHAPTER ONE

The Russian Americans
The Approach by Sea

Map Number 1, following page 58

I

ON JUNE 4, 1741, AN EXPEDITION OF TWO SMALL PACKET BOATS, the *St. Peter* and the *St. Paul*, under the command of Vitus Jonassen Bering, a Dane in the service of the Russian navy, sailed from Petropavlovsk on the Siberian peninsula of Kamchatka with the intention of exploring the unknown seas that lay between Asia and North America. The two ships, each 70 feet long and crowded with a complement of 80 men and all the stores that could be crammed on board, were pitifully small vessels to challenge the stormy waters that separated the two continents.

For Captain-Commander Bering, on the *St. Peter*, and for Captain Alexei Chirikov of the *St. Paul*, it was not the first venture into these inhospitable seas. In July 1728, Bering, with Chirikov as a lieutenant, had sailed from the same port to search for the land bridge which many geographers and eminent scientists believed linked the continent of Asia to that of North America, somewhere in the mists and the ice of the northern seas. On that occasion Bering had set a northerly course, keeping the Siberian coast in view whenever possible. In August, in very bad weather, he had passed through the strait that today bears his name, still hugging the west side of the narrow passage and unaware that had the fog lifted and the storms abated, the coastline of North America would have been clearly visible. The coast which he had been following now veered sharply to the west, and as he had seen no land to the east or to the north, he was satisfied in his own mind that he had proved that the land bridge between the two continents did not exist. Rather than risk being trapped in the polar ice, he had continued on course only until 67° 18′ north was reached. No land having yet been sighted, he had given the order to sail for home.

Though this was an eminently practical move with respect to the safety of his ship and crew, it had nearly been the end of his naval career. On his return to St. Petersburg in 1730, instead of receiving at the Tsar's court the praise and rewards that he had so confidently expected, his act in turning back when he did had been attacked and ridiculed, and the report of his voyage, when published, had not been generally accepted as conclusive proof that the land bridge did not exist. In the face of this abuse, the dismayed Bering in self-defence had petitioned the court for permission to lead a second Kamchatkan expedition that would prove beyond a doubt, by thorough examination of the waters between the two continents, that his conclusions regarding the geography of the region were correct. This petition had eventually been approved. Now, thirteen years after his first voyage, he had embarked at Petropavlovsk for a second time, on what he hoped would be a journey of vindication.

Almost from the time they left port, the *St. Peter* and the *St. Paul* were lashed by gales and hampered by fog. On June 20 they finally became separated and were unable to re-establish contact — each continued to bear to eastward on their own.[1] Navigation became almost impossible. Though the crossing was one that should easily have been accomplished in eight days, for Bering and his men it was over a month before they caught their first glimpse of the American coast. The sighting was on July 16, St. Elias Day, and in honour of the saint, his name was given to a long, narrow, jutting cape, the westerly tip of Kayak Island, and also to a prominent, snow-covered mountain peak on the mainland itself. It was the first place name bestowed on the coast of northwestern North America by explorers of a European nation, and it was eventually applied to the entire range of towering peaks and vast ice fields that straddle the Yukon-Alaska boundary along the 141st meridian.

A month later, on August 30, a precarious anchorage was found among a group of islands which the sailors named Shumagin, after the first man of the ship's company to die from scurvy — a debili-

---

[1] Chirikov went on to make an independent landfall on the Alaskan coast, and returned to Petropavlovsk in October 1741. He too was severely buffeted by storms, and a number of his men were killed by natives, and both his ship's boats lost, in an abortive attempt to land and explore the coast.

tating disease that was then almost inescapable on a long sea voyage. In the vicinity of this landing came the first encounter with the natives: a rather skittish meeting during which each of the participating sides watched with deep suspicion every action of the other. Sven Waxell, Bering's second-in-command on the *St. Peter*, and author of an account of the voyage, had with him "an English book, de la Hontan's Description of North America ... in which there is a whole number of American words in alphabetical order, with an English translation added," and through this unlikely medium he was able to carry on a limited conversation with some of the natives. "As they answered all my queries to my satisfaction," Waxell concluded triumphantly, "I was completely convinced that we were in America."[2]

The dreadful voyage dragged on through September and October, as the crew struggled in vain to make headway in the face of almost constant storms. Scurvy continued to take a frightful toll. By the end of October only ten of the sailors were strong enough to work the ship: the remainder, including Bering, were unable to leave their hammocks. Waxell was in active command.

Disaster struck early in November. They finally sighted one of the islands of the Commander group — later named Bering Island — and ran in close to shore in a desperate search for shelter, only to have the *St. Peter* driven up on the beach, and a great hole ripped in her hull below the water line. The men scratched out crude shelters in the dunes along the water's edge, but they could do little to check the appalling inroads caused by exposure and disease. On December 8 Bering died, and was buried in a sandbank on the side of a bleak, wind-swept hill. By the end of the year only 45 men remained alive of the 80 who had sailed from Petropavlovsk six months before.

Miraculously, most of these survived. Their uninhabited island prison had fortunately a fresh water spring, and was the habitat of great numbers of sea otters. The tough and sinewy flesh of these

---

[2] Sven Waxell, *The Russian Expedition to America*, (New York, Cromwell-Collier, paperback, 1962), p. 94. Waxell's original manuscript, which was in German, became part of the Tsar's private archives, and after surviving somehow the ransacking of the Imperial Palace during the Bolshevik Revolution, re-appeared in a bookshop in Leningrad in 1938. A Danish edition appeared a few years later, and this was eventually translated into English and published under the title *The American Expedition*, nearly 200 years after the events described.

animals sustained the sailors for most of the winter. In March came fur seals, and later manatees or sea cows, to vary their diet: also with warmer weather herbs and plants appeared, which could be used for eating, or for making broth. With these improvements the men began to plan their escape from the island, and it was decided to build, from the wreckage of the *St. Peter*, a smaller boat in which all the survivors could travel together.

The project was started early in April, but it was slow work: the sailors were still feeling the weakening effects of their long ordeal, and it was necessary to employ continually over half of them on the daily chore of hunting and collecting food. It was not until August 13 that they were able to put to sea: on August 27 they landed at Petropavlovsk. "I am not able to describe," wrote Waxell fervently, "the joy and heart-felt delight we one and all felt and exhibited on our deliverance. From the utmost misery and distress we plunged into a veritable superabundance, for there was a whole storehouse full of provisions, comfortable warm quarters and other amenities, none of which we had been able to have that last winter. All that made our joy and the sense of contrast so overwhelming that it just cannot be expressed in words."[3]

II

THE GEOGRAPHICAL CONTRIBUTIONS OF THE KAMCHATKA EXPEDITION were significant, but the information was of concern only to a small group of scholars and map-makers, and was soon buried and almost forgotten in libraries and government archives. The more immediate effects of Bering's explorations came from the spreading of word-of-mouth reports by the survivors of the abundance of the sea otters they had seen on the island on which they had been forced to spend the winter. Even before the voyage of the *St. Peter* a lucrative trade in the beautiful fur of these animals had sprung up between Kamchatka and the Chinese merchants along the Sino-Russian frontier — a trade which, however, had been limited by the fact that sea otter were not numerous along the Asian coast. The word of rich new peltries to the eastward was, therefore, eagerly received. The Cossack fur traders of the Pacific, who had already crossed the grim

[3] *Ibid.*, p. 127.

4

interior of Siberia, lost little time in launching still further into the unknown.

Few of them were seamen, but they sailed in ever-increasing numbers from Kamchatka, often in badly-constructed and overcrowded ships, without compass or map, and with neither the means nor the knowledge to take observations or put down on paper the routes they travelled. Their first journeys were to Bering Island, but the uncontrolled slaughter of the fur-bearing animals there soon forced the traders to travel farther afield. They worked their way gradually along the Aleutian chain, continuing to deplete the peltries with reckless abandon. In a very short time their greed, and the insatiable demands of the market, forced them to venture into the distant waters of the Gulf of Alaska, and approach the great bays and inlets of the mainland coast.

For these longer voyages, the hit-or-miss navigation methods of the early fur-hunters no longer satisfied the traders' needs, and voyages devoted primarily to exploration rather than to killing were dispatched by some of the Kamchatka syndicates, in attempts to plot usable maps of the maze of islands and coves into which they were venturing. The Empress Catherine II, hearing in her distant capital of St. Petersburg of these efforts and this rich market in furs, lent her support to the cartographers. In 1768, two naval surveyors, Krenitsyn and Levashev, led an expedition to the Aleutians that, by careful astronomical observations made over a two-year period, fixed the true position of Unalaska, a large island in the Fox group — an essential first step in the accurate charting of these waters. Unfortunately, just after the completion of this phase of the work, Russia became embroiled in a war with Turkey, and funds for the continuation of the project were diverted to military expenditures.

It was an expedition dispatched by the British Admiralty that made the next important contribution to the geographical knowledge of the North Pacific coast. The English came, not as merchants or traders, but as eager seekers after the fabled Northwest Passage, which they above all nations were anxious to locate. This route, if it existed, would afford them direct access to the rich Oriental spice trade, unhindered by the maritime ambitions and claims of Spain and Portugal on the North Atlantic. Many eminent British sea captains had already penetrated far into the Canadian Arctic from the east in a vain search for open water discharging into the Pacific. Now Bering's charts — which, even if largely ignored by the Russians, were carefully studied by the British naval authorities — had led to increased interest in the Pacific northwest; an interest fueled by such imaginative contributions to the maps of the day as the Straits of Anian, which a Greek pilot who called himself Juan de Fuca claimed to have entered; the "River of the West" of Bartholemew de Fonte, a passage which supposedly led from the west coast of North America to Hudson Bay; and J. von Staehlin's map of the *New Northern Archipelago*, which showed a large island called Alaschka lying west of the coast of North America. This flood of new information in time led the Lords of the Admiralty to decree that still another attempt would be made to find the Northwest Passage. This time the approach would be from the west coast of North America.

In command of the expedition was England's greatest scientific navigator, Captain James Cook of the Royal Navy. Born in Yorkshire in 1728, the son of a farm labourer, he started his career as an able seaman, and rose through the ranks by sheer ability. He had already made two great voyages of exploration, during which he had, among other achievements, discovered and charted New Zealand and the dangerous east coast of Australia, as well as numerous islands in the South Pacific, and had circumnavigated the globe in Antarctic waters, spending the winters on these protracted journeys refitting at bases in New Zealand or Tahiti. In 1776, though the sinecure of a shore posting could have been his, he volunteered to lead this expedition that the Admiralty was assembling. His offer was accepted with alacrity.

The two ships of his command, the *Resolution* and the *Discovery*, left England in July 1776, sailing by way of the Cape of Good Hope, New Zealand, the Society Islands, and a previously unknown group of islands in the central Pacific that Cook named "Sandwich's Isles" after his patron the Earl of Sandwich, but which later became collectively known as the Islands of Hawaii. It was not until March 7, 1778, after nearly two years at sea, that a landfall was made on the coast which Sir Frances Drake had named New Albion, near Cape Blanco, the most westerly point in the present-day state of Oregon. Almost immediately, squalls of hail and sleet, accompanied by hazy weather, forced the ships to stand out to sea again, and obliged them to set a course that would clear the coast. They did not sight land again until March 28, when they approached the west coast of Vancouver Island. Because of the storms, Cook missed the mouth of the Columbia River and the strait at the south end of Vancouver Island, and believed that the coast that was now visible was part of the American mainland.

The expedition's immediate need was a secure anchorage, protected from the storms, and they found it in Nootka Sound. Here they refitted, and shipped new masts, then started north in their search for the Northwest Passage, keeping as close to the coast as the frequent squalls and storms permitted. Cook was no believer in the existence of the Straits of Anian or the river of de Fonte. He thought that the passage, if it existed, would be found far to the north, possibly at the exit to the strait shown on von Staehlin's map. "We were now," he wrote in his journal, "upwards of 1,560 miles to the westward of any part of Baffin or Hudson bays. Whatever passage there may be, it must be, or at least part of it must be, north of Latitude 72°. Who could expect to find a passage or strait of such extent?"[4] This opinion was reinforced as he found that his course in following the shoreline soon became more westerly than north, increasing the overland distance between himself and the Atlantic. Before his exploration of this coast ended, he was to find himself 8° 45' west of his navigational fix in the Hawaiian Islands!

Cook's ideas on the probable location of the passage did not mean that a sharp lookout for an inland channel was not kept at all times, and at least twice the sailors had reason to believe that the search might be over. On May 12, they entered an inlet much larger than any that they had investigated before, but a day or so of exploration convinced them that it was not the entrance to a northwest passage. Cook named this great arm of the sea Prince William Sound. On May 26 their hopes were raised again when, according to John Rickman, a lieutenant on the *Discovery*, "We perceived the land very high on both sides of us E. and W., and saw two burning mountains at a considerable distance. As the fog cleared up, we perceived ourselves in the entrance of a vast river, supposed to be about four miles over, with a strong current setting to the southward. . . . We were once more flattered with having found the passage, of which we were in pursuit, being in the latitude of 60 degrees north."[5] Cook

---

[4] James Cook and James King, *A Voyage to the Pacific*, 3 vols., (London, G. Nicol and T. Codell, 1784) quoted by Paul W. Dale, *Seventy North to Fifty South*, (Englewood Cliffs, N.J., Prentice-Hall, Inc., 1969), p. 216.

[5] John Rickman, *Journal of Captain Cook's Last Voyage to the Pacific Ocean*, (Amsterdam, N. Israel, 1967), pp. 251-253.

spent several days investigating the coastline here, eventually sending the ships' boats some 20 miles inland. "The water was fresh," Rickman's account continued, "and the current rapid, all hopes therefore of a communication with any other sea in this passage vanished; and the ships returned to the sea again by the same passage." This inlet was named Cook's River; one of its arms, in disappointment or frustration, they called Turnagain. Today the busy port city of Anchorage is located on it.

For two months more the ships followed the increasingly bleak coast, hampered by atrocious weather; in July they encountered a snow storm so severe that it "wounded" several of the watch on deck. The ships finally found a channel to the northward through the islands of the Aleutian chain, but because of shoal waters and "the most dreadful tempest of thunder, lightning and hail that ever blew,"[6] they were not in these reaches able to approach the coast.

In August, in a last effort to find the passage, the ships passed through Bering Strait, following the American coast, and when this coast receded in an easterly direction, at a point which Cook named Cape Prince of Wales, they pushed on northward into the Arctic seas. "On the 17th," wrote Rickman, "the weather began to grow piercing cold. The frost set in and froze so hard that the running rigging was soon loaded with ice, and rendered almost impossible to make the sheaves or blocks traverse without six men to do the work of one."[7] On the 18th "hot victuals froze while we were at table," and the next morning "we saw nothing but fields of ice." For a week an open passage was vainly sought, and finally, on August 25, at a conference of the officers of both ships held on the *Resolution*, the decision was made to turn back. "On observation being made at noon," Rickman noted, "we found we were in Lat. 71 and Long. 197 when the ships put about."

Cook made a brief landing in northern Siberia and then passed through Bering Strait south-bound, following the American coast again, and carrying out extensive small boat surveys, in spite of the lateness of the season. In the course of this investigation, Norton Sound was discovered and named, after Sir Fletcher Norton, the Speaker of the British House of Commons. The vast extent of the sound, and its shallowness, prevented detailed exploration. "From

[6] *Ibid.*, p. 268.

[7] *Ibid.*, pp. 275. Other quotations in this paragraph are from pp. 276 and 278.

the masthead," wrote Cook, "the sea appeared checkered with shoals — the water very much discoloured and muddy, and considerably fresher than at any of the places where we had lately anchored. From this I inferred that a considerable river runs into the sea in this unknown part."[8] It was indeed a correct deduction, for in the vicinity of Norton Sound discharge the waters of the Yukon River.

Except for one more landfall in the Aleutians for yet another refit, and a convivial meeting, hampered by language problems, with a Russian trader and navigator, Gerasim Izmailov, who was at the time making his headquarters in Unalaska, Cook's exploration of northwestern North America was over. He was murdered by the natives while wintering in Hawaii — a distressing end to a distinguished career. Charles Clerke, captain of the *Discovery*, assumed command of the expedition, and after his death in August of consumption he was in turn succeeded by John Gore, the officer next in line.

The summer of 1779 was devoted to one more attempt to find a passage north of Bering Strait, but the ships were again halted by the pack ice in about the same latitude that they had reached the year before. Both on their journey north and on their return they did not touch on the American coast, using instead the Russian port of Petropavlovsk as a refitting and supply base. On the long journey home they avoided Sandwich's Isles, and their unhappy memories, skirting instead the coast of Japan, and stopping at Macao (now Macal) one of the centres of the East India Company's trade, and a port-of-entry for Canton. Early in October 1780, they dropped anchor finally in the Thames, their long journey over. They had been at sea four years, two months and twenty-two days — the longest single voyage in the history of exploration.

Other European expeditions followed Cook. Hard on his heels came the Spaniards, from bases in Mexico, first to the Queen Charlotte Islands, and in 1779 to a landfall in the vicinity of Cape St. Elias, where they carried out a reconnaissance of the immediate area. A French scientific expedition under La Perouse spent six weeks in the same waters before putting in to Petropavlovsk, from which port they sailed into the South Seas and were never heard from again. Shortly after La Perouse's departure the Spanish were back again.

[8] Cook, in Dale, *Seventy North*, p. 261.

Two of them, Martinez and De Haro, made contact with the Russians on Kodiak Island in 1788, while a third, Alejandro Malaspina, explored Yakutat Bay in 1791, his name later being given to the vast piedmont glacier to the west of it. Between 1790 and 1793 the Russians themselves mounted a "Geographic and Naval Astronomy Expedition" that acquired valuable information concerning northeastern Siberia and the Bering Sea, and completed the work of Krenitsyn and Levashev by producing the first accurate charts of the Aleutian Islands.

Finally, the touchy and temperamental Captain George Vancouver of the Royal Navy, a brilliant cartographer who had sailed as a midshipman on Cook's second and third voyages, was instructed by the Admiralty "to repair to the north-west coast of America, for the purpose of acquiring a more complete knowledge of it,"[9] and spent three summers, those of 1792, 1793 and 1794, surveying the gaps and making corrections in Cook's charts of 1778. Among his many accomplishments in the course of carrying out his instructions were the first circumnavigation of Vancouver Island and the discovery and charting of both Portland and Lynn Canals, the latter being named by Vancouver after the town of his birth, King's Lynn, a seaport in Norfolk. In Dean Channel, at the mouth of the Bella Coola River, he missed by one month a meeting with Alexander Mackenzie, who completed his notable journey to the Pacific "from Canada, by land," on July 22, 1793.

III

OUT OF THE WORK OF THESE EXPLORERS, AND FROM THE CHARTS OF Cook and Vancouver in particular, the coasts of northwestern North America began to emerge on paper in recognizable form. Of greater immediate import, however, was the trade that was established with the Indians on the coasts and islands. Wherever a strange ship dropped anchor, it was soon surrounded by dug-out canoes, and natives quickly climbed aboard, ready to barter formally with the officers, more informally with the crew.

[9] Bern Anderson, *The Life and Voyages of Captain George Vancouver, Surveyor of the Sea*, (Toronto, University of Toronto Press, 1960), Appendix, p. 234.

The articles which they offered to sell [wrote Cook] were skins of bears, wolves, foxes, deer, racoons, polecats, martens, and in particular sea otters. They also brought weapons such as bows, arrows, and spears, fishhooks, instruments of various kinds, and wooden visors of many different monstrous figures. The most extraordinary of all articles which they brought to the ships for sale were human skulls and hands not yet quite stripped of the flesh, which they made our people plainly understand they had eaten. . . .

Our articles of traffic consisted for the most part of mere trifles, and yet we were put to our shifts to find a constant supply of these. Nothing would go down with our visitors but metal. Brass had by this time supplanted iron, being so eagerly sought after, that . . . hardly a bit of it was left in the ships. Whole suits of clothes were stripped of every button, bureaus of their furniture, copper kettles, tin cannisters, candlesticks and the like, all went to wreck.[10]

The most exotic of the items traded were the skins of the sea otter which, Cook noted, were "fully described in the accounts of the Russian adventurers in their expeditions eastward from Kamchatka. The fur of these animals, as mentioned in the Russian accounts, is certainly softer and finer than that of any others we know of."[11] As Cook's expedition continued its course north and west along the coast, sea otter fur was still offered to the sailors for barter. In the higher latitudes and the colder climates, in areas still untouched by the Russian traders, the Indians used the skins for clothing, and many of the sailors followed this example and purchased the fur to provide extra warmth when working on deck or sleeping.

Cook from the first believed that these furs would become a valuable article of commerce, and that " a very beneficial fur trade might be carried on with the inhabitants of this vast coast."[12] For the sailors, however, it was only during the voyage home, after Cook's death, that the possibilities of this development became apparent. While anchored at Macao, Captain James King, who had assumed command of the Discovery — and who had also become the official chronicler of the expedition — took a party of seamen into Canton to purchase supplies. There, rather to their surprise, those of the men who still had their sea otter fur were able to sell these old, badly cared for skins for over £2,000, a fortune in the economy of the

[10] Cook, in Dale, *Seventy North,* p. 196.
[11] *Ibid.,* pp. 197-198.
[12] *Ibid.,* p. 227.

day, particularly for sailors in the ill-paid Royal Navy. "The rage with which our men were possessed," wrote King, "to return to Cook's River, and, by another cargo of skins, to make their fortunes, at one time was not far short of mutiny. And, I must own, I could not help indulging myself with the thought of the project."[13]

In the 1780's this exciting fact — that sea otter pelts and other valuable furs could readily be obtained in Russian American territory and sold at enormous profits in Canton — was broadcast to the English-speaking world by the publication of accounts, both official and unofficial, of Cook's third voyage. The results were inevitable. Peace had been restored to Europe, and the English seaports swarmed with half-pay, out-of-work naval officers, including several of Cook's own veterans. For them a bonanza beckoned, and another rush to the North Pacific began. The search was no longer for the Northwest Passage, but for the rich peltries, the existence of which had been until now deliberately suppressed. This new invasion from the west ended the thirty-year monopoly of the Cossack fur traders.

The first English trading vessel, the appropriately named *Sea Otter* under Captain James Hanna, appeared in 1785, and obtained a considerable cargo of furs. Encouraged by this success, other merchants followed, until by 1788 there were eight British ships along the coast, some operating as far north as Prince William Sound and Cook's River, where the Russians were still active. That same year the first American traders arrived, the *Columbia*[14] under Captain John Kendrick, and the *Lady Washington*, under Captain Robert Gray, both sailing out of Boston. They too were soon followed by others, until in time the Americans, and the Boston merchants in particular, came to dominate this profitable trade, developing a three-way exchange between New England, Russian America, and China, carrying the sea otter pelts to the Orient, and chests of tea on the voyage home. The term "Boston man" was to become synonymous for "American" up and down the northwest coast.

The more far-seeing of the Russian traders were justifiably disturbed by this turn of events. Two veteran Siberian merchants, Grigori Shelekhov and Ivan Golikov, anticipating the trading rush that followed the map-makers, quickly formed a partnership with the

---

13 King, in Dale, *Seventy North*, p. 347.

14 This vessel was later commanded by Gray, who discovered the Columbia River, which he named after his ship. The first exploration of the river, however, was carried out by Vancouver.

objective of more vigorously exploiting the fur harvest by establishing a permanent colony and trading post close to the American mainland. In 1784 Shelekhov led an expedition of three ships — one of which was lost at sea — to Three Saints Bay on the northeast coast of Kodiak Island, where a small settlement was planted, and the adjoining coast claimed for Russia. In 1786 Shelekhov returned to Petropavlovsk, and continued on to St. Petersburg where, as the next stage in his plans, he presented to the Empress Catherine II an account of his accomplishments, and requested that he and his partner be granted a trade monopoly in the area. This showing of the flag and the ending of the internecine struggle for the peltries would, according to his petition, consolidate Russia's claims to the coast.

Catherine did not grant the request, but Shelekhov, knowing the long road that a seeker of favours at the court must follow, was not discouraged. To oversee his new policy on the coast he appointed in 1791 as manager of his American interests Aleksandr Andreyevich Baranov, a one-time glass maker and unsuccessful independent trader, whose capacity for rum was already legendary, but whose energy and ability would do much to consolidate Shelekhov's Russian American holdings. In 1792 Baranov moved the settlement on Three Saints Bay to a more favourable location at the site of the present community of Kodiak, on the opposite coast of the island. A second settlement was established on Yakutat Bay, and trading posts built at Cook's River and Prince William Sound. Shelekhov died in 1795, but his shrewd and ambitious widow, Natalie, and his partner Golikov continued to press his petition for exclusive trading privileges.

Catherine's long reign ended in 1796. She was succeeded by her son, the Emperor Paul I, an unstable and erratic middle-aged man who had lived so long in his mother's domineering shadow that he had grown to hate her policies and ideas. In this new regime, Golikov and Natalie Shelekhov saw their opportunity. Playing skillfully on Paul's vanity they presented their case again, this time successfully. On July 8, 1799, a charter establishing the Russian American Company was promulgated by the Imperial court. The Company was granted a 20-year monopoly to trade on the coast of America and the adjacent islands from 55° north latitude to the Bering Sea and beyond, and all other trading companies were forbidden to encroach on this preserve. In return, among other rights and privi-

13

leges, the Company was to continue the exploration of its domain, and occupy all new lands discovered as Russian possessions. Shelekhov's heirs and his partner received a one-third interest in the Company, and Baranov remained as its first governor.

During the period of the first charter, little was done in the way of further exploration, as most of Baranov's energies were absorbed by the not inconsiderable task of consolidating his position. He moved his settlement from Kodiak to a site near present-day Sitka, a location he considered more suitable as an administrative centre for the Company. This brought him into direct conflict with the Tlingit Indians, who had a village on the same bay as Baranov's establishment. In 1802 the Tlingits sacked the Russian post, and massacred most of the inhabitants. Baranov had to wait two years for his revenge, but when it came it was brutal and direct — he bombarded the Indian village from the sea, and rebuilt his fort Novarkhangelsk (New Archangel) or Sitka, on the smoking ruins of the Tlingit homes. Russian and native then settled down to an uneasy truce.

Living conditions in Sitka and the other Russian establishments were primitive, the cost of food and supplies was high, and their availability uncertain. In order to maintain their operations, the Russian American Company was forced to rely with increasing frequency on goods and staples purchased from British and American traders, who were operating in territory over which Russia claimed exclusive sovereignty. The breakdown of the supply system finally had to be officially recognized. In the early 1820's, shortly after the charter was renewed for a second 20-year term, negotiations were initiated with the governments of both Britain and the United States to place the surreptitious trade with their merchants on a diplomatically recognized basis. Russia's desire was to abrogate her maritime claims without losing face.

An agreement with the United States was quickly reached, as essentially only commerce was involved; the Russian-American treaty of 1824 granted American merchants trading rights in the Russian colonies for a ten-year period. The Anglo-Russian talks, on the other hand, were protracted and bitter, as the boundary between British and Russian possessions in North America had to be delimitated as part of a trade agreement. Bargaining revolved around several crucial points, one of them being a decision as to which meridian (i.e. degree of longitude) would constitute the extension of the boundary from the Gulf of Alaska to the Arctic coast. During most of the negotiations the British insisted that this part of the line should follow the 140th meridian, while the Russians insisted on the 139th, which touches the west side of Kluane Lake and passes 15 miles east of the mouth of the Klondike River. This was not the most important issue to the Russians, who were more concerned with the southern limits of their coastal territory; and when at long last, over a year after the talks began, a settlement appeared within reach, they were prepared to make a longitudinal concession to the British in exchange for a favourable agreement in the panhandle. When the British finally conceded that 54° 40′ north latitude should mark the southern extremity of Russia's American possessions, they insisted that the northern part of the boundary should follow the 141st meridian. The Russians agreed.

In making this concession, and incorporating it into the Anglo-Russian convention of 1825, the Russians quite unintentionally ensured that the richest of the Yukon goldfields, including the whole of the Klondike, would be located in Canada and not in American territory.

IV

IT WAS NOT ONLY THE LACK OF SUPPLIES THAT WAS CAUSING difficulties for the Russian American Company, but also the depletion of the fur harvest. The years of unrestrained slaughter in the Aleutians and in the Gulf of Alaska had brought the sea otter to the verge of extinction. New peltries were urgently needed if the Company was to survive. The search for these turned the attention of its administrators to the barren, windswept lands that bordered the Bering Sea. One of the most able of Baranov's successors, Ferdinand Petrovich Wrangell, a veteran Arctic traveller and one of the founders of the Russian Geographical Society, ordered in 1832 the construction of a post upstream on the Kuskokwim, Alaska's second largest river, which after being missed by Cook, had finally been discovered in 1818, and its lower reaches to some extent explored. From this new establishment — named Fort Kolmakov after its builder, Fedor Kolmakov — came not only rich shipments of fur, but also reports of an even larger river farther to the north. Wrangell's interest was aroused.

He was not the first white man to hear of this "great river" in the interior of Alaska. In 1789 Alexander Mackenzie of the Northwest

Company made the first descent of the vast waterway that today bears his name.[15] Near the Arctic coast, according to his journal, he met an Indian who informed him that "there is another river on the other side of the mountains to the South-West, which falls into the *Belhoullay Toe*, or White-man's Lake, in comparison of which that on whose banks we then were, was but a small stream; that the natives were very large, and very wicked, and kill common men with their eyes; that they make larger canoes than ours; that those who inhabit the entrance of it kill a kind of beaver, the skin of which is almost red, and that large canoes often frequent it. As there is no known communication by water with this river, the natives who saw it went over the mountain."[16]

The indefatigable Mackenzie was anxious to explore this other river, and he diligently sought further information concerning it. He persuaded one Indian, who appeared to have some knowledge of the terrain to the west "to describe the circumjacent [*sic*] country upon the sand. This singular map he immediately undertook to delineate, and accordingly traced out a very long point of land between the rivers, though without paying the least attention to their courses, which he represented as running into the great lake, at the extremity of which, as he had been told by Indians of other nations, there was a *Belhoullay Couin*, or White Man's Fort. This I took to be Unalascha Fort [Unalaska], and consequently the river to the West to be Cook's River; and that the body of water or sea into which this discharges itself . . . communicates with Norton Sound."[17]

Neither threats nor bribes, however, would induce any of the Indians whom Mackenzie met to guide him across the mountains. They countered his insistence by telling him increasingly fantastic stories, elaborating on the tales that he had already heard. The people who lived on this river, they told him with great seriousness, were "of a gigantic stature, and adorned with wings, which, however, they never employed in flying: they fed on large birds, which they killed with the greatest of ease, though common men would be certain victims of their voracity if they ventured to approach them.

---

[15] Mackenzie himself called the waterway he descended the River of Disappointment, as he had believed that it would lead him to the Pacific.

[16] Alexander Mackenzie, "Journal of a Voyage Through the North-West Continent of America," in *Voyages From Montreal . . . to the Frozen and Pacific Ocean*, (New York, G. F. Hopkins, 1802), p. 60.

[17] *Ibid.*, pp. 61-62.

They also described the people who inhabited the mouth of the river as possessing the extraordinary power of killing with their eyes, and devouring a large beaver at a single meal."[18] Mackenzie was certain that "these people knew more about the country than they chose to communicate or at least reached me," adding shrewdly that "the interpreter, who had long been tired of the voyage, might conceal such a part of their communications as, in his opinion, would induce me to follow new routes, or extend my excursions."

Mackenzie's journal was translated into Russian and published in St. Petersburg in 1808. For Wrangell it became a much-thumbed reference, and it strengthened his resolve to act upon the reports of an interior river that were reaching him from the Kushokwim. As a first step, two naval officers, A. K. Yetolin and Mikhail Tebenkov, were sent in 1832 to complete the charting of Norton Sound, and the following year Tebenkov returned to the area to build a fort on St. Mikhail Island. First called Mikhailovsky Redoubt, and later St. Michael or St. Michael's, this post was intended as the base for an economic and scientific examination of the surrounding region.

Shortly after its completion the Redoubt was the starting point for a penetration into the interior by one of Wrangell's traders, a creole,[19] Andrey Glazunov. In 1835, in the winter, using dogs and sleds, he crossed from Norton Sound over a native portage to the Anvik River, which he followed to its mouth, where it was absorbed by a much larger river flowing from the northwest on a tortuous course to the sea. For this river Glazunov adopted the name given to it by the natives he encountered on its banks, the Kvikhpak (or Kwikpak), a name that in translation meant "great river."[20] This was almost certainly the waterway for which Wrangell was seeking, and the one of which Mackenzie had been told.

Glazunov made his way back to St. Michael's after the breakup by paddling downstream to Norton Sound. The following year he returned to the river and established a post at Ikogmyut — now

18 *Ibid.*, p. 63, as is the other quotation in this paragraph.

19 In Russian America, a creole was the offspring of a Russian father and a native mother. Though this was an illegal union, many creoles were given a rudimentary education by the Company, and in return had to remain in its service for a specified term of years.

20 In other areas, Glazunov's River was known as Yuk-khane or Yuna, the meaning of which was the same — great river. Kwikpak survives on present-day maps as the name of one of the channels in the Yukon delta. For the sake of clarity, "Yukon" will generally be used when referring to the river.

Russian Mission — near the delta, and then crossed the height of land to the Kuskokwim, in search of a route to Cook's Inlet.[21] In 1838 another Company trader, Vasiliy Malakhov, continued the exploration of the Kwikpak (or Yukon). He made his winter crossing from Norton Sound by a portage that followed the Unalakleet River, which brought him to the river at a point considerably farther from its mouth than did the Anvik route previously used. From here, he started upstream on the ice, in spite of attempts by the natives to dissuade him by their tales of dangers that lay ahead. Early in March he reached the village of Nulagito, at the mouth of the Nulato River, and was told that every spring at this place many natives gathered to trade and to prepare dried salmon. Malakhov noted the fact that this would be a good location for a post, and continued his journey upstream as long as it was possible for his dogs to travel. By the time he reached the mouth of the Koyukak River, at the end of the month, the snow was too soft for further progress. He waited there until the ice went out, and then obtained a native skin boat and followed the Yukon to its mouth — a distance of slightly over 400 miles.

In November of 1839 he repeated his journey over the Unalakleet portage, under instructions to establish a post at his suggested location in the vicinity of Nulagito. Reaching the village in March 1840, he found that a smallpox epidemic was raging, with several deaths, and that food was very scarce, and the dogs starving. The disruption of the native economy and the lack of supplies made the project for the present impractical, and he returned to the Redoubt early in the summer, though not before he had collected 500 beaver pelts, in spite of the difficulties of carrying out trade.

The following summer another attempt was made to reach the Nulato by travelling upstream by boat, instead of using the winter portage, but this expedition turned into a fiasco when the leader of it got lost in the sloughs and channels of the delta. In 1842 Wrangell, still determined to exploit the "great river," assigned the task of building the new post to Deryabin, an illiterate but energetic creole who had been with both Glazunov and Malakhov on all their journeys. Deryabin arrived at his destination just before freezeup, and immediately began construction of a fort which he named

---

21 Cook's River was changed to this more correct name by Vancouver while charting the area in 1794.

Nulato, after the river. It was to become the principal bastion of the Russian American Company's trade on the lower Yukon.

The creoles who spear-headed the Russian entry into this region were redoubtable travellers, but their only motivation was the extension of the fur trade: they lacked the education or the specialized training necessary to map their routes or prepare reports on the country and the people with whom they came in contact. As a professional geographer, Wrangell had long been disturbed by this lack of scientific knowledge of the region, and when in 1840 he received an unsolicited letter from a young naval officer offering to undertake exploration on behalf of the Company in the interior of Alaska, he quickly accepted the proposal.

The writer, Lieutenant Lavrentiy Alekseyevich Zagoskin, seemed ideal for Wrangell's purpose. His service background was conventional: graduation from the Kronshtadt Naval Cadet Corps in 1822; service in the combat navy in the Caspian and the Baltic; and finally, to escape the low morale that was prevalent in the fleet at that time, an application for temporary duty in his country's American colonies, which was approved. When he made his offer to Wrangell, he had already spent two years with the Company in command of ships on trading cruises.

In other respects, however, Zagoskin was no run-of-the-mill naval officer. He read widely, ranging from the poetry of Pushkin and the novels of Gogol to the books of Russian geographers and world travellers. He had something of a literary flair: the first of his several published works — a reminiscent essay on his naval experiences in the Caspian Sea — appeared in 1826. He possessed a catholic intellectual curiosity which lured him into a study of ethnography and the natural sciences, and though he had no formal training in these disciplines, a fortunate meeting during his early period in Russian America with a field officer from the Academy of Science gave him an opportunity to learn the principles of collecting. The two men were able to spend a month together at Sitka, and at the end of this period Zagoskin wrote that he had become "a mineralogist, an entomologist, a conchiologist, a zoologist, and others, and . . . my hut is arranged and hung about with every possible kind of curiosity."[22]

[22] L. A. Zagoskin, *Lieutenant Zagoskin's Travels in Russian America 1842-44,* ed. Henry N. Michael for Arctic Institute of North America, (Toronto, University of Toronto Press, 1967), p. 15, introduction.

The expedition was formally commissioned in the spring of 1842, and in May Zagoskin left Sitka with a number of creole hunters and his naval orderly. He arrived at St. Michael's in August, and busied himself with preparations for the journey ahead. As one of his objectives, he had been rather casually instructed "to follow from Fort St. Michael to their sources the two rivers Kvikhpak and Kuskokwim ...; to put down the most satisfactory description possible of the country drained by these rivers and to ascertain the most practical and shortest portages from one river to another."[23] This, and a further task, that of checking possible routes north of the Redoubt along which furs for Siberia were reportedly by-passing the Russian posts, could, he felt, be best carried out from a base at Nulato.

On December 4, the party, consisting of Zagoskin, three hunters, and an interpreter, and using five sleds and 27 dogs, crossed to the Yukon over the Unalakleet portage, and reached Nulato on January 15, 1843. Here Deryabin, with a detachment of four Russians and a creole from California,[24] was still struggling to complete the permanent buildings of the fort, and at the same time live off the land. Zagoskin put his men to work assisting with the construction, but the problem of finding food continued to plague them. In the six weeks that the explorers spent at Nulato before their first venture into the interior, the four fish-traps at the post yielded a paltry 383 fish, or approximately two per day for each man. The only supplement to this sparse diet was an occasional grouse or partridge that was snared or shot, and some dried salmon that Zagoskin was able to purchase locally for blue beads and some other cheap baubles that he had providently brought with him. "Thanks to God," he wrote in his account of the expedition, "we did not suffer great want, though in all honesty we should confess that often when we finished eating, we could easily have eaten again. Lunches were unknown during the whole time of our stay in Nulato."[25]

Between February 25 and March 18 he was away from the fort,

---

[23] *Ibid.*, p. 15, introduction.

[24] In 1812 the Russian American Company established a colony at Fort Ross, near the present site of San Francisco, to grow agricultural produce for the northern posts. The project was abandoned in 1841 as being uneconomical. During the same period, a badly-bungled attempt was also made by the Company to start an agricultural colony in Hawaii.

[25] Zagoskin, *Travels*, p. 145.

carrying out a rather casual investigation of the access routes to the coast north of St. Michael's, which he confirmed were being used to transport furs to Siberia; but he made no specific recommendations as to the location of a post that might intercept this trade. A month after his return came the first harbingers of the northern spring, and the end for a time of the period of hunger. "On April 18th," Zagoskin noted, "the first duck ... appeared at Nulato; on the 20th the first goose flew over and was brought down. It is a bad omen to kill a sentry-goose; this means that there will not be many birds that year. But there was no help for it — the goose meant two day's full rations for a man. From the 24th on everyone was shooting, and all the remaining days of the month we ate our fill."[26]

On May 1 the Nulato River, blocked by ice, flooded its banks, and on May 5, the ice on the Yukon moved.

After the first crack, mountains of ice reared up on the sandbars; after a minute everything broke loose: the ice heaped up again, and again broke apart ... In case the heaping of the ice should cause the banks and buildings to be flooded, all our supplies had been carried onto the roof. The umiaks [skin boats] of the post were held in readiness. The ice went out smoothly, however, and by morning the water, which had risen with the first pressure of the ice, had begun to go down. Blue sky was reflected in places in the river, and the banks were freed of ice; nature was reborn.[27]

With the coming of the breakup, it was possible to start the last task remaining to be carried out from Nulato — to locate the source of the Yukon River. Zagoskin and his men had built a large skin boat with room for six paddlers and a helmsman: now they loaded it with provisions and supplies — biscuit, ham, tea, sugar, salt, astronomical instruments, a tent, and trade goods, including 517 dentalium shells.[28] On June 4, 1843, at 10 p.m., "we prayed to God and took leave of our Nulato comrades. We ourselves did not know where we were going, but we entertained hopes of reaching the ridge that divides the British possessions from ours. I proposed that we

[26] *Ibid.*, p. 159.

[27] *Ibid.*, p. 159.

[28] Dentalium shells were a species of mollusk, long and narrow in shape, that were much used for personal adornment, and therefore an important trade item. They were found off the the Queen Charlotte Islands, and were purchased by the Russian American Company there for distribution to the northern posts.

undertake to prove Mackenzie's supposition about the true direction of the 'Great River' that flows westward from the Rocky Chain."[29]

Unfortunately, good intentions were not sufficient to make progress upstream on the Yukon, and the expedition ran into difficulties from the start. The Russians were admittedly novices in handling a boat of the type that they had built, and they found it gruelling and awkward work forcing their craft against the strong current. They lacked sufficient sea-mammal fat to keep their boat adequately greased, with the result that the skins frequently became waterlogged, and had to be dried in the sun. Their basic ration of biscuit was inadequate to sustain hard physical labour, and they had to stop and hunt whenever fresh tracks on the river banks indicated the presence of game. Yet, in spite of all their problems, they persevered for nearly a month in their slow and painful journey towards their nebulous goal.

The end of their journey came on June 30. They had been detained in camp for three days by "foggy drizzle and rain," while the river level rose steadily. Ahead were supposed to be shallows, but when they finally launched their boat again, "the noise of the churning and plunging waters could be heard a long way from the place. When we reached the shallows in an hour of redoubled work at the paddles, we could not advance a foot"[30] They tried poling, but made no headway; they did not have enough line for tracking; they could not reach either bank for the purpose of making a portage without losing a great deal of ground. After nearly wrecking their boat on a rock, they abandoned their plan of exploring the Yukon's source.

They were close to the mouth of a river that Zagoskin called the Noggoyya (now the Nowitna), roughly 40 miles above the present settlement of Ruby. Before turning back he tried to find out as much as possible from the local natives concerning the nature of the river and the country above them. In spite of language difficulties, he gained the impression that "the river at its source is so broad that one bank cannot be seen from the other." Some traders whom he met later were more specific, informing him that

... they travel up the Yukon beyond the Noggoyya River for a distance of four nights, or about 60 miles, and that the river is in places

[29] Zagoskin, *Travels*, p. 162.
[30] *Ibid.*, p. 174.

broad and broken up by islands, and in places it flows in one stream and has towpaths. In general it is fast, shallow, and interspersed with shallows, and beyond the limit where they have gone, there are rapids. They do not meet many people along its banks, and those they do meet have come down for the fishing from the upper waters of the tributary streams. The distance from the place we turned back to the source of the Yukon where it comes out of the lake they estimate to be one and one-half times the distance we had come from Nulato, that is, over 300 miles.[31]

The explorers completed their return journey to the post on July 7, a welcome contrast to their rate of upstream travel. Zagoskin now had only one assignment remaining, the exploration of the Kuskokwim; but before starting on this task he edited his notes and maps, and made a duplicate set to send to St. Michael's with the furs for forwarding to Sitka — a precaution in case of accident to the expedition while carrying out their remaining task. He summed up his conclusions to date by noting that "the Yukon is our only fairly easy route to the heart of the interior and there is no doubt that some as yet unknown rivers will lead the traveller through to the Arctic Ocean. Judging from the vegetation and the wealth of fur-bearing animals in the part we surveyed, one can hope that further exploration will be rewarding."[32] He pointed out that the Nulato post, between September 8, 1842, and August 1, 1843, took in 3,125 beaver pelts, "a number unsurpassed so far at any other post, not to mention in any other division or region. And these figures are as yet no real indication of the riches of the upper Yukon."

Zagoskin left Nulato early in August, and explored and mapped the Kuskokwim River and some of its tributaries during the winter of 1843-44. He returned to St. Michael's by the Yukon River in June 1844. "At 7 a.m. on June 21st," he wrote, "we completed the tasks of the expedition. We had been gone 1 year, 6 months, and 16 days, and had travelled during that time on foot and by skin boat about 5,000 versts [i.e. approximately 3,300 miles]."[33] It was not without justifiable pride that he listed the results of his expedition:

[31] *Ibid.*, p. 175. The location described by the Indians as being the "source" of the Yukon appears to be the maze of islands and channels in the vicinity of the mouth of the Porcupine River, which are over 1000 miles downstream from the actual headwaters!

[32] *Ibid.*, p. 183, as in the other quotation in this paragraph concerning the Nulato fur harvest.

[33] *Ibid.*, p. 282.

mapping along portions of the Yukon and the Kuskokwim and adjacent tributaries, and numerous inland points located astronomically; in zoology, 38 species of birds collected, and 70 species of insects; "herbs" from St. Michael's and Nulato; 50 "principal species" of rock; and "varied statistical and ethnographic information" about the native tribes encountered, "together with some examples of the weapons, clothing, and cooking utensils of these tribes."[34]

Most of Zagoskin's exploration was over routes which the Russian American traders had already travelled. Nonetheless, his was the first scientific investigation of the Yukon basin, and the first map of any part of the interior. Wrangell the geographer must surely have appreciated the results.

V

AT THE SAME TIME THAT THE RUSSIANS WERE BEGINNING TO venture into the interior, the last great project remaining to be accomplished from the sea — the mapping of the northern coast of northwestern North America — was successfully completed. Sir John Franklin began this task when, in the course of his second expedition of 1825-27 "to the shores of the Polar Sea" he followed and charted the Arctic coast westerly from the mouth of the Mackenzie River to Return Reef at longtitude 149° 37' west, at which point he was forced by the pack ice to turn back. At the same time, and working in conjunction with Franklin, Captain Frederick William Beechey of the Royal Navy charted the south coast of what is now the Seward Peninsula as far as Cape Prince of Wales, and then led a small boat survey party to Point Barrow, where he too was stopped by the ice. Beechey had hoped to meet Franklin there, but a gap of 100 miles still remained, unknown and unmapped.

In 1837 this last blank space was filled in by a strangely assorted pair of Hudson's Bay Company officers. Chief Trader Peter Dease, nominally in charge of an expedition dispatched by the Company to explore the Arctic coast, was a veteran of two of Franklin's overland journeys, but was now aging, with failing eyesight, and looking forward to the retirement on pension which was almost his due. His companion, Thomas Simpson, was a brilliant Scotsman still in his twenties, a graduate with the degree of Master of Arts from King's

[34] *Ibid.*, p. 83.

College, Aberdeen. He had studied for the church, but instead of taking orders he had accepted an offer of service in Canada with the Hudson's Bay Company, as secretary to Governor George Simpson, his cousin. After several years of routine work in this position, he did not hesitate when given the opportunity of accompanying Dease north as a surveyor.

In June 1837, Dease and Simpson, with 12 men, left Fort Chipewyan for Fort Norman on the Mackenzie River, where five men were left for the purpose of establishing a winter base on Great Bear Lake. The two officers and the remaining men continued on to the mouth of the Mackenzie, where they turned westward, following in Franklin's footsteps. With great difficulty, and by resorting to such risky expedients as putting far out to sea in their small boat to get around some of the ice fields, they managed to follow the shoreline to longitude 154° 25' west, from which point further progress by boat was impossible. Determined to connect with Beechey's exploration, the young and active Simpson, with five men, continued to follow the coast on foot. On August 4, 1837, they sighted Point Barrow, "the long strip of land reaching out into the Arctic wastes." Simpson knew that he had reached his goal, and that the entire Alaskan coastline had now been traced. Returning the way he had come, he rejoined Dease, and the whole party made their way back to the winter quarters that had been prepared for them. They were to spend two more years in the Arctic, but their remaining work was carried out east of the Mackenzie.[35]

After this journey to Point Barrow, the exploration of northwest North America from the sea became a matter of refinement and the adding of details — a never-ending process. The interior of this subcontinent, however, was still almost unknown: the few so-called "maps" of the area published at this time were largely conjectural and wildly inaccurate once the coastline was drawn. The Russians

[35] Rather surprisingly, the men who led this Arctic exploration are commemorated by two place names at locations considerably south of their exploits. Dease Lake in the Cassiar district of British Columbia was named for Peter Dease by John McLeod, another Hudson's Bay Company explorer, and the Thomas River, flowing into the east arm of Frances Lake in the south-central Yukon, was named after Thomas Simpson by Robert Campbell, also of the Hudson's Bay Company. (See Chapters Two and Three.)

Thomas Simpson died under mysterious circumstances in 1840, on his way from Fort Garry to England. The case is fully treated in Vilhjalmur Stefansson's *Unsolved Mysteries of the Arctic*, published in paperback edition by Collier Books, New York.

lifted a corner of the veil, but Zagoskin's hopes of further Russian exploration of the Yukon basin were not to be realized. It was the traders of the Hudson's Bay Company, pushing overland into the northwest from their Mackenzie River posts, who were to provide the next glimmerings of knowledge of this vast hinterland, and it was their sketch maps and journals that were to flesh out the map that Zagoskin had begun.

CHAPTER TWO

The Hudson's Bay Company
The Approach by Land

Map Numbers 1, 2 and 3, following page 58

I

IN 1830, A TALL, STRAPPING SHEEP-FARMER'S SON IN PERTHSHIRE, Scotland, named Robert Campbell met a cousin of his, James Mc-Millan, a Chief Factor in the service of the Hudson's Bay Company, who came home on a year's furlough leave. The meeting was to change young Campbell's life. "Through him," Campbell wrote later in his journal, "I heard for the first time of the Great North-West and the free and active life that awaited one there ... I became possessed with an irresistible longing to go to that land of romance and adventure."[1] Learning through McMillan that a sub-manager was needed for an experimental farm the Company proposed to establish near the Red River settlement, Campbell applied for the position, and to his delight was accepted.

On June 2, 1830, at the age of twenty-two, he left the home farm

---

[1] Robert Campbell, *Two Journals of Robert Campbell (Chief Factor, Hudson's Bay Company), 1808 to 1853*, (Seattle, Washington, limited edition privately printed by John W. Todd, Jr., 1958), p. 1. The early journal covered the period 1808-1851, and according to Mr. Todd, "was copied from a typed copy that reposed for years in the fine library of the late Geo. W. Soliday of Seattle. No record has been found as to where the original of this lies — or if it still exists." The later journal covered the period Sept. 1850 to Feb. 1853. This manuscript "is in the possession of Mrs. J. W. Waddy of Canada, a granddaughter of Robert Campbell." Mrs. Waddy gave permission to have the diary copied for this publication. Mr. Clifford Wilson, for many years editor of the Hudson's Bay Company's magazine *The Beaver*, and author of *Campbell of the Yukon* states that the original journal was destroyed by fire and rewritten by Campbell from memory after his retirement. The old man's recollection of events was excellent, Wilson noted, "and comparison with material from other sources revealed only minor discrepancies."

for the last time. On July 1 he sailed from Stromness on a Company ship bound for York Factory on Hudson Bay. On board, besides "4 apprentice clerks and 30 or 40 labourers," were McMillan, whose furlough had expired, and Chief Trader Donald Ross, another experienced Company officer. At Fort Garry, which was reached on September 22, the young greenhorn met a third veteran trader, Chief Factor Donald Finlayson. Campbell never forgot the kindness and encouragement that these men gave him as he started his career in a new and strange environment.

Most important of all, however, he attracted the attention of George Simpson, the governor of both the Northern and Southern Departments of the Hudson's Bay Company, who happened to be wintering at Fort Garry when Campbell's service with the Company began. This energetic and able administrator, a short and stocky Scotsman with a bland manner and an iron will, was born of illegitimate parentage at Loch Broom in Ross-shire in 1793, and was brought up by relatives who ensured that he received a well-rounded education. He entered the service of the Hudson's Bay Company directly from the office of a London mercantile firm, his potential having been noted by Andrew Colvile, then a member of the Company's Governing Committee. Simpson arrived in British America in 1820, only a year before the union with the Northwest Company, when the bitter rivalry between the two companies was approaching a climax. The newcomer was placed in charge of the Athabasca District, "the very storm centre of the fur trade battle and the last stronghold of the enemy. . . . From the stranger — 'reputedly a gentlemanly man,' one Northwester wrote — they did not anticipate 'much alarm.' It turned out to be as strenuous a season of competitive fur trading as any Canadian party had ever encountered."[2]

Out of the delicate compromise that finally brought about the union and the end of wasteful competition, Simpson emerged as the most powerful officer, in Canada, of the combined companies. His was the task of binding up the wounds, assuaging the injured pride, removing the deadwood — in short, of making the union work. He achieved this in part by travelling constantly over his vast domain, yet finding time to keep in touch with every aspect of the operation, no matter how trivial. One of his particular interests was explora-

2 Douglas McKay, *The Honourable Company*, (Toronto, McClelland & Stewart, 1966), p. 177.

tion, which he encouraged as part of Company policy; he was always on the lookout for men of ability and courage who were temperamentally suited to undertake these exacting pioneer journeys. By the time Campbell joined the Company, Simpson had already sent Samuel Black up the Finlay branch of the Peace River, and John McLeod up the Liard and into the Coast Range mountains. McLeod discovered and named Dease Lake, after Peter Dease, and penetrated into the headwaters of the Stikine, which he called the Pelly. The Liard he ascended as far as the mouth of the Frances River, which he followed until he was opposite a lake that he named after Simpson. This was the most westerly point of his journey; beyond, farther to the northwest, was still much unknown country. When the right man came along, this area too would be opened up for the fur trade.

Simpson was apparently impressed by the capabilities of the young Scottish recruit. Learning that Campbell was not happy on the farm, and that he regarded it only as a stepping-stone to the more stirring and active life of a trader, Simpson encouraged him to apply for a transfer; and when he did so, the governor appointed him to the Mackenzie River District. "His last words to me," Campbell noted, "were 'Now, Campbell, don't you get married, as we want you for active service.' "[3] Already, possibly, the "Little Emperor" was hoping that this recruit would in time fit into the Company's exploration program in the northwest.

In the early years of his service in the Mackenzie District, Campbell had ample opportunity to show his mettle. In 1835 he was placed in charge of the post at Fort Liard. In 1837 he volunteered to establish a new post on Dease (or Dease's) Lake, after the man who had originally been dispatched for this purpose returned in panic to Fort Simpson "when an alarm was got up that hundreds of Russian Indians were advancing on the camp to murder them all."[4] Campbell, leading a rather reluctant party, was able to prove, by finding the abandoned trade goods undisturbed except by wild animals, that the war-party of hostile Indians was, as he suspected, a figment of someone's imagination. After this, Campbell's men followed him with far more confidence than they had shown before.

They would have reached Dease Lake too late in the season to

[3] Campbell, *Two Journals*, p. 27.
[4] *Ibid.*, p. 30.

start building the new post, so they wintered instead at Fort Halkett, on the Liard at the mouth of the Smith River. With the fall trading outfit came a letter for Campbell from Simpson in which the governor ordered that "your attention be particularly directed to pushing the trade across the Mountains and down the Pelly [i.e. Stikine] River."[5] Accordingly, Campbell and his men moved out of their winter quarters as soon as possible after the spring breakup: they reached Dease Lake early in July; selected a site for the post on the east shore of the lake five miles above its outlet; and immediately started the task of new construction. Campbell was now free to carry out the investigation Simpson had requested.

July 20 [1838]   Leaving the men under Mr. McLeod [Campbell's apprentice clerk] to put up the fort, I started with Hoole and 2 fine young Indians Lapie and Kitza, to carry out my instructions to explore the West side of the Mountains.

We took pine [i.e. spruce] bark canoes with us to the South end of the lake, 20 miles off, & then shouldering our blankets and light equipment such as small axe, kettle etc., we started on foot trusting to our guns to keep us in provisions.

21 July   The first day's tramp took us over 2 low ridges and 2 mountain streams. On the next morning we passed over the shoulder of a lofty snow-clad mountain, whence we saw a river that looked like a thread running through the deep valley below. By 6 o'clock at night . . . we came to 'Terror Bridge' whence Mr. J. McLeod & exploring party had turned back in 1834. He had named the river *the Pelly*, but as a matter of fact, the river in question was the upper part of the Stikine, (the Tooya R.) as I was presently informed by the Indians I met there. . . .

[The bridge] was a rude ricketty structure of pine poles spliced together with withes and stretched high above a foaming torrent; the ends of the poles were loaded down with stones to prevent the bridge from collapsing. This primitive support looked so frail and unstable and the rushing waters below so formidable that it seemed well nigh impossible to cross it. It inclined to one side which did not tend to strengthen its appearance for safety. . . . The 2 Indian lads & myself attempted the crossing which we succeeded in making, the flimsy bridge swaying and bending with our weight and threatening to precipitate us into the boiling waters beneath.[6]

On the other side, they were told by Indians who were guarding the trail that a large camp was not far away, and that "the great

[5] *Ibid.*, p. 36.
[6] *Ibid.*, pp. 37-39.

Chief 'Shakes' from the sea was there and Indians from all parts without number."[7] This powerful chief was an agent and middle-man for the Russian traders at the mouth of the Stikine, who supplied him with trade goods, and for whom he collected furs: the Russians themselves did not venture inland. This assembly was the gathering at which the annual trade was carried on. Campbell's informants added that if he went on to the camp, Shakes would surely kill him, as the Russians had told the chief that all white men from east of the mountains were trade rivals and enemies. Campbell, however, was not that easily dissuaded from his purpose. He was doggedly loyal, and he had his duty to the Company to perform.

"From the top of a hill," he wrote, "we caught our first glimpse of the immense camp (about 13 miles from the bridge) of which we had heard so much, and indeed the description given us was not exaggerated. Such a concourse of Indians I had never before seen assembled."[8] He descended alone into the closely-packed throng which, alerted by the Indians at the bridge, was expecting his arrival. A great din arose, and there was much jostling and shoving for several dangerous minutes. Finally, however, a lane was cleared, and the chief strode along it to greet Campbell, shaking hands with him, and escorting the visitor to his tent. There, probably to Campbell's considerable relief, Shakes produced a bottle of whiskey and a cup. Campbell, a devout Presbyterian, "merely tasted" the liquor; the others imbibed much more freely. The din outside continued, and the tent was eventually swept away by the crush, but there was no bloodshed.

I was well armed, having pistols and dirk in my belt, and a double barrelled percussion gun, which was a great source of wonder to them as the only guns they were familiar with were single-barrelled flint locks. Shakes wanted me to fire so that he might see how the gun went off. Fearing this was only a ruse to render my gun harmless, I took the precaution to have ball, powder & cap in my hand ready to slip in immediately after firing a shot. At every report, the whole camp yelled, clapping their hands on their mouths at the same time, & the noise was frightful.

[7] *Ibid.*, p. 40. According to Dr. George Dawson of the Geological Survey of Canada, who led a scientific expedition into the Yukon and wrote a comprehensive report on the area — which is the basis of Chapter Six — Shake or Shakes was the traditional name always given to the chief of the Coast Indians at the mouth of the Stikine.

[8] *Ibid.*, pp. 41-42.

I was glad to find that some of the Indians knew Dr. McLoughlin and Mr. (afterward Sir) James Douglas, both prominent H.B.C. officers on the Pacific slope. This induced me to write notes addressed to them and others, giving particulars of my trip and informing them that I had ascertained that the so-called Pelly and the Stikine were identical, and requesting them to forward the information to headquarters. I may here add that these notes duly reached their destination.

I remained in the camp for some time, the object of much curiosity till at length getting clear of Shakes and the crowd on the plain in safety, (which was more than I expected when I first went among them), I found my small party also all right on top of the hill, where I forthwith hoisted the H.B.C. flag, & cut H.B.Co. & date on a tree, thus taking possession of the country for the Company.[9]

It was at this trade gathering that Campbell met "the Chieftainess of the Nahanies . . . [who] commanded the respect not only of her own people, but of the tribes they had intercourse with. She was a fine looking woman above the middle height and about 35 years old. In her actions and personal appearance she was more like the Whites than the pure Indian race. She had a pleasing face lit up with fine intelligent eyes, which when she was excited flashed like fire. She was tidy and tasteful in her dress. . . . At our first meeting, she was accompanied by some of her tribe and her husband, who was a nonentity."[10] Campbell added that the lack of an interpreter made conversation difficult. In spite of this poor communication, however, the friendliness of the Chieftainess to the Hudson's Bay trader was soon obvious, and she was able to demonstrate before the day was over the very real authority that she exercised in that savage and unruly assembly. Learning that some small personal items "indispensable for the return journey to Dease's Lake" had been pilfered in his absence from Campbell's campsite of the day before, "she gave some directions to 2 young Indians, who started off to the great camp, & who to my astonishment soon returned with the missing articles." When Campbell finally rejoined his men, the Chieftainess "came back with us for some miles & urged us on no account to stop until we were across Terror Bridge, as some of the young bloods, with the sanction of Shakes, were likely to slip after us & kill us or do us harm." It is very possible her openly-bestowed favour saved Campbell's life on more than one occasion during that

[9] *Ibid.*, pp. 43-44.

[10] *Ibid.*, p. 44. All other quotations referring to the Chieftainess in this paragraph are from pp. 44-45.

day. It would certainly save him the next time their paths crossed, during the hard winter that lay ahead.

Returning to Dease Lake, where he had been instructed to winter, Campbell found the construction of the buildings well in hand; but he was alarmed to learn that the daily yield of fish from the nets in the lake was decreasing, and that his hunters were having little success in finding game. In view of this, he determined to make a trip to the Depot at Fort Simpson to report his contact with the Coast Indians and his discovery that the so-called Pelly and the Stikine were identical, and at the same time to request more provisions for the winter. Taking Lapie with him, he made the descent of the Liard in a frail birch bark canoe, arriving at the Depot on August 20. "Though I went there at the risk of my life," he commented bitterly, "it availed me little. Mr. McPherson [Chief Trader Murdock McPherson, in charge of the Mackenzie District] though glad to hear of my success, was deaf to all my entreaties for a few extra & much wanted supplies."[11] The outfit that Campbell did obtain was in fact so skimpy that by the time he and Lapie arrived back at Dease Lake in October, most of the supplies were already consumed. They were faced with the prospect of a wretched and unhappy winter.

The buildings were ready for our use, but our prospects were very gloomy. The produce of our nets, on which we depended principally for subsistence, was inadequate to our daily wants, & the hunters were unable to add anything to our slender means. We were now thrown entirely on our own resources, a long dreary winter approaching, ten men, one family, a clerk & myself to provide for, a distance of about 600 miles between us & the nearest Company's Post (Fort de Liard), shut in by barren mountains surrounded by a host of Indians rendered by Shakes' instigations and our high tariff, anything but amicably disposed towards us . . . It was not without reason that I looked forward to the winter with apprehension. . . .

Our efforts all winter to procure a bare living were never relaxed. We were scattered in twos & threes trying with nets & hooks for fish, & with traps, snares & guns for any living thing, bird or beast, that came in the way. Everything possible was used for food: 'tripe de roche,' skins, parchment, in fact anything. But much as we felt these privations, our greatest trouble was the passing & repassing of the Russian Indians, who kept us night and day in a state of alarm & uncertainty, particularly as it was impossible for us to be all together. . . .

Our circumstances were such that we could do nothing but grin &

11 *Ibid.*, p. 46.

bear it. We were completely at their mercy. Most of us were so weak & emaciated that we could hardly walk. . . . To resent the outrageous conduct of the Indians would have been suicidal folly. But if we had been in a stockaded fort with plenty of provisions & all our men inside, I venture to say we would have taught these aggressive gentlemen a wholesome lesson.[12]

In February, at a time when the wretched traders were "perfectly destitute of food of any kind," the Chieftainess accompanied by some of her tribesmen made a most providential visit to the Dease Lake post. Assessing at a glance the miserable conditions under which the white men were living, and undeterred by the fact that Shakes had ordered their harassment as a potential menace to his lucrative trade, "she ordered her servants (all leading Indians there had slaves) to cook the best they had for our use, & it was served under her directions. We partook of a sumptuous repast — the first for many a day — consisting of excellent dried salmon & delicious fresh caribou meat. I felt painfully humiliated that I could not make a suitable return."[13] The whole band stayed overnight at the post, a visit marred only by one quick and violent outburst of hostility which was, however, instantly suppressed by the Chieftainess, who, when she found out the name of the man who was causing the trouble, "walked up to him, and, stamping her foot on the ground, repeatedly spat in his face, her eyes blazing with anger. Peace & quiet reigned as suddenly as the outbreak had burst forth." The next month, another party from her tribe also passed by the fort, but she was not with them. Without her presence, the Nahani were as obnoxious to the Hudson's Bay men as any of the other "Russian Indians" who caused so much unpleasantness during the Dease Lake sojourn.

Somehow the traders survived the winter with only one death at the post and the loss of two hunters who disappeared in an attempt to reach Fort Liard. Spring and open water brought reports of wild fowl and caribou, and the men lost little time in preparing to leave the establishment at which they had endured so much misery and privation. On May 8, 1839, they prepared a final meal — a "savoury dish" consisting of the webbing of their snowshoes and the parchment from the windows, boiled until the mixture reached the consistency of glue. Once heading downriver, however, they soon killed

[12] *Ibid.*, pp. 47-48 and 50-51.
[13] *Ibid.*, p. 49, as are all other quotations referring to this visit.

enough wild fowl to enjoy a satisfying feed, "a luxury to which we had been strangers for a long time." For the present, the period of terrible hunger was over.

Campbell sent one canoe on to Fort Simpson, and took the remainder of the men back to Fort Halkett, which had been abandoned when the Dease Lake post was built. Eventually, instructions came back from the Depot that they were to refurbish Fort Halkett and spend the winter of 1839-40 there. This was a happier prospect, even though the winter's trading outfit, when it arrived in September, was still a niggardly one. "The Indians in the surrounding section of the country," Campbell reported, "knew of our presence, they visited us regularly, bringing in their furs, &c., and enabled us to pass a pleasant & profitable winter."[14]

II

NONE OF THIS ACTIVITY ESCAPED THE ATTENTION OF GOVERNOR Simpson. He had already written to Campbell commending the "spirited tender of your services to establish Dease's Lake, which has called forth approbation of the Council and led to your promotion to the rank of Clerk with an advance in salary."[15] In the September dispatches which reached Fort Halkett there was a more important letter from the governor dated 16 June 1839 that was to initiate a new phase in the young Scot's career.

Simpson began by expressing his "entire satisfaction with your management in the recent voyage down the Pelly or Stikine River, bearing ample evidence that the confidence reposed in you was well placed."[16] He then went on to tell Campbell that an agreement had just been concluded with the Russian American Company for the lease of "the whole of the Russian mainland territory," that is, the coastal strip today known as the Alaska panhandle. "This arrangement," Simpson continued, getting to the meat of his letter, "renders it unnecessary for us now to extend our operations from the East side of the Mountains or McKenzie River [sic], as we can settle

[14] *Ibid.*, p. 56.

[15] *Ibid.*, p. 36. Campbell had previously held the rank of postmaster, the lowest commissioned rank in the Company's hierarchy.

[16] *Ibid.*, p. 56. All other quotations from this letter and from the one received in February 1840, are on pp. 56-57.

35

that country from the Pacific with greater facility at less expense. Your services will now therefore be required to push our discoveries in the country situated on the Peel & Colvile[17] Rivers, and I am quite sure you will distinguish as much in that quarter as you have latterly done on the West side of the Mountains." More definite orders were received at the end of February 1840, when a successor to take charge of Fort Halkett arrived from the Depot. "I was instructed," Campbell wrote, "to follow the North (or West) branch of the Liard and from its source to cross the height of land and try to discover any large river flowing westward." The governor had obviously decided that he had indeed found the right man to continue the Company's program of exploration in the northwest.

In accordance with the instruction I had received, I left Fort Halkett about the end of May in a canoe with a crew of 7, 4 engaged men and 3 Indians, among them my faithful Indians Lapie and Kitza and the interpreter Francis Hoole. We had a pleasant trip, living luxuriously on *beaver*, which were very abundant & traces of which in the shape of houses, freshly cut trees, etc., could be seen all along the river; on fine *trout*, which could easily be caught with hooks & any sort of bait in the clear mountain streams; and on Game of all kinds. After passing the Nahany [Dease] which led to our old quarters at Dease's Lake, our route up the Liard took us in serpentine curves against a swift current, through a valley well wooded with Pine & Poplar,[18] the mountains on both sides increasing in altitude as we advanced, & showing lovely slopes of bright verdure facing the South.

After ascending the stream far into the mountains, on this date [July 19, 1840] we reached a beautiful sheet of water which, in honour of Lady Simpson, I called Frances Lake. About 4 miles further on, the lake divides into two branches round "Simpson's Tower" (which I named after Sir George).[19] It is of considerable altitude — over 2,000 ft. The West wing extends about 30 or 40 mis., the East about 20 or 30, each being on the average about a mile broad, & the water clear and

---

[17] The mouth of the Colvile River was discovered by Dease and Thomas Simpson in 1837 (see Chapter One), and named after Andrew Colvile, a member of the London Committee and later home governor of the Hudson's Bay Company. As the Colvile where it flowed into the Arctic Ocean was nearly two miles wide, there was considerable speculation that this might be the mouth of the "Great River" of the interior.

[18] The Liard River, or Riviere au Liards (poplar) of the voyageurs, was named by them for the abundance of these trees along its banks.

[19] Simpson was knighted in 1841, the year after this journey. The journal, as already noted, was prepared for publication after Campbell's retirement.

deep ... The Hills slope off from the edge of the lake, along which are many picturesque coves, while the scenery in general is very striking.[20]

Leaving the "engaged men" at Frances Lake, "with a canoe & nets & guns to fish & hunt round there & wait our return" — a rather idyllic-sounding assignment — Campbell pushed on.

I went off on foot with Hoole and the 3 Indians carrying our blankets, etc., on our backs & our guns in our hands, to cross the mountains in quest of any river we might find flowing from the West side. Traversing a rough wooded country along the base of the hills, we ascended the valley of a river ... [which] we traced to its source in a lake 10 miles long and about 1 mile in bredth [sic], which with the river I named Finlayson's Lake and River (after Chief Factor Duncan Finlayson, afterwards a member of the H.B. Co. Board of Directors.) The lake is situated so near the watershed that, in high floods, its waters flow at one end down one side of the mountain, & at the other end, down the other side.

For 3 days on this trip, we had neither the luck to kill nor the pleasure to eat; but having managed to make pine bark canoes we paddled to the W. end of Finlayson's Lake & shortly after that we got deer & beaver more than sufficient for our wants. On the 6th day of our journey from 'Simpson's Tower' we had the satisfaction of seeing from a high bank a large river in the distance flowing Northwest. I named the bank from which we caught the first glimpse of the river 'Pelly Banks' & the river 'Pelly River', after our home Governor[21] Sir H. Pelly. Descending to the river we drank out of its pellucid water to Her Majesty & the H.B. Co.

We constructed a raft & drifted down the stream a few miles, & threw in a sealed can with memoranda of our discovery, the date, etc., with a request to the finder, if perchance the can should fall into anyone's hands, to make the fact known. After taking possession in the name of the Company by marking a tree 'H.B.C.' with date & flying the H.B.C. ensign the while overhead, we retraced our steps to Frances Lake, highly delighted with our success. ... In due time we rejoined the rest of the Party, who during our absence had built a rough shanty at the foot of 'Simpson's Tower' on the point at the forks of the lake. This edifice was dignified by the name of "Glenlyon House". We now returned down stream to Fort Halkett, which we reached about the middle of September with our canoe loaded with provisions. We saw no Indians, nor trace of them, during the entire trip.[22]

[20] Campbell, *Two Journals*, pp. 57-58.

[21] The home governor presided over the meetings of the Governing (or London) Committee, the Hudson's Bay Company's supreme authority, which met in London, England. Sir John Henry Pelly was governor 1822-1852.

[22] Campbell, *Two Journals*, pp. 58-60.

Campbell was not yet aware that in making this portage, he had crossed, for the first time in his travels, from the watershed of the Mackenzie into that of the Yukon River system.

He spent the winter quietly at Fort Halkett, though "again on the verge of starvation," a state of affairs to which he was by now becoming resigned. In the spring he accompanied the returns to Fort Simpson, where he was delighted to learn that the tight-fisted Mc-Pherson had gone on furlough in 1840, his successor as officer in charge being Chief Factor John Lee Lewes. "From him," Campbell reported, "I received a kind welcome & the promise of cordial support in the work I was engaged in."[23] In this happier atmosphere, Campbell passed the summer at Fort Simpson, and returned to Fort Halkett for yet another winter's trade.

III

GOVERNOR SIMPSON, ABOUT TO EMBARK ON A TRIP AROUND THE world, was enthusiastic at the news of this discovery, and wrote to Campbell in June 1841, suggesting that "every information respecting it be acquired as early as possible," at the same time hazarding a guess that the Pelly River would be found to flow into the Pacific. He also told Campbell that "you speak so favourably of the country in the neighbourhood of Frances Lake, both as regards the means of living and the prospects of trade, that we have determined on extending our operations in that quarter."[24] Carrying out this latter instruction was to absorb Campbell's energy for some time to come: it was almost two years after receiving Simpson's letter before he was able to undertake further exploration of the Pelly.

The first step was to establish a post at Frances Lake. In June 1842, he was again at Fort Simpson to receive his outfit: "2 fine boats, manned by 10 men & 2 Indians, & ample supplies"[25] — certainly a more generous issue than he had been given by McPherson before he set out for Dease Lake. The party did not reach their destination until August 13, after the usual difficult trip upstream on the Liard. The new post was started immediately at the site of

23 *Ibid.*, p. 60.

24 *Ibid.*, p. 61. The letter was dated 24 June 1841.

25 *Ibid.*, p. 62. All other quotations referring to the founding of Fort Frances are on p. 64.

Glenlyon House, and "fisheries" were established. These, unfortunately, were not very successful.

"Our fisheries proving insufficient to meet our daily wants," Campbell wrote, "much less to allow us to lay aside fish for the winter, and strangers as we were to the resources of the country, I deemed it inadvisable to keep all the men we had, so I sent off our guide Francis Whiteford with 4 men to Fort Simpson at the end of Oct., a tough trip at that time of year & inadequately equipped as they were. It was fortunate that I did so, as even with our reduced establishment, we found it hard to keep the wolf from the door during the winter till our hunters began to kill deer on the crust in Spring. Then came better times, the Indians finding us out & spreading the news that we were stationed at Frances Lake, & gladly coming in to trade furs and provisions with us." This post, which was renamed Fort Frances or Frances Lake, was the first to be built by the Hudson's Bay Company within the present-day boundaries of Yukon Territory.

With Fort Frances successfully established, Campbell felt justified in proceeding with further exploration of the Pelly. Preparations for the journey had been going on throughout the winter. Hoole, an expert canoe maker, had been sent with some men to Pelly Banks to put up a shelter and start building the framework for a large canoe. Later, Campbell sent birch bark across the portage to them by dog team: a delicate cargo that had already been brought some 600 miles from Fort Liard, the nearest source of supply. By the spring of 1843, Campbell could hardly contain his impatience to be on the trail.

As soon as the river opened . . . I crossed over the mountains with my remaining 2 men to resume exploring work during the summer months. We reached Pelly Banks on the 6th day & a cold and fatiguing tramp it was too. We found all well & Hoole had the canoe finished and ready for the trip.

On [June 10, 1843] we embarked, our crew consisting of Hoole, 2 French Canadians, & 3 Indians, including of course my 2 inseparables, Lapie and Kitza. Our supplies were very limited, consisting of 3 bags pemmican brought all the way from Edmonton, a little Powder and Shot, a few pounds of Tobacco and Beads, & a few knives, axes, awls, flints & gunworms. . . .

As we descended the river it increased in size, and the scenery presented a succession of picturesque landscapes. Our first obstruction was a bad rapid (Hoole's) about 25 miles from Pelly Banks; where we had to make a portage, then for about 90 miles we had a fine flowing current till we came to another rapid ('Desrivieres' after one of the French Canadians with me) between 2 high walls of rock, about ¼ mile long; strong current which we ran.[26] Ranges of mountains flanked us on both sides, those on the right were well-wooded, while on the left the hills were covered with grass, only the ravines being wooded.[27] Moose and bear we often saw as we passed along, & at points where the precipice rose abrupt from the water's edge we frequently observed the 'Big-Horn' or wild sheep above us. These were very keen-sighted & quick to take alarm, & when once started would file off swiftly & gracefully. When we chanced to get one we found it splendid eating. On the 2nd day we saw 2 Indians with whom we had a smoke & talk. Next day as we rounded a point, we surprised an Indian family camped on the bank. The wife & children ran off & hid, but they came back when they found we were friendly. They belonged to the 'Knife' tribe[28] of Indians & had never seen a white man before. We had a talk & smoke with them and after eating we gave them some small presents & went on our way, leaving them apparently well pleased at the meeting.

Every now and then we passed the mouths of tributaries which I named; the largest of these, entering from the N.E. was christened the McMillan after Chief Factor McMillan.[29] On the 6th day we reached the junction of a large river flowing from the S.W., which I named the Lewes after J. Lee Lewes. There we camped for the night. Early next day a short distance below the forks, we came upon a large band of 'Wood'[30] Indians, whom we took completely by surprise, which almost amounted to awe, as they had never seen white men before. Two of their leading Chiefs, father & son, named Thlin-ikik-Thling and Hanan were tall, stalwart, goodlooking men, clad from head to foot in dressed deer skins, ornamented with beads & porcupine quills of all colours. We smoked a pipe of peace with them & I distributed some tobacco & presents among them. They spoke in very loud tones, as do all Indians in their natural state, but seemed peaceable & kindly disposed towards us. When we gave them to understand as best we could that we proposed going on down the river, they all raised their voices against it.

---

26 This rapid on present-day maps is named Hoole Canyon. The rapid that Campbell called Hoole's is today unnamed.

27 This must be an error in recollection or in transcription; the right and left sides should be reversed.

28 Knife Indians was the traders' name for the Indians of the Upper Pelly.

29 Among others he named Ross River, after his old ship-board friend, Chief Trader Donald Ross, and the Hoole River and the Kitza (Ketza on present-day maps) after his canoe maker and one of his "2 inseparables." Incidentally, the McMillan River of Campbell for some obscure reason appears on modern maps as the "MacMillan."

30 Wood Indians were those who lived below the confluence of the Pelly and the Lewes.

They said that inhabiting the banks of the Lower river were many tribes of bad Indians, who would not only kill us but eat us. We would never return, & our friends coming after us would unjustly blame them. All this frightened my men so much that I had reluctantly to consent to turn back, which perhaps under the circumstances was the best thing we could do, as we were not equipped for a longer trip, and I learned afterwards it would have been madness to proceed unprepared as we were for such an enterprise.[31]

Campbell was in low spirits as they started the return journey; but on the third day the sight of signal fires burning on the hill tops on both sides of the river quickly snapped his mood of depression. "I conjectured," he wrote, "that as in Scotland in the olden times, these were signals to gather the tribes so that they might surround and intercept us. This awakened me to a sense of our situation, & we made every effort with paddle & tracking line to get up stream as fast as we could."[32] It was too late, however, to elude their unseen pursuers.

The morning of the next day the confrontation took place: a large band of Indians stood waiting on the river bank, and made signs for the travellers to cross over to them. "They were very hostile," Campbell reported, "standing with bows bent & arrows on the string. . . . We ascended the bank to them, as they would not come down to us, and our bold and at the same time conciliatory demeanour had the effect of cooling them down. We had an amicable interview with them, carried on with words & signs. It required some finessing however to get away from them; but once in the canoe, we quickly pushed out of range of their arrows and struck obliquely down the stream for the opposite bank, while I faced about, gun in hand, to watch their actions."

They travelled hard for the remainder of the day, trying to put as much distance as possible between themselves and the Indians, but no additional attempt was made to detain them, though Campbell learned later that he and his men had continued under surveillance for at least one more day and night. Once the traders felt safe from further trouble, they continued their journey at a more leisurely pace, arriving at the Frances Lake post late in July. Campbell estimated the distance from Pelly Banks to the Lewes as "over 300 miles." Dr. Dawson of the Geological Survey, making the same

[31] Campbell, *Two Journals*, pp. 65-68.
[32] *Ibid.*, p. 69, as are all other quotations relating to this confrontation.

journey in 1887, and using a sextant and chronometer to establish latitude and longitude as he travelled, reported the distance as being 320 miles; with the distance in a straight line being 219 miles. Campbell's rough estimate was remarkably close.

The report and sketch maps of this exploration evoked an enthusiastic response from the perambulatory Sir George Simpson, when they finally reached him. "Pelly River, from what you say of it," he wrote to Campbell in a letter dated June 3, 1844, "appears to be either 'Turnagain' or 'Quikpok' River ... the former falling into Cook's Inlet & the latter into Norton Sound. The country is evidently rich both in large & fur bearing animals, & from your description of the Forks of Pelly and Lewes Rivers, that appears a good situation for an establishment. I, therefore, think the first post ought to be formed there. You seem to have been anxious to have proceeded down to the sea; that, however I think at present unnecessary, & would be impolitic, as it would bring us into competition with our Russian neighbours, with whom we are desirous of maintaining a good understanding."[33]

For reasons over which he had no control, it was to be four years before Campbell was able to build the fort proposed by Simpson, and seven years before he could continue his explorations of the Pelly "down to the sea." For the present, the mundane business of consolidating the fur trade on Frances Lake and the upper Pelly, in the face of considerable obstruction and incompetence on the part of individuals in his own Company, kept him chained. The governor firmly believed that exploration should not only contribute to geographical knowledge but should also pay its way.

IV

ABOUT THE SAME TIME AS CAMPBELL WAS TRAMPING THE PORTAGE from Frances Lake to Pelly River, exploration was beginning far to the north of a second inland route to the Yukon basin. Sir John Franklin[34] inadvertently laid the groundwork for this investigation

[33] *Ibid.*, p. 75.

[34] Franklin (1786-1847), English Rear Admiral and explorer, is credited by some with the discovery of the Northwest Passage. After a distinguished naval career, he led two overland polar expeditions to the Arctic coast in 1819-1822 and 1825-1827, which together mapped 1,200 miles of shoreline. In

when, returning from the Mackenzie delta after his second expedition of 1825-27, he accidentally ascended for some distance a wide river which he thought at first was a branch of the Mackenzie, but which he finally realized was a separate tributary. He named it Peel's River, after Sir Robert Peel, then Home Secretary, later Prime Minister of England. He wrote a glowing account of the river and its valley, including the observation that the natives who lived there dressed in furs, and that many prime pelts from this region eventually by a process of intertribal barter reached the Mackenzie River trading posts. In time this report was brought to the attention of Governor Simpson, and he promptly decided that the Peel warranted further exploration.

Another experienced Hudson's Bay Company officer, John Bell, was selected for the task. A native of the Isle of Mull, off the Scottish coast, he joined the fur trade in 1818, at the age of 19, as a clerk with the Northwest Company, and transferred to the Hudson's Bay Company after the union of 1821. He was sent to the Mackenzie District in 1824, where he was placed in charge of the post at Fort Good Hope, then the most northerly and the most prosperous of the Company's Mackenzie River establishments. It was from this post that in 1839 Bell made his first excursion into the Peel River country.

Bell was a reluctant writer: his reports made difficult reading, and contained meagre and often confusing information: as a result his contribution to the exploration of the northwest is a most neglected one. However, his first ventures into the Peel had, briefly, a chronicler. He was Alexander Kennedy Isbister, an articled clerk in the employ of the Hudson's Bay Company, whose initial assignment was to accompany Bell into the Peel, and who wintered there in charge of the first post established in the region. Isbister possessed the literary ability that Bell lacked, and he prepared from the older man's notes, and from his own experiences in the country, a more readable account of the first reconnaissance of the Peel. In 1845 the article, with a map drawn by Isbister, was published in the *Journal of the Royal Geographic Society*, and though it covered only the

---

1845 he commanded an expedition by sea of two ships and 129 officers and men, which attempted to sail from the Atlantic to the Pacific by way of the Arctic. When the expedition did not return Franklin and his men became the object of many searches over a span of 14 years before his fate was determined and records of his journey recovered.

beginnings of Bell's investigation, it is still the principal record of his achievements in this region.

Isbister, though of Scottish blood, was born in 1822 at Cumberland House on the Saskatchewan River. His father was an Orkney man in the service of the Hudson's Bay Company who, when Isbister was 11 years old, was killed in an accident at Norway House. The widow and children moved to the Red River settlement, where Isbister attended school. He showed an aptitude for learning, particularly for rhetoric and for the florid style of composition that was very popular at that time. At the age of 16 he joined the Company's employ, a most desirable recruit, well-built and over six feet in height, who had lived all his life at trading posts or at Red River, and who therefore had little to learn about travel in the bush.

Bell's first ascent of the Peel was in the summer of 1839, when he "was commissioned to make a preliminary examination of the river, and apprise the natives of the Company's intention to open trade with them in the ensuing season."[35] Isbister did not accompany Bell on this occasion, but he later was given Bell's journal, and travelled through the country himself, though on snowshoes and not by boat. It is apparent from the account Isbister prepared, and from his survey and map, that Bell in actual fact followed the Peel only as far as the mouth of the Snake River — about 200 miles — which he then followed to its headwaters under the impression that it was the main stream. It was an understandable error, caused partly by the many islands in the river at this locality; a technicality that had no effect on his contribution to the opening up of northern Yukon.

A rapid was encountered about 60 miles from the river mouth. "The natives at this place," wrote Isbister, "had constructed a barrier of basket-work, which extended entirely across the stream, sufficiently open however to permit the water to pass freely through its interstices, for the purpose of catching the fish which ascend from the sea during the summer."[36] Above the rapids the current became swifter, as the explorers entered the mountains. "The banks of the river had now entirely changed their aspect, and instead of [flowing] through the low, unvarying mud-cliffs, with the sombre and cheerless appearance which the recent deposits of alluvium had

[35] A. K. Isbister, "Some account of the Peel River, N. America," *Journal of the Royal Geographic Society*, (Vol. XV, 1845), p. 335.

[36] *Ibid.*, p. 336.

imparted to them, the water-course was [now] not unfrequently through bold, romantic defiles, so steep and lofty as often to hide the midday sun from view."[37]

Eventually the current became too strong, and tracking and rowing too difficult, and the "cumbrous boat" was abandoned. A canoe had been brought along for just this eventuality, and Bell and half his men continued their upstream struggle in the lighter craft. However, this vessel too was soon abandoned.

The party continued on foot among the mountains, fording such streams as crossed their path, and after no slight hardships and not a few complaints from some of the men of numbness in the limbs, produced by wading in water whose temperature was scarcely above the freezing point, though it was then the middle of summer, Mr. Bell reached what seemed to be the headwaters of the Peel. The minute streamlets into which it had now ramified had become so insignificant . . . that he considered it useless to prolong the survey any farther, more especially as the short Arctic summer was more than half over, and he still had the exploration of the Rat River before him.[38]

The Rat, which Bell had first glimpsed on his upstream journey, was a large tributary flowing into the Peel from the west, about 30 miles from its mouth. This river, the Indians had told him, led through the mountains to a portage across a height of land where the "Tramontane Loucheux" — the Mountain Indians — would probably be camped, as this was an annual rendezvous for the purpose of trading with the Indians of the Peel. On his way out of the country, therefore, Bell determined to turn aside and explore it, at least as far as the Indian camp. He was happy to find travel along it relatively smooth, "compared to what they previously had been engaged in." At the portage, "they found [the] large band of Indians they had expected already encamped. After some time had been spent in bartering such furs as the Indians had to dispose of, Mr. Bell commenced his return and reached his winter quarters [Fort Good Hope] . . . in safety, after spending a little more than two months on the river."[39]

At the Fort Simpson Depot the hard-headed McPherson was sufficiently impressed by the account of the country to decide on the

[37] *Ibid.*, p. 337.
[38] *Ibid.*, p. 338.
[39] *Ibid.*, pp. 338-339.

immediate construction of a new post on the Peel, and he sent word to Bell at Fort Good Hope to make arrangements to carry out this assignment in the summer of 1840. Isbister would be in charge of the new post, and he would be sent from Fort Simpson to make the journey to the Peel with Bell as soon as river travel on the Mackenzie was possible.

On May 25, 1840, hard on the heels of the breakup of the ice, Isbister left the Depot for Fort Good Hope, where he found "everything in readiness for our immediate departure. Our party consisted of Mr. Bell and myself, twelve Orkney-men and Canadians, and four Indians with their families, who were engaged to act as fort hunters."[40] The journey downstream was continued on June 3, in two well-stocked boats, and the mouth of the Peel reached on June 6. Here the traders were met by a band of local Indians, who were waiting for the white men "with the view of acting as an escort to our party in the event of a collision with the Esquimaux, whose uniform hostility to the whites rendered a meeting with them anything but desirable." The natives were given the traditional gifts of tobacco, but were persuaded, in view of the size of the Company's party, that an escort would not be necessary.

Aided by a following wind, the men made good time on the upstream portion of their journey, and on the first night "encamped about 30 miles from its mouth in sight of the Rocky Mountains[41] . . . Next day we resumed our march, and passing the Rat River found, about 10 miles above it, another large party of Indians encamped. This being the spot selected for the site of the establishment, we encamped; and as Mr. Bell had traced the river to its source the previous year, and it being desirable to get the buildings erected as soon as possible, [the] survey for the time being had to be postponed."[42] The new establishment was at first known simply as Peel's River Post, though it was also sometimes referred to as Fort McPher-

---

[40] *Ibid.*, p. 335, as is the other quotation in this paragraph.

[41] The "Rocky Mountains" west of the Peel were the Richardson Mountains, named by Franklin for Sir John Richardson, (1787-1865), surgeon and naturalist on both of the Franklin overland polar expeditions. In 1848, when over 60 years of age, he commanded a Franklin searching expedition based at the mouth of the Mackenzie. His book on this experience, *Arctic Searching Expedition*, contained material on the Yukon, all of it, however, second-hand. He was knighted in 1846.

[42] Isbister, "Peel River," p. 335.

son. It was not until about 1898, however, that the latter name came into general use in the Company's records.

A survey of this unmapped area was a project that Isbister had cherished ever since he had known of his assignment to the Peel. During his first days at Fort Simpson, Dease and Thomas Simpson had passed through the Depot on their way back from the Arctic, and Simpson had given the eager young clerk a pocket sextant and a spirit level. "As I had besides," Isbister wrote, "two very good compasses and the free use of Mr. Bell's valuable watch . . . I unexpectedly found myself in possession of the means to make a survey."[43] His only regret was that he did not have as much time to devote to the project as he would have liked. "The party to which I was attached," he explained, ". . . was fitted out solely for the purpose of establishing a trade with the Indians, towards which it was of course expected by our employers our undivided attention should be directed. The duties of an Indian trader are of sufficiently multifarious a nature to occupy the attention of any man."[44] It was not until the winter of 1840-41 that Isbister was able to resume his self-imposed task.

For the next few months he was almost constantly on snowshoes, examining the topography along the river, and searching for lakes in the vicinity. He retraced Bell's route to the "source" of the Peel, though the snow cover made comparisons in some locations rather difficult. As the young man was guided by Bell's notes while making the journey, he inevitably followed the same route, and also missed the right-angled bend that the Peel makes where the Snake flows into it.

Later, he turned his attention to the Rat, following Bell's footsteps along it as well. The notes he made on this journey provided the first detailed description of its headwaters and of the country that for over 20 years was to be a lifeline of the Company's northern operations. It was a terrain, Isbister noted

. . . of a very different character from that through which the Peel takes its course. It derives its waters from numerous small lakes, with which the flat country W. of the mountains is studded. . . . Its water has the peculiar swampy taste which indicates its origin. Its banks are

[43] *Ibid.*, p. 335.
[44] *Ibid.*, p. 334.

low, with little or no wood, but clothed instead with a long rank grass and some dwarf willows, with occasionally a few interspersed clumps of stunted pines. The soil is composed of strata of various coloured sands, overlying clay [that encloses] gravel and small water-moved boulders, and supporting a thin vegetable coat, in many places going to peat. The river ... trends to the S., and, according to the Indians, extends to a considerable distance into the interior.[45]

After returning to Peel's River Post, Isbister, in intervals during the business of trading, added the information concerning the Rat River to his map. "For the interstitial data," he acknowledged, "I was here, as before, in the case of the Peel, indebted to the notes of Mr. Bell."[46]

Isbister's three-year contract with the Company had nearly run its course, and as he did not plan to renew it, intending instead to return to school to further his education,[47] he was instructed to report to Fort Simpson after the breakup. While waiting for warmer weather — the thermometer during the winter had ranged between "40° and 70° minus" — he undertook one more short journey. "On the 15th of April," he wrote, "I left Peel River along with four men, and crossing the country with a view of falling upon some part of the [Arctic] Red River. It was a quarter of a mile wide where I saw it, and rises, according to the Indians, in the mountains, and flows through a district similar to that which borders the Peel."[48] The course of the lower reaches of this river was the last addition to the young man's map.

Bell's work in the Peel area, however, continued, though with the departure of Isbister only the bare record of it survives. In 1842 he was instructed to cross the Richardson Mountains again by the Rat River route, and to investigate the country still farther to the west. He started downstream on a river since named after him, but which

---

[45] *Ibid.*, p. 339.

[46] *Ibid.*, p. 341.

[47] In 1842 Isbister went to England to continue his education, and after obtaining his M.A. and LL.B. degrees, became a barrister. Though he never returned to the northwest, he retained a life-long affection for the land of his birth. In his will, he left $60,000 and his considerable library to Manitoba College, the forerunner of the University of Manitoba. He was always happy to entertain Company officers in his rooms, and among others Robert Campbell was a frequent visitor when in London on furlough.

[48] Isbister, "Peel River," p .341.

was then generally known as the Rat, in spite of the fact that this was also the name given to the tributary that flowed eastward into the Peel.[49] In time he came to a junction with a larger stream — the Porcupine, named for the large numbers of these animals found along it — which he followed for a further three days before turning back, reaching a point close to the present-day location of the international boundary.

In 1844 Governor Simpson issued orders that the Porcupine was to be explored to its mouth. Once again Bell crossed the portage and began another descent of the river beyond the Richardsons. Several days later he came to the end of his journey, on a sprawling alluvial plain on which the Porcupine was swallowed by a much larger river that at the junction swept in a great right-angled arc from a northerly course to a westerly one. To this river Bell gave his version of the name for it used by the natives he encountered on its banks — the Youcon. It was his most significant contribution to the geography of the northwest, and is today almost forgotten.[50]

When this information reached him, Simpson digested it with his usual thoroughness, and reached a typically brash decision. He would establish a new Hudson's Bay Company's post on the Yukon, at the mouth of the Porcupine — a location in good fur country, and strategically situated to attract the trade of the Indians who lived in the vicinity. What he did not officially acknowledge was that this post would be well to the west of the 141st meridian, in Russian American territory. Even as he was advising Campbell that it would be "impolitic" to risk competing with "our Russian neighbours," he was himself planning to throw down the gauntlet and meet them on their own ground.

---

[49] This confusion is not lessened by the fact that there are still two Rat Rivers in the area, one flowing westward from the Richardson Mountains, and the other eastward, into the Peel. This latter stream is the one explored by Bell and Isbister in 1839-40, while the river beyond the portage that for a time was also called the Rat is now the Bell. The Rat River of today west of the mountains is a tributary of the Bell, flowing into it not far upstream from Lapierre House.

[50] Bell, who was promoted to the rank of Chief Trader in 1840, continued to serve in the Mackenzie District until 1850, though he was seconded to Arctic exploration in the season 1847-48. He retired from the Company's service in 1860, and died in 1863. He married a daughter of Peter Warren Dease, and had one daughter.

V

TO BUILD HIS NEW ESTABLISHMENT, SIMPSON SELECTED ANOTHER Scotsman, Alexander Hunter Murray, a 27-year-old bachelor, born in Kilum in Argyllshire. Though at the time of his appointment he was new in the service of the Hudson's Bay Company, he already had acquired a wealth of experience with the American Fur Company in various parts of the United States. The assignment started auspiciously. Murray left Fort Garry in June 1846, with the fur brigade, and by rare good fortune one of his travelling companions chanced to be a young and attractive single girl — Anne Campbell, 17 years old, the daughter of Chief Trader Colin Campbell of Fort Chipewyan, who was returning to her father's post after completing her formal education at the Red River settlement. During the journey the inevitable happened. Murray, a talented artist, undertook to teach Anne to sketch, to help pass the time while travelling; but before they reached Anne's destination, the teacher had asked the hand of the pupil in marriage, and had been accepted. The ceremony was performed at Fort Chipewyan "in the manner of the country" by the officer in charge of the brigade. The honeymoon was the remainder of the long journey to Peel's River Post, and there the newlyweds spent the first winter of their married life.

The party that was to erect the post — which it had been decided would be called Fort Yukon — left the Peel on June 11, 1847. Murray had already taken his wife by dog team, before the breakup, to Lapierre House,[51] at the head of navigation on the Porcupine, and had then returned to the Peel to lead his men across the portage, using the trail which Bell had pioneered, and which by now was sufficiently used to have an established summer and winter route. Crossing the mountains in spring when the ground was no longer frozen, and with the rivers in spate, was a much more difficult undertaking than the winter journey. The first obstacle was the muskeg on the low ground immediately west of the Peel, which Murray described in his journal as being

---

[51] Lapierre House was established as a satellite post of the establishment at Peel's River, and was under the control of the same officer. It was actually located on the Bell River, about 35 miles above its confluence with the Porcupine. Its spelling varied widely, that adopted here being the one used on the National Topographic Series mapsheets — not because it is necessarily the correct one, but because a choice of the several variants had to be made.

... overflown by the river in May, and now in an almost impassable state. We waded most of the way knee-deep; but often up to our middle in sludge and water. The day was clear and warm, and the mosquitoes had already begun their ravages, which rendered the commencement of the voyage anything but pleasant. In three hours we cleared the 'Slough of Dispond' [sic], and another hour brought us to top of hills nearest to Peel's River, where we rested for awhile and partook of pemmican and moss water. The party being now assembled and fairly 'en route' in the open country, I cautioned them to be careful of the Company's property, that each was responsible for what he carried, advised them not to separate on the way, and left instruction with Mr. McKenzie [Murray's assistant clerk] to look after things in general. I then started ahead with Manuel, the best walker among the men, and an Indian not so heavily loaded as the others, intending to reach L.P. House in three days, so as to have my letters answered and things in order, that the voyage might not be delayed on that account.

Although now on high ground and gradually ascending sloping hills, the ground was completely saturated with water, very little vegetation appeared, tufts of heath and moss thinly interspersed on a bottom of soft mud, but only thrived about 6 inches from the surface, passed a range of small lakes extending toward the north, they were only open around the sides, the ice in the centre appearing quite solid. Several large flocks of geese were seen here, but we were too hurried to go after them ...

It was past 10 o'clock, before we reached a place with sufficient *brush* to make a fire, and had some difficulty in finding a spot dry enough whereon to sit. Each picked out his own moss knole [sic], and rolled up in his blanket composed himself to sleep. We came only about 25 miles to-day in a westerly course, and to the north of the winter route.

Although stiff in the joints and otherwise fatigued, I could sleep little, from my moss bed having sunk into the water, and from a severe attack of heartburn occasioned by the raw pemmican which generally disagrees with my stomach.[52]

The next day the three men approached the treeless, open terrain of the Yukon divide. "We now joined," wrote Murray, "that portion of the winter trail known as the 'Barren Traverse', here every place was flooded, every snow bank sent forth a stream, what appeared in winter to be diminutive brooks were now foaming rivers, several of these intersected our path and caused some detention."[53] They saw a few caribou, and many small game birds, mostly

[52] A. H. Murray, *Journal of the Yukon, 1847-48*, ed. L. J. Burpee, (Ottawa, Government Printing Bureau, 1910), pp. 21-22. This journal is much livelier than most of its kind, and is illustrated by many of Murray's sketches.

[53] *Ibid.*, p. 23.

grouse and ptarmigan, which Murray called white partridge. "Some of their nests were also found," he added, "and the eggs of course we devoured raw."

The flooded creeks continued to delay their progress. At one point at which the trail followed a small canyon known as the Chute "where the sleds and dogs have to be lowered over with lines in winter," it was now completely impassable because of high water, and they had to make a detour of several miles before they were able to rejoin it. The crossing of the swollen Bell River was also accomplished only with difficulty, at a location much farther upstream than the usual ford. Equipped with a strong pole, Manuel made the first attempt, "and got about two-thirds across when it became too deep and rapid, on attempting to turn, his pole gave way and he was carried down stream, most fortunately the current set in to the opposite bank, and after rolling him once or twice over, he scrambled ashore, with the loss of his gun and bonnet."[54] With Manuel soaking wet but safe on the far shore, Murray threw him a rope weighted with a rock, and with this as a support managed to cross without being swept downstream. The Indian, however, "not admiring this method, refused to make a trial, he went further up, and crossed without difficulty at a much broader place," — a wry commentary on the white man's efforts.

Their troubles were not over. Having waded the Bell in unfamiliar terrain, they had trouble locating themselves once they crossed it, and after wandering most of the day in a landscape in which there were "no 'verdant hills' . . . not a vestige of animation," they found themselves to their chagrin back at the Bell River only a few miles below the point where they had crossed it. "I expected to have slept at Lapiers [sic] House," Murray commented, in exasperation, "and here we were farther by a few miles than we had camped last night."

The advance party finally reached Lapierre House on the fourth day, and Murray enjoyed a brief reunion with his bride. "Once alongside of my young wife," he wrote, "before a table well replenished with venison steaks, and the usual accompaniments, the fatigues of the journey were soon forgotten."[55] When the rest of the men caught up with him four days later, Murray moved on, reluctantly leaving his wife at "the Small House" in the care of an Indian

---

[54] *Ibid.*, p. 25. Other quoted references to the crossing are on p. 26.
[55] *Ibid.*, p. 28.

woman. Anne was expecting their first child, and her husband did not dare take her on the strenuous journey to the Yukon. It was to be over a year before they saw each other again.

Below Lapierre House, the going was easier: travel was by river with the current, in a York boat that had been built the previous winter on Murray's instructions, and that was waiting for them when they arrived at the post. There was considerable rain during the journey, and even, on June 21, some snow squalls and sleet. When the weather did clear up and the sun beat down, the mosquitoes quickly became almost unbearable, and forced them to travel as much as possible at night. Even though, in these latitudes at this time of year, there was no darkness, the late hours of the day at least were cooler, and the insects less voracious.

At the mouth of the Bell, where it flowed into the Porcupine, the traders were hailed by a party of Indians, including five from the Yukon River who had been at Lapierre House when Murray arrived there, and who had assured him that Russian traders had been at the mouth of the Porcupine the year before. This story haunted Murray, and when he reached, according to his reckoning, the vicinity of the boundary between British and Russian territory, he admitted to having been "on the look-out, as we came along, for a site whereon to build, should it so happen, that we are compelled to retreat upon our own territory."[56]

The Porcupine when they first started down it was found to be generally broad and sluggish, with the main channel not always easily identifiable, so that several times they ran aground. The river's course was meandering, the banks low and muddy, with only occasionally glimpses of "high but smooth mountains" to the north "where it is said Rein deer resort in numerous numbers during summer."[57] They missed the mouth of the Old Crow River as it was obscured by an island.

On June 22 Murray noted the "commencement of the great ramparts, the river becomes quite narrow and the current much stronger." The length of the canyon which constituted the ramparts he estimated as 68 miles, running between "rocky hills and precipices

[56] *Ibid.*, p. 35. Murray was actually about 50 miles out in his dead reckoning, as when he wrote this he was still over a day's travel from the ramparts of the Porcupine, which lie just west of the boundary.

[57] *Ibid.*, p. 35. These were the Old Crow Mountains, to the north of the Old Crow flats.

varying from 30 to 120 feet in height." At one place, he noted, "the principal body of the river rushes through a small channel of about thirty feet wide, between the rocks on one side and a high strong batture [ledge] on the other, this is named the 'Carribeux Leap' from one being able to leap over it, so say the Indians."[58] This last phrase is perhaps the true explanation of what sounds suspiciously like a traveller's tale.

Below the ramparts the current continued stronger than in the upper reaches, the trees were larger, and the maze of channels increasingly difficult to follow, but the party continued to make good progress. On June 25 they reached the Yukon River. Indians whom they encountered there told them that there was no high ground below the mouth of the Porcupine, but they might find a suitable site for a fort a short distance upstream. They turned their boats in this direction, and found themselves exposed for the first time to "the full force of a *Youcon current*; that of the Mackenzie is nothing to it, it was with much difficulty — at certain places — [that] we could make any headway against it with the oars; the banks are so overhanging, thickly wooded, and choked with fallen trees, that tracking was equally laborious, and the water too deep for using poles."[59] The mosquitoes descended on them in swarms, to Murray's disgust.

We could neither speak nor breathe without our mouths being filled with them, close your eyes and you had fast half a dozen, fires were lit all around but of no avail. Rather than be devoured, the men, fatigued as they were, preferred stemming the current a little longer, to reach a dry and open spot a little further on, of which the Indians informed us. Another half hour's hard *tugging* brought us to it, and we camped on the banks of the Youcon.

I must say, as I sat smoking my pipe, and my face besmeared with tobacco juice to keep at bay the d—d mosquitoes still hovering in clouds around me, my first impressions of the Youcon were anything but favourable. As far as we have come (2½ miles), I never saw an uglier river, everywhere low banks, apparently lately overflowed, with lakes and swamps behind, the trees too small for building, the water abominably dirty and the current furious; but I was consoled with the hopes held out ... that a short distance further on there was higher land.[60]

[58] *Ibid.*, pp. 36-37.

[59] *Ibid.*, p. 42.

[60] *Ibid.*, pp. 42-43.

Murray was not made any happier by a talk, through his interpreter, with the local Indian chief, who told the traders that he had been in contact with the Russians on the lower Yukon; that they had many trade goods; that they were expected soon at the mouth of the Porcupine "as they had promised to come up with *two* boats, not only to trade, but to explore this river to its source."[61] They were described as being "well armed with pistols, their boat was about the same size as ours . . . but made of sheet iron, [and] carrying more people." "This was not very agreeable news to me," Murray added wryly, "knowing that we were on their land, but I kept my thoughts to myself, and determined to keep a sharp lookout in case of surprise."

With some difficulty a site was selected for the new post — a dry ridge three miles above the Porcupine, on the right bank — and "little bark cabins" were erected as temporary shelter for the men during the construction period. They quickly had visitors, not Russians but Indians, and the ritual of making gifts of tobacco to them, watching their dancing, and listening to what Murray called "speechifying," was meticulously observed. On July 1, 1847, construction of the establishment was started, and even though most of the men were inexperienced and "could scarcely square a log," progress was good. By fall the dwelling house was completed, and the men moved in for the winter; the work would be continued in the spring. "When the fort is finished," wrote Murray proudly, "as I hope it will be next fall, I calculate on it being the best and strongest (not excepting Fort Simpson) between Red River and the Polar Sea."[62] The Russians were very much on his mind as he planned his buildings and lay-out; he insisted on strong fortifications. "The pickets will not be pointed poles or slabs," he continued, "but good sized trees dispossessed of their bark and squared on two sides to fit closely and 14½ feet in height above ground, 3 feet underground . . . the bastions will be made as strong as possible, roomy and convenient. When all this is finished, the Russians may advance when they d—d please."

Trading began while construction was still in progress, using a temporary store. From the first Murray was handicapped and frustrated by the skimpy outfit supplied to him by the parsimonious Murdock McPherson, who had returned from furlough in 1844,

---

[61] *Ibid.*, p. 45, as are the other quotations in this paragraph.

[62] *Ibid.*, p. 66. Other quotations referring to the fort are from pp. 66-67.

and was again in charge of the Mackenzie District. All too soon Murray found himself in the humiliating position of having to turn down opportunities to acquire prime pelts because of the lack of articles to offer in trade. "The box of beads were gone," he wrote unhappily in the fall, "the box of guns ditto, except two guns kept for the defence of the place, the roll of tobacco was on its last legs, and our shop, except cloth and ammunition, nearly empty."[63] To make matters worse, in November Indians arrived from the lower Yukon, with information concerning the Russians, which Murray noted.

[They] had a large stock of goods with them, were trading at much lower prices than formerly, and had better goods than us. The Russians were trying to incite the Indians here against us by telling them, that it was on account of our being in their country that so many of them had died in summer, that we were bad people, etc., and inviting the Indians to go to them with their sick friends, as they had medicines to cure all diseases, that they were sorry they had not been able to keep their promise with the Indians here and visit them in summer, they had been unfortunate in having necesary boats built, but next summer they would meet them farther up the river with plenty of goods.[64]

It was difficult to counteract such promises with a warehouse bare of trade goods. As a last resort, Murray sent men and dogs, as soon as it was possible to travel, to Peel River with an urgent request for extra supplies "to be taken from the year's outfit," but they returned early in January 1848, with pitifully little. Murray wrote bitterly "that I was greatly mortified to find so limited a supply of the articles most needed (beads and guns) being sent; I notice that there are only a quarter of a box of beads (16 lbs.). I would have been better satisfied had none at all been sent, as then I could have settled with the Indians alike, without displeasing one more than the other."[65] A short time later he echoed the same sentiments in a letter he wrote almost in despair to McPherson: "Guns and beads, beads and guns, is the cry in all our country. Please to excuse me for repeating this so often, but I cannot be too importunate, the rise or fall of our establishment on the Youcon depends principally on the supply of these articles."[66]

[63] *Ibid.*, p. 68.
[64] *Ibid.*, p. 69.
[65] *Ibid.*, p. 93.
[66] *Ibid.*, p. 100.

By spring, however, he was more optimistic. The trade had not after all gone too badly, considering the "means at hand": there had been no hunger at the post, as both game and fish were plentiful, and the pickets of which he was so proud were now squared and ready for erection. Anxious for a reunion with his wife, Murray left his assistant in charge and accompanied the returns to Lapierre House as soon as the Porcupine River was free of ice. After a three week's journey, the anxious husband had a joyous reunion with his bride, and saw for the first time his infant daughter Helen — the first white child born in present-day Yukon Territory. Husband and wife resolved that this would be their last parting, and when Murray returned to Fort Yukon later in the year he took Anne and Helen with him.

The Murrays remained at Fort Yukon for three years, and they were busy ones for both of them. Anne while there gave birth to two more daughters, Elizabeth and Margaret, and the care of her children and the chores of setting up housekeeping kept her occupied. To her relatives and in-laws she wrote sober letters full of domestic chit-chat: "We have a good house. I have now another daughter, Elizabeth. Our little Helen now speaks well. My husband is preparing for a summer trip and will be away about a month."[67] Occasionally, however, a cry from the heart broke through the brave veneer, as when to her mother-in-law she wrote, in the midst of the trivia, that "We are far from old friends, and have no society but ourselves." The worst periods were during her husband's absences on the business of the Company.

For Murray there was the time-consuming task of developing the trade at the new post and establishing good relationships with the Indians of the vicinity, 300 of which he estimated traded regularly with the Company. After a shaky start Fort Yukon began by degrees to prosper, a fact partly accounted for by the departure of McPherson from the Mackenzie District in 1849, and the more open-handed policy of his successors. To increase his knowledge of the Indian tribes and the country they inhabited, Murray began to compile a vocabulary of the local Indian dialects. "Since my arrival here," he explained, "and also while at Peel's River, it was my study to obtain from the different bands of Indians a description of their respective

[67] Nan Shipley, "Anne and Alexander Murray," *The Beaver*, (Winter 1967), p. 36.

lands and river . . . [and] I have been able to form some idea of the courses of the Youcon and other rivers, of which hitherto very little was known."[68] He divided the Yukon Indians, or "Kutchin," into eight tribes, and he calculated that "the population of the country from the Polar Sea to the Pelly — I mean along the Youcon and its tributaries — is from what I can ascertain close upon 1,000 *men*, or men and boys able to hunt."[69] Much of this information, and several of his sketches, were used by Sir John Richardson in his book *Arctic Searching Expedition*, written by the famous explorer after a visit to the mouth of the Mackenzie, and published in London in 1851.

As his family grew, Murray became increasingly anxious for a posting closer to civilization, and he did not hesitate to make his feelings known. In 1851 his request for a transfer was granted, and as soon as travelling conditions permitted, he made his last crossing of the portage to the Peel, this time with his wife and three small daughters, on what must have been for them an arduous and difficult journey. The fort that he had established at the mouth of the Porcupine was to operate profitably for 22 years, although it was the most isolated of the Company's posts. In spite of Murray's initial concern, the Russians made no attempt to force its removal, and there is no historical evidence to support the statement made more than once by the Indians that the Russians had been at the site of the fort before Murray got there. Contact between the rival traders, when it was made, was at the mouth of the Tanana River, about mid-way between Fort Yukon and Nulato, and it was not until 1861 that a creole in Russian employ, I. S. Lukin, finally travelled as far upstream as the Hudson's Bay Company's Porcupine River post. Even this was not a belated challenge, but an isolated journey, not repeated. For the present, the illegal British post on Russian soil was undisturbed.

[68] Murray, *Journal*, p. 74.
[69] *Ibid.*, p. 81.

Maps

Numbers 1 to 7 by J. G. Callan

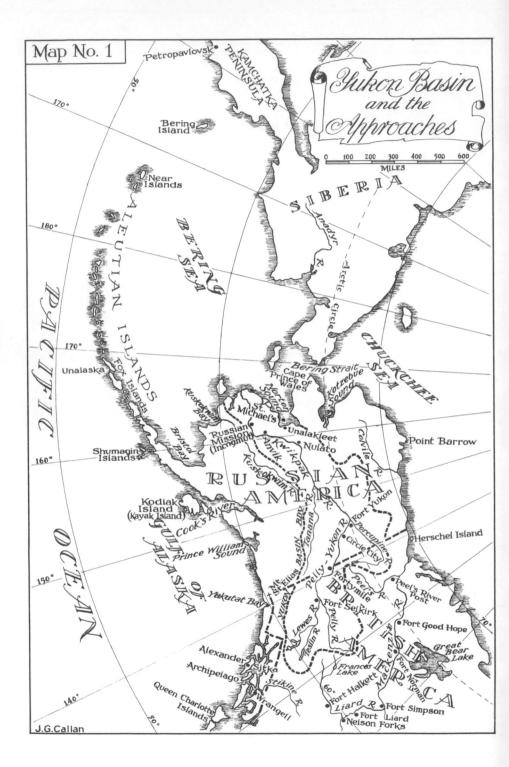

Map No. 1

Yukon Basin and the Approaches

0   100   200   300   400   500   600
MILES

Petropavlovsk

KAMCHATKA PENINSULA

Bering Island

Near Islands

ALEUTIAN ISLANDS

BERING SEA

SIBERIA

Anadyr R.

Arctic Circle

CHUCKCHEE SEA

Bering Strait
Cape Prince of Wales

Kotzebue Sound

Unalaska

Fox Islands

Norton Sound

St. Michael's

Unalakleet

Nulato

Colvile R.

Point Barrow

PACIFIC

Kuskokwim Bay

Bristol Bay

Russian Mission (Ikogmute)

Anvik

Kwikpak

Kuskokwim R.

RUSSIAN AMERICA

Shumagin Islands

Fort Yukon

Porcupine R.

Circle City

Herschel Island

Kodiak Island (Kayak Island)

Cook's River

Tanana R.

Birch R.

Yukon R.

Pelly R.

Fortymile

Peel's R.

Peel's River Post

GULF OF ALASKA

Prince William Sound

Mt. St. Elias

OCEAN

Yakutat Bay

Yukon R.

Pelly R.

Fort Selkirk

Lewes R.

Teslin R.

Fort Pelly R.

BRITISH

Fort Good Hope

Great Bear Lake

Alexander Archipelago

Sitka

Stikine R.

Wrangell

Frances Lake

Fort Halkett

Liard R.

Fort Nelson

Fort Norman

Mackenzie R.

AMERICA

Queen Charlotte Islands

Fort Simpson

Fort Liard

Nelson Forks

J.G.Callan

170°   180°   170°   160°   150°   140°

70°   60°   50°

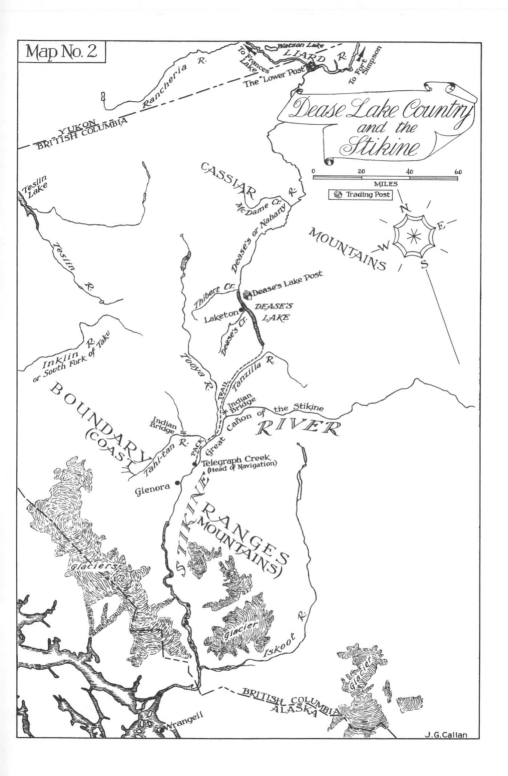

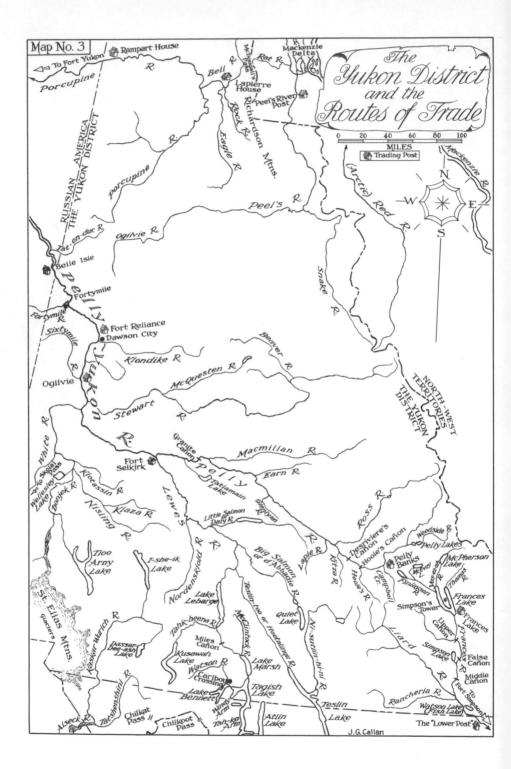

Map No. 3

Rampart House

To Fort Yukon

Porcupine R.

Bell R.

McDougall's Pass

Rat R.

Mackenzie Delta

Lapierre House

Peel's River Post

Richardson Mtns.

RUSSIAN AMERICA
THE YUKON DISTRICT

Porcupine

Rock R.

Eagle R.

Peel's

Snake R.

(Arctic) Red R.

Mackenzie R.

The Yukon District and the Routes of Trade

0 20 40 60 80 100
MILES
Trading Post

N
W   E
S

Tat-on-duc R.

Ogilvie R.

Belle Isle

Fortymile

Pelly

Fortymile R.

Sixtymile

Fort Reliance

Dawson City

Klondike R.

McQuesten R.

Beaver R.

NORTH-WEST TERRITORIES
THE YUKON DISTRICT

Ogilvie

Stewart R.

Yukon R.

White R.

Granite Cañon

Macmillan R.

Earn R.

Ross R.

To Skagway
Wellesley Lake

Klotassin R.

Donjek R.

Fort Selkirk

Pelly

Tatlmain Lake

Gegdan

Lapie R.

Ketza R.

Desriviere's Cañon

Hoole's Cañon

Woodside R.

Pelly Lakes

Nisling R.

Klaza R.

Lewes

Little Salmon or Daly R.

Big Salmon or d'Abbadie R.

Hoole's R.

Pelly Banks

Campbell Cr.

Mt. Roy

McPherson Lake

Moose R.

Tloo Army Lake

I-she-ik Lake

Nordenskiold R.

Lake Lebarge

Teslintoo or Hootalinqua R.

Quiet Lake

Ni-sutlin-hi-ni

Finlayson

Simpson's Tower

Thomas R.

Frances Lake

St. Elias Mtns.

glaciers

Kaskawulsh R.

Dassar-bee-ash Lake

Tank-heena R.

McClintock R.

Lake Marsh

Liard

Frances R.

Upper Cañon

Simpson Lake

False Cañon

Miles Cañon

Kusawah Lake

Watson R.

Tagish Lake

Teslin Lake

Middle Cañon

Tatshenshini R.

Caribou Crossing

Lake Bennett

Windy Arm

Atlin Lake

Rancheria R.

To Fort Simpson

Alseck R.

Chilkat Pass

Chilkoot Pass

Tah-ko Arm

Watson Lake (Fish Lake)

The "Lower Post"

J. G. Callan

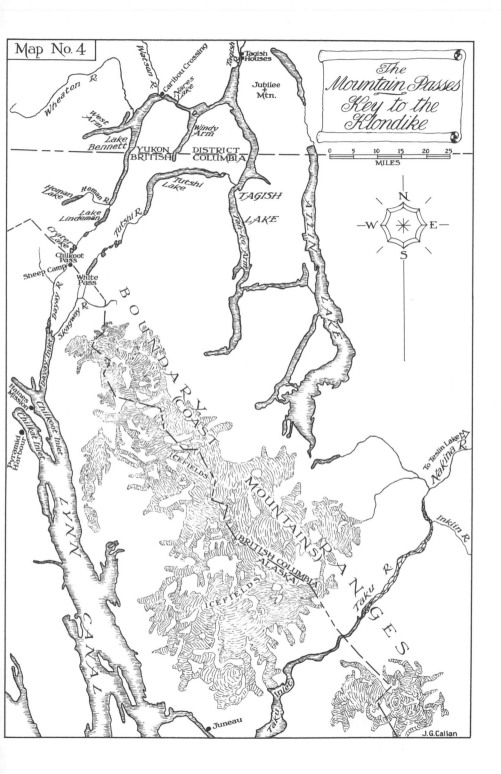

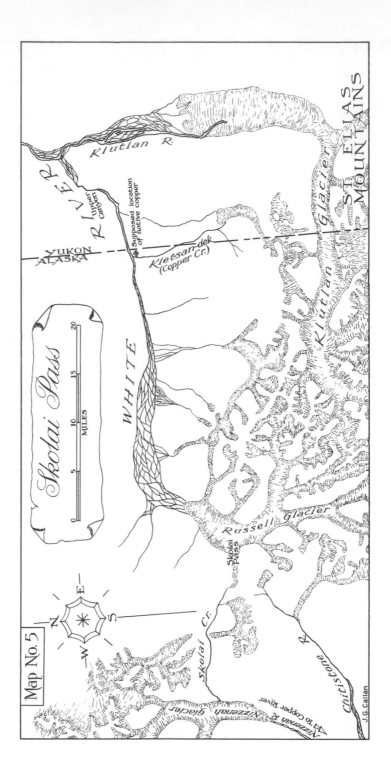

Map No. 5

Skolai Pass

MILES
0 5 10 15 20

N E S W

YUKON
ALASKA

RIVER

Klutlan R.

Upper
canyon

Supposed location
of native copper

Kletsan-dek
(Copper Cr.)

WHITE

ST. ELIAS
MOUNTAINS

Glacier

Klutlan

Russell Glacier

Skolai
Pass

Skolai Cr.

Chitistone R.

Nizzenah Glacier

Nizzenah R.

to copper River

J.G. Callan

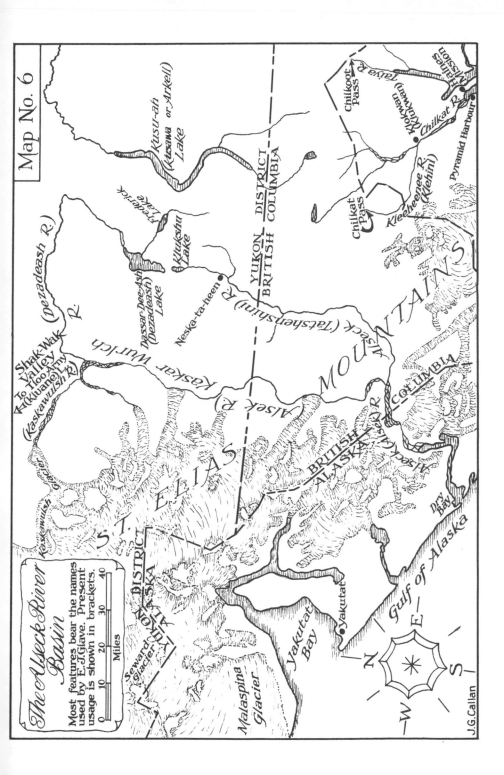

Map No. 6

The Alsek River Basin

Most features bear the names used by E.J.Glave. Present usage is shown in brackets.

Miles
0 10 20 30 40

Kusur-ah (Kusawa or Arkell) Lake

Chilkoot Pass

Taiya R. (Taiya)

Dayay Haines Mission

Klokwan (Klukwan)

Chilkat R.

Pyramid Harbour

Chilkat Pass

Kleeheenee R. (Klehini)

Frederick Lake

Klukshu Lake

YUKON DISTRICT
BRITISH COLUMBIA

Dassar-Dee-Ash (Dezadeash) Lake

Neska-ta-heen

Alseck R. (Tatshenshini) R.

Shak-Wak (Dezadeash R.) Valley
To Tloo Army (Kluane L.)
(Kaskawulsh R.)

Kaskar Wurlch R.

Alsek R.

Alsek or Alseck R.

Alseck or COLUMBIA

MOUNTAINS

S T. E L I A S

BRITISH ALASKA

Kaskawulsh Glacier

DISTRICT
ALASKA

Seward Glacier

Dry Bay

Gulf of Alaska

Malaspina Glacier

Yakutat Bay

Yakutat

N
W · E
S

J.G.Callan

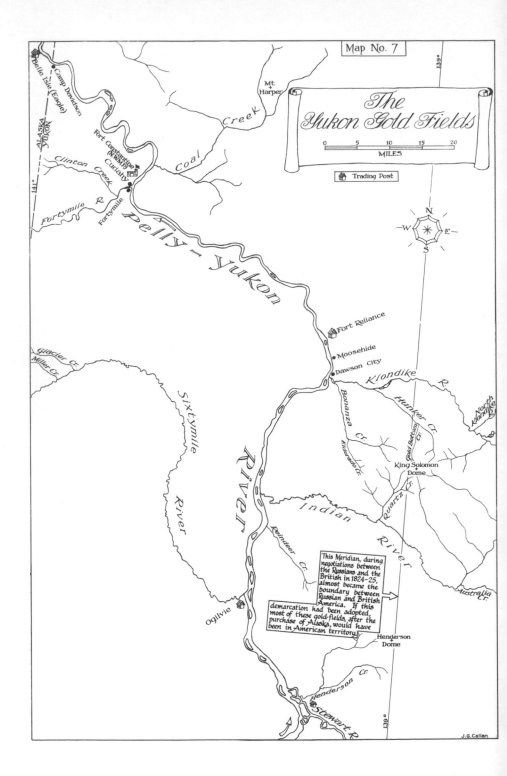

Map No. 7

The
Yukon Gold Fields

0   5   10   15   20
MILES

🏠 Trading Post

Belle Isle (Eagle)
Camp Davidson
ALASKA
YUKON
141°
Clinton Creek
Fort Constantine (N.W.M.P.)
Cudahy
Fortymile R.
Fortymile
Coal Creek
Mt Harper
Pelly – Yukon

N
W E
S

Fort Reliance
Moosehide
Dawson City
Klondike R.
North Klondike
Bonanza Cr.
Hunker Cr.
Gold Bottom Cr.
Eldorado Cr.
King Solomon Dome
Quartz Cr.
Glacier Cr.
Miller Cr.
Sixtymile River
River
Reindeer Cr.
Indian River
Australia Cr.
139°

Ogilvie

This Meridian, during negotiations between the Russians and the British in 1824–25, almost became the boundary between Russian and British America. If this demarcation had been adopted, most of these gold-fields, after the purchase of Alaska, would have been in American territory.

Henderson Dome
Henderson Cr.
Stewart R.
139°

J.G.Callan

CHAPTER THREE

The Hudson's Bay Company
Linkup and Expulsion

Map Number 3, following page 58

I

WHILE FORT YUKON WAS BEING CONSTRUCTED AT THE MOUTH OF the Porcupine, Campbell was building on the Pelly. In 1845 he established a post at Pelly Banks, near the hills from which he had first seen the river, and spent two winters there, the second one largely occupied in building boats to use for the journey to the site of the proposed station at the confluence of the Pelly and the Lewes. Unhappily, Campbell was dependent again for his supplies on the handouts of Murdock McPherson, who had no enthusiasm for the expansion, in spite of Governor Simpson's approbation, and who issued a "miserably insufficient outfit" for the new venture. "Of such essential staples as ammunition & tobacco," Campbell wrote angrily in his journal, echoing Murray's complaints, "we were furnished as follows: — 1 keg powder weighing 66 lb. & a corresponding quantity of shot & ball, & 1 roll of Tobacco *84 lb.* with the rest of the outfit to match. Such were the meagre means placed at my disposal for the new post ... to be established among hundreds of Indians — who to begin with had to be conciliated with the customary presents in order to start our dealings with them on a friendly basis."[1]

By the spring of 1848 the boats were ready, and the trade at both Frances Lake and Pelly Banks was on a sound footing "as more Indians were finding us out." Then Campbell received another shock. His replacement at Pelly Banks, who would be responsible for the trans-shipment of supplies and goods to the new post on the

---

[1] Campbell, *Two Journals*, pp. 78-79.

Lewes, turned out when he arrived not to be the man whom he had been promised, and was expecting, but rather a man — identified in his journal only as "Mr. P."[2] — who "was well-known to possess neither the judgment nor the foresight nor the energy requisite at a remote & isolated charge, where everything so much depended on his own efforts."[3] Nonetheless, whatever his doubts and forebodings, Campbell pushed on.

As early in May as circumstances permitted, we embarked at Pelly Banks on our journey. . . . My party consisted of Mr. Stewart[4] & 8 men & some of my Liard hunters. We had a boat carrying our apology of an outfit, a skiff, & some canoes; also a raft of building boards which we started ahead. We met hardly any Indians till within 50 miles of our destination. They were in large camps along the river watching, with eager and friendly feelings for our coming, as the news had gone before that we were to do. The boat, so many white men & in fact the 'tout ensemble' astonished them beyond expression. . . .

The Indians we met were all most friendly, & it was to be regretted that from our limited stock of tobacco we could spare only 1 inch to each Indian as we met him instead of the usual 6 inches, which constituted the gratifying emblem of peace handed to Indians on arriving at a post.

On 1 June, 1848, we safely reached the forks of the Pelly & Lewes with boat, skiff, canoes & raft, all of which were of great service to us afterwards. On selecting a site we proceeded with the erection of the building in earnest & got on rapidly, naming the new Post Fork Selkirk.[5] Parties of local Indians, "gens de bois" were coming and going freely

---

2 Mr. P. was Pierre Chrysologue Pambrun, Jr., son of one of the Company's Chief Traders, and a graduate of St. John's College in Winnipeg. He was hired as a clerk and sent to the Mackenzie District in 1841, remaining there until 1852. In 1898, at the age of 72, he was brought to Ottawa to appear as an expert witness before a special committee of the Senate that was enquiring into the possibility of constructing a rail link "to the navigable waters of the Yukon." On the stand he gave evidence of the Pelly River portage as he recalled it. His evidence was literate and lucid, and he emerges from this appearance in a more sympathetic light than presented by Campbell. The kindest comment must be that his talents did not suit him in a position of responsibility in the fur trade, to Campbell's understandable exasperation.

3 Campbell, *Two Journals*, p. 80.

4 James Green Stewart, Campbell's assistant clerk since 1847, whom he identified in a note to Dr. Dawson as "son of the Hon. John Stewart of Quebec," and for whom Campbell had a high regard.

5 After Thomas Douglas, 5th Earl of Selkirk, who founded the Red River colony in 1811, as a settlement for dispossessed Scottish crofters, after starting a similar venture in Prince Edward Island. He later lost control of the colony, through dubious legal proceedings initiated by rivals for the land.

among us — all very friendly and strictly honest — gazing with wonder at the work of putting up a building, never having seen a house before — in fact nothing in the shape of a dwelling place but their leather tents. . . . The 2 Chiefs, father & son, whom I met here on my first exploring visit in 1843, often visited us with their bands, and were more than pleased at our coming among them with articles of civilized useage for barter.[6]

Later in the summer, Campbell had visitors of a different sort.

One evening early in August, when a good many of these local Indians were about us, we heard a noise of shouting & singing up the Lewes. The Indians explained to us as best they could who the strangers were (they were Chilcats) [*sic*] & advised us to hide our working tools and everything movable unless we wished to have them stolen by the strangers who were adept at pilfering. They also gave us a ready hand to put everything out of sight, which was hardly done when the Chilcats arrived, about 20 in number & a hard looking set, on several rafts on which they had drifted down the Lewes from near its source. We soon found out their thieving propensities, which were in such marked contrast to the honesty of the native Indians. These poor people, though so destitute of everything that a knife was looked upon by them as an invaluable treasure, were so thoroughly straightforward, that even if they found an article that was lost or mislaid, they would bring it back.
The Chilcats belong to the Coast Indians along Lynn Canal, who had long carried on a bartering trade with the Indians in that quarter; & the only articles from the outside world — indifferent though they were in quality — these poor Indians had ever obtained in trade came from the Chilcats. I may add that such a thing as fair dealing was unknown among the Chilcats, whose motto was 'might is right,' & who were civil only when they were the weaker party.[7]

The Chilkats — a "kwon" or tribe of the Tlingit Indians — had for several generations regarded the Chilkat River as their traditional trading route to the interior, and the coming of the white men into their area was an infringement on their established rights as middlemen between the Indians who lived in the Chilkoot Pass country and the coast. Campbell, for his part, could do nothing, because of his paltry supply of goods, to intercept their trade: he could only watch impotently while his unwelcome rivals obtained, and prepared to carry away on their backs, several bales of fur. These weighed, he noted with reluctant admiration, "from 100 lbs.

[6] Campbell, *Two Journals*, pp. 80-82.
[7] *Ibid.*, pp. 82-83.

to nearly 200 lbs. — I weighed some of them out of curiosity to see."[8]

Before his visitors departed, however, Campbell was able to obtain at least one useful and constructive service from them. Northern explorers and traders learned quickly that even the most hostile natives could be trusted to deliver printed matter to its destination, and the relatively sophisticated Chilkats were no exception. Campbell managed to gather from them the information that "they traded on the Coast with Capt. Dodd of the H.B.C. steamer 'Beaver,'[9] & I availed myself the chance of opening up communications with him, & thus for a small consideration had a yearly exchange of letters. Indians are proud to be intrusted with letters, which they regard with awe, as a mysterious form of speaking."[10]

With this diversion ended, the interrupted schedule was resumed. For the moment, there were no apparent problems: good progress was being made on the buildings, and fish and game were plentiful.

During the fall, we caught some kind of sea trout in the river at our door. They averaged fully 2 ft. long, wieht [sic] 10 or 12 lb., bluish colour with white spots or stars on the side. They are not as good eating as the river trout. I do not know their proper name,[11] and never saw them elsewhere.

Salmon of the best quality ascend the river in their season, in the fall on their return downstream they are seen in any number, in a thin rusty state, dying in the shoal water along the river banks. The Grizzly Bear live on them then to such an extent that their flesh acquires so fishy a taste that the Indians even won't eat it. . . .

We made every provision with our limited means to face the winter. Our twine & nets we used to the best advantage, establishing several

---

[8] *Ibid.*, p. 83.

[9] The *Beaver*, the first steam vessel to operate in the North Pacific, was built for the Hudson's Bay Company in England and launched in 1835, and made the voyage around the Horn under sail. Her engines and machinery were in place but her sidewheel paddles were not attached — they were installed when the *Beaver* reached the mouth of the Columbia River. Until 1860 she plied between Puget Sound and Alaska as a floating trading post of the Company. After this career she served successively as a passenger vessel, a hydrographic survey ship, and after 1880 as a tow boat. In 1888 she ran aground on the rocks off Prospect Point, outside Vancouver Harbour, and broke up before salvage could be attempted.

[10] Campbell, *Two Journals*, p. 83.

[11] This species, according to the Whitehorse branch of the Fisheries Service, was probably from the description lake trout, though they are not found in this part of the river today.

fisheries at Lakes in different quarters in the mountains — one in particular — Tatlamain — about 40 miles to the back of us, being a fine
fishing lake. As it turned out our efforts, hunting & fishing, met with
great success, as we passed the winter enjoying an abundance of country
produce; but we were not in a position to make any big fur trade for
lack of goods.[12]

Even though there was no famine at Fort Selkirk, it was a frustrat-
ing time for Campbell as his fragile lines of communication steadily
deteriorated. The 1848-49 outfit from Fort Simpson was a month
behind schedule in reaching Frances Lake, arriving at the beginning
of the hiatus in northern ground transportation when it was too late
to move goods by water, as the first ice is running, yet too early to
use sleds, as there is not yet sufficient frost or snow. Stewart, who had
gone to the Frances Lake post in September to bring back the supplies, instructed Mr. P. to freight the outfit with dogs during the
winter over the portage to Pelly Banks, where a party from Fort
Selkirk would pick it up in the spring. Two reliable men, dispatched
by Campbell for this purpose in April 1849, returned in June empty-
handed. They had found everything in confusion at Pelly Banks, and
the Fort Selkirk outfit not yet delivered there. "Part of it," Campbell
wrote in exasperation, "was left scattered & abandoned along the
route, part of it still unmoved on the other side."[13]

Desperate for trade goods, he sent Stewart with a boat and six
men up the Pelly again in July, with orders to pack as much of the
freight as they could from Frances Lake to Pelly Banks, and to return
with these supplies to Fort Selkirk. Five of the men arrived back in
September with a load that, in spite of their best endeavours, was
pitifully small. They also brought word from Stewart that he had
stayed behind, with the other man, in order to bring the mail and
"any little thing" from the Fort Simpson boat when it arrived with
the 1849-50 outfit, and that they expected to be back by November.
However, the two men did not arrive at Fort Selkirk until late in
December, in a desperately emaciated condition. "They waited at
Frances Lake in vain for the boats till near the close of navigation,"
Campbell reported bitterly, "then seeing that further delay was useless, they crossed to Pelly Banks without provisions. Mr. P. had nothing or next to it; they passed by Mr. P's fishery on their way, but got

12 Campbell, *Two Journals*, pp. 83-85.
13 *Ibid.*, p. 85.

little help there; they managed to live from hand to mouth as they struggled along; killed a wolverine which kept body and soul together & that was all, & had made up their mind to lie down and die when they came on the 'caches' which I had caused to be made; thence they got to Tatlamain, & home to my inexpressible joy."[14]

The winter of 1849-50 was similar to the previous one. "Flour, tea, & such luxuries," Campbell commented, "were beyond our reach, except on rare occasions; & trade without goods was of course limited."[15] Noting that they had now been nearly two years without contact with the Depot, Campbell decided in April 1850, to send Stewart, "who was always ready for any enterprise," and one other man, direct to Fort Simpson, by-passing the incompetent Mr. P. If this mission failed, then Campbell and the remaining men, rather than risk another winter without supplies, "would drift down stream till we would reach the Russian trading posts along the river on the Pacific Coast."[16] He sent word of this possible evacuation to Dodd "per the Chilcats," and he was gratified to learn later that the message was duly received, that the Russian governor at Sitka was informed, and that he had issued an order to the Yukon posts of the Russian American Company instructing them that "if Mr. Campbell with his people turned up among them, every attention & kindness was to be shown them, and all their wants supplied."

Happily, this plan did not have to be utilized. On August 23 an Indian arrived at Fort Selkirk with a report that Stewart had reached Frances Lake with a boat load of supplies, and Campbell immediately rounded up the men still at the post and set out to help transport these much-needed goods across the portage and down the Pelly. In the course of this journey Campbell was nearly drowned, and many of his personal papers were lost, when an "old" canoe that he and one of his men were using to cross Finlayson Lake filled with water and sank. "The canoe came up, bottom up," he wrote, "& we held on to it, swimming at the same time, though badly tossed

---

14 *Ibid.*, p. 87. Campbell had made some caches of fish along the section of the trail adjacent to Fort Selkirk in case Pambrun and his men should be forced by hunger to abandon Pelly Banks. Before leaving that miserable post to return to his base, Stewart tried to persuade its people to return with him to Fort Selkirk, where there would probably be enough food for the combined parties to get through the winter, but the offer was declined.

15 *Ibid.*, p. 87.

16 *Ibid.*, p. 88, as are other quoted references to this emergency evacuation plan.

by the waves & almost paralyzed with the intensely cold water. . . . We had little hope of reaching the shore which was a long way off, but we struggled desperately & at last reached bottom, so weak & benumbed that we could hardly drag our feet after us, but deeply thankful for our delivery."[17]

The news, when Campbell and Stewart finally met, was both bad and good. At Pelly Banks, tragedy had struck. Early in the winter, all the buildings except one small house had been accidentally destroyed by fire, and two white men and several Indians had starved to death before spring. Stewart lost no time in pushing on to Fort Simpson, taking with him two of the survivors, Mr. P. and the faithful Lapie. At the Depot the news, for a change, was good. The famous Arctic explorer, Dr. John Rae,[18] had arrived to take charge of the District, though too late to prevent the fiasco of the previous winter's supply boats which, Stewart eventually learned, had never reached Frances Lake, but had turned back "on some paltry excuse" at Fort Liard, without even sending on the letters or word that they would not be arriving. Dr. Rae had listened to Stewart's story with sympathy, and had immediately procured a boat with adequate supplies and goods, which he dispatched towards Fort Selkirk in Stewart's care.

For the first time since the post was built, it seemed possible that the struggle for survival might be succeeded at last by a vigorous trade.

II

WITH THE IMPROVED PROSPECTS AT FORT SELKIRK, CAMPBELL DARED to hope that he would at last be given the opportunity to take the final step in the exploration of the Yukon River — the linkup of its known courses. At the mouth of the Porcupine, the Hudson's Bay traders had already proved that the stretch of the "Youcon" which

---

[17] *Ibid.*, p. 89.

[18] Dr. John Rae, physician and explorer, was born in 1813 near Stromness in the Orkney Islands, and graduated in medicine from Edinburgh University. His service with the Hudson's Bay Company began in 1833 with a ten year stint as clerk and surgeon, and until his retirement in 1856 his career varied between periods of Arctic exploration and periods spent at company posts, including his time in the Mackenzie District. A man of exceptional endurance, he once snowshoed 1200 miles in two months. He was made a Fellow of the Royal Society (London) in 1880, and died in London, England in 1893.

they occupied and the "Kwikpak" of the Russians, were one stream, as many of the Indians who visited them at Fort Yukon had also traded with the Russians on the lower reaches of the same river. It only remained to be proved that the "Youcon" and the river below the Pelly-Lewes confluence, which Campbell called the Pelly, were also the same. This would confirm that one continuous waterway flowed from the interior to Norton Sound.

Governor Simpson, possibly thinking aloud, in turn had favoured Cook's River, the Kwikpak, and the Colvile as the mouth of the river that Campbell had discovered. Campbell himself, however, from the beginning had little doubt that the Pelly flowed into the Kwikpak — hence his emergency evacuation plan to reach the Russian trading posts by floating down it. Murray, busy studying the Indians at Fort Yukon, also had no doubts of this. "The Youcon and Pelly," he wrote with great definiteness, "are one and the same. Two Indians who had been at the Pelly were here in summer, and with them another Indian belonging to . . . a band near to the forks of the Lewis [sic] and Pelly, who had two years before been at the great lake [Teslin] the principal source of the river; they described the Forks of the Lewis and Pelly where Mr. Campbell had been, the [Pelly] River and the house on the west side of the mountains near Frances Lake where some of the people had traded deer skins."[19]

To confirm the theories, one voyage of proof was all that was required.

At this auspicious moment Campbell received, in April 1851, the dispatch from Sir George Simpson for which he had waited so long — "instructions to explore the Pelly downwards as far as I might deem advisable, & authorizing me to make my own arrangements to that end."[20] He lost no time in carrying out the governor's orders. As soon as possible after the ice went out, around the end of May, he was on his way, leaving Stewart in charge of the post.

We travelled night & day [he wrote] only putting ashore to cook or

---

19 Murray, *Journal*, p. 76. Murray was apparently convinced that the forks of the Lewes and Pelly and the mouth of the Teslin River, which gave access to the Great Lake, were in the same location, and he was obviously uncertain which river gave access to Frances Lake. However, this in no way detracts from the fact that, several hundred miles away at the mouth of the Porcupine, he had done a commendable piece of research on the geography of the upper Yukon.

20 Campbell, *Two Journals*, p. 93.

speak to Indians whom we met in bands along the river. At this season of the year, there is no night in these latitudes.

The river increased in size & beauty as we advanced, its waters swelled by many tributaries, some of considerable size, like the White & Stewart Rivers, to all of which we gave names,[21] & had them afterwards entered on the map. The river is skirted with 2 ranges of mountains on both sides, the further range being of greater altitude, many of the peaks covered with perpetual snow. The slope & bottom flats on our right are generally covered with poplar, spruce, &c., while the left, facing the midday sun, presented beautiful slopes of verdure. Bears & Moose were often seen as we moved along.

But the great attraction was the natives, whom we came across generally in large bands in camps; they all were very friendly & we always landed to have a talk with them. They were astonished at seeing us & our boat, as they had never seen either a white man or a boat before ... They were destitute of almost every article of civilized usage. The only arms that they had were the bow & arrow; their substitute for axe & knife was a bone or stone; their "kettle" was made of small fibres of the roots of trees, mostly split & then knitted up tight & close like a blanket; after using it for a time it becomes water proof & is then fit for cooking purposes; the method being to heat stones in the fire & throw them into the "kettle" with a pair of tongs formed by bending a stick, and keep on doing so until the water is boiling & the food cooked. By the time this is accomplished to the satisfaction of the "chef," the water is converted into a pretty thick soup — not with vegetables like Scotch broth — but with sand & ashes conveyed into the cooking utensil by hot stones. ...

Their dress which when new is pretty & picturesque, is made of the skin of the moose or the reindeer, principally the latter. The skirt or coat is finished in a point, both before & behind, & reaches down to the knees, being frequently ornamented with coloured beads, porcupine quills, or long hair. The coat has a hole large enough to admit the head, but does not open in front, & is provided with a hood which can be used when wanted, as a head-dress. The trowsers [sic] or leg covering, & shoes are made of the same material, & trimmed the same way. The winter costume is the same, except that the skin is dressed with the hair left on, & the garment made with the hair inside for warmth. Their socks in winter consist of grass & hair, over which is drawn the shoe. Their tents of course are made of leather. These Indians are very fond of ornaments of any kind, such as ear-rings, & also decorate their dress freely with ermine or squirrel skins or tails, ducks wings, long hair, &c. They also often daub their faces with red earth or ochre &c. ...

After descending the river some hundreds of miles, the Indians gave us to understand that there were some white people like us at a fort on

[21] The White River Campbell named for the milky colour of its glacier-fed waters, and the Stewart after his assistant — surely a deserved tribute to that long-suffering young man.

the bank of the river some distance down. After a time the ranges of mountains skirting the river on both sides recede, the river widens, & for miles wanders among countless islands. After travelling about 45 miles after entering this level stretch of country, we had the satisfaction of coming in sight of the fort spoken of by the Indians. It turned out to be Fort Youcon, situated at the confluence of the Porcupine River ... I had thus the satisfaction of demonstrating that my conjectures from the first — in which hardly anyone concurred — were correct & that the Pelly & the Youcon were identical.[22]

Campbell wasted no time savouring his triumph. He was informed at Fort Yukon that Murray and his family had just started up the Porcupine for Lapierre House with the returns, and that they would then continue on to Fort Simpson for a new posting. "The following morning," Campbell wrote, "we steered our boat up the Porcupine after Mr. Murray, whom we overtook in the afternoon. . . . The water was very high, weather very warm, with the sun continually overhead, as we were now within the Arctic circle; mosquitoes very troublesome, so much so that the reindeer were often seen swimming in the river to rid themselves of their pestiferous attendants."[23] At Lapierre House the furs were stored to wait for winter, when they would be taken across the portage by dog sled. The men from Fort Yukon started downstream immediately with their outfit, which had been "rendered there from Peel River the winter before," while Campbell and the Murrays started across the portage on foot, heading towards Peel's River Post. For Mrs. Murray and the children it was undoubtedly a trying journey, and the little fort, when it finally came into view, must have been a most welcome sight.

The remainder of the journey to Fort Simpson was comparatively routine, as the Mackenzie during the brief summer season was by now almost a Hudson's Bay Company highway, with flotillas of boats carrying returns and supplies constantly coming and going. Campbell and his party reached the Depot on August 12, 1851. By this time he realized that not only had he proved his theory concerning the Pelly, but that he had also opened up a new access route to the Fort Selkirk post. The journey by the Mackenzie, the Porcupine, and the Pelly-Yukon, in spite of the Rat River portage, was much preferable to that by the Liard River and Frances Lake, though it was longer. The Liard was a vicious and dangerous river to travel.

[22] Campbell, *Two Journals*, pp. 96-98.
[23] *Ibid.*, p. 98, as is the other quotation in this paragraph.

Chief Trader James Anderson, who was appointed officer in charge of the Mackenzie District in 1851, wrote of it with feeling in a letter to Sir George Simpson:

You can hardly conceive the intense horror the men have to go up to Frances Lake, they invariably on re-hiring endeavour to be exempted from the West Branch [the Liard]. The number of deaths which have occurred there is Fourteen, viz. 3 in connection with Dease Lake, and 11 in connection with F.L. & P.B.; of these last, 3 died from starvation and 8 from drowning — even instances of cannibalism are pretty well established at Pelly Banks and when we consider the dreadful sufferings many have undergone there and at F.L. we need not be surprised at the antipathy that exists towards these posts.[24]

Campbell himself called the Liard the "River of Malediction," and bitterly regretted that he had not been allowed to make this journey sooner, as both lives and money would have been saved. His bitterness, however, was tempered by the hope that his discovery might be an augury of better things to come.

He returned to Fort Selkirk following his same route in reverse, arriving there about the middle of October "to find Mr. Stewart & men all well, having passed the summer in comfort and uneventfully, but for a diversion caused by the Chilcats"[25] — the "diversion" so casually referred to being nothing less than an attempt to ransack the post, which was foiled only by the timely arrival of a band of the local Wood Indians. In spite of the shadow cast by the enmity of the Chilkats, the winter passed in comfort, and in the early summer of 1852 Campbell received from the Depot, by way of the Porcupine, "the first real outfit ever rendered at Fort Selkirk." Optimism was in the air.

James Anderson, however, did not share these sentiments. Shortly after his arrival at Fort Simpson he wrote to his friend Eden Colvile, a member of the Governing Committee, that

... I have been much occupied in getting through my business and acquiring a knowledge of this extensive Dist. —
Mr. Campbell got a large outfit at Fort Selkirk. . . . We will now see what Fort Selkirk can do — I must own that not withstanding Mr. Campbell's sanguine representations, I have my doubts on the subject.

[24] Letter, James Anderson to Sir George Simpson, dated Fort Simpson, 20 November 1852, photostat in possession of the Provincial Archives of British Columbia.

[25] Campbell, *Two Journals*, p. 123.

I fear it is too near the Coast — only about 8 days from Lynns Canal, whence I should suppose the natives could produce goods at a cheaper rate than we could afford to sell them — Hitherto from various misfortunes Selkirk has been a dead loss and that not a trifling one. . . .

I have a much higher opinion of Campbell's Zeal and Enterprise than of his judgement.[26]

Obviously, in the opinion of his superiors, even if not in his own mind, the viability of Campbell's operation was yet to be proved.

III

AS AN ADMINISTRATOR, ANDERSON HAD GOOD REASON TO VIEW HIS new district with a jaundiced eye. Several of the account books were missing, while others had not been kept up-to-date, or were so "cooked" as to be meaningless. Confidential documents were strewn about the mess hall and the store room "at the mercy of every one." Discipline had become lax. A firm hand was certainly needed to restore a measure of efficiency to the badly disorganized operation, and this Anderson moved energetically to apply.

He was quick to identify his most serious problem. "I am now pretty well acquainted with the affairs of the District," he informed Colvile on March 16, 1852, "the only place I am not satisfied with is Selkirk."[27] In a "private and confidential" letter written about the same time to another old friend, Chief Factor Donald Ross at the Red River settlement, he expanded on the same theme.

Campbell at Selkirk has only £66 worth of Furs in October. . . . The Chilcats from the Coast swept off everything. I expressed an opinion to Mr. Colvile, and perhaps to yourself — that this post was too near the coast to pay — these Chilcats undersell us — I now learn that Stewart, who is a clear headed clever fellow, is of the same opinion, he wishes the post to be removed 100 miles lower down the river, where there are plenty of Indians who do not visit Fort Youcon, willing to trade at our own prices or even below them — and thinks that we would also draw down most of the upper trade, there we should be quite out of the sphere of the Chilcats, and it is also a better situation for Provisions.

26 Letter, James Anderson to Eden Colvile, Esq., dated Fort Simpson, 22 November 1851, photostat in possession of the Provincial Archives of British Columbia.

27 Letter, James Anderson to Eden Colvile, Esq., dated Fort Simpson, 16 March 1852, photostat in possession of the Provincial Archives of British Columbia.

— No accounts have been kept here since '47, documents are missing, and everything is in a chaos of confusion, so that I cannot tell exactly the Profit & Loss of the posts across the mountains — The Loss on Selkirk has however been very serious — The first Outfit was sent in '47, and including the supplies that have been furnished up to this date, & the wages — without charging Interest — the sum of £2153 has been expended on that post for which not a single 6ᵈ of Returns has hitherto reached market — The first instalment amounting to £546 is now at Peels River, and will reach England in October 1853, and I doubt much if the Returns of that year will amount to that sum. This is a disheartening state of affairs.[28]

One result of Campbell's journey over the northern route to the Mackenzie was a decision to abandon the Frances Lake Fort, which was primarily only a staging post between the Liard and the Pelly. Anderson was quick to assure Simpson that this action "will not be attended with any loss, as most of the Indians will resort to Fort Halkett, some to Fort Norman and others to Fort Selkirk, in fact I think there will be a considerable gain by having abandoned it. — From the loss of life and starvation which have occurred there and on the West Branch it was difficult to get men to go there."[29]

Spring turned into summer, and at the Depot there was still no hint of the tragedy that was in the making "across the mountains," though Anderson was keeping a firm finger on the pulse of the District's far-flung operations. In July he advised Simpson that a "few" of the Frances Lake Indians had already turned up at Fort Halkett, "and a large band was daily expected to arrive there."[30] At the same time he told Colvile that "two Esquimaux visited LaPierre's House last winter, they were kindly treated and encouraged to resort there. I fear however owing to the deadly hostility that exists between them and the Loucheux this need not be expected."[31] He was in regular touch with most of his posts: Campbell alone, he com-

---

[28] Letter "Private and confidential," from James Anderson to Donald Ross, Esq., Red River Settlement, dated Fort Simpson, 11 March 1852, original in possession of the Provincial Archives of British Columbia.

[29] Letter, James Anderson to Sir George Simpson, dated Fort Simpson, 26 November 1851, photostat in possession of the Provincial Archives of British Columbia.

[30] Letter, James Anderson to Sir George Simpson, dated "en route," 10 July 1852, photostat in possession of the Provincial Archives of British Columbia.

[31] Letter, James Anderson to Eden Colvile, Esq., dated Athabasca River, "en route," 10 July 1852, photostat in possession of the Provincial Archives of British Columbia.

plained to Colvile, was "very chary of information" in his reports to the Depot.

At Fort Selkirk rumours of an impending attack on a more determined scale than that of the previous year drifted down from the mountain passes, but Campbell seemed remarkably unconcerned. True, the local Wood Indians, who had always been friendly, remained of their own accord in the close vicinity of the fort for most of the summer as a deterrent to a possible assault, and he probably counted on this assistance to keep him unmolested. Yet, incredibly, as August approached — the time of year when the Chilkats might be expected to appear — the Wood Indians left the post on an excursion down the river, Stewart and four men were absent on a trading trip that would take them as far afield as Fort Yukon, and the buildings, which were being moved to a new location, were unprotected by a stockade. At the peak of this period of ill-preparedness, disaster struck, as Campbell later reported to Anderson:

At the fort I had two men and two engaged Indians with me, and the business was going on peaceably and prosperously, much to my satisfaction, and would have continued to do so but for the arrival of twenty-seven of these demons on the 20th of August.

They took us by surprise, as we were then absent at work, but arrived as we were landing. . . . Though their turbulence occasionally subsided into partial quiet, it was like a volcano, ever ready to burst anew. They were never for a moment out of mischief, and it defied our vigilance to watch them in every corner of our premises.[32]

The next day this volcano erupted. The occupants of the fort were overwhelmed and forcibly expelled, and the buildings were ransacked.

We were without a blanket amongst the party, and none of the men but myself had even a capot; nothing but their trousers, and in their shirt sleeves, with but two guns and a few shots of powder amongst us.

The roaring and yelling of these painted fiends, smashing everything that came their way — and firing — beggars description. The only alternative now was to proceed down the river to meet Mr. Stewart, some of the natives, or both, to revenge the blow, and this I did without delay.

Mr. Stewart we had not the good luck to meet, but we reached the

---

[32] Report, Robert Campbell to James Anderson, dated Fort Simpson, 4 November 1852, original in the possession of the Provincial Archives of British Columbia. The other quotations following which also describe the Chilkat's raid are taken from this same report.

camp of one of the Indian chiefs about noon the next day. He was furious at what had happened, and with all his band we returned immediately, say about ten men, making in all twelve guns. The evening of the following day (23rd) we reached and surrounded the fort, never in the least doubting that the Chilcats were still there, but to our inexpressible vexation all were gone, and all the goods, furs and private property taken or destroyed. . . .

I regret to say that except ammunition and tobacco, but little else of the entire outfit had been traded. Not a grain of powder or rag of clothing was left. Cassettes, dressing cases, writing desks, kegs and musical instruments were smashed into a thousand atoms and the house and store strewed with the wreck, a sight to madden a saint.

Campbell's first thought was to set off in pursuit of the fleeing Chilkats, but the Wood Indians quickly lost their enthusiasm for the chase: with Fort Selkirk stripped of trade goods, they would obviously have little choice but to resume their trade with the natives from the coast. For the Hudson's Bay men, there remained only the bitter choice of abandoning the fort. All Campbell's hope and plans for the Yukon lay buried in the wreckage of his post.

IV

THE IMMEDIATE NECESSITY NOW WAS TO GET TO FORT SIMPSON AS soon as possible and appeal to Anderson for the men and supplies required to return to Fort Selkirk and avenge the attack. Accordingly, the disconsolate traders started down the river for a meeting with Stewart, to whom they broke the dismal news. It was decided that the latter would take most of the men, the boats, and the few salvaged stores back to Fort Yukon, where they would winter. Campbell himself, with a light canoe and two men, would follow the shorter Pelly-Liard route to the Depot. He arrived there safely in October, though the ice was running on the Liard before he finished his journey. He told his story to the startled Anderson, who sympathized with his feelings, but who felt that retaliation was a luxury that the Company could not afford. He asked Campbell to prepare a report on the expulsion, and forwarded copies of it to both Simpson and Colvile, with his own comments appended. To the latter he wrote:

It strikes me there was a want of due caution on our part. A large fort had been built, but the stockades though cut were not planted — in my opinion a small defensive post should have been first built, and after that the permanent Establishment, the menacing conduct of the Chilkots [*sic*] last summer should have put them on their guard & Cap. Dodd gave them repeated warnings.

The motives that induced the Chilkots to perpetrate this outrage was undoubtedly the fear of losing their long established Traffic with the natives, the same motive caused the pillage of Dease Lake in 1838 and its consequent abandonment, poor Campbell was at that place also.[33]

To Simpson, Anderson repeated this comment, and also reiterated his opposition to the Fort Selkirk establishment, and to Campbell's operation of it.

Campbell has urged me most strongly to send him back next summer, but on mature consideration I determined on abandoning the post for next year, referring its future fate to your decision. My opinion is that it should be abandoned, it appears to me a hopeless speculation which can never pay — 1stly From the Expenses of Transport — 2ndly From the length of time (7 yrs.)[34] that the Returns of an Outfit take to reach Market — 3rdly From the large establishment of Men and Officers which must be kept up there, and which it would now be necessary to augment — 4thly From the apparent poverty of the Country and the bad quality of the Furs — 5thly From the cheap rate at which we must sell to compete with the Chilkots. . . .

Mr. Campbell's conviction that Selkirk will ultimately prove a profitable post still remains unshaken. . . . It is my opinion that his sanguine disposition has caused him to estimate the prospects of Selkirk far too favorably — his views have been so long and intensely directed to one absorbing object that they have become distorted and he can no longer see things in their true colors.[35]

[33] Letter, James Anderson to Eden Colvile, Esq., dated Fort Simpson, 20 November 1852, photostat in possession of the Provincial Archives of British Columbia.

[34] Dawson, in his report of the Yukon Expedition of 1887 (see Chapter Six) described the 7-year cycle entailed in shipping goods into Fort Yukon and getting the furs purchased by these goods to market as follows: "*Goods* — 1st year, reach York Factory; 2nd year, Norway House; 3rd year, Peel River, and were hauled across the mountains to La Pierre's House; 4th year, reach Fort Yukon. *Returns* — 5th year, reach La Pierre's House and are hauled across to Peel River; 6th year, reach depot at Fort Simpson; 7th year reach market." The new route to Fort Selkirk would have followed the same course, with an additional journey on the Yukon River. George M. Dawson, *Report on an Exploration in the Yukon District, N.W.T. and Adjacent Northern Portion of British Columbia*, (Ottawa, The Queen's Printer, re-issued 1898), p. 140.

[35] Letter, James Anderson to Sir George Simpson, dated Fort Simpson, 20 November 1852, photostat in possession of the Provincial Archives of British Columbia. The quotation following this extract, and referring to Campbell's future disposition, is from the same letter.

Anderson concluded by informing Simpson that as there was now no place for Campbell in the District "he will accompany the Express to Isle à la Crosse and proceed hence next spring to meet with you at Norway House."

This proposed timetable was much too slow for Campbell, once it was apparent that he was not going to obtain satisfaction at Fort Simpson. The governor was wintering at Lachine, near Montreal, and Campbell felt he must talk to him as quickly as possible, without waiting for the meeting at Norway House, which would not take place until the following June at the earliest. Late in November, therefore, as soon as the snow was firm, he started up the Mackenzie on the first leg of a journey that would take him to the governor's winter quarters. Over 3,000 miles of this trek were covered on snowshoes, with dogs to carry his supplies, traversing in the dead of winter a country almost uninhabited except for scattered trading posts and wandering Indian bands. He was of course hospitably received at the Company establishments, often by old friends, and in many cases he was urged to extend his stay. His fierce yearning to confront Simpson, however, permitted him little rest. Early in March 1853, he finally arrived at Crow Wing, Minnesota, and by the end of the month, using more prosaic methods of travel — horse and wagon, stage coach, steamer, and train — he reached his destination. He lost no time in repeating to Simpson the plea that he had made to Anderson a few months before and the width of a continent away.

The governor, in view of Anderson's dispatch, would not countenance reprisals against the Chilkats, assuring Campbell that his exploits were too well known in the north for anyone to "fancy" a charge of cowardice against him. Instead, with his usual glibness of tongue, Simpson made a counter-proposal. He sympathized with Campbell's feelings, but suggested that in view of his previous requests for furlough leave it would be "cruel" for him to turn back while so close to his homeland. Campbell had little choice but to allow Simpson's eloquence to persuade him, and in early April he departed, however reluctantly, on a well-earned furlough in Scotland.

A final decision regarding Fort Selkirk was not made until the following year, at a Council meeting held at Norway House in June 1854. Campbell, newly returned from leave, was present, as was Stewart, and from these two men "the Councilors had learnt more detailed information regarding the Pelly/Youcon area than they had known before."[36] The earlier decision, however, was not changed. "The conclusion we arrived at," Simpson informed the Governing Committee, "was the inexpediency of an attempt to re-establish Fort Selkirk, unless with such a force as would enable us to punish the Chilcats for the pillage of the Post in 1852 — which we were not at present prepared to do." This decision ended Campbell's Yukon career.

He continued in the Company's service for another 20 years, first in the Athabasca District, and later at Swan Lake. He received his belated commission as Chief Trader in 1856, and in 1859 he married at Norway House Miss Ellenora Stirling, to whom he became engaged during his furlough, and who made the long journey from Scotland to the wilderness trading post accompanied only by her sister. Campbell was made a Chief Factor in 1867, and retired in 1872, settling at Strathclair, in Manitoba, where he died in 1894.

The founding of Fort Selkirk should have been the climax of his fur trading career: instead, with the expulsion, everything that he had accomplished up to that time had apparently come to naught. The posts that he established — Dease Lake, Frances Lake, Pelly Banks, Fort Selkirk — were all abandoned for one reason or another. Only Fort Yukon, the one post in the region with which he had not been involved, remained in active operation. Anderson characterized him as "a hardy, enterprising officer who has undergone great hardship and privations in the service, but a bad man of business and always in difficulties."[37] Simpson, reporting to London after the interview at Lachine, praised Campbell for his energy and hardihood, but mentioned "a singular fatality that seems to have attended all his undertakings, which has reached its climax in the destruction of the establishment, rendering abortive the labour & outlay of so many years."[38] It was a hardheaded assessment, and not strictly a fair one.

[36] Letter, Sir George Simpson to the Governor, Deputy Governor and Committee of the Hudson's Bay Company, London, dated Red River Settlement, 30 June 1854. (H.B.C. Arch. A 12/7 Fos. 140-141.), as is the other quotation in this paragraph.

[37] Letter, James Anderson to Eden Colvile, Esq., dated Fort Simpson, 16 March 1852, photostat in possession of the Provincial Archives of British Columbia.

[38] Letter, Sir George Simpson to Archibald Barclay, Secretary, Hudson's Bay Company, London, dated Lachine, 2 April 1853. (H.B.C. Arch. A 12/6, Fos. 344-5d.)

In the course of time Campbell's faith in the Pelly-Lewes area was vindicated, and the country in which he had laboured for so long became an important source of fur, Anderson's opinion notwithstanding. In the 1890's an independent trader moved back to the Fort Selkirk site, and the Hudson's Bay Company itself finally re-established a post there in 1938, which did not close down until 1950, when the whole settlement moved to a new location on the expanding Yukon road network. Yet the man who first built there, and who discovered and named nearly every principal river in the Territory, was until recently only commemorated by a minor tributary of the Pelly, named for him by Dr. Dawson in 1887, and by a bridge in Whitehorse spanning a stretch of river that he had never seen. In 1966 a development road was completed between Watson Lake on the Alaska Highway and Carmacks on the Yukon River, which follows for much of its length the same route along the Frances and the Pelly that Campbell followed when he first entered the country. The Yukon Territorial Council by a happy choice bestowed the name of Campbell Highway on this road. It was recognition long overdue.

V

THOUGH DISASTER HAD STRUCK THE OTHER POSTS ACROSS THE mountains, Fort Yukon continued to flourish. An appreciable volume of traffic continued to move each year across the Rat River portage — trade goods and supplies in one direction, and bales of furs for the London auction houses in the other. Between Peel's River Post and Lapierre House freight was moved during the winter, by dog teams and sleds, when the overland carry was easier. Between Lapierre House and Fort Yukon transportation was by boat, during the brief summer period of open water. The portage was the life line that made the Company's operations in this remote area possible.

In 1860-61 the posts along this trade route received a visitor, a young American naturalist named Robert Kennicott, the first English-speaking scientist to enter the Yukon basin. Though only 25 years old at the time of the visit, Kennicott was already pre-eminent in his chosen field. Born in a small village near Chicago, he was the son of a physician who gave up the practice of medicine to become a horticulturalist, and who encouraged his boy's early interest in natural history. Kennicott's initial collections and reports on the fauna of his native state attracted considerable attention because of their thoroughness and clarity, and led to his appointment as curator of the Museum of Natural History of Northwestern University, and later to a similar position with the newly-formed Chicago Academy of Sciences.

This work eventually brought him into contact with the man who became his sponsor — Spencer Fullerton Baird, assistant secretary (and later secretary) of the Smithsonian Institution.[39] Baird encouraged the young naturalist in his plans for the future: one of these was to extend the study of the distribution[40] of the birds and mammals of North America into those parts of the continent which were still unknown territory from a scientific point of view. In particular, Kennicott longed to carry his investigations into the northwesterly extremities of Britain's American possessions, and into the fringes of the adjoining Russian colonies, both of which were regarded as exciting areas for zoological work. To this project Baird gave his full support.

The scheme could be carried out only with the full co-operation of the Hudson's Bay Company, which controlled all the living facilities and means of travel in the region. Through Baird, Kennicott obtained the backing of the Smithsonian and of the Audubon Society of Chicago, and Governor Simpson was approached by these distinguished sponsors with a request for logistic support. Simpson's response was most generous. In a departure from the usual policy of discouraging visits by outsiders to the trading posts, Kennicott was offered free transportation with the fur brigades to anywhere in the Company's territory, the hospitality of all its establishments, and free passage for his collections. This offer made the undertaking possible,

[39] The Smithsonian Institution was a centre of learning established in Washington, D.C. by Act of Congress in 1846, as the result of a large bequest in the will of an English scientist, James Smithson. One of the first projects undertaken by the Smithsonian, as it was popularly known, was to begin zoological and ethnological studies in the newly accessible American west. The work of Kennicott and his fellow collectors in the northwest (see Chapter Four) was an extension of this project.

[40] As the camera was not yet a practicable tool for exploration, the distribution of species could only be determined by personal observation, and detailed studies of form and colouration made by the examination of specimens shot or snared in the field. The preparation and preservation of skins was part of every naturalist's training.

and in the spring of 1859, Kennicott left Chicago for Fort William, where he made connections with the westbound freight canoes.

In the first year of his travels Kennicott eventually reached the Mackenzie District, and the area of his particular interest. Here he spent his first winter and the following summer, and in September 1860, made his first crossing from Peel's River Post to Fort Yukon, where he passed his second winter and most of the summer of 1861, collecting frantically during the spring influx of wild fowl, and watching with interest the ritual of the annual trade. In August, in the company of some Indians, he began the return journey to Peel's River Post. They reached Lapierre House early in September, where they were detained for such a length of time by interminable rains that finally they could wait no longer for the weather to improve. Leaving behind the Fort Yukon zoological specimens "on account of the risk of wetting" they began a miserable crossing of the portage.

We traveled some twenty miles in the rain the first day, sleeping (or lying awake) at night on the sand and stones in a river bed, where we found driftwood enough to cook by, though not enough for drying our clothes. It cleared up and commenced freezing shortly after we camped, so that sleeping in wet blankets and clothes was just a *little* chilly.
The next day we had alternately to plunge through wet moss, wade across small mountain streams, swollen by rain, and climb slippery banks, where bruised shins were rather plentiful. Towards noon the weather, which had been fine, changed, and after a sort of thunderstorm, with the thunder left out, settled into a quiet rain, which turned first to a sleet and then to a snow, as we got higher on the mountains. Such of us as did not know the track had to keep close to those who did, for during a good part of the afternoon there was thick mist which hid any object fifty yards distant — a very common thing on the mountains, and a rather dangerous one too.[41]

The bad weather slowed down their rate of travel, forcing them to camp out for two more nights in exposed locations where firewood was scarce, though at the highest point in the pass they found the ground "hard frozen and got on fine." By the third night on the

---

[41] Robert Kennicott, "Journal of Robert Kennicott, May 19, 1859 - February 11, 1862," in James Alton James, *The First Scientific Exploration of Russian America and the Purchase of Alaska*, (Evanston, Ill., Northwestern University, 1942), p. 89. Professor James in the preface to his book (p. ix) states that Kennicott's journal was initially published in the first volume of the *Transactions of the Chicago Academy of Sciences* in 1869. The original manuscript and most of the printed copies were destroyed in the Chicago fire of 1871.

trail they could see the post, and could have reached it "by carrying on late. But it is a great breach of voyaging etiquette to arrive late at a strange fort; so we camped within sight of Peel's River, and made amends for our two vile, fireless camps, by keeping up, all night, such a fire as even voyageurs seldom take the trouble to make. Next morning we arrived at the fort early, with the usual firing of guns and noise that takes place on such occasions."[42]

Kennicott stayed at the Peel's River Post for three months, keeping himself occupied by trapping marten and carrying on an endless feud with the carcajou (wolverine) that did their best to play havoc with his efforts. In December he left for Lapierre House with a brigade of eight dog sleds that were carrying the year's supply of trade goods destined for Fort Yukon. He was driving his own team, and though he was slight in build, and not very strong because of consumption suffered in his boyhood, he managed to keep up with the others, and do his fair share of work on the trail. He was quick to observe that these "voyageurs," who travelled on snow instead of water, had customs and habits that were as strictly observed as were those of their fellows in the canoe brigades. Kennicott noted a number of these rituals in his journal:

On a voyage, where several sleds go together, all go on without stopping or unnecessary delay for from five to seven miles, when they stop to smoke and give the dogs a spell, and the distance thus made is called a *pipe*, or *spell*. In speaking of the stopping place, the voyageur always says "where we smoked," or "where we spelled," or "the end of such pipe." On well-known roads the spelling places are always the same. The stoppages thus made are very short, not over fifteen minutes, unless the dogs are very tired; and often, where going light, only long enough to strike fire and light the pipes. . . .

At the end of each pipe the foremost sled goes behind the whole, and the second sled goes ahead, and thus all in their turn make a "spell ahead," the front being the hardest place. . . . When a sled cannot keep up and take its proper place in the brigade at each spell, it is said to be "planted," which is considered something very disgraceful; and a good voyageur will push (i.e. help his dogs by pushing with a long pole always attached to the top of a loaded sled) till he is nearly knocked-up rather than be planted, even though his dogs are known to be weak, or his load extra heavy. . . . My pushing stick is my fourth dog, for in ordinary trains there are but three. By the rules of voyaging etiquette four dogs are not obliged to do more than three, so I manage to get on

[42] *Ibid.*, p. 91.

without much "forcing" (hard work) when on a voyage, only using the pushing stick on bad banks. . . .[43]

To ride on my sled, so long as I did not own to being tired, was creditable, as showing what my dogs could do; but had the others known of my being *forced* to do it, on account of fatigue, I would have been laughed at consumedly, as I would have been also at getting frozen. It is very comical, sometimes, to see the pains taken by the old voyageurs to [conceal] a frost bite, or any fatigue.[44]

Whatever the nationality of the voyageur, the dogs were invariably addressed in French, or at least in "a language they call French here." The progress of a team was marked by "queer cries of *'sacre chien mort!' 'sacre crapaud noir!' 'marche!' 'yeu!' 'chah!'* etc., with the occasional *'ta ta'* of a whip, as loud as a pistol shot, and the call of the unfortunate dog that is getting his lugs warmed."[45]

The attempt to reach Lapierre House was short-lived; gale force winds on the height of land forced them to abandon their loads and return in the teeth of the storm to Peel's River, to await its passing, and to reprovision. According to Kennicott, "this was the hardest gale ever experienced by the oldest voyageur among us. . . . In one place where the wind took us sideways as it came down a 'cooly' (ravine), several of us, with dogs, sleds, and all, were blown clean off the ground and down the hillside for some yards. Altogether it was the jolliest and most exciting race I have had since I was last on horseback."[46]

The wind did not stop blowing until December 23, when the drivers of four sleds, including Kennicott, immediately began preparation for a fresh start, "determined to 'mouch' [travel light], and reach Lapierre's House in two days; but it was, finally, after midnight before we got off. It made little difference at what hour we started though, for there were but two or three hours of daylight then."[47] In the early morning of December 25 they approached the height of land.

We crossed the highest part of our track over the mountains just at the first appearance of the gray light in the southeast, which precedes

[43] *Ibid.*, pp. 99-100.
[44] *Ibid.*, p. 109.
[45] *Ibid.*, p. 113.
[46] *Ibid.*, p. 104.
[47] *Ibid.*, p. 106.

the first real daylight by several hours at this season, and here, about nine o'clock on Christmas morning, I stopped and smoked the last of my cigars to the health and "conduction" of the family circle.... But the temperature was more than 40° below; too cold for cigars or sentiment, so I got on my sled, relieved my feelings by a yell, which started my dogs off on a gallop, and rode down the mountain singing *La Claire Fontaine* and other voyaging songs, to encourage my dogs, for dogs, and horses, seem to like singing, and what the sounds I produced wanted in melody they made up in volume.

It is singular, that on the mountain tops it is warmer (in very cold weather at least) than in the valleys between them. When we 'put ashore' [stopped] for dinner we found it intensely cold and I froze my fingers by handling the iron buckles in unharnessing my dogs. My Christmas dinner you will hardly guess. The men with me had pemmican,[48] which I dislike, but one of them by some lucky chance, had brought a large, fresh white fish. They *chopped* the skin off this, and, cutting it up with an axe, boiled it for me, and it, with a pound or so of melted moose tallow, and a few quarts of tea, a little weaker than would skin one's mouth, made up my Christmas *festin*.... After dinner we determined to have some kind of jollification in honor of the day, and decided on a Louchioux [*sic*] dance, a form of exercise which is decidedly calculated to promote the rapid circulation of blood. So we left our dining place quite warm.[49]

They reached their destination about nine o'clock Christmas night, in the coldest weather of the season to date, estimated at 60° below zero. Kennicott was warmly received "even for this hospitable country" by James Flett, an Orkneyman with 17 years of service with the Company, who was in charge of the post. Kennicott described the place in some detail in his journal:

La Pierre's House is situated literally in a *hole* in the west side of the Rocky [Richardson] Mountains. The bare mountains rise some thousands of feet high on every side, the river escaping through a crooked valley. On the banks of this small river (the head-waters of Porcupine River) are some large spruces, and a little birch and balsam poplar,

48 Pemmican was a cake made of dried and pounded meat mixed with fat, sometimes flavoured with currants or other wild berries. It kept indefinitely and was nourishing, but was usually tasteless and required a strong stomach to digest. Elsewhere in his Journal (p. 86), Kennicott wrote feelingly of this universal voyageur's food that "hair, sticks, bark, spruce leaves, stones, sand, etc. enter into its composition, especially if the meat has been pounded by Indians.... I was a little shy of it for awhile after learning how two packet men were made into pemmican near Fort Good Hope, a few years since, by starving Indians."

49 Kennicott, in James, *The First Scientific Exploration*, pp. 107-108.

forming pretty heavy timber in places. I have seen some spruces here over eighteen inches in diameter, but not very high. . . .[50]

La Pierre's House is the smallest establishment in the district, and has but two men besides the one in charge. It belongs to Peel's River, and the two are, theoretically, but one post, and both under the general charge of the gentleman at Peel's River. For this reason it is generally known under the name of "The Small House," and the Indians call it *Ko-ah-ze* (little house). It was formerly better entitled to that name than now. . . . Since Flett has been in charge, he has put up a larger dwelling-house, with two rooms, which he has fitted up very comfortably. . . . It is an old saying, that a good voyageur with an ax, crooked knife, and a gimlet, will build a house, make furniture, prepare sleds, snow-shoes, etc., for winter, and, in short, make himself quite comfortable; and with a saw, in addition, he will do all this work rapidly, and with ease.[51]

Kennicott, in spite of the fact that he had already eaten a large dinner, had more food pressed upon him by his host, and managed "to make a supper of caribou steak, back-fat, tongues, bango, and tea, that would have been three days' 'prey' for you miserable outsiders."

The day after Christmas, Flett gave a Christmas ball, whereat were assembled the largest number of whites ever seen at La Pierre's House, besides a dozen or so of Indians. The only representatives of the fair sex present, however, were Flett's Indian wife and daughter, and the wife of one of the La Pierre's House men. . . . The dancing was, I may say without vulgarity, decidedly "stunning." I should hardly call it remarkably graceful. The figures, if they may be called such, were only Scotch reels of four, and jigs; and, as the main point to which the dancers' efforts seemed to tend, was to get the largest amount of exercise out of every muscle in the frame in a given time, I must confess that an Indian boy and a fat wife were the best dancers. The music consisted of a very bad performance of one vile, unvarying tune, upon a worse old fiddle, accompanied by a brilliant accompaniment upon a large tin pan. All seemed to enjoy it very well, and as to the dancing, I must say that I found as much amusement in it as I have done in that at some gatherings of "youth and beauty" in the civilized world.[52]

Kennicott quickly settled into the easy-going routine of a small trading post in winter-time. There was little wildlife in evidence, and therefore little opportunity for collecting. "The only species of mam-

[50] *Ibid.*, p. 88.

[51] *Ibid.*, pp. 110-111.

[52] *Ibid.*, pp. 109-110.

mals I have seen here in winter," he wrote, "are foxes, rabbits, and mice; of birds, ptarmigans and whiskey jacks. There are porcupines, deer, fur animals, and mountain sheep nearby, but I have no time to hunt them."[53] He left with Flett instructions for the preparation and shipping of skins the following spring, when warmer weather would bring more abundant animal life.

Food at the Small House was plentiful, though lacking in variety — it would have been the despair of a professional dietician. Kennicott described the usual daily menus as consisting of "boiled caribou rump, with a respectable showing of back-fat" for breakfast; "caribou steaks fried in tallow" for dinner; and for supper "a rib of large caribou roasted, and some 'bangs' — cakes made by frying a batter of flour and water in tallow, improved by the addition of some pounded white-fish roe."[54] Elsewhere in his journal, he mentioned that a dog's daily ration was "half a man's and the same as a wife's — that is, four pounds of fresh meat, one and a half pounds of dry meat, two fresh white fish, or two pounds of dry fish."[55] Apparently there was not often fresh meat to spare for either dogs or women.

At the post he usually worked until late at night, and slept late in the morning, until perhaps ten o'clock, about the time of the January sunrise. During a typical day he would yarn with Flett for perhaps an hour or so, feed his dogs, skin and measure a rabbit or a ptarmigan, smoke several pipes, sing several songs in an impromptu musical entertainment, and work on his journal and other memoranda. For a "constitutional" he and Flett would often take their dogs on a run to haul wood "from about two and a half miles off, in a temperature more than 40° minus now and again. Wood hauling is cold work, however, as the dogs go slowly, from there being many banks to mount. A cord of dry poplar or pine is usually taken at three loads. But, on a reasonably good track, three strong dogs will go at a trot with half a cord of dry pine. Wood is hauled on short, broad, sleds, provided with a high rack. The dogs seem to know, when harnessed to a wood-sled that no long voyage is before them, and carry on willingly."[56]

[53] *Ibid.*, p. 112.

[54] *Ibid.*, p. 116.

[55] *Ibid.*, p. 115-116.

[56] *Ibid.*, p. 113.

About the middle of January "some Indians came in to announce that the deer killing had commenced, and that sleds must be sent for meat."

At this place, after the summer and fall hunt [Kennicott explained] few deer are killed till January or February. The Indians are not permitted to disturb the deer near the fort at first, that they may collect in large numbers until spring, when they are more easily killed, and the meat is thus obtained near at hand. In the fall the Indians hunt at a great distance, coming gradually nearer as the deer are driven off from their vicinity, until in spring they are killed within a "pipe," or even less of "The Small House." When I first arrived here the Indians had their camps about forty miles off — some even further. Flett then gave orders for them to commence hunting in earnest at the first opportunity afforded by warm or windy weather. This they did, and have already some twenty or thirty deer for the fort, besides what they use themselves. At about this time they are to remove their camps to within thirty miles of the fort, where the deer are still more plentiful. There are but twenty-seven Indians, men and boys, that can hunt, belonging to La Pierre's House, and they all camp together at this season. They do not kill deer much in barriers[57] here, but shoot them, either by stalking, "surrounding" them, or "running" them. When the snow is deep in spring a single Indian has killed an entire band of thirty deer in a day by running them down. With their large snow-shoes the Indians run over the snow without sinking, while the deer go through the crust and get tired out.... The average weight of the meat alone (without the head, shanks, feet, or hide), of a female caribou here, is about one hundred pounds; of a male, about one hundred and fifty pounds.[58]

The Small House supplied most of the caribou needed to provision Peel's River Post, as well as its own modest domestic requirements. It was also a fantastic source of fish for both establishments.

In the fall, the small rivers about here are all barred with fences of willow wicker work, through which an opening leads into a basket, and thus the fish are caught as they descend from the mountains where they have passed the summer. In this way Flett caught five thousand bluefish in one basket, just at "The Small House" this fall, and in all obtained twelve thousand. One year he caught sixteen thousand. A few small suckers are taken early in the fall, and a good many of a very small kind of salmonoid, a little like the whitefish, known here as the "mountain fish." But only the bluefish are caught in such immense numbers. These are a species peculiar to the northern part of the Rocky Mountains, belonging to the genus *Thymallus*. They are allied to the

[57] That is, kill the deer (i.e. caribou) by driving them into fenced enclosures.
[58] Kennicott, in James, *The First Scientific Exploration*, pp. 114-115.

brook trout, and are generally rather smaller than that species. They are a bonnie fish, with a much elongated dorsal fin; the colors are not, however, near so elegant as those of the brook trout, as they are of a dark color, of various shades, the larger ones bluish black, whence the name. I have never had an opportunity to try them with the hook, but I fancy they would afford good sport to the fisherman.[59]

Kennicott left the Small House at the end of January 1862, on the first stage of a homeward journey that would not be completed until the following October. He took his departure with regret, as he had become very attached to this isolated corner of the world and its uncomplicated way of life. For their part, Flett and his people were sorry to see him go. The advent of this high-spirited and learned young man was a notable event in their lonely lives. He took part in their activities and shared their hardships without grumbling. More than this, however, he told them of great museums in distant cities, and of their need for natural history objects, which the traders could help supply. That he was successful in obtaining their support became evident after his return home. "For more than ten years," wrote a colleague, "collections poured into Washington from the North until those who had been inspired by Kennicott retired from active service."[60]

Lapierre House, when Kennicott left, had almost served its purpose. The sale of Alaska was already being secretly negotiated, and its eventual purchase by the United States would lead to further expulsion for the Hudson's Bay Company, this time from Fort Yukon, its illegally occupied establishment at the mouth of the Porcupine River. With the closing of this post the traffic through Lapierre House would lessen, and its usefulness decline.

VI

BEFORE THE CONSUMMATION OF THE SALE, HOWEVER, STRANGERS would once more cross the Rat River portage, as the first missionaries entered the upper Yukon basin. In 1861, while Kennicott was

---

[59] *Ibid.*, p. 111.

[60] W. H. Dall of the Smithsonian Institution, (see Chapter Four), quoted by James in *The First Scientific Exploration*, p. 11. Kennicott's own Arctic collections, when delivered to the Smithsonian, consisted of "forty boxes and packages, weighing in the aggregate 3,000 pounds." *Ibid.*, p. 29.

still in the country, Rev. William West Kirkby, the Anglican incumbent at Fort Simpson, used the pass to make a one-week visit to Fort Yukon, though the journey necessitated a three-months' absence from his mission station. This was one of the final moves in a race for souls that had spread across the Canadian west in the 1850's and early '60s. The efforts of the Anglican Church in this contest were supported by funds raised in England by the Church Missionary Society, an organization devoted to the propagation of the Anglican version of Christianity among the heathen in all parts of the world. Their rivals were the Oblates of Mary Immaculate (O.M.I.), the Roman Catholic specialists in work among the unconverted. In the northwest in particular the Oblates generally held the upper hand. Along the Mackenzie River they had established mission stations in the vicinity of most of the Hudson's Bay Company's posts, while the Anglicans' only church on this vast waterway was at Fort Simpson. Farther to the west, however, was one more prize — the bands of Loucheux or Kutchin Indians who traded at Fort Yukon and at Lapierre House. In this field Kirkby was determined to be first.

At Fort Yukon he found the officer in charge of the post sympathetic, and the Indians enthusiastic: the latter perhaps encouraged by the gifts that were distributed as part of the ritual of establishing contact with any Indian band. In any event, Kirkby started his long journey home well satisfied with his foray across the height of land. "On the whole continent of North America," he wrote enthusiastically from Fort Simpson, "it would be difficult to find a more important and interesting field of Missionary operation. Gladly would I, if it were not for my family, live permanently among them. They require a single man to be their Missionary."[61]

Kirkby made a second trip to Fort Yukon in 1862. This time he was followed across the portage by Father Sequin from the Oblate mission at Fort Good Hope, but the Indians remained loyal to Kirkby, and the officers at Fort Yukon and Lapierre House, who were both Protestants, offered Sequin no support. He remained in the area until June 1863, but could make no headway, finally withdrawing discomfited to the Mackenzie. It was the first of several unsuccessful efforts by the Roman Catholic Church to establish a

[61] Quoted in "Tidings from the Yukon," *The Church Missionary Intelligencer,* (May 1867), p. 144.

mission for the Indians in the Yukon. In the race for converts in the west, this was one area in which the Anglicans arrived first, and dominated the field.

Kirkby, meanwhile, had found a permanent worker for Fort Yukon. Robert McDonald, at a church missionary meeting in the distant colony of Red River, heard of this need and volunteered to fill it. He was well qualified for the task. "Country-born" — to use a word beloved by the missionary magazines — he was well able to withstand the rigours of northern travel: he had already worked for nine years among the Ojibway Indians in Manitoba, and he had a gift for languages. The congregation of the Anglican church at Red River quickly raised the funds for his transportation, and in October 1862, he arrived at Fort Yukon ready to begin his labours.

The work started auspiciously. McDonald quickly gained the respect of the Fort Yukon Loucheux — or the Tukudh, which the missionaries claimed was the name these Indians called themselves. He made rapid progress in learning the language, and soon could talk to them freely without requiring an interpreter. He began the task of translating hymns, prayers, and excerpts from the bible into the Tukudh language, and teaching his converts to read or memorize these passages. Two years after he arrived at Fort Yukon, however, all these accomplishments were threatened. He became seriously ill with influenza, and for some time his recovery was in doubt. Reluctantly he requested that he be relieved, and this message was sent by the slow and uncertain mail routes of the day to the headquarters of the Church Missionary Society in London, England.

It turned out that the young "country-born" missionary, the veteran of a score of long journeys by canoe or snowshoes, was physically tougher than even he suspected. Instead of the fatality that had been feared he began a remarkable recovery, and by the summer of 1865, though not fully restored to health, he was making preparations to return to the Yukon from Fort Simpson. It was to be a sad and busy year for the missionaries. An epidemic of scarlet fever, brought into the country by the boats' crews supplying the trading posts, spread throughout the Mackenzie valley, causing much distress and many deaths. "Fort Halkett was the only place that escaped," Kirkby reported to the Society, "and that was in consequence of the boat which should have gone there not being able to accomplish the journey from the illness among its crew. The fever reached the Youcon, and even the Esquimaux along the Arctic coast,

88

and was as fatal there as anywhere. Altogether hundreds must have been swept away by it."[62]

The epidemic was still running its course in September when McDonald started back to Fort Yukon. Sickness amongst the boat's crew made it a slow and laborious journey.

I arrived at Peel-River Fort on the evening of the 12th of September [he wrote], and received a cordial welcome from Mr. and Mrs. Andrew Flett, and a large number of Indians who were there assembled. Owing to ... my being not quite well I did not attempt holding more than one religious public service with the Indians, but was otherwise actively employed during my short stay there in doing what I could for the sick, giving directions as to the treatment of scarlet fever, putting up medicines to be left with Mr. Andrew Flett, and making up packages of articles which I required to be brought on at once. Two days afterwards I proceeded on my journey. I performed the portion of it across the mountains from Peel-River to La Pierre's House much more satisfactorily than I had anticipated. Not having as yet recovered from influenza, I had rather feared the walking through the cold water, but I found myself better at the end of it than at its commencement. I reached La Pierre's House on the 18th September, partially recruited in health and strength....

On my arrival [at Fort Yukon] I received a hearty welcome from the Indians, of whom there were a good many assembled here; also from Mr. James McDougall, the officer at present in charge of this Fort, and others belonging to the Fort. Most thankful was I to arrive here again after an absence of more than a year; and more so as it was doubtful when I went away whether I should be able to return again, owing to the ill state of my health....

Since my return my time has been much occupied in rendering what assistance lay in my power to the sick, both in a medical way and also to their spiritual necessities, and I have felt encouragement in the hope that my efforts have not been in vain.[63]

Indirectly, McDonald's illness had an incalculable effect on the work of the Anglican Church in the Canadian northwest, in that it brought William Carpenter Bompas into this field. McDonald's request for relief did not reach London until the spring of 1865, just before the anniversary service of the Church Missionary Society, held every year in May. In 1865 the preacher was Bishop Anderson, formerly of Rupert's Land, who, unaware of the recovery in health that was even now taking place, used as the theme of his sermon the

---

[62] *Ibid.*, p. 150.
[63] *Ibid.*, p. 151.

story of this sick and lonely man whose faithful ministry, just now starting to bear fruit, might come to naught. "Shall no one come forward," Anderson thundered in his peroration, "to take up the standard of the Lord as it falls from his hands, and to occupy the ground."[64] It was Bompas who volunteered to undertake the task.

A native of London, he was then 34 years old. His father was a lawyer who had died suddenly when his children were still at school, leaving his family in straitened circumstances. Bompas was forced to give up the promise of a brilliant scholastic career and work unhappily for a time in a solicitor's office. He had always had a strong religious bent, however, both his parents being staunch Baptists, and in his late twenties he decided to quit his clerkship and present himself as a candidate for ordination, though in the Anglican Church and not in the faith of his family. For a time after completing his studies he served as a rural curate in a small village in Lincolnshire, but he found little satisfaction in the humdrum routine of this post. He turned his attention to the mission field, hoping to find there more meaningful service. Bishop Anderson's clarion call was an irresistible challenge.

Within three weeks Bompas was on his way to the Mackenzie, and on Christmas Eve he was greeting the surprised but delighted Kirkby at Fort Simpson, where visitors did not normally arrive in the dead of winter. For the newcomer there was the news of McDonald's recovery and his return that fall to Fort Yukon, a fact that both pleased and disappointed Bompas, whose heart had been set on that assignment. However, at a conference of the three missionaries — Kirkby, McDonald and Bompas — held at Fort Simpson in the spring of 1866, it was decided that the latter would become a priest-at-large rather than be given a fixed station, an arrangement that gave Bompas much pleasure, and more than compensated for his disappointment in not getting the Fort Yukon assignment.

This arrangement marked the beginning of Bompas' extensive travels in the northwest. At first his journeys were confined to the valley of the Mackenzie River, which he followed from its headwaters to its delta in a search for the hunting camps of the scattered Indian and Eskimo bands. Later, as his responsibilities increased so did the scope of his travels, which eventually ranged from the Peace

[64] H. A. Cody, *An Apostle of the North*, (New York, E. P. Dutton and Company, 1908), p. 20.

River country to the Arctic, and from Lake Athabasca to the northern coast of British Columbia. He visited more of the northwest than did any other man who was in the country before the gold rush, but his journeys were usually unsung and unrecorded. He was not, as were most of those in the district, seeking personal gain: instead, he was bringing Christian instruction to the natives, whereever they happened to be. For him, the hardship was a joy: beyond a doubt, the man who was to become the first Anglican bishop of the Yukon had found his true vocation.

CHAPTER FOUR

The Lower Yukon
The End of an Era

Map Number 1, following page 58

I

BY THE 1860'S, THE FORTUNES OF THE RUSSIAN AMERICAN COM-
pany were deteriorating. The third, and last, charter which had been
signed in 1844 after a long period of negotiation, had reduced the
Company from the status of a great mercantile institution to that of
a governing body for the American colonies, which many of the
Tsar's advisers in St. Petersburg no longer considered as worth
retaining. In the Gulf of Alaska the peltries were depleted; the
British by their commercial agreement with the Russians were firmly
entrenched in the panhandle; and the once-proud fleet of merchant
ships, that had carried sea otter skins to China and brought back
cargoes of tea in return, was now ignominiously hauling ice from
Sitka to the booming port of San Francisco. The moment to dispose
of Alaska was at hand. Yet the dream of an imaginative and elo-
quent American financier named Perry McDonough Collins almost
brought at this time an important development to the valley of the
lower Yukon River, that might well have changed its history, and
brought jobs and people to it ahead of the search for gold.

Collins was probably the first American Russophile. The California gold rush had made him wealthy, and he was searching now
for new investment opportunities: American whalers, returning from
the Amur (or Amoor) River, on the border between Siberia and
China, brought back tales of exciting commercial developments in
that region. Collins became convinced that here was an unparalleled
field for capital investment and the application of American tech-
nology. He arranged in 1855 to have himself appointed commercial

agent for the United States on the Amur, and he returned home in 1857 advocating the construction of an overland telegraph line from the United States to Europe by way of Alaska and Siberia. Attempts by a company to lay a submarine telegraph across the Atlantic had met with repeated failures, and Collins was able to persuade Hiram Sibley, president of the newly-formed Western Union Telegraph Company, to adopt his scheme. Sibley's company had just completed the construction of the first land line across the United States, and its extension to Europe did not seem any more difficult or impractical.

It was, nonetheless, an ambitious proposal. It would involve the building of 16,000 miles of line, which would originate in Portland, Oregon, traverse the interior of British Columbia by way of New Westminster and the Fraser valley to Fort St. James, follow the valley of the Yukon River to the sea, cross Bering Strait at its narrowest point, and push into Siberia as far as the mouth of the Amur. From this point the Russians would complete the construction to St. Petersburg, where the system would connect with the European telegraph network. Collins had already obtained from the governments concerned permission to acquire the necessary rights-of-way, and these he transferred to Sibley and the Overland Telegraph Company, the organization formed to carry out the work. In a message to Congress on December 6, 1864, President Lincoln formally announced the start of the project, "with the cordial good will and support as well of this government as of those of Great Britain and Russia."[1]

Colonel Charles L. Bulkley, a military engineer who had become a specialist in telegraphic communication during the Civil War, was borrowed from the United States Army to serve as engineer-in-charge of the new Company. He organized the work on quasi-military lines, bestowing army titles on his officers, and seeking out young men for the key positions, as he felt that they had greater endurance and perseverance. One of those he approached was Kennicott, who was offered the position of officer-in-charge of the Yukon party, with the rank of major. Seizing this opportunity to expand the work that he had begun in the northwest, Kennicott agreed to leave his new position at the museum, on condition that he be allowed to select a number of assistants who would carry out scientific investigations and collect natural history specimens in the country through which

[1] Quoted in James, *The First Scientific Exploration*, footnote, p. 13.

the line was to pass, the collections to be divided between the Smithsonian and the Chicago Academy of Sciences. These terms were agreed to, and Kennicott was given the additional appointment of Director of the Scientific Corps. From the younger scientists on the staff of the Smithsonian he chose to accompany him J. T. Rothrock, botanist, and W. H. Dall, H. W. Elliott, Charles Pease, H. M. Bannister, and Ferdinand Bischoff, zoologists and geologists. In addition, a young man named Frederick Whymper, who had just returned from an expedition to the interior of Vancouver Island, was hired in Victoria as official artist for the expedition. The bulky wet plate cameras then in use were not a practical device for recording activities in the wilderness.

The exploration and construction parties for the British Columbia section of the line left San Francisco for the field on May 17, 1865, and the northern parties, including Kennicott's, followed in quick succession, until the supply lines stretched from the Fraser River to Siberia. Yet in little more than a year, the purpose behind the planning and expense was nullified. On July 22, 1866, the laying of the first trans-Atlantic cable was successfully accomplished, and the Overland Telegraph Company collapsed like a house of cards.

It took another year to inform all the field crews that the project was abandoned, and bring them back to civilization. Three million dollars had been spent, and miracles of logistics performed, but when the workers were recalled their only visible legacy was a few miles of telegraph poles standing in lonely hinterlands, instead of the long string of wire, the line maintenance roads, and the repeated stations of a permanent installation, which would certainly have contributed to the opening up of the country. Yet there were intangible contributions: the mass of information gathered in the course of the reconnaissance that preceded construction was perhaps the most obvious of these. As one of the participants wrote: "It is needless to state that an expedition employing several hundred explorers, who examined six thousand miles of country on both sides of the Pacific — from Fraser River to Bering Straits and thence southward to the Amur — has added something to our knowledge of these countries."[2]

The printed word helped to disseminate this knowledge. Several

[2] Frederick Whymper, *Travels in America and on the Yukon,* (New York, Harper & Brothers, 1869), p. 90.

of the explorers and scientists on the project, fortunately, were keepers of journals, and when the work was halted and the men removed, four of these daily records were rewritten and expanded into books. Two of these publications recorded events that took place in Siberia. The other two were accounts of the Company's exploration of the lower Yukon River and, most topically, they offered the first description in English of Alaska — the Great Land — the almost unknown sub-continent that by the stroke of a pen had become an American possession just before the books appeared.

II

DALL, THE SCIENTIST, AND WHYMPER, THE COMPANY ARTIST, WERE the writers on Alaska. They travelled together during a considerable portion of their Company service, but they were not particularly compatible associates. Dall combined an impeccable and strait-laced New England background with impressive scholastic credentials and the cocksureness of extreme youth. Whymper, on the other hand, was a footloose and pleasure-loving Englishman, typical of many who were flocking to the colonies in growing numbers to escape the nagging restrictions of life in the Victorian era in their homeland. Because of these differences in background and outlook, their observations and emphasis on the country and its people often varied. Taken together, however, their books offer a composite picture of the last days of the Russians in North America, and of the river on which this final act was played.

Dall was born in Boston in 1845, and graduated in medicine from Harvard University. He soon, however, became more interested in natural history than in the care of the sick, and returned to college for further training in this field. For a time he was a special student of Louis Agassiz, an eminent naturalist, geologist, and teacher, who was developing at Harvard an institute for advanced biological research. With this academic background, Dall had no difficulty in obtaining a staff position with the Smithsonian Institution, in spite of his youth. He was only 19 when he was seconded to the Overland Telegraph Company: he was 21 when he began his northern service.

Whymper's antecedents are more obscure. He was obviously well-educated and possessed of some financial means: he was also a skillful artist, a talent he put to good use in satisfying his desire to see other parts of the world. "In 1862," he wrote of his trip to America, "the Pacific coast, and especially British Columbia, attracted much attention at home. Having, thank God, like a good proportion of my countrymen, a little superfluous energy — which was lying fallow — I determined to see something of these coasts, and accordingly commenced getting together my traps for the voyage."[3] When he signed on with the Overland Telegraph Company he was offered a free hand in his choice of assignments, and he requested service in the Yukon region, "which had been, from the commencement of our explorations, more spoken about than any other."[4] Because there were at that time no vacancies in the Yukon crews, he had to wait almost a year before his posting to the area was possible.

Dall and Whymper finally both set foot in Alaska for the first time in September 1866, though they arrived on different days and in different ships. Dall was actually on his way from Sitka to Siberia, to carry out scientific studies with one of the parties there, when the vessel on which he was travelling put into Norton Sound to unload supplies at St. Michael's. Shocking news greeted him. Kennicott had died suddenly at Nulato the previous May, of a heart attack, though because of the difficulty of communication, this fact was only now becoming generally known. He had, it appeared, reached St. Michael's in August 1865, and during the winter had crossed the Unalakleet portage to Nulato, with Charles Pease, also of the Smithsonian, and two Canadians, Frank E. Ketchum of St. John, New Brunswick, and Michael Lebarge[5] of Chateaugay, Quebec, who were in charge of exploration and construction between Nulato and Fort Yukon. Kennicott had already, while in San Francisco, suffered a stroke brought on by the strain and worry of organizing the work, and at Nulato his companions soon noted that he was still depressed and subdued, very unlike his usual ebullient self. One morning, he did not appear for breakfast, and was missing from his room. A search was organized, and he was soon found, dead, on the riverbank, his pocket compass in his hand, and bearings to prominent

---

[3] *Ibid.*, p. 21.

[4] *Ibid.*, p. 170.

[5] "Lebarge" is Dall's spelling; others used "Labarge," while the lake near Whitehorse that was named after him is, on present-day maps, spelled "Leberge." Dall's spelling will be used in the text for the name when not in a quotation, and Leberge for the lake.

topographic features in the neighbourhood sketched in the sand. To the very end he was gathering material for his studies of the country.

Kennicott's death caused Dall to change his plans. Instead of going on to Siberia, he resolved to seek permission to remain in the Yukon valley, and use "my best energies to complete the scientific exploration of the northwest extremity of the continent."[6] Bulkley happened to be in the harbour, and the request for a change of assignment was quickly given official approval. Dall was appointed to succeed Kennicott as Director of the Scientific Corps, and in addition was made "surgeon in general charge of the district between Bering Strait and the Yukon,"[7] a rather nebulous position with apparently little work or responsibility attached to it. Pease was preparing to leave the country, to escort Kennicott's body home for burial, but Ketchum and Lebarge were at St. Michael's, waiting to return across the portage as soon as it was possible to travel with dogs. Dall proposed to accompany them — Nulato, he decided, would be the logical base from which to continue scientific work.

His arrangements completed, he gathered together his gear and went ashore in a night that matched his sombre mood. "Having pocketed some biscuit," he wrote, "I was provisioned, and, picking out a soft plank in a back room, I rolled myself in a blanket, and, after some difficulty, got to sleep. The rain continued; the Russians were holding an orgy with liquor obtained from the vessels; the dogs howled nearly all night; the roof leaked, not water, but fine volcanic gravel, with which it is covered. If this is a sample of the country, I thought, it is not prepossessing!"[8]

While waiting for the right conditions to start his inland journey, Dall had ample opportunity to absorb more of the atmosphere of the harsh society of which he was to become temporarily a part. He found little reason to revise his initial impressions. The St. Michael's Redoubt was dismal and dirty, with log living quarters and storehouses built around a hollow square that was protected by a ten-foot palisade. For defence, there were a "number of pieces of artillery of very small calibre and mostly very old-fashioned and rusty.... One of the bastions is without cannon, and is used as a guardhouse

[6] W. H. Dall, *Alaska and Its Resources*, (Boston, Lee and Shepherd, 1870), p. 6.

[7] *Ibid.*, p. 6.

[8] *Ibid.*, p. 7.

for refractory subjects."[9] It was soon apparent that this room saw frequent use: discipline was, of necessity, brutal and strict.

The workmen of the Russian American Company [Dall wrote] were, almost without exception, convicts, mostly from Siberia, where the Company was originally organized. They were men convicted of such crimes as theft, incorrigible drunkenness, burglary, and even manslaughter. . . . They work with little energy and spirit as a general thing, but can accomplish a great deal if roused by necessity. Small offences are punished by confinement in the guardhouse, or *boofka*, and greater ones by a thrashing administered by the commander in person; those who commit considerable crimes are forced to run the gauntlet, receive one or two hundred blows with a stick, or in extreme cases are sent for trial to Sitka, or, in case of murder, to St. Petersburg.
 The present Uprovalisha [District Commander], Stepanoff, has been in office about four years. He is a middle-aged man of great energy and iron will, with the Russian fondness for strong liquor . . . generous in his own way, and seldom does a mean thing when he is sober, but nevertheless is a good deal of a brute. He will gamble and drink in the most democratic way with his workmen, and bears no malice for a black eye received in a drunken brawl; but woe to the unfortunate who infringes discipline when he is sober, for he will certainly receive his reward, and Stepanoff often says of his men, when speaking to an American, "You can expect nothing good of this rabble: they left Russia because they were not wanted there."
 The commanders, or "bidarshiks", of the smaller posts in the district of St. Michael's are appointed by Stepanoff, who has absolute authority over them, and does not fail to let them understand it, making them row his boat when the annual supply-ship is in port. . . . But Stepanoff trembles before the captain of the ship or an old officer of the Company, much in the same way that his workmen cringe before him. This sort of subserviency, the fruit of a despotic government, is characteristic of the lower classes of Russians; and to such an extent is it ingrained in their characters that it seems impossible for them to comprehend any motives of honor or truthfulness as being superior to self-interest.[10]

Early in October, Dall, Ketchum, and Lebarge thankfully left by boat for Unalakleet, where, at the start of the portage to the Yukon River, the Russian American Company had established a small post to serve as a way station for travellers to the interior. This move, though it took them closer to their objective, brought no improvement in their living conditions. Not only was the Unalakleet post even more primitive than St. Michael's, but it was crowded beyond

[9] *Ibid.*, pp. 10-11.
[10] *Ibid.*, pp. 11-13.

capacity by 40 telegraph labourers preparing to start construction on the line.

Whymper, already waiting to make the crossing to Nulato, had noted the inevitable effect of the sudden increase in population on local trade.

The men [he wrote] had very naturally a strong desire to obtain skin clothing for winter use, and also as curiosities, and in the excessive competition for the limited quantities in the hands of the Russians and Indians, prices went up about 200 per cent! This was generally known as the "parka mania," (from "parka," Russian for skin or coat), and was a great benefit to some of the more enterprising Russians, who set their Indian wives to work making coats, boots, caps and fur-socks in great variety, while they reaped themselves a harvest of five-dollar pieces.[11]

On October 27 the Nulato party was finally able to start the journey over the portage, using four sleds, each pulled by five dogs, and "very well laden with a miscellaneous collection of boxes, barrels, tools, furs, blankets and snow-shoes. Each load averaged 350 pounds weight."[12] For everyone except Ketchum and Lebarge it was their first experience in using dogs, and those who had purchased the fur clothing of the Norton Sound natives soon found that these garments were much too warm for the trail. With rueful thoughts of the inflated prices that they had paid at Unalakleet, the neophytes switched back to the use of ordinary heavy woollen clothing brought from the United States. Native skin boots, however, were found to be superior to all other types of footwear, and were universally used on the trail.

It was a difficult journey, slowed by inclement weather. Towards the end of November, however, the travellers finally glimpsed the Yukon River ahead of them, and Dall, for one, approached it with an almost religious fervour.

A natural impatience urged me forward, and after a smart tramp of several miles we arrived at the steep bank of the river. It was with a feeling akin to that which urged Balboa forward into the very waves of a newly discovered ocean, that I rushed by the dogs and down the steep declivity, forgetting everything else in the desire to be first on the ice, and to enjoy the magnificent prospect before me.

[11] Whymper, *Travels in America,* p. 168.

[12] *Ibid.,* p. 172.

There lay a stretch of forty miles of this great, broad, snow-covered river, with broken fragments of ice-cakes glowing in the ruddy light of the setting sun; the low opposite shore, three miles away, seemed a mere black streak on the horizon. ... On its banks live thousands who know neither its outlet nor its source, who look to it for food and even for clothing, and, recognizing its magnificence, call themselves proudly *men of the Yukon.*

Stolid indeed must he be, who surveys the broad expanse of the Missouri of the North for the first time without emotion.[13]

On November 26 the party arrived at the Nulato post, after a quick trip along a well-travelled trail on the river ice. By now this establishment was as large as St. Michael's: it had the same type of drab, dirty buildings around a hollow square, protected by a log stockade. They were pleasantly received by the bidarshik, Ivan Pavloff, who had been forewarned of their coming. A large room had been cleared out for their use, with fresh straw laid on the floor, and a fire lighted in the stove. They all enjoyed a "delicious steambath," and settled down with anticipation for their stay. At that moment, life in Russian America seemed endurable after all.

III

THE FEELING OF WELL-BEING WAS SHORT-LIVED. IT SOON BECAME apparent to the newcomers that relations between the Russians in the fort and the natives in the vicinity were poisoned by a cloud of fear, a lingering heritage of a long period of brutal treatment by the Company's officers that had culminated in a massacre of the inhabitants of the post 15 years before, in 1851.[14] A regular watch was still

---

[13] Dall, *Alaska*, p. 41.

[14] The details of the massacre are obscure, and vary with the telling. All accounts agree, however, that the killing was precipitated by a visit of a Lt. Bernard (or Barnard) of the Royal Navy, a member of one of the Franklin searching expeditions, who was investigating a report that strange white men had been seen in the Yukon valley. While staying at Nulato, he appears to have offended the natives in some way, probably unintentionally, and so lighted the powder keg that led to an attack on the undefended fort at night by the Indians, and the slaughter of its people, including Bernard. The unfortunate officer's action was, however, only the incident that triggered simmering forces: the true cause of the killing was the continuing ill-treatment of the natives by the Russians.

kept from the bastion, though, typically, most of the firearms supplied by the Company were in disrepair, and the heavy armament consisted of two rusty, useless six-pounders. "During our stay," Whymper wrote, "the gate was always shut at night, and Indians excluded when present in large numbers."[15]

Inside the fort, the atmosphere was little better. Pavloff was a creole who could not read or write: because of this handicap, he was servile to full-blooded Russians, though he was treated with open contempt by most of them, in spite of his position of authority. Usually "good humoured," he was a heavy drinker, and violent when drunk. "He was continuously pestering us with requests for liquor," Dall commented, "until I was obliged to poison all the alcohol intended for collecting purposes."[16] Besides the bidarshik, there were at the post two Russians, one old Siberian native, and two other creoles, one of whom kept the accounts for Pavloff: in addition a few Indians and a considerable number of Indian women were employed at the fort. The internal ill-will was not tempered by the fact that Nulato was still a "hungry place," and fish, though often in short supply, was, for most of the year, the principal article of diet for Company workmen and natives alike.

In fact, little had changed on the lower Yukon River since Zagoskin's journey. Nulato was still the eastern limit of the Russian American Company's expansion, and the British were still unchallenged in Fort Yukon: occasionally the rival traders met at the mouth of the Tanana, midway between the two establishments. As in Zagoskin's time, the considerable portion of the trade that by-passed the Russians through Kotzebue Sound was still unchecked.

Inter-tribal commerce [wrote Whymper] goes on to such an extent that clothing worn hundreds of miles up the Yukon, and in other parts of the interior of Russian America, is of Tchuktchis [Siberian] origin, and is made up by the women of the coast tribes, who sew better than those of the interior. This trade is principally for tame reindeer skins, of which the Tchuktchis have an overplus, and in exchange they recieve bone, oil, and the furs of smaller animals. . . .

A large portion of the [coast] natives have guns — both flint-lock and percussion-cap — obtained in trade. Guns obtained from as far off as

[15] Whymper, *Travels in America*, p. 194.

[16] Dall, *Alaska*, p. 45.

the Hudson's Bay Company's fort at the junction of the Porcupine, find their way to the coast by inter-tribal barter.[17]

For the Overland Telegraph men the winter was not a period of idleness. Much time was spent in discussing and refining their plans for the coming year. "Whymper and myself," Dall wrote, "decided to ascend the Yukon together, as far as Fort Yukon, by water in the spring. Ketchum proposed, in company with Mike Lebarge, to make the same journey over the ice, with dogs and sleds, in February."[18] Meanwhile, everyone kept active. They worked on their quarters, making the rooms more habitable by chinking the logs and lining the walls and floor to keep out the increasing cold. Whymper busied himself sketching. Ketchum and Lebarge started preparations for their winter journey. Dall began his notes on the Indian tribes of the lower Yukon, and also started the acquisition of a "vocabulary" of Indian words, as well as some basic Russian. On December 4, he recorded a temperature of 56 degrees below zero, and noted that "on the 27th of December an observation was made, which showed the day to be just three hours long. As nearly as our watches could determine, the sun rose at a quarter before eleven, and set at a quarter of two."[19]

At the end of January Ketchum and Lebarge returned to the coast to obtain supplies and gear for their journey to Fort Selkirk. They did not get back to Nulato until March 2, when they brought with them 22 dogs and enough dried salmon for 25 or 30 days of travel, but none to spare for the period of waiting while final preparations for the trip were made. Feeding 22 dogs at "hungry" Nulato was a serious problem; the solution arrived at was "to get together every eatable thing that was available, and to make soup for them, as the Russians also do at times, of oil, fish, scraps of meat, bran and rice. We even sacrificed our last beans for their benefit, and found that they would eat them when properly softened. . . . It evidently suited them, for they fattened on it."[20] This feeding regime lasted for nine days. The two explorers finally started their journey on March 11, a gray and dismal day that threatened snow. They left amidst much head-shaking and gloomy prognostications by the

[17] Whymper, *Travels in America*, pp. 162-163.
[18] Dall, *Alaska*, p. 56.
[19] *Ibid.*, p. 58.
[20] Whymper, *Travels in America*, p. 203.

Russians and Indians, who felt, with justification, that the departure had been too long delayed.

By early April, there were signs of spring at Nulato, as the climax of the northern year approached once more. Dall through the eyes of a naturalist, catalogued the cycle of change as winter yielded its long grip:

The continued warm weather was melting the snow rapidly, and although we had cleaned off the roof as much as possible, still the melting ice caused a continual dripping during the day....

The Nulato and other small rivers had felt the effects of the melting snow, and the ice on the edge of the Yukon, which rests on and is frozen to the beach, was covered with water from them.

Flies, to all appearance the common universal house-fly, as well as the blue-bottle, had appeared in large numbers, and might be seen on the sunny side of every wall.

On the 10th I found the first fully expanded willow catkins, and the pretty red catkin of the alder....

The white ptarmigan began moulting, or rather brown feathers began to appear in their necks and on the edges of their wings, where the first change may be looked for....

On the [29th] the first goose was seen, the solitary advance-guard of the thousands to come.... The weather had become extremely warm. Shirt-sleeves were the rule, and the little children enjoyed themselves on the broad river-beach, building houses with pebbles and making mud pies....

On the 3d, Kurilla [a local Indian hired by the Overland Telegraph party] killed a goose.... He received the annual pound of tobacco, the perquisite of him who kills the first goose in the spring....

On the 7th of May the first swans were seen.... The geese did not arrive in large numbers until the 9th of May, ten days later than on the previous year. The commonest ducks were the pin-tail and the green-winged teal....

On the 12th of May the mosquitoes made their appearance, though the snow still lay on the ground in abundance. They were larger than our home mosquitoes, and very bloodthirsty. After a few days it was impossible to sleep without a net.[21]

On May 19, the breakup of the ice came quietly and without pyrotechnics. Dall and Whymper, watching from the roof of their quarters, were disappointed — the spectacle was certainly not up to their expectations. Nevertheless, the open water that followed was a siren call, and the song of spring is difficult to resist. Fort Yukon beckoned. It was time to be on the move.

[21] Dall, *Alaska*, pp. 66-70.

ON MAY 26, 1867, ONE WEEK AFTER THE ICE WENT OUT, DALL AND
Whymper began their journey from Nulato to Fort Yukon in pouring rain, travelling in a type of native sealskin boat similar to that
used by Zagoskin for his abortive upstream journey, and known to
the Russians as a "bidarra." It was of flat-bottomed, open construction, adapted from the cargo-carrying "oomiak" of the Eskimos.
The explorers' craft carried a substantial load, consisting of "five
persons, a tent, blankets, cooking utensils and guns, two bags of
biscuits (100 lbs.), 150 pounds of flour, with smaller packages."[22]
The crew, besides the two white men, was made up of the steersman,
Kurilla, and two other Indians. The Russians left at the same time
in a much larger bidarra on a trading journey to Nuklukahyet, at
the mouth of the Tanana River, and the two parties stayed more or
less together for this portion of the voyage.

The explorers quickly established a routine, allowing themselves
only four or five hours sleep a night, and eating sparingly, except for
the luxury of numerous cups of sweetened tea, usually followed by
a pipeful of tobacco. At first they had to be wary of ice-floes and
driftwood. "The banks in many places are undermined by the rapid
current," Dall observed, "and frequently fall into the river in large
masses, with the trees and shrubs upon them, startling the unaccustomed ear with a noise like thunder."[23]

After four days, the rain stopped, and on every side, and overhead, the rich pageant of the north's awakening continued to unfold.
Wild life was everywhere. "Swans, brant, and sandhill cranes were
seen," Dall noted, "the former abundantly. . . . Every step added
some new plant, insect, or bird to our collections."[24] They supplemented their food supplies from this rich harvest: Whymper reported
that "in three days we obtained one heron, two or three ducks and
geese, and a few eggs; also some beaver-meat. The heron was
decidedly tough eating; the beaver-meat was musk-like in flavor, the
tail alone excepted, which is the trapper's greatest luxury, and was
really delicious. The natives here, when very short of supplies, eat

[22] Whymper, *Travels in America*, p. 219.
[23] Dall, *Alaska*, pp. 77-78.
[24] *Ibid.*, p. 78.

the flesh of marten, owls, hawks, etc., but it is from necessity rather than choice."[25]

On June 3 the explorers arrived at Nowikakat village, where the Indians told them that Ketchum and Lebarge had reached Fort Yukon in safety on the ice, and were now on their way to Fort Selkirk by water. "It is surprising in this thinly-populated country," Whymper commented, "how fast news of any kind will travel from tribe to tribe. Should a vessel call at St. Michael's, in a week or two it will be known on three parts of the Yukon."[26]

Before resuming their journey, Dall and Whymper replenished their supplies by acquiring about 300 pounds of dried meat, as well as fat, tongues, and dried moose noses, which, according to Dall, were delicious when "thoroughly boiled." Trade was by barter, and was not without its inconveniences.

We were not over well provided with trading goods [wrote Whymper] and in common with all the men of our expedition, I had at times to give away my shirts, socks, pocket knives, etc. The chief at this village took a great fancy to my towel and soap, and as my companion Dall was well provided in this matter I gave them to him. At this juncture he caught sight of my tooth brush, and immediately asked for that. I need not say he did not get it; but I would recommend any future traveller to take nothing but absolute necessaries, or else take all the little luxuries of civilization by the dozen, as whatever [the Indians] are unaccustomed to and see you make use of they immediately want.[27]

Nowikakat was well-known for the skill of its canoe makers, and several of their graceful craft accompanied the Overland Telegraph Company's explorers and the Russian traders when the journey was resumed. In spite of the fact that they were now approaching the latitude of the Arctic Circle, the travellers found themselves, to their surprise, suffering from the extreme heat. The weather was so warm that in the middle of the day they were often compelled to pull into the bank and rest for an hour or two to escape the worst of its effects.

The sun hardly dipped below the horizon at midnight [Dall commented], and his noontide rays scorched like a furnace. The mosquitoes

---

[25] Whymper, *Travels in America*, pp. 226-229.

[26] *Ibid.*, p. 211.

[27] Frederick Whymper, "Russian America, or 'Alaska'; the Natives of the Yukon River and adjacent country," *Transactions of the Ethnological Society of London*, Vol. 7 (1869), p. 175.

were like smoke in the air.... [They] were distinguished from the civilized species by the reckless daring of their attack. Thousands might be killed before their eyes, yet the survivors sounded their trumpets and carried on the war. A blanket offered them no impediment; buckskin alone defied their art. At meal-times, forced to remove our nets, we sat until nearly stifled in the smoke, and, emerging for a breath of air, received no mercy. My companion's hands, between sunburn and mosquitoes, were nearly raw, and I can well conceive that a man without a net, in one of these marshes, would soon die from nervous exhaustion. The mosquitoes drive the moose, deer, and bear into the river, and all nature rejoices when the end of July comes, and their reign is at an end.[28]

On June 8 they reached the mouth of the Tanana River, the Yukon's largest tributary, and parted company with the Russians, though several of the Nowikakat canoes continued upstream with them. The nature of the country was changing — the distant hills, sometimes not even visible from the river, were now crowding closer to the banks, while the channel was becoming narrower and the current more swift. On June 10 Dall wrote:

We entered, about three o'clock in the afternoon, between high bluffs and hills rising perhaps fifteen hundred feet above the river, which here was exceedingly deep and rapid and not more than half a mile wide. The bends were abrupt, and the absence of sunlight and the extreme quiet produced a feeling as if we had been travelling underground. The appropriate and expressive English name for these bluffs is "The Ramparts."

We were approaching the so-called Rapids of the Yukon, of which we had heard so many stories. The Russians had predicted that we would not be able to ascend them. The Indians joined in this expression of opinion, and had no end of stories about the velocity of the current and the difficulty experienced in ascending them.... About midnight we arrived at the Rapids. The river is very narrow here, and the rocky hills rise sharply from the water. The rocks are metamorphic quartzites, and a dike or belt of hard granite rock crosses the river. The fall is about twelve feet in half a mile. The rapid current has worn the granite away

[28] Dall, *Alaska*, pp. 100-101. The ultimate mosquito story from the pre-Klondike, incidentally, must be that of Mrs. Frederick Schwatka, wife of a Yukon explorer (see Chapter Five), who, in one of the many pot-boilers that appeared as "guides" to the gold rush Klondike, was quoted as saying that "at some seasons in the country mosquitoes are in such dense swarms that at night they will practically cover a mosquito netting fairly touching each other, and crowding through any kind of mesh. I have heard it asserted by people of experience that they form co-operative societies and assist each other through the meshes by pushing behind and pulling in front."

on either side, forming two good channels, but in the middle is an island of granite, over which the water rushes in a sheet of foam during high water. There are several smaller "rips" along the shore, especially near the left bank, but nothing to interrupt steamer navigation, except the very rapid current.

Several Indians attempted to ascend in their small canoes. We saw them reach a point just below the island, and by dint of the hardest paddling keep stationary there a few minutes; when, their strength being exhausted, away went the canoes downstream like arrows.

We joined our tracking-line with several rawhide lines belonging to the Indians, and by keeping close to the rocks succeeded in tracking over the worst part without much difficulty. Taking our seats again, we had a hard pull to pass one jutting rock, and our troubles were over. We then enjoyed a well-earned cup of tea, and took a parting glance of the Rapids from above.[29]

Their first camp beyond the rapids was by a small tributary stream, where, wrote Whymper, they found "wild gooseberry and currant bushes on the bank. I had previously seen a quantity of wild rhubarb, which the Indians gather in quantities, and it is really very little inferior in flavor to the cultivated kind."[30] Moose, he continued, were also abundant on this section of the river, often being driven into the water by the fierce mosquitoes. "The natives do not always waste powder and shot over them, but get near the moose, manoeuvring round it in their birch-bark canoes till the animal is fatigued, and then stealthily approach and stab it in the heart and loins."[31] The natives killed one moose for the white men in this fashion and shot several others. Whymper shot a moose calf swimming in the river, not, he admitted, without some qualms of conscience, which quickly vanished when he tasted the delicious flavour of the meat. Bear and Canada lynx were also seen in this vicinity.

For another fortnight they pushed on doggedly in the scorching heat and the clouds of mosquitoes. On June 23 they reached the mouth of the Porcupine River, where they paused briefly to set their colours and load their fire-arms.

Rounding a bend in the river, about noon we saw the white buildings of the fort on the right bank, about a mile above the mouth of the

---

[29] *Ibid.*, pp. 96-98.

[30] Whymper, *Travels in America*, p. 242.

[31] *Ibid.*, p. 246.

Porcupine.[32] We gave them a hearty salute, which was returned by a fusillade from a large crowd of Indians who had collected on the bank. Landing, we received a cordial greeting from an old French-Canadian and two Scotchmen, who were the only occupants. The commander and Antoine Houle[33] were daily expected with the remainder of the men and the annual supply of goods from La Pierre's House, by way of the Porcupine River. . . .

The [travel time] . . . had occupied less than twenty-seven days, and the distance travelled we estimated at about six hundred and thirty miles. In a straight line the distance from Nulato to Fort Yukon is over four hundred and eighty miles.

We were much elated at the successful issue of our journey, and I confess to having felt a pardonable pride in being the first American to reach Fort Yukon from the sea.[34]

V

DALL WAS IMPRESSED BY THE LAY-OUT OF THE POST. "ALL THE houses were strongly built," he wrote, "roofed with sheets of spruce bark pinned and fastened down by long poles. The sides were plastered with a white mortar made from shell-marl, obtainable in the vicinity. . . . The yard was free from dirt, and the houses, with their white walls and red trimmings, made a very favourable comparison with any of those in the Russian posts."[35] They were, however, almost the only kind words written by the young American about the Hudson's Bay Company.

The fare for men and dogs at this place is the same [he commented] i.e. dry moose meat alternating with dry deer meat, occasionally varied by fresh meat of the same kind, and the slight supply of game and fish which is now and then obtainable. . . . The men should receive three pounds of tea and six of sugar, annually, to flavor their diet of dry meat; but I was informed that this supply was exceedingly irregular, and often failed entirely.

[32] The construction of a new post at Fort Yukon was begun in 1864, as Murray's original site was being undermined by the river. Dall mentioned that at the time of his visit only the erection of a stockade was needed to complete the establishment. Most of the old buildings had been moved to the new location, and many of the original foundation timbers that had been left in place now "projected far over the water." *Ibid.*, p. 102.

[33] Antoine Houle (or Hoole), the interpreter, was the son of Campbell's Francis Hoole. The spelling "Houle" is that used by Dall.

[34] Dall, *Alaska*, p. 102.

[35] *Ibid.*, p. 103.

The Indian chiefs often obtain a small present of tea, sugar, or flour, but the latter is quite inaccessible to the men, except through the favor of the commander. These men are allowed two suits of clothes annually, if the supply holds out; but for anything else they must wait until the furs are all purchased, and then, if anything remains after the Indian are satisfied, the men are allowed to purchase.... Every effort is made, to make these men marry Indian wives; thus forcing them to remain in the country by burdening them with females whom they are ashamed to take back to civilization, and cannot desert. They perform a larger amount of manual labour for smaller pay than any other civilized people on the globe.

The hardships and exposures to which they are subjected are beyond belief. In fact, the whole system is one of the most exacting tyranny; and only in the north of Scotland could men of intelligence be found who would submit to it. The systematic way in which the white "servant of the Company" is ground down below the level of the Indian about him, is a degradation few could bear.... There is some comfort in reflecting that a few years will put an end to this. Free traders already pass through the greater part of the Hudson Bay territory with out restraint, and they will not be long in reaching a district so rich in valuable furs as that of Fort Yukon.[36]

Dall certainly did not share the feelings of his mentor Kennicott concerning the life-style of the Hudson's Bay Company's posts.

It was a propitious time to arrive at the fort, as the annual trade was about to begin. On June 26, Mr. J. McDougall, who was in charge of the post, four "Scotchmen," and "the Rev. Mr. Mc-Donald, a missionary of the Established Church,"[37] arrived with the eagerly-awaited trade goods. The next day came the Tanana River Indians, travelling in a flotilla of 25 single canoes. Dall recorded their spectacular arrival with admiration:

The occupants kept perfect time with their paddles, advancing in three platoons, and passed over the water as swiftly and beautifully as a flock of ducks.

Sakhniti [Senatee] the chief of the Kucha Kutchin, or Fort Yukon Indians, stood on the bank dressed in his gayest costume, with a richly embroidered blue blanket wrapped about him. He hailed the foremost canoes as soon as they were out of the current. After a harangue of a few minutes a fusillade was commenced by the Indians on shore, and returned by those in the canoes, after which they landed. The Tenan

[36] *Ibid.*, pp. 103-105.

[37] *Ibid.*, p. 103. McDonald was Rev. Robert McDonald, already referred to in Chapter Three. Dall's "Established Church" was of course the Anglican Church.

Kutchin (people of the mountains), or Indians of the Tananah, are known to the Hudson Bay men as Gens des Buttes. They are without doubt the tribe of all others which has had the least to do with the whites. . . . Of their mode of life nothing is known, except that they obtain their subsistence principally by hunting the deer. . . . The most striking peculiarity about them was their method of dressing their hair. Allowed to grow to its full length, and parted in the middle, each lock was smeared with a mixture of grease and red ochre. These then presented the appearance of compressed cyclinders of red mud, about the size of the finger. This enormous load, weighing in some of the adults at least fifteen pounds, is gathered in behind the head by a fillet of dentalium shells. A much smaller bunch hangs on each side of the face. The whole is then powdered with swan's-down, cut up finely, so that it adheres to the hair, presenting a most remarkable and singular appearance. The dressing of grease and ochre remains through life, more being added as the hair grows.

The fat is soon rancid, and a position to leeward of these gentry is highly undesirable.[38]

Other tribes present for the trading Dall identified as "the *Natche Kutchin*, or Gens de Large, from north of the Porcupine River; the *Vunta Kutchin*, or Rat Indians, from farther up the Porcupine; the *Han Kutchin* (Wood people), or Gens de Bois, from the Yukon, above Fort Yukon; and finally, the *Tutchone Kutchin* (crow people), or Gens de Foux, from still farther up the Yukon."[39]

On June 29, to Dall's great pleasure, Ketchum and Lebarge arrived from Fort Selkirk, carrying as a memento "a piece of one of the blackened timbers which remained."[40] They reported that the site of the former post "was a fine one, well timbered, abundantly supplied with moose and game, and inhabited by friendly Indians." Their sled journey to Fort Yukon had been a difficult one, due largely to the soft snow. It had lasted nearly two months, or twice their estimated time, and they reached their destination through rotten ice and water just before the breakup of the river. The rest of the trip had been comparatively easy — 29 days by boat from Fort Yukon to Fort Selkirk, camping every night, and four days back, without camping. The two parties of Overland Telegraph men decided that they would return to Nulato together, but that, at Dall's request, they would stay at Fort Yukon until the trading was completed.

[38] *Ibid.*, pp. 107-108.

[39] *Ibid.*, p. 109.

[40] *Ibid.*, p. 110, as are the other quotations in this paragraph referring to Fort Selkirk.

Dall and Whymper occupied their spare time at the fort in collecting and sketching. The heat continued unabated. At the end of June Dall noted that "at noon, out of the direct rays of the sun, one of Greene's standard thermometers stood at 112° Fahrenheit. The men informed me that on several occasions spirit thermometers had burst with the heat. In the depth of winter the spirit falls sometimes as low as sixty-eight and sixty-nine below zero, making a range for the year of one hundred and eighty degrees Fahrenheit! Nevertheless, potatoes, turnips, lettuce, and other hardy garden vegetables mature during the short, hot summer, and barley was said to have succeeded once, but only reached a few inches in height."[41]

By the end of the first week in July most of the Indians had departed, and the year's fur returns were being prepared for shipment to Lapierre House and winter forwarding to Peel's River Post. The visitors were allowed to view the results. "It was a sight seldom witnessed by other than traders," Dall wrote, "the large loft over the storehouse was literally overflowing with valuable furs. Among other trophies of the chase were forty-five silver foxes. The commander confessed to five thousand sable [marten] purchased the previous year. The men in the fort said that the amount was nearer eight thousand, with half as many beaver, and five hundred foxes of all kinds. Few otter, and very few mink are obtained here, but black bearskins, dressed mooseskins, and black and silver foxes are especially abundant. The value of the furs annually obtained at this post cannot be estimated at less than fifty thousand dollars."[42]

On July 8, 1867, the four men left on their downstream journey to Nulato, after a flurry of good-byes and the customary fusillade.

In the broad channel, out of reach of the mosquitoes, we drifted on without impediment at the rate of four or five miles an hour. Points appeared, were passed, and faded out of view, almost without perceiving it; while between them, going up, we had passed many hours of paddling in the hot sun. . . . We tied our canoes together and floated down, sometimes sleeping, sometimes in a revery which recalled the lotus-eaters of the Nile. We did not camp anywhere. We boiled the chynik [tea-kettle] and cooked our meals ashore, and, pushing out into the broad stream, ate them while calmly drifting with the current. Sometimes the mosquitoes would try to follow us, and we could see them vainly endeavoring to make headway against the fresh breeze

[41] *Ibid.*, p. 105.
[42] *Ibid.*, p. 115.

usually to be found in midstream. They were always unsuccessful, and we discarded our nets and laughed at the discomfited insects. About three o'clock in the afternoon of the 9th we re-entered the Ramparts, and here, in the swiftest current, our progress was more rapid.

Large fires were burning in the forests, and on the side of the hills. They had been kindled by some neglected campfire, and spread rapidly over the mossy sod and leaves dried by the midsummer sun. The smoke hung over all the country, obscuring everything with a lurid haze.[43]

On the afternoon of July 10 they passed the rapids, scarcely recognizing the place because of the low water. On the 12th they reached Nulato, where orders awaited them to continue on to St. Michael's, taking all moveable property belonging to the Overland Telegraph Company with them. The post was rife with rumours, mostly relating to the alleged sale of the country, but nothing was certain. "Near midnight, July 15th, we started down the river," wrote Dall, "full of anxiety, not knowing what changes lay ahead."[44] The weather suited their gloomy mood: "much of it hot, cloudy, and disagreeable, with occasional rain, forming a marked contrast to that which we had experienced farther inland."

They reached St. Michael's on July 25, and found that all the members of the exploring and construction parties in the Yukon were already assembled there. "The news was soon told. The Atlantic cable was a triumphant success.... Our costly and doubtful enterprise was abandoned.... The ill-fed and hard-worked constructors hailed their deliverance with joy, but the weather-beaten explorers with their carefully matured plans for more extended exploration during the coming year, felt a regret and disappointment which could hardly be overestimated, as with a few words these prospects were destroyed."[45]

During the interminable wait for the arrival of a steamer to take the men home, the inevitable happened.

Some of our men [wrote Whymper] found a keg of specimens preserved in alcohol, belonging to one of our Smithsonian collectors. Having had a long abstinence from exhilarating drinks, the temptation was too much for them, and they proceeded to broach the contents. After they had imbibed to their hearts' content, and become "visibly affected thereby," they thought it a pity to waste the remaining contents of the

---

[43] *Ibid.*, p. 116.

[44] *Ibid.*, p. 118, as is the other direct quotation in this paragraph.

[45] *Ibid.*, pp. 119-120.

barrel, and feeling hungry, went on to eat the lizards, snakes, and fish which had been put up for a rather different purpose! Science was avenged in the result, nor do I think they will ever repeat the experiment.[46]

It was a typical northern ending to a grandiose construction scheme.

VI

FORTUNATELY FOR HIS PEACE OF MIND, DALL THE DEDICATED AND serious-minded young scientist was not a witness to the desecration of the hard-won natural history material. He had decided that he would not leave the country with the others, and he had already moved into separate quarters.

A pretty thorough examination had been made [he explained] of the geology and natural history of the Yukon above and at Nulato, and on the shores of Norton Sound. The Lower Yukon and the delta had yet to be examined. I felt unwilling that the plans of Mr. Kennicott, so far carried out successfully, should be left uncompleted. I therefore proposed to carry them out alone, and at my own expense.[47]

Arrangements were made with Stepanoff, on Dall's assurance that he would not "interfere" with the fur trade, to provide accommodation at the Company's posts. The telegraph company had no provisions to spare, but they sold Dall some trade goods at cost, and paid him a portion of the back salary owing to him. Individual members of the telegraph parties gave him "many articles useful in the country." The die was cast; yet on August 28, when the time came for his companions to leave St. Michael's, Dall watched the departure of their ship with very mixed feelings. "As I saw her white sails disappear in the distance," he wrote, "I realized more thoroughly the loneliness of my position, and that I was the only person in the whole of that portion of the territory who spoke English. If I needed companions, I must seek them among alien convicts or Indians, in a foreign tongue."[48]

Dall passed a miserable winter at Nulato, plagued by illness and

[46] Whymper, *Travels in America*, p. 272.
[47] Dall, *Alaska*, p. 122.
[48] *Ibid.*, p. 123.

by unseasonably mild, wet weather that played havoc with the salmon catch, and forced the Russians in the post to exist largely on bread and tea. On February 3, 1868 however, the dull routine was suddenly broken, when dog teams were seen approaching in the distance. "A rumour spread that Stepanoff was coming," Dall wrote, "and it was amusing to watch the unaccustomed energy with which the Russians hastened to clean out the yard, removing the accumulated dirt of months, and sweeping the path clean from the gateway down to the ice."[49] These frantic preparations were wasted: the visitor, it turned out, was not the St. Michael's commander, but a courier. The dispatches he carried, however, were electrifying. They reported the sale of Alaska to the United States, and ordered the Russians to evacuate Nulato.

This was good news [Dall commented] and I lost no time in hoisting the stars and stripes on our flagstaff. The news was soon made public, and all received it with joy. Old men, who had been many years in the country, detained by trifling debts to the Company, which they had no means of paying, were extravagant in the expression of their delight in the hope, so long deferred, of seeing Russia once more. The native women, who could not accompany their husbands if the latter chose to leave the country, were in tears at the prospect of parting; while others, whose husbands had treated them with brutality, did not conceal their pleasure at the hope of getting rid of them.[50]

Dall took advantage of the presence of the courier and his drivers by returning with them to St. Michael's for additional supplies. "I obtained two bags of flour, some powder, and tea from Stepanoff. At home it would sound queerly to talk of going three hundred and fifty miles for a bag of flour, but here it was well worth the trouble."[51] He also brought back a small pane of glass for the window in his quarters. "After getting light all winter only through parchment, it was a great relief to be able to peep out occasionally, and to admit a few rays of pure sunlight."[52]

The breakup of 1868 was much more spectacular than the disappointing performance of the year before; for a time the buildings of the fort were threatened by the water backed up by ice jams.

[49] *Ibid.*, p. 181.
[50] *Ibid.*, pp. 181-182.
[51] *Ibid.*, p. 184.
[52] *Ibid.*, p. 192.

Dall started downstream on June 2, just ahead of the Russians, travelling with two Indians — one of them the faithful Kurilla — in a well-laden bidarra that had been hauled over the portage by dog sled during the winter. He was retracing his route of the previous season, but earlier in the year, and under less pressure to reach his destination. In particular, his passion for collecting received free rein. His course lay through one of the world's great wild fowl nesting areas, and Dall's excitement grew as he saw mile after mile of sloughs and river bars alive with birds.

The report of a gun [he wrote] will often raise such immense flocks of geese as literally to darken the air; sometimes a flock will be four or five miles long, and two or three rods wide, flying as close together as they can with safety. Swans whitened the surface of several lagoons, and from them down to the tiniest snipe, not weighing more than an ounce, every kind of wild fowl abounded in profusion. Their eggs were scattered over the sand-bars, and a hatful could be obtained on any beach. . . .

The [collecting] had been well commenced at Nulato but partially suspended since we left, as we had procured but few birds new to the collection, since leaving that point. Now I had my hands full, and leaving the task of navigation to Kurilla, I was constantly occupied skinning the birds which we obtained at every turn. I passed many a night without getting an hour's sleep, in order that rare birds might be preserved; and the work of preparing birdskins is anything but a pleasant one. The results to be obtained for natural history were so great, that it was impossible to grudge a moment of time so spent, or to neglect any opportunity of adding to the note-book or the collection.[53]

The greatest prize from this scientific orgy was two specimens of the rare Emperor goose, shot by Kurilla on June 18.

On June 23 Dall and his Indians reached the Eskimo settlement of Pastolik on the Yukon delta, at a time when it was temporarily deserted. On the beach near the village Dall picked up "a large portion of the skull of the extinct elephant (*Elphas Primigenius*). . . . The natives have no tradition of any other large animal than the reindeer or moose, and regard the elephant and musk-ox bones as the remains of dead 'devils.' The tusks are not so well preserved as those found in Siberia, which are usually buried in the earth."[54] The ancient bones and teeth of extinct mammals were in fact a popular

[53] *Ibid.*, p. 229.
[54] *Ibid.*, p. 238.

trade item on many parts of the Yukon River: Robert Campbell, while still at Fort Selkirk, sent an elephant's leg-bone which was found near his post to the British Museum.[55]

Dall's journey to the river-mouth was nearing its end — "the trees were now reduced to low willows, and the level character of the country to the north and west showed that we had passed all the mountains. A few low hills still fringed the right bank, but the general level of the country was only a few feet above the sea."[56] On June 27 he ventured into Norton Sound, and made the crossing to St. Michael's. To Dall's surprise and delight, Michael Lebarge was there; he was now working for one of the American trading companies that were moving into Alaska as the Russians left. Yet, when he began to talk with his old friend,[57] Dall encountered an unexpected difficulty. "Speaking English, after a year of nothing but Russian dialects, was anything but easy, and for several days I was

[55] Dawson, in a paper read to the Geological Society of London on November 8, 1893, quoted Campbell as saying that he "saw the bones, heads, and horns of buffaloes (Musk-Oxen); but this animal had become extinct before our visit, as had also some species of elephant, whose remains were found in various swamps." Concerning the bone that Campbell presented to the museum, Dawson noted that "The skeleton of which it formed part was said to be complete when found; but most of the bones were lost by the Indians who extracted them for Campbell." Dawson, "Notes on the Occurrence of Mammoth-remains in the Yukon District of Canada, and in Alaska," *The Quarterly Journal of the Geological Society of London*, Vol. L, (February 1894), p. 2. The skeleton was located close to Fort Selkirk, but the attack by the Chilkats made further investigation of the site out of the question. It is interesting to note that about this same time remains of the identical species, *Elphas Primigenius*, were found at "Burlington Heights, near Hamilton, Ontario."

[56] Dall, *Alaska*, p. 232.

[57] Lebarge was an obvious favourite of Dall's; he was the only one of the Overland Telegraph Company's men whom Dall in his book consistently referred to on a first name basis. Writing in the April 1898, issue of the *National Geographical Magazine*, under the title "A Yukon Pioneer," Dall gave more biographical details of his friend. Lebarge was born in Chateaugay, Quebec, in 1837, and in 1865 left for California by steamer "by the Nicaraguan Route." Kennicott, on his way to take up his duties with the Overland Telegraph Company, was a fellow passenger, and "impressed by the excellent qualities displayed by Lebarge in trying circumstances" — which included a shipwreck on Lake Nicaragua — he persuaded the young French Canadian to join the Company's "Corps of northern explorers." After the chance encounter with Dall at St. Michael's, Lebarge remained in the Alaskan fur trade until 1875, until he retired on a small pension to his native village. "Frank Ketchum lies under the green turf of an Unalaska Hillside," Dall concluded eloquently, "may his faithful companion, and our good friend survive for many happy years."

obliged to resort to Russian when fluency was required."[58] Nonetheless, it was a warm and happy reunion; each had a great deal to tell the other, and Dall after his long isolation had much he wanted to learn of events in the outside world.

On August 9, 1868, Dall left Alaska on a schooner bound for San Francisco by way of the Aleutians. He had witnessed the end of the Russian era on the lower Yukon, an interlude that had lasted for thirty years. While he waited for his ship he had watched the American traders bring casks of rum ashore, and he had misgivings as to what lay ahead. For all its harshness, he had come to love this bleak, lonely, and almost timeless land.[59]

[58] Dall, *Alaska*, p. 240.

[59] Dall returned to Alaska from 1871 to 1874, in charge of a scientific investigation of the Aleutian Islands for the United States Coast and Geodetic Survey. On the completion of this survey, he transferred to the Geological Survey in Washington, D.C., as a palaeontologist: he also came to be regarded as one of the leading American authorities on Alaska. He retired in 1923, and died in 1927, the strongly opinionated outlook of his youth much mellowed by the passage of time.

CHAPTER FIVE

Soldiers, Sailors, Miners
and Missionaries

Map Numbers 1, 3 and 4, following page 58

I

THE PURCHASE OF ALASKA WAS GREETED WITH LESS THAN ENTHU-
siasm in the United States. The negotiations had been carried on in
secret, and even the final agreement, for a sale price of $7,000,000
in gold and $200,000 for title clear of all encumbrances, was signed
at four o'clock in the morning at a hasty ceremony in the White
House on March 30, 1867. The American press and public awoke
suddenly to the realization that, willy-nilly, they were now the land-
lords of an almost unknown country equal in area to that of all the
states east of the Mississippi River. A storm broke over the head of
the architect of the transaction, William H. Seward, the Secretary
of State. The new acquisition was reviled as "Seward's Folly" or
"Seward's Icebox," and described as "a dreary waste of glaciers,
icebergs, white bears, and walruses." The sale was "a dark deed
done in the night."[1] So prolonged and vociferous was the opposition,
even after the ratification of the agreement by the Senate, that the
House of Representatives balked at passing the appropriation for
the sale, and when the formal takeover ceremonies took place at
Sitka on October 18, 1867, the $7,200,000 had not yet been paid.
The money was not voted until the following summer, and then only
after some frantic lobbying and the placing of some judicious bribes.

Alaska became the ward of a somewhat reluctant Department of
War, and remained under the control of the army for the next ten

---

[1] The newspaper comments on the Alaska purchase are quoted by James, *The
First Scientific Exploration*, pp. 24-25.

years: civil government, in the opinion of the policy-makers in Washington, was not possible in an area so remote and so sparsely populated. Instead, two companies of soldiers, about 500 men, were sent north for garrison duty, and were stationed at Sitka, the capital, and Wrangell. A collector of customs at Sitka was the only other government official in the territory: a town council elected in the capital resigned in frustration when it became apparent that, without civil government or courts of law, there was no basis for the enforcement of its ordinances and regulations.

A mercantile partnership from San Francisco, Hutchinson Kohl & Company, was successful, despite some rugged competition, in purchasing for $350,000 the physical assets and goodwill of the Russian American Company. The new firm, operating as the Alaska Commercial Company, lost little time in re-opening the trading posts, and in 1869, through its considerable influence in Washington, was able to persuade the military authorities to undertake a survey of the lower Yukon. Captain Charles W. Raymond, United States Corps of Engineers, was the officer assigned to this task, and at Fort Yukon his astronomical observations effectively demolished the old tongue-in-cheek claim that the post was located on British soil.

"On the 9th of August at 12n.," Raymond wrote in his report, "I notified the representatives of the Hudson's Bay Company that the station is in the territory of the United States; that the introduction of trading goods, or any trade by foreigners with the natives is illegal, and must cease; and that the Hudson's Bay Company must vacate the buildings as soon as possible. I then took possession of the buildings, and raised the flag of the United States over the Fort."[2] The Hudson's Bay Company moved their people back up the Porcupine to Rampart House, the alternate site selected by Murray many years before, and the Alaska Commercial Company occupied the well-kept buildings of Fort Yukon.

This unfortunately was one of the few positive government actions in the first ten years of American control of Alaska. A boom had followed the takeover, but it was of short duration, and as economic conditions worsened, lawlessness increased. The importation of liquor into the territory was supposed to be prohibited, but whiskey was sold openly: among the best customers for it were the soldiers who were supposed to be the upholders of law and order. Only the Tlingit

[2] Quoted by Dawson, *Report on an Exploration*, p. 139.

Indians were ever arrested for drunkenness, and it was not surprising that they could evoke little enthusiasm for American justice "when they found themselves in the guardhouse, but never saw the officers in when in like conditions."[3]

In this atmosphere of permissiveness for the whites and creoles, and repression for the Indians, some unknown opportunist — reputedly either an army deserter or an escaped convict from British Columbia — taught the Tlingits the technique of distilling liquor from molasses and sugar. None of the tribes adopted this art more eagerly than did the Hootchinoo of Admiralty Island. Eventually the name "hooch," applied to the product of all the stills, entered the language, immortalizing in a modest way the misdirected enthusiasm of these people.[4]

The size of the army garrisons in Alaska had been steadily declining, due to a lack of replacements, and in 1877 the last of the troops were withdrawn. Administrative responsibility for the territory was transferred to the Revenue Cutter Service of the Treasury Department, but for the two years following this change the country was ignored. The Tlingits, swilling without restraint their foul brews of hooch, became more restless and unruly: in Sitka in particular the residents, recalling their past, lived increasingly in fear of another massacre. Repeated appeals to the American government for protection brought no response.

The situation came to a head in February 1879, when two ugly episodes involving the drowning of some Indians and the murder of a white man almost blew the lid off the powder keg. A meeting of

[3] Morgan B. Sherwood, "Ardent Spirits: Hooch and the Osprey Affair at Sitka," *Journal of the West*. Vol. IV, No. 3, (July 1954), p. 312.

[4] The basic ingredient for making hooch was molasses: to each gallon of it could be added, according to Sherwood, "some flour, sugar, yeast or hops, potatoes, elder and other berries, apples, perhaps a few beans, a little rice, and some alcohol, if it happens to be handy.... For additional tang, ginger, and mustard may be added." (*Ibid.*, p. 320). This was made into a thin batter, and a gallon of lukewarm water stirred into each gallon of the mixture, which was then set aside in a warm place to ferment, after which it was distilled. One gallon of the mixture made about three-quarters of a gallon of hoochinoo.

The Yukon Liquor Control Board now markets a liquor under the name of "Yukon Hooch," which is popular as a distinctive gift or souvenir. It is not made by this technique, but is in fact a rum-based product. Fortunately, the frightful taste of the original concoction is lacking: a committee formed to sample the Tlingits' hooch decided that "there might be a worse beverage, but they should not like to taste it." (*Ibid.*, p. 321).

the alarmed citizens of Sitka voted in favour of appealing as a last resort to the British authorities in Victoria for protection, and a signed petition to this effect was sent to the Esquimalt naval station, and eventually was turned over to Captain H. Holmes A'Court, in command of H.M.S. *Osprey.* A'Court, after consulting the American consul and receiving non-committal advice, sailed for Sitka more or less on his own initiative. Once there, he promised that he would remain until an American gunboat arrived to relieve him.

This action finally forced the reluctant authorities in Washington to make a move. Captain L. A. Beardslee, in the U.S.S. *Jamestown,* was sent to Sitka, and instructed to remain in Alaskan territorial waters. The *Osprey* returned to her home port, and her captain received the grudging thanks of the American government. Whether there actually was danger of an Indian attack was heatedly debated after the *Osprey*'s departure, but it is certain that without some action Sitka would have been at the mercy of the Indians if they had got out of hand. The whole bizarre episode was a wry commentary on the measure of neglect by the United States of her new possession.

II

SOME OF THOSE IN SITKA WHO SIGNED THE PETITION TO THE BRITISH authorities were miners — a breed of lonely, restless men new to the Gulf of Alaska and the Alexander Archipelago. They had been a long time coming, but their arrival was almost inevitable. The discovery of gold in California in 1848 had brought them to the west coast, following a long trail that led through the mining camps of Arizona, Colorado, Nevada, and Idaho. For most of them there was no reward, except perhaps a drunken spree, and the continuation of the search. The Pacific halted their further travel westward; they began instead to move slowly north by west, parallel to the coast. Gold was discovered on the Fraser River in 1858, and late in 1859 at Quesnel Lake in the Cariboo. Victoria, like San Francisco, became a boom town, and Barkerville, rising overnight, enjoyed its brief and riotous hour of glory.

Still the searchers pushed on. The vanguard of them came in time through Sitka and Wrangell to the Stikine, and followed that river inland into Robert Campbell's unhappy, hungry country. Late in

1871 two of these miners met casually on the Liard River, and spent the winter together near the site of abandoned Fort Halkett. One of them, Henry Thibert, was a French-Canadian who in 1860 had left a dull life on a Red River farm to go hunting and prospecting in the west. His chance companion was a Scotsman named McCullough. Their first winter was, as usual in that area, a struggle to survive: there was nothing to indicate that the end of their search for wealth was little more than a year away.

Their prospecting began auspiciously when, with the coming of spring, they found gold in a river bar on the Liard River, near their camp. They worked this discovery for part of the season, and then continued on to Dease Lake where, remembering the winter they had just been through, they intended to obtain a supply of fish to tide them over the one ahead. Here they were told by Indians that white men were mining on the Stikine quite close at hand. The two men quickly decided against returning to the Liard; instead they crossed over to the river and wintered there, at a small mining camp called Buck's Bar. Their prospecting was without reward in this location, so after breakup the following year, 1873, they returned to Dease Lake on the way back to their original find near Fort Halkett.

They never reached their goal. In true prospector fashion, they panned all likely-looking ground that they encountered, and on a creek at the north end of the lake — later known as Thibert Creek — they found gold in abundance. This changed their plans. They worked their ground with conspicuous success for the remainder of the summer, soon being joined by thirteen of the miners from the Stikine. Paydirt was encountered on another tributary, Dease Creek, before the year ended.

The news quickly spread, and a rush to the scene of these new finds began. By 1874 there were 1500 men in the area, and those who were not successful on Dease Lake spread out over the surrounding countryside. Rich placer deposits were discovered on McDame Creek, a tributary of the Dease River. Much of the Liard River was prospected and worked, including the bar on which was located Thibert's and McCullough's original find. A small settlement, Laketon, was established on Dease Lake, and beef and cattle were driven overland from the Cariboo to feed the miners. Total production for the year from all the creeks and bars was probably in excess of $1,000,000.

In 1875 the population dropped to a little over 1,000 persons, and production to an estimated $830,000. These were the Cassiar district's[5] two best years: in 1876 the yield dropped again, to half that of the year before, and the search for gold became even more widespread, extending in time to headwaters of the Liard and to Frances Lake. Henry Thibert, who was visited by Dawson at Dease Lake in 1887, where he was still mining, told the geologist of a prospecting trip to the west arm of Frances Lake, including a journey up the Yusezyu River to McPherson Lake. Later, in Vancouver, another miner told Dawson that he too had been on Frances Lake during this period, and that he had worked the mouth of the Finlayson River for a short time, where the gravel had yielded pay at the rate of $8 to $9 a day.

There was a fresh influx of miners into the Cassiar in 1876, as optimistic reports of the district — unfortunately without foundation — continued to circulate outside. Most of the newcomers were too late. A few new discoveries were made, but they were quickly worked out, and though the main creeks — Thibert, Dease and McDame — continued to yield moderately for many years, there was not enough profitable ground available to support all who sought it. Those for whom there was no livelihood simply moved on, fanning out over the islands of the Alexander Archipelago and the adjacent mainland, using Sitka as a base. Rumours of finds kept that little settlement in a turmoil of anticipation during 1877, 1878, and 1879, and for the first time since the purchase, the town's population increased rather than declined.

III

AS CASSIAR WANED, STORIES BEGAN TO REACH THE MINERS OF wealth to be found beyond the barrier of the coastal mountains, in the creeks in the Yukon basin. Whymper, in his travel book on Alaska published in 1869, made the first reference in print to this possibility, when he noted cautiously that "minute specks of gold have been found by some of the Hudson's Bay Company's men in the Yukon, but not in quantities to warrant a rush to the area."[6] Earlier, a young clerk at the Fort Yukon post, in a letter sent to his

[5] Cassiar is probably a corruption of "Kaska," the name given to the two small bands of Indians indigenous to McDame Creek and the mouth of the Dease.

[6] Whymper, *Travels in America*, p. 258.

parents in Toronto in 1864, also made casual reference to the same subject:

I had some thoughts of digging the gold here, but am not sure about it. I do not think it is in paying quantities at the Fort, but if I could only get time to make an expedition up the Yukon, I expect we should find it in abundance, but I am always on the voyage or busy at the Fort during the summer, and in the winter nothing can be done in the way of gold hunting. I think that next fall, after arriving from my trip down the Yukon, I shall be able to go up the river. There is a small river not far from here that the minister, the Rev. McDonald, saw so much gold on a year or two ago that he could have gathered it with a spoon. I have often wished to go, but can never find the time. Should I find gold in paying quantities I may turn gold-digger, but this is merely a last resort when I can do no better.[7]

To a man named Arthur Harper, poring over the crude existing maps of the North-West Territories, such an off-hand attitude would have been akin to heresy, for to him the pursuit of gold and mineral wealth was the goad that was to drive him all his life. He was born in Ireland, and emigrated to the United States as a young man, where he drifted west to the diggings in California and British Columbia: here, the riches that he pursued had to date eluded him. Now he turned his attention north. Studying his maps, he noted that the Liard and the Peace, important branches of the Mackenzie, had their sources in the proven auriferous areas of British Columbia, and that the upper tributaries of the Yukon River had their sources in the same area. He soon convinced himself that if gold were plentiful on the headwaters of the Mackenzie, it should be equally plentiful on the Yukon. He persuaded four other miners of his acquaintance to test this theory with him, by going into the area and mining it for themselves. In September 1872, they completed their preparations for a protracted journey into an almost unknown wilderness.

Starting their odyssey in the Peace River country, they crossed during the winter the height of land that separated them from the Liard basin, and the following spring, after the breakup, came by way of the Sikanni Chief and the Fort Nelson River, to the confluence now known as Nelson Forks. Here they encountered by chance another party of miners, led by Leroy Napoleon McQuesten, a footloose New Englander who as a boy had made his way to the

---

[7] Quoted, but not identified, in William Ogilvie, *Early Days in the Yukon, and the Story of Its Gold Finds*, (Ottawa, Thorburn & Abbott, 1913), p. 86.

west, and then north to British Columbia and the Territories, working as a prospector, trader, and, briefly, as a voyageur for the Hudson's Bay Company. In the Hay River area, McQuesten and his two partners, one of them an ex-circus acrobat named Albert H. Mayo, "had heard a great deal about the Yukon River from men that were in the H.B. Company employ, and we concluded we would go and see for ourselves what the country was like."[8] They had started up the Liard in July 1872, but had made very slow progress, and had decided to winter at Nelson Forks, where game was plentiful. They had not yet resumed their journey when Harper and his men arrived, and the two leaders agreed to join forces. McQuesten abandoned his struggle to ascend the Liard: instead they would all return to its mouth and drift downstream on the Mackenzie, as soon as the ice went out in the spring of 1873. Their entry to the Yukon would be by way of the Hudson's Bay Company's portage to the Porcupine.

They did not travel all the way together, as McQuesten and Mayo had some business to attend to at Great Slave Lake; when they reached Fort Simpson, therefore, Harper started on ahead. He was busy with his gold pan all along the way, and later, in conversation with William Ogilvie, a government surveyor, he tersely summed up his results: "On the Peace everywhere colours were found more or less, on the Liard colours, on the Mackenzie nothing, on the Peel fair prospects, on the Porcupine some colours, and on the Yukon colours everywhere."[9] Almost as soon as he arrived at Fort Yukon, one of the Indians showed him an interesting piece of native copper, and parted with the information, after some persuasion, that it came from the vicinity of White River. It was by now well into August, but Harper was on his way immediately, with two men, to try and locate the source of the ore. They did not find any copper, but they missed the possibility of a more valuable find on their way to the White, when some natives discouraged them from prospecting a stream which appealed to them. It was later to be known as the Fortymile River, and the first discovery of coarse gold in the Yukon was to be made not far from its mouth.

[8] Leroy N. McQuesten, *Recollections of Leroy N. McQuesten, Life in the Yukon 1871-1885*, (privately printed, June 1952), p. 1. This pamphlet, according to a notation on the title page, was "copied from the original in possession of the Yukon Order of Pioneers."

[9] Ogilvie, *Early Days*, p. 95.

Harper had already left Fort Yukon on his wild-goose chase when McQuesten and Mayo arrived, with 1400 pounds of supplies and four dogs. The Alaska Commercial Company's agent at the post, Moses Mercier, a French Canadian from Montreal, received them most hospitably. "He let us have fifty pounds of flour," McQuesten wrote gratefully, "It was all that he could spare. That was quite a treat to us, as that was the first we had had for two years."[10] McQuesten and Mayo, and the men who had not gone to the White River with Harper, pushed on upstream to establish winter quarters. They killed "three moose and one large bear," as well as netting "the largest and fattest whitefish that we had seen in the Northwest. They would fry themselves; one pint of oil was very common to get out of one fish. They weighed from eight to twenty pounds each." This was not to be a repetition of Robert Campbell's hungry winter at the Dease Lake post!

In spite of the abundance of food at this location, trading was poor, and late in the winter they hauled their remaining supplies back to Fort Yukon, completing this chore on April 2. McQuesten had business with the Hudson's Bay Company, and promptly set out with one man for "La Pear House [sic]," though the most difficult time of the year for overland travel was fast approaching. "It was about four hundred miles," he reported off-handedly, "the snow was very deep and we made slow progress going there. We got short of provisions and we had to stop and hunt rabbits for our supper, but we made the trip alright."[11] They arrived back at Fort Yukon on May 10, the day that the ice went out at the post, and following its retreat they went down to the Alaska Commercial Company's station at the mouth of the Tanana. Here Harper and his party soon turned up: they had wintered on the White River, where they had killed plenty of moose and lived like kings, even if their prospecting had been unsuccessful.

Supplies at both Fort Yukon and the Tanana were very low, and the whole party decided that they would accompany Mercier on his spring trip to St. Michael's, where he would deliver his fur returns, and pick up fresh goods and provisions. They arrived at the Redoubt on June 25, where McQuesten, Mayo, and two others signed as agents for the Company, and Harper and another three men received

---

[10] McQuesten, *Recollections*, p. 3, as are the other quotations in this paragraph.
[11] *Ibid.*, p. 3.

supplies. On July 7 they started their return journey on the Company's little steamer, the *Yukon*, the first vessel to operate on the Yukon River.

We had five boats in tow [McQuesten wrote]. We made about three miles an hour up stream. When we would get out of wood we would tie up to some drift-pile and pile up the boat with wood. She would take about four cords at a time, it took us about three hours to fill her up. That would last about ten hours. We were fourteen days getting back to Station [Tanana]. . . . We only had one boat in tow when we left [the] Station but the current was getting very strong and it was about all the steamer could do to make any headway. We arrived at Fort Yukon on the 7th of August. We remained there a few days and it was finally arranged that I should go up the Yukon and locate at some suitable place. . . . As it was the first time the Steamer had been on that part of the River, we had considerable trouble keeping the channel, which necessarily delayed us some. We had only about three ton of merchandise aboard and a Whale boat in tow. We selected a location near the Trundeck [*sic*] about 350 miles from Fort Yukon.
We arrived there on the 20th of August, 1874. The steamer discharged and returned the next day leaving F. Barnfield and myself to build our winter quarters. I employed some Indians to carry logs and some went out to hunt. The hunters returned in a few days with plenty of meat before it froze up. We had our house and the store completed and the Indians brought in plenty of dried meat to last us all winter. I sold all the goods we had for furs during the winter.[12]

This new post, which its founders named Fort Reliance, was only six miles downstream from the mouth of the Klondike — McQuesten's "Trundeck" — and its untapped treasures. The search for gold was to range far and wide throughout this area. Ironically, it was to reach its climax 22 years later almost at the spot where it began.

IV

PARALLELING THE GROWTH OF TRADING FACILITIES IN THE YUKON was the increasing influence of the missionaries. McDonald, still at Fort Yukon when the Hudson's Bay Company was expelled, moved with the Company's men to Rampart House, and continued to make periodic journeys down the Porcupine. In 1873, Bompas accompanied him on one of these trips, crossing from Fort McPherson by way of the Rat River portage to join him. From Fort

---

[12] *Ibid.*, pp. 4-5.

Yukon, Bompas travelled for a considerable distance both upstream and downstream on the Yukon, and was impressed with what he saw. "It is a splendid river," he wrote in a letter to his brother in England, "with high wooded hills on each bank, occasionally broken into bold and craggy rocks. The margin of the river is rather flowery with lupins, vetches, bluebells, and other wildflowers; and I was surprised to see a few ferns in the cleft of the rock, so close to the Arctic circle. Gold has not yet been found in the Yukon, but I brought down with me some good specimens of iron ore, of which there seems to be a great quantity close to the river's mouth. This may some day be utilized."[13]

This visit was interrupted by a summons to return to England to be consecrated Bishop of Athabaska, one of four new dioceses[14] created in the Canadian west as the result of a decision to partition the huge and now unmanageable episcopate of Rupert's Land, which covered the whole of Canada west of the Great Lakes. Bompas left unwillingly, hoping to persuade the ecclesiastical authorities that the selection was an error: when he was unable to have the appointment changed he found consolation in the fact that Athabaska was at least the most remote of the new charges. In spite of the fact that it was formed in an effort to make the administration of the Anglican Church in the northwest less burdensome, it still covered an immense territory, embracing "an area about twenty times that of England and Wales, but the population . . . is estimated at only 10,000, consisting of Chipewyan and Tukuth [sic] Indians, and Esquimaux. The missionaries have constantly, therefore, to be travelling about in order to meet the little wandering bands of hunters and fishermen, and that in a climate where the temperature in winter ranges as low as 50 degrees below zero. . . . Three missionaries and four lay-assistants are engaged in this field of labour at present, and as the Bishop of Rupert's Land could not visit them

---

[13] Cody, *An Apostle of the North*, p. 141.

[14] A diocese in the Anglican Church is a local administrative unit presided over by a bishop, who controls personnel and finances within the diocese. A senior clergyman is usually appointed to act as his assistant, with the title of archdeacon. A missionary diocese is usually not financially self-supporting. In the Roman Catholic Church a diocese in the mission field is an apostolic vicarate, headed by an apostolic vicar, the equivalent in power and duties to a bishop, except that he does not have a cathedral. His principal assistant is a coadjutor, who has some apostolic authority.

and their converts without a two year's absence from his own diocese, the appointment of a Bishop is most desirable."[15]

Before returning to Canada in May 1874, Bompas married his cousin Miss Charlotte Selina Cox, the daughter of a successful physician, and a cultured, gracious, and well-travelled woman, who had lived for several years in Italy. She had once dismissed missionary meetings, to which she was frequently exposed in her youth, as "the dullest affairs," and the clergy who addressed them as "the most dismal old slow coaches it was anyone's unhappy fate to attend to."[16] This sentiment she obviously later abandoned, for after she met Bompas she freely exchanged her comfortable and refined existence for life in a rude cabin in the wilds of the northwest. She became a true helpmate and strong support throughout the remainder of her husband's strenuous ministry, even though her health and his travels did not permit that she be always at his side.

Their first home together was at Fort Simpson, where the bishop promptly established a diocesan school, at first doing most of the teaching himself. The work in the diocese he divided into four parts: Athabasca Mission; Great Slave Lake Mission; Mackenzie River Mission; and the Tukudh Mission, the latter consisting of the area along the Rat River portage and the Porcupine River. Bompas moved McDonald to Fort McPherson, from which location he supervised the work of this mission, and also, by watching the only route into the country, was in a position to "forestall any Roman Catholic attempts to open missions in the Yukon."[17] A native catechist (lay worker), Henry Venn, was at Lapierre House, while Kenneth McDonald, a brother of Robert, was catechist at Rampart House, though he spent most of his time on the trail visiting the scattered bands in the vicinity.

Bompas had hoped in his new position to be able to devote more time to teaching and to the study of classical languages, but he now

[15] "From the Youcon to London," *Church Missionary Gleaner*, Vol. I, (1874), p. 57.

[16] Cody, *An Apostle of the North*, p. 154.

[17] George E. Gartrell, "The Work of the Churches in the Yukon During the Era of the Klondike Gold Rush," unpublished M.A. thesis, University of Western Ontario, London, Canada, 1970, p. 18. Father Petitot in 1870 and Coadjutor Bishop Isadore Clut in 1872 had followed Father Sequin across the portage, but their efforts to proselytize the Indians were no more successful than his.

had, as an added responsibility, "the care of all the churches," and the long and time-consuming pastoral journeys were more than ever necessary. He now had to visit and encourage his own workers as well as the Indians.

The Bishop [Mrs. Bompas wrote later in a parish magazine] was a good traveller in those days. Starting off on one of his itinerary expeditions, with dog-sleigh, snow shoes and a couple of Indians, the "Yalti" (praying man) would always run ahead of his dogs, only occasionally taking to his sleigh for a few miles to rest. In this way he would get over long stretches of country — camping out in the snow by night (for there were no roadhouses in those days). A good carpet of brush laid under him and, wrapped in robe and blanket, with the poor tired dogs acting as foot warmers, he would sleep until the loud "leve, leve" of the Indians roused the traveller to another day's laborious travel.[18]

Bompas concerned himself with the practical as well as the spiritual problems of the Indians to whom he ministered. One of his great worries was the terrible cycles of famine that they endured when game was scarce, and in an effort to alleviate this scarcity he established two mission-farms in the southern part of his diocese, near Dunvegan. The prevalence of disease among the natives was also a cause of anxiety, and he often nursed them personally, calling on empirical skills acquired of necessity in his own long years of travel and isolation. Eye diseases were particularly rampant, and to aid in the treatment of this scourge, he found time when in England for his consecration to attend several lectures at a London eye hospital. But hard as he worked to aid his Indians, there was always at the back of his mind the gnawing regret that the vastness of his territory made it impossible to visit systematically all the wandering bands, and that all too often the fragile accomplishments of one sojourn in a native camp were dissipated before it was possible to visit them again. Such thoughts, of course, were never allowed to cloud the pages of the missionary magazines.

V

THERE IS SOME DIFFICULTY IN FOLLOWING THE PROSPECTING AND trading activities of McQuesten and Harper in the years immediately

---

[18] Charlotte S. Bompas, "Bishop Bompas, (A Short Sketch of His Work)," *St. Paul's Parish Magazine*, Dawson City, Y.T., Vol. I, No. 5, (March 1902), unpaged.

following 1874, as dates and movements during this period are dependent almost entirely on McQuesten's recollections, set down some time after the events, and varying somewhat in different versions. Ogilvie noted that McQuesten "had regularly chronicled events of note for many years, but had loaned his records to a would-be author of a history of the region. He had often tried to have his manuscript back but had not succeeded. . . . He never got it, but years after when I wrote to him asking for a statement, he sent me what he recollected."[19]

Some things are reasonably certain. In 1875, when the partners again went to St. Michael's for supplies, and to deliver their furs, they found that the Alaska Commercial Company had reorganized its system, and that the traders on the river were to work on a commission basis. "A. Mayo, Harper, and myself had from Fort Yukon and the upper country," McQuesten reported, "Harper and Mayo went to Fort Reliance and I stopped at Fort Yukon. They remained at Fort Reliance three years, they came down in a boat every Spring and the little steamer would tow them back in the summer."[20] McQuesten eventually abandoned Fort Yukon, and moved down to the mouth of the Tanana.

Sometime during these years Mayo and Harper had trouble with the Indians at Fort Reliance, apparently over the pilfering of tobacco, and were forced to leave, after storing most of the trade goods in a cache. In 1877 McQuesten decided to re-open this post, as "another company" had moved into the Tanana country, and the resulting competition had depressed prices to such an extent that it was no longer possible to make a living working on commission. While still on the river, however, he learned that the buildings at Fort Reliance had been broken into and two old Indian women and a blind girl had died from eating a mixture of arsenic and grease that they mistook for flour. His approach to his old post, therefore, was a cautious one, as he was uncertain of the reception that awaited him.

When we arrived in sight of the station they began firing off guns to salute us — they kept shooting until we were very near the landing. Being received so friendly relieved the feelings of my interpreter and the Indians I had with me as they were opposed to coming, thinking they

[19] Ogilvie, *Early Days*, p. 92.

[20] McQuesten, *Recollections*, p. 5.

131

would all be killed. Before landing the goods I had a talk with the Indians in regard to the goods they stole from Mayo. Catsah the Chief had taken charge of the goods and received pay for them and turned the furs over to me so that part was settled.

In regard to the poison, they had to break the lock to get into the Store — I told them that the poison was put into the store to destroy mice and it was out of the way of children and the old people ought to know better and the people that died it was their own fault for breaking into the store and taking things that didn't belong to them. There was one blind girl about sixteen years old that got poisoned — her father said she was a great deal of help to her mother and he had taken one of our dogs to replace the girl, but if I would pay for the girl he would return the dog. I told him I would think the matter over and let them know later on. Finally I told them the girl's Mother could keep the dog, so that settled the matter and that was the last I ever heard about the poison.

The next day we unloaded the steamer and prepared to buy furs. The Indians had a large amount of furs and they traded them all without any trouble.[21]

During these years, Harper was able to find the time for several prospecting ventures. Before the trouble at Fort Reliance, he travelled downriver to the present site of Eagle in Alaska, from which point he went overland to the Fortymile River, and then across the divide to the Sixtymile. On this river he found "such good pay" that he decided to go mining there the following summer, but later had to abandon the idea when he found that he could not afford the time or the cost of an outfit. After Fort Reliance was re-opened, McQuesten himself prospected the Sixtymile. "I found Gold on all the bars in small quantities," he reported, "I found some places where a man would make $6.00 to $8.00 per day, but not extensive enough to put in a string of sluices."[22] Harper returned twice to the Tanana, the first time ascending it as far as he could in the steamer, with McQuesten at the helm, and the second time travelling by land from the Yukon to its headwaters.

In 1878 a second steamer, the *St. Michael* appeared on the lower river. It was owned by the Alaska Commercial Company's "opposi-

---

[21] *Ibid.*, p. 7. Ogilvie in his book has an account of this episode, which was presumably also told to him by McQuesten, in which many of the details vary considerably from those recounted here. This is a hazard which often faces anyone who delves into the records of this period, which are to a considerable extent based on hearsay.

[22] *Ibid.*, p. 7.

tion," though the rival firm did not last long, and McQuesten's organization soon acquired this new vessel. About the same time the original steamer *Yukon* which had been hauled up on the beach at Fort Yukon for the winter, was smashed by the ice during an exceptionally violent spring breakup. Fortunately, because of the old vessel's great age and unreliability, a replacement was already on order, and the new boat, also named the *Yukon*, was assembled and launched at St. Michael's on August 20 of the same year her predecessor was lost — in time, fortunately, to supply the posts before freezeup. She was 75 feet long with a 20-foot beam, a veritable behemoth compared with her namesake. "The old steamer was so small," wrote McQuesten by way of a requiem, "that she had to tow all the goods in barges and she only had accommodation for the crew to handle her. She had no cabin; the stove was in the fire room and four could sit down to the table at a time. The traders in the lower river had to go in the barges, and at meal time we would stop and let them come aboard for their meals."[23]

Both McQuesten and Harper were prolific letter writers, and they bombarded their many friends in the closely-knit mining fraternity with glowing reports of their new area to the north. Some of these letters reached Sitka, and several of the miners who read them were, with the restlessness of their breed, eager to be on the trail at once to this unknown and beckoning land. Only the Indians, still barring the mountain passes, stood in the way. And then in the late '70s, a spark was added to the smouldering desire to enter the country. A man arrived in Sitka who had actually crossed the Chilkoot Pass.

His name was George Holt, though little else is known about him. Even the year of his passage is uncertain, being sometime between 1875 and 1878, as the details of his journey varied with the telling. Certainly how he got past the Chilkats is a mystery. Dawson, after careful investigation, wrote that "He was accompanied by two or more Indians, and crossed by the Chilkoot or the White Pass to the head of the Lewes. He followed the river down to the lower end of Lake Marsh and walked over the Indian trail thence to the Tes-lin-too, returning to the coast again by the same route. On his return, he reported the discovery of 'coarse gold', but none of the miners who afterwards prospected the region mentioned, have been able to confirm his statement in this particular.... The date and route

[23] *Ibid.*, p. 9.

assigned to Holt [is], however, probably correct, being the result of inquiry among miners who knew him, followed his route through the country, and came in contact with the Indians whom he had met."[24]

The moment for unlocking the gateway into the Klondike was at hand.

VI

APPROPRIATELY ENOUGH, HOOCH, WHICH PLAYED A PART IN THE *Osprey* affair, also contributed to the opening up of the Canadian Yukon.

Fortunately for both Alaska and Canada, Captain Beardslee, the American naval officer reluctantly sent by his government to Sitka, was an intelligent man who did not hesitate to use initiative and imagination in carrying out his orders. He was well aware, for example, of the role the drinking of hooch played in fomenting Indian troubles, but he was also aware of the futility and unfairness of the total prohibition to the natives of its use. He instigated instead a series of "restrictions" which would control consumption but not prevent it, and he promised that if liquor was abused by anyone, the offenders would be treated alike, be they white men, creoles, or Indians. Instead of armed military detachments, he appointed native policemen to see that the restrictions were obeyed. His ultimate weapon when dealing with the Tlingits was the threat that the distillation of hooch would be prohibited to recalcitrant bands, and the old discriminative system would be enforced. He could back up this threat if necessary: a ship of war, supported by disciplined boats' crews that could penetrate the most remote inlets, was a much more efficient enforcement agency than bored and drunken soldiers on fixed garrison duty in the settlements.

[24] Dawson, *Report on an Exploration*, p. 179. A popular Alaskan story of the day credited a red-headed Scotsman, a deserter from the Hudson's Bay Company, with being the first to cross the Chilkoot Pass, from the interior to the coast, in 1864 or 1865. Dawson, however, after a careful investigation, questioned the veracity of the story, claiming that it grew in the telling from the fact that some items from Campbell's ransacked Fort Selkirk eventually found their way to traders on the coast.

Holt not long after his appearance in Sitka took off again on another mysterious journey, this time up the coast, where he was murdered by the Copper River Indians. Beyond this bald fact, the details of his death are as little-known and obscure as those of his life.

In 1879 many of the miners, including some who had been previously turned back by the Chilkats, requested Beardslee's assistance in obtaining for them an unhindered passage to the Yukon basin. "This privilege (of crossing the passes) had never been accorded," Beardslee explained in a report to naval headquarters, "the Indians (Chilkhats) [sic] fearing that the whites would interfere with the Stich [sic] Indians who live in the interior, and whose trade the coast Indians monopolize. The Chilkhats were estimated as from two to four thousand in number, and considered the most warlike of all the tribes."[25] It would require hard bargaining to persuade the Chilkats to abandon this old and rigidly-policed taboo.

Ammunition for the start of negotiations turned up on September 25, when Indian canoes arrived with the news that "there had been a big fight up in the Chilkhat country, between two families of the Chilkhats, viz. the Klockwateries (warriors) and the Onochtades, and that the chief of the former, Klotz-Kuch (who is head chief of the tribe), was seriously wounded, and that a number on both sides had been killed; the inciting causes having been a barrel of molasses with which Klotz-Kuch had given a pot-a-latch."[26] This episode gave Beardslee the leverage he needed. There were several Chilkats living at Sitka: one of them, whom the white men called Dick, was a nephew of Klotz-Kuch and a member of Beardslee's police force, and another, a chief called Sitka Jack, was a crafty veteran of the hooch trade, whom Beardslee had found at first to be a worthy adversary,[27] and later a firm supporter. These two men were placed in charge of a force of 30 other Chilkats recruited in the Sitka area who were sent on October 3 to visit their own people and emphasize to them "the value of white friendship and the danger of the opposite."

[25] L. A. Beardslee, *Reports of Captain L. A. Beardslee, U.S. Navy, Relative to Affairs in Alaska*, (Washington, Government Printing Office, 1882), p. 60.

[26] *Ibid.*, p. 60.

[27] One of their early meetings was during a raid on the stills at the rancheria (settlement) just outside of Sitka where Jack lived. Jack apparently remorseful, led the way to his own still, which he demolished in spectacular fashion. It was only later that Beardslee learned that by this diversion Jack had successfully concealed from the raiding party the fact that he had two more stills hidden in the bush. His ingenuity, however, backfired: the owners of the other stills that were casualties of the raid lost no time in smashing Jack's hidden installations as soon as the sailors had gone. In this case, the authorities had the last laugh, but many of the wily old chief's schemes were more successfully executed.

The party [wrote Beardslee] ... were directed to report to Klotz-Kuch, and say that I had sent them to help him keep his people in order, and that in return I expected him to always use his influence to secure good treatment to any white men who should come to his country to trade, and that I would be pleased if he would let white miners go into the interior to prospect for precious minerals, which, if found, would enrich the Indians also. ...

On the 12th of February, 1880, Dick and most of the party returned. ... They brought an invitation from Klotz-Kuch for the white miners to come, and promises of welcome, and thanks to me. This invitation I extended to the miners, of whom there were a number in town deterred from work on Baranoff Island by the great amount of snow still remaining on the mountains. ... These men were very ready to undertake such an expedition, and were of such characters as were best adapted. The project was freely discussed, meetings held, and an expedition to the Chilkat country organized, and for the ensuing two months Sitka was quite lively with the preparations for the expedition.

Several boats were built, some from timber which was growing in the forest when the idea was conceived, and in May the party of pioneers were ready to start.[28]

On May 11 a public meeting was held, and an agreement drawn up between Beardslee and the miners, in which the latter pledged, among other things, "to acquit ourselves as becomes orderly, sober, reasonable men," and not to carry "spirituous liquor ... into the Indian country for the purposes of trade or barter with the natives."[29] One of their number, Edmund Bean, was chosen as leader, and he and 18 other men signed the document.[30] To ensure that the Chilkats kept their word, Beardslee ordered the *Jamestown*'s launch to accompany the party and sent three naval officers, 13 men, two interpreters and a pilot, under the command of Lieutenant E. P. McLellan, to support them. On his arrival at the Chilkat village McLellan and the officers who accompanied him to interview Klotz-Kuch were under orders to wear uniforms and side arms, and to leave one officer and a strong guard in the naval launch at all

[28] Beardslee, *Reports*, p. 60.

[29] *Ibid.*, p. 61.

[30] For the record, the signatories of the agreement, besides Bean, were as follows:

Robert A. Duggan	William Zoble	J. Newton Massen
Geo. G. Langtry	M. A. Hayes	Fred Cushman
Thomas Liveham	Antone Marks	Preston Vontenien
Dankert A. Petersen	Dennis Barrett	James McCluskey
James Tallon	Thomas Keirnan	John Lemon
Patrick McGlivichey	Geo. Haukrader	S. B. Matthews

times. These precautions fortunately proved unnecessary. The miners, as promised, were permitted without hindrance to make their pioneer crossing of the Chilkoot Pass, and the Indians, for a fee, packed some of their gear to the Yukon headwaters, the first loads in what was to become a lucrative trade. For both the Indians and the white men it was, unknowingly, a momentous occasion. The future development of the gold fields beyond the mountains was ensured.

Success in mining was not instantaneous. Bean and his party reached Lake Lindeman on June 17, 1880, and after building boats started down the lake on July 4. They eventually reached the mouth of the Teslin, which they ascended and prospected for some distance, but only traces of gold were found. Two more miners, Johnny Mackenzie and a man known only as "Slim Jim" followed hard on the heels of this large group, and others may have entered the country this same year. All of them had to cut their prospecting season short in order to make their way back to the coast before winter set in.

In 1881, two men who had been with Bean, and two other miners, again climbed the Chilkoot. They reached the mouth of the Big Salmon River, which they called the Iyon, and which they ascended by their own reckoning some 200 miles. They panned "colours" along almost this entire distance, and encountered some remunerative river bars. "This," Dawson noted, "may be characterized as the first discovery of paying placers in the district."[31]

In Juneau, a new mining town which had replaced Sitka as the prospecting centre of the area, this find caused much excitement, and in the spring of the following year, 1882, some twenty men made the crossing to the upper river. It was probably during this season that two parties made the first ascent of the Pelly as far as Hoole Canyon, or possibly beyond, and it was during this season also that twelve miners, instead of returning outside the way they had come, pushed on to Fort Reliance for the winter. McQuesten supplied them as best as he could; there were shortages, but there was no danger of starvation. "They all built cabins," he wrote happily "and went into winter quarters. . . . It was the first time, with the exception of one year, that anyone was living near that I could converse with. Most all of the men would meet at the Station in the evening and we would play cards, tell stories, and the winter eve-

---

[31] Dawson, *Report on an Exploration*, p. 180.

nings passed away very pleasantly."[32] These gatherings became the nucleus of a fraternal organization, that grew with the increase of miners in the district, and in time was formally incorporated as the Yukon Order of Pioneers.

At Christmas and New Year's, McQuesten gave parties that established an enduring tradition at all his posts.

Christmas . . . we had a good dinner [he wrote] and all the Indians that were near the Station had all they wanted to eat. New Year I gave the Indians ammunition to celebrate on and they had a splendid time. The Indians got a large moose skin and as many as could get around it would take hold of the edge and then some young Indian would get on top of the skin and they would toss him up. The white men thought it great sport and they joined in the game. After a while the men began to throw the women in the Moose skin and tossing them up. After the women had been tossed they turned to and caught the white men and they had to take their turn to be thrown up in the air — it was great sport for those not in the Moose skin as a man is perfectly helpless when he is thrown ten up. Some time he will come down on his head but they never get hurt. . . . Everyone living near the town had to be tossed up and they most all took their medicine in good humor.[33]

The men who wintered at Fort Reliance worked at Fortymile and Sixtymile Rivers in the summer of 1883, and though, like Harper and McQuesten, they found plenty of "prospects," they did not encounter pay dirt. At the end of this second season most of them were forced to return over the Chilkoot pass to Juneau, but two of the party, William Moore of Victoria, B.C. and Joseph Ladue, a French Canadian born in New York State, remained in the country. Moore was to become well known as a steamboat captain and dog musher, while Ladue was to become a trading partner of McQuesten and Harper, a sawmill operator, a saloon keeper, and an unquenchable enthusiast for whom every reported strike was the Eldorado which all the miners on the river were seeking.

In this same year, four men from Juneau, Dick Poplin, Charles McCoskey (or McConkey), George Marks and Ben Beach, were the first miners to work the Stewart River bars, with encouraging results. They too decided to continue on to Fort Reliance, rather than face the time-consuming upstream journey in the fall. However, McQuesten's supply steamer had broken down on the lower river,

[32] McQuesten, *Recollections*, p. 11.
[33] *Ibid.*, p. 11.

and Fort Reliance in consequence was deserted when they reached it: they had to continue on to the mouth of the Tanana, where they wintered. In the spring, Marks and Beach returned to the coast by way of the Kuskokwim, while Poplin and McCoskey went back for another season on the Stewart. Their results on this trip were disappointing.

About the same time, a curious figure appeared briefly on the scene, when Edward L. Scheiffelin led a well-equipped prospecting party that entered the country by the long journey up the Yukon from the sea. Scheiffelin was no penniless prospector supported by a grub-stake, but a self-made millionaire who had already discovered and brought into production the famous Tombstone Silver Mines in Arizona. He organized his party in 1882. To get from San Francisco to St. Michael's he chartered a schooner, and for the trip upstream from St. Michael's a small paddle-wheel steamer was brought along as deck cargo. The little vessel, curiously named the *New Racket*, succeeded in reaching the Tanana River before freezeup in 1882, and in the summer of 1883 continued on to the Lower Ramparts. The party found placer gold, but no lode deposits, in which Scheiffelin was chiefly interested. Discouraged by the vast, empty distances and the long, harsh winters, he cut short his exploration program early in its second year, sold his riverboat to McQuesten, and dismissed the Yukon as a sterile wilderness in which there was no hope of finding mineral wealth. He was to be proved wrong in spectacular fashion, but it was to take a decade to do so.

Not only miners were excited by the potential of the Yukon basin. The first scientific explorers reached the Chilkoot Pass only two years after Beardslee ensured its unmolested passage. They were the brothers Arthur and Aurel Krause, geographers sent to the northwest by the Geographical Society of Bremen, Germany, to extend geographical research into this remote region, and in particular to initiate a study of the Tlingit Indians and their environment. Out of these investigations came a classic ethnographic report by Aurel, *Die Tlinkit-Indianer*, published in 1885, and a map of the area that was characterized by Dawson as being "worthy of note on account of its conscientious accuracy."[34] Five years later he gratefully incorporated this work into his own maps of the territory.

The mapping was done by Arthur Krause who, while his brother

[34] Dawson, *Report on an Exploration*, p. 180.

was studying the culture and language of other Tlingit tribes, accompanied the Chilkats on two of their journeys across the passes into the valley of the Yukon. "The first of these," wrote Aurel in the introduction to his book, "he started in the company of two young Indians on May 28 [1882] when the snow was not yet completely melted."[35] In their company he crossed the Chilkoot Pass, but was prevented by bad weather and ice from undertaking a detailed survey of the lakes. He started back to the Chilkoot on June 1, though travel in the pass was still hazardous because of ice and snow.

While crossing the coast range to the Yukon had been done before by prospectors [Aurel's account continued], my brother was the first scientific traveler to pass this way and render an exact description and sketch maps of it.

He started a second trip into the interior through entirely unknown territory on trails never before trod by a white man. On June 17 he left the station and started up the Chilkat River to the Chilkat village of Klokwon [Klukwan].... From here he went out with two Indians whom he took as guide and packer into the valley of the Chilkat River and up its right tributary, the Tlehini [Klehini] to the high tundra which in contrast to the wild, almost impenetrable thicket in the valleys offered no hindrance beyond the numerous mountain streams which had to be forded at hip depth. On June 25 my brother reached the divide of the waters that flow to the Altsech [Alsek] and those that flow into the Yukon. Unfortunately, the illness of one of his Indian companions ... forced him to turn back after he was in sight of the Kusooa [Kusawa], the largest lake through which the western source of the Yukon flows.... The return was accomplished without delay and on July 2 they reached the station.[36]

Krause's report, in the form of soberly written "travel letters," was circulated without fanfare in scientific and academic circles. The following year, a much more flamboyant figure followed in the footsteps of the Germans. Lieutenant Frederick Schwatka of the United States Army led a military expedition of five soldiers and one civilian across the Chilkoot Pass to the headwaters of the Yukon. Here they began a journey that would take them from the source to the mouth of the Yukon, the first traverse of the entire lake and river system. The task of investigating the areas that lay beyond the limits of the coastal charts was finally underway.

[35] Aurel Krause, *The Tlingit Indians*, (Seattle, University of Washington Press, paperback, 1970), p. 5.

[36] *Ibid.*, p. 6.

VII

IT WAS SURPRISING THAT THE UNITED STATES ARMY'S EXPEDITION to the Yukon and Alaska ever got under way. Plans for a series of reconnaissance surveys of the territory had been drawn up by the Department of War after the purchase, but Congress had consistently refused to grant funds for these projects, with the exception of Raymond's work on the lower Yukon, which had the blessing of powerful commercial interests. After the withdrawal of the last of the military garrisons, the army's legal right to exercise any further control in Alaska was ended by Presidential order, and specific disapproval by the General of the Army and the Secretary of War for any further exploration in the north by military forces had hardly been issued when, somehow, an expedition was organized and dispatched.

Schwatka was chosen to lead it; possibly he was one of the behind-the-scenes promoters of the scheme. The main objective, he wrote in his book *A Summer in Alaska*, a "popular" account of his journey published in 1894, "was to acquire such information of the country traversed and its wild inhabitants as would be valuable to the military authorities in the future, and as a map would be needed to illustrate such information well, the party's efforts were rewarded with making the expedition successful in a geographical sense."[37] But in fields other than topography — such as geology, botany, or natural history — the army was unable to supply men, and the unknown bureaucrats in Washington who were stubbornly organizing the group, decided reluctantly that for political reasons it would not be possible to add specialists from civilian sources to the party. This was a regrettable decision, though understandable under the circumstances: certainly the lack of even one trained scientist affected the value of the contribution to knowledge which the expedition made.

With all the secrecy of the preparations for a modern-day commando raid, the men assembled at Vancouver barracks in Washington Territory, near the mouth of the Columbia River. Besides Schwatka, the members of the party were Dr. George Wilson, sur-

---

[37] Frederick Schwatka, *A Summer in Alaska*, (St. Louis, Mo., J. W. Henry, 1894), p. 9. This book was also published under the title *Along Alaska's Great River*. Because many of the miners on the Yukon were Americans, the casual and infuriating use of "Alaska" as the name of the whole territory drained by the Yukon River was in general use.

geon, United States Army; Topographical Assistant Charles A. Homan, United States Engineers, topographer and photographer; Sgt. Charles A. Gloster, United States Army, artist; Cpl. Shircliff, United States Army, in charge of stores; Pvt. Roth, assistant; and a lone civilian, listed as Citizen J. B. Mitchell, who was described as a miner experienced in living and travelling in Alaska. The plan was to build a raft once the lakes at the head of the Yukon were reached; the wind and the current would provide the motive power.

Schwatka, a dapper, arrogant little man with a goatee and pince-nez, was an experienced Arctic traveller who had led one of the numerous Franklin searching expeditions, and had to his credit the longest sledge journey then on record, "being absent from his base of supplies for eleven months and 20 days, and travelling 3241 statute miles."[38] He was born in Galena, Illinois, in 1849, and when he was ten he moved west with his family and settled in Salem, Oregon, where he eventually attended Willamette University. In 1867 he received an appointment to West Point, and after graduation in June 1871, he was commissioned in the Third Cavalry.

His army career appears to have been somewhat unorthodox. Besides serving in various posts in the United States, he found time to study both medicine and law. He was admitted to the Nebraska bar in 1875, and received a medical degree from Bellevue Hospital Medical College in New York the following year, but he did not become active in either of these professions. Instead, his consuming interest became geographical exploration. His Franklin searching expedition, which he persuaded the American Geographical Society to organize, not only set impressive travel records, but also resolved any last, lingering doubts concerning the fate of all members of the Franklin expedition. To a man of this background, the opportunity to attempt a traverse of the Yukon River could only be a challenge to be welcomed.

The party left Portland, Oregon, on May 22, 1883, on the coastal steamer *Victoria*, bound for Alaska by the Inland Passage. Even their departure was secretive, as recall was still possible if news of the project reached the ears of the wrong officials in Washington. Schwatka wrote, with justifiable bitterness, that the little expedition "stole away like a thief in the night, with far less money in its hands

[38] William D. MacBride, "Lieutenant Schwatka's Northern Expeditions," *The Whitehorse Star*, January 20, 1966.

142

to conduct it through its long journey than was afterwards appropriated by Congress to publish its report."[39] Nonetheless, in the hold of the *Victoria* were three tons of supplies for which he would have to find packers once the head of Lynn Canal was reached.

The steamer dropped anchor on June 2 in a little port on Chilkat Inlet called Pyramid Harbour. There were just-completed salmon canneries on each side of the inlet — for a new industry was becoming established in Alaska — and farther inland, on the Chilkat River, were the villagers from which Schwatka proposed to recruit his packers, some 60 or 80 of them. The expedition arrived at an inauspicious moment, as an important chief had just died, and the funeral festivities, which were about to get underway, would last at least a week or ten days. To wait until these festivities ended, and the Indians recovered, was a delay the expedition could not afford. Schwatka, however, "by being a little bit determined managed to persuade enough strong sturdy fellows away to do my proposed packing in two trips over the pass, which had the effect of inducing the others to come forward in sufficient numbers to accomplish the work in a single journey, and preparations were commenced accordingly. These preparations consisted mostly in assorting our effects with reference to everything that we could possibly leave behind, taking as little as we could make our way through with, and putting that little into convenient bags, boxes, and bundles of about one hundred pounds each, that being the maximum load the Indians could well carry over such Alpine trails."[40]

The manager of one of the canneries loaned the expedition a small steam launch belonging to his company, and this towed the Indians in their canoes southward down Chilkat Inlet and northward up Chilkoot Inlet to the mouth of the "Dayay" (now Taiya) River at its head, passing on the way Haines Mission[41] and the future site of Skagway. They camped that night at the river mouth: three days later they were at its headwaters. "All around us," Schwatka wrote, "was snow or the clear blue ice of the glacier fronts, while directly northward, and seemingly impassable, there loomed up for

---

[39] Schwatka, *A Summer in Alaska*, p. 11.

[40] *Ibid.*, p. 38.

[41] Haines Mission, now Haines, was established in the late 1870's by the Presbyterian Church, and was named for Mrs. Francina E. Haines, the first secretary of the Committee of Home Missions.

nearly four thousand feet the precipitous pass through the mountains, a blank mass of steep white, which we were to essay on the morrow."

On the morning of the next day [June 11] about five o'clock we commenced the toilsome ascent of this coast range pass ... and by seven o'clock all my long pack train was strung up the precipitous pass, making one of the prettiest Alpine sights that I have ever witnessed, and as seen from a distance strangely resembling a row of bowlders [sic] projecting from the snow. Up banks almost perpendicular they scrambled on their hands and knees, helping themselves by every projecting rock and clump of juniper and dwarf spruce, not even refusing to use their teeth on them at the worst places. Along the steep snow banks and the icy fronts of glaciers steps were cut with knives, while rough alpenstocks from the valley helped them to maintain their footing. In some such places the incline was so steep that those having boxes on their backs cut scratches in the icy crust with the corners as they passed along, and often-times it was possible to steady one's self by the open palm of the hand resting against the snow. In some of these places a single mis-step, or the caving in of a foot-hold would have sent the unfortunate traveler many hundred feet headlong to certain destruction. Yet not the slightest accident happened, and about ten o'clock, almost exhausted, we stood on the top of the pass, enveloped in a cold drifting fog, 4,240 feet above the level of the sea.... How these small Indians, not apparently averaging over one hundred and forty pounds in weight, could carry one hundred pounds up such a precipitous mountain of ice and snow, seems marvelous beyond measure. One man carried one hundred and thirty-seven pounds, while boys of twelve to fourteen carried from fifty to seventy pounds.[42]

Beyond the summit, they descended rapidly for a few hundred yards, following the trail past Crater Lake, which was still frozen over. "We caught sight of the main lake in the afternoon, and in a few hours were upon its banks at a point where a beautiful mountain stream came tumbling in, with enough swift water to necessitate crossing on a log."[43] To Schwatka's surprise, his Indian packers, though they had just completed a long and fatiguing climb, immediately demanded their pay — $10 to $12 apiece — claiming that they wanted to start their return journey at once, and that they would travel as far as the mouth of the Dayay River before they would stop to rest. Incredible as it may seem, Schwatka found out

42 Schwatka, *A Summer in Alaska*, pp. 83-84.
43 *Ibid.*, p. 88.

on later enquiry that this estimate of their homeward progress was not exaggerated — in fact, one of them kept on going as far as Haines Mission before resting, and remained there for only a very brief period before continuing on his way.

VIII

EXERCISING A TOPOGRAPHER'S PREROGATIVE, SCHWATKA ON HIS MAP attempted to name the pass he had just climbed Perrier Pass, after Colonel J. Perrier of the French Geographical Society, but Chilkoot was already too well-established to be changed by a map-maker's fancy. Many of the other names that he bestowed, however, have been more kindly treated by time, and are still in use. He ignored, or did not know, the popular names given by the miners to many of the rivers and creeks, and he made little attempt to retain native place names, claiming that they were difficult to pronounce, and that there were often conflicting names for the same location. Instead he filled the blank spaces of his map with the names of geographers or other scientists of the day, or with the names of patrons of exploration. Most of the men he honoured are almost forgotten now, but on modern maps, because of Schwatka's journey, a little of them endures.

His "main lake" beyond the pass, where the packers ended their task, he named Lindeman, in honour of Dr. Lindeman, secretary of the Bremen Geographical Society. Here the raft was constructed. "The best logs available," Schwatka wrote, "which were rather small ones of stunted spruce and contorted pine [were] floated down the little stream, and a raft made of the somewhat formidable dimensions of fifteen by thirty feet, with an elevated deck amidships. The rope lashings used on the loads of the Indian packers were put to duty in binding the logs together, but the greatest reliance was placed in stout wooden pins which united them by auger holes bored through both, the logs being cut or 'saddled out' where they joined, as is done at the corners of log cabins. A deck was made on the corduroy plan of light seasoned pine poles, and high enough to prevent ordinary sized waves from wetting the effects, while a pole was rigged by mortising it into one of the central logs at the bottom, and from this was suspended a wall tent as a sail. . . .

A large bow and stern oar with which to do the steering completed the rude craft."[44]

The raft was taken down the lake by three of the men — the remainder walked — and on June 16, was "shot" through the turbulent little river that drained Lake Lindeman into the much larger body of water that lay beyond it. Here more substantial logs were available, and the party set to work immediately enlarging their craft "on a scale commensurate with the carrying of our entire load." The new dimensions, when the alterations were completed, were 16 feet by 42 feet: the deckwork was improved; and provision for the use of two side oars was added to the structure. "One of the delights of this raft-making," Schwatka commented with feeling, "was our having to stand a greater part of the day in ice-water just off the mountain tops, and in strange contrast with this annoyance, the mosquitoes would come buzzing around and make work almost impossible by their attacks upon our heads, while at the same time our feet would be freezing."[45] By June 19, in spite of the discomforts, the refit was completed.

The lake that stretched ahead of them as far as they could see, which the miners called Boat Lake, Schwatka named Lake Bennett, after James Gordon Bennett, a newspaper man and a patron of exploration.[46] On the lake their craft depended entirely on a following wind to make progress. Fortunately for the explorers, the prevailing winds at this time of the year were from the south, though they were alarmed shortly after starting their journey by being caught in one of the area's frequent gales. "A perfect hurricane was howling," Schwatka reported, "the high waves sweeping the rowing space so that no one could stand on his feet in that part, much less sit down to the oars."[47] After being blown uncomfortably close to a rocky beach, they managed to anchor in a sheltered cove. Here they found logs longer than any they had encountered yet, and four stiffeners were added to the raft, a much needed improvement.

[44] *Ibid.*, pp. 95-96.

[45] *Ibid.*, p. 99.

[46] Bennett was founder and editor of the New York *Herald*, and noted as an innovator of many journalistic practices which were at the time rather radical, but which are now in standard use. He subsidized several exploration parties in various parts of the world, including Stanley's search for Livingstone, in return for the exclusive rights to their stories.

[47] Schwatka, *A Summer in Alaska*, p. 105.

About 5 p.m. on June 21 they reached the outlet of the lake, at a narrows in which the reconstructed raft felt for the first time the force of the current.

This short stretch of the draining river of Lake Bennett [wrote Schwatka], nearly two miles long, is called by the natives of the country "the place where the caribou cross," and appears on the map as Caribou Crossing.

At certain seasons of the year, so the Tahk-heesh [Stick] Indians say, these caribou — the woodland reindeer — pass over this part of the river in large numbers in their migrations to the different feeding grounds. . . . Unfortunately for our party [no] crossings occurred at this time of the year, although a dejected camp of two Tahk-heesh families not far away from ours had a very ancient reindeer ham hanging in front of their brush tent, which, however, we did not care to buy. The numerous tracks of the animals, some apparently as large as oxen, confirmed the Indian stories, and as I looked at our skeleton game score and our provisions of Government bacon, I wished sincerely that June was one of the months of the reindeers' migration, and the 21st or 22nd about the period of its culmination.

The very few Indians in this part of the country — the "Sticks" — subsist mostly on these animals and on mountain goats, with now and then a wandering moose, and more frequently a black bear. . . .

The country was now decidedly more open, and it was evident that we were getting out of the mountains. Many level spots appeared, the hills were less steep and the snow melting from their tops. Pretty wild rose-blossoms were found along the banks of the beach, with many wild onions with which we stuffed the wrought-iron grouse that we killed, and altogether there was a general change of verdure for the better. There were even a number of rheumatic grasshoppers which feebly jumped along in the cold Alpine air, as if to tempt us to go fishing, in remembrance of the methods of our boy-hood's days . . . Grand terraces stretching in beautiful symmetry along each side of the lake plainly showed its ancient levels, these terraces reaching nearly to the tops of the hills, and looking as if some huge giant had used them as stairways over the mountains. Similar but less conspicuous terraces had been noticed on the northern shores of Lake Bennett.[48]

Before they reached the crossing, Schwatka named two large streams which flowed into Lake Bennett from the north — the Wheaton River, after Brevet Major-General Frank Wheaton, U.S. Army, military commander of Alaska, and the Watson River, for Professor Sereno Watson of Harvard University. A small lake beyond the narrows he named Nares Lake, after George Strong Nares, a Brit-

48 *Ibid.*, pp. 109-111.

ish Arctic explorer, and the larger lake beyond it he called Bove Lake, after Lieutenant Bove of the Italian Navy, noting at the same time that the native name for it was Tahk-o. Although Nares Lake was only three or four miles long, the explorers were delayed there three days waiting for a favourable wind. It was not until the afternoon of June 26 that they succeeded in reaching the outlet of Bove Lake, and entered "the first considerable stretch of river that we had yet met with on the trip, about nine miles long. We quitted the river at five o'clock, which was quite an improvement on lake travel even at its best."[49] On the right bank of the river, about four miles from its entrance, Schwatka noted a "tolerably well-built 'Stick' Indian house."

Beyond the river was yet another lake, which "also had a few terraces visible on the eastern hillsides, but they were nearer together and not so well marked as those we observed on some of the lakes further back. Along these, however, were pretty open prairies, covered with the dried, yellow grass of last year. . . . I have no doubt that they furnish good grazing to mountain goats, caribou, and moose."[50] The weather was miserable, with rain and thunder showers; soft clay and shallow mud banks along the shore made camping difficult; "horse-flies" attacked them when they attempted to bathe in the warmth of the afternoon. One of their stops in particular moved Schwatka to considerable vehemence. "The raft lay far out on the lake," he wrote, "a hundred yards from the shore, across soft white mud, through which one might sink in the water to one's middle. When to this predicament the inevitable mosquitoes and a few rain showers are added, I judge that our plight was about as disagreeable as could well be imagined."[51] This lake Schwatka named for Professor O. C. Marsh,[52] a prominent American scientist. The miners had called it Mud Lake, which was certainly a more descriptive title.

[49] *Ibid.*, p. 119, as is the reference to the Indian house.

[50] *Ibid.*, pp. 126-127.

[51] *Ibid.*, p. 130.

[52] Othniel Charles Marsh, 1831-1899, professor of vertebrate paleontology at Yale University, was a pioneer in the study of the fossil beds of the American west, and active in national scientific affairs, being president of the National Academy of Sciences for 12 years. When the United States Geological Survey was formed in 1881, Professor Marsh was put in charge of its work in vertebrate paleontology.

On June 29, to their great relief, the explorers at last entered the main river. A tributary stream, flowing into the lower end of Marsh Lake, was named the McClintock River, after Vice-Admiral Sir Leopold McClintock, of the Royal Navy,[53] and a prominent peak to the east of the lake was given the name of Mount Michie, after a professor on the staff of West Point. Somewhere ahead of them lay what Schwatka called "the Grand Cañon of the Yukon River," and beyond that one more lake to cross, and then some 1900 miles of river travel. Their unwieldy craft had brought them safely across the lakes; now their progress would be dependent on the current rather than the wind. It would be faster, but there would be new problems to overcome.

IX

THEY ENTERED THE RIVER CAUTIOUSLY, AS THEY WERE UNDER THE impression that the canyon was less than five miles from the outlet of Lake Marsh. As the Indians who were accompanying them as guides and interpreters — two Chilkats and two Stick Indians — had cheerfully predicted that the raft would "go to pieces" in the rapids, the explorers were understandably anxious to inspect this obstacle to navigation before running it. By the time, however, that they discovered that the distance from Lake Marsh was closer to 50 miles than five, they had somewhat relaxed their lookout, and almost charged unwittingly into the maelstrom with all hands and supplies on board. They succeeded in snubbing their awkward craft to the bank just in time.

Schwatka walked ahead "exposed to heat and mosquitoes" to make a reconnaissance, and was impressed with what he saw.

The walls of the cañon are perpendicular columns of basalt, not unlike a diminutive Fingal's cave in appearance, and nearly a mile in length, the center of this mile stretch being broken into a huge basin of about twice the usual width of the stream in the cañon, and which is full of seething whirlpools and eddies where nothing but a fish could live for a minute. . . . Through this narrow chute of corrugated rock the

[53] McClintock, 1819-1902, had a distinguished naval career, highlighted by service in four Franklin searching expeditions, including that of 1857-59, which finally discovered evidence of the fate of Franklin himself and the main body of the explorers. For this accomplishment he was promoted to Vice-Admiral and knighted in 1877.

wild waters of the great river rush in a perfect mass of milk-like foam, with a reverberation that is audible for a considerable distance, the roar being intensified by the rocky walls which act like so many sounding boards. . . . At the northern outlet of the cañon, the rushing river spreads rapidly into its former width, but abates not a jot in its swiftness, and flows in a white and shallow sheet over reefs of bowlders and bars thickly studded with intertwining drifts of huge timber, ten times more dangerous for a boat or raft than the narrow cañon itself, although perhaps not so in appearance. This state of things continues for about four miles further . . . when the river again contracts, hemmed in by low basaltic banks, and becomes even narrower than before . . . making a veritable horseshoe of boiling cascades, not much wider than the length of our craft, and as high at the end as her mast. Through this funnel of foam the waves ran three or four feet high, and this fact . . . made matters very uninviting for navigation in any sort of craft.[54]

Most of July 1 was spent on this investigation of the canyon and rapids, and in making the raft ready for its trip through the white water. Schwatka was not very specific as to the nature of these preparations, but presumably the supplies were off-loaded and carried to the foot of the rapids. On July 2, with a skeleton crew on board, the raft was unmoored and pushed with some difficulty "out of the little eddy where she lay, the poor vessel resisting as if she knew all that was ahead of her, and was loth to go." Finally she was gripped by the current and sucked irrevocably towards the hazardous passage.

A moment's hesitation at the cañon's brink, and quick as a flash the whirling craft plunged into the foam, and before twenty yards were made had collided with the western wall of columnar rock with a shock as loud as a blast, tearing off the inner side log and throwing the outer one far into the stream. The raft swung around this as upon a hinge, just as if it had been a straw in a gale of wind, and again resumed its rapid career. In the whirlpool basin of the cañon the craft, for a brief second or two, seemed actually buried out of sight in the foam. . . . I was most afraid of the four miles of shallow rapids below the cañon, but the raft only received a dozen or a score of smart bumps that started a log here and there, but tore none of the structure, and nothing remained ahead of her but the cascades. These reached, in a few minutes the craft was caught at the bow by the first high wave in the funnel-like chute and lifted into the air until it stood almost at an angle of thirty degrees, when it went through the cascades like a charge of

54 Schwatka, *A Summer in Alaska*, pp. 165-166.

fixed bayonets, and almost as swiftly as a flash of light, burying its nose in the foam beyond as it subsided.[55]

Three days of repairs were necessary to make their battered craft seaworthy again, but the men attacked the work with a light heart "for our greatest obstacle was now at our backs."

Schwatka was an enthusiastic fly fisherman, and he and the doctor had been trying their luck at every opportunity since the start of the journey, so far without success, except for a few trout caught near the discharge of Lake Bennett on a "trout line" set overnight. It was not until just before they entered the canyon that grayling had finally begun to rise to their lures, and now, while the repairs were being made, they lost no time in getting out their rods again. "Our favourite fishing place," Schwatka reported, "was just below the cascades, where a number of disintegrating columns of basalt had fallen in, forming a talus along which we could walk between the water and the wall."[56] In the three days they landed, according to Schwatka's count — and who can doubt a fisherman's word! — "between four and five hundred grayling," the largest weighing two and a quarter pounds, and the average about a pound. The Indians who had gathered to watch the raft's descent and to assist in the portaging were fascinated by this novel method of catching fish, and were delighted when given a few of the flies as a gift.

The patched-up raft resumed the downstream journey on July 6. The explorers passed the mouth of the "Tahk-Henna or Tahk River" shortly after noon, Schwatka noting that "By following to its head, where the Indians say is a large lake, the travellers arrived at the Chilkat portage.... From this point on, my guides were much more familiar with the country, having been over the Chilkat Trail many times."[57] A prominent hill between the Tahk and the Yukon was named Haeckel Hill, after Professor Ernst Haeckel[58] of Jena, Germany.

[55] *Ibid.*, p. 167.

[56] *Ibid.*, p. 168.

[57] *Ibid.*, p. 177.

[58] Ernst Heinrich Haeckel, 1834-1919, was for many years professor of comparative anatomy and director of the Zoological Institute of Jena, Germany. He was an early and enthusiastic supporter of Darwin's theory of organic evolution. He was also a field naturalist of note, and in 1866 he coined the term "ecology," which is so much in evidence today.

Late that same afternoon they came to the last of the lakes that they had to traverse. "This lake was called by the Indians Kluk-Tas-Si; and, as it was one of the very few pronounceable names of Indian derivation in this section of the country, I retained it, though it is possible that this may be the Lake Lebarge of some books."[59] The first day on it they made 13 miles, the wind dying down and springing up several times. The next day they made only nine miles, but the evening, Schwatka noted, "was a still and beautiful one, with the lake's surface like a mirror, and the reflection of the red rocks in the quiet water made the most striking scene on our trip ... The eastern shores of the lake seem to be formed of high rounded hills of light gray limestone, picturesquely striped with the foliage of the dark green evergreens growing in the ravines."[60]

The capriciousness of the winds, and of northern weather in general, was fully demonstrated on the lake on July 8. The morning was calm, and as they could make no headway it was devoted to the taking of astronomical observations.

At 1:30 p.m. a favorable breeze from the south sprang up, and by 2 o'clock was raging a gale, blowing over the tent where we were eating our midday meal, filling the coffee and eatables with sand and gravel, and causing a general scampering and chasing after the lighter articles of our equipment, which took flight in the furious wind. Most exasperating of all, it quickly determined us to break camp, and in less than half an hour we had all of our effects stored on the vessel, and were pulling off the beach, when just as our sail was spread the wind died down to a zephyr hardly sufficient to keep away the mosquitoes. At 7 o'clock the lake was as quiet as can be imagined, and after remaining almost motionless for another hour we pulled into the steep bank, made our beds on the slanting declivity at a place where it was impossible to pitch a tent, and went to sleep only to be awakened at night by showers of rain falling upon our upturned faces. We congratulated ourselves that we were in a place where the drainage was good.[61]

The next day the wind blew hard all morning, "upsetting all our prognostications," and by early afternoon they were finally clear of the lake. "I doubt," Schwatka commented feelingly when they reached the outlet, "if the beseigers of a fortress ever saw its flag go down with more satisfaction than we saw the rude wall-tent sail

[59] Schwatka, *A Summer in Alaska*, p. 178.

[60] *Ibid.*, pp. 182-183.

[61] *Ibid.*, pp. 183-184.

come down forever, and left behind us the most tedious and uncertain method of navigation that an explorer was ever called upon to attempt — a clumsy raft on a motionless lake, at the sport of variable winds."[62] They found themselves travelling now through a burned-out area, with some of the fire damage obviously very old, and some "so recent that the last rain had not yet beaten the white ashes from their blackened limbs."

The party was now averaging over 40 miles a day, and on July 10, even after a late start, they drifted 59 miles, their best single day's mileage during the journey. They quickly discovered that travelling with the current had its problems as well as it obvious advantages. For one thing, it made the selection of their nightly camping spot very difficult. Good locations "were not to be had in every stretch of the river, and, worse than all, they had to be selected a long way ahead in order to be able to make them, with our slow means of navigation, from the middle of the broad river where we usually were."[63] There was more chance too of running aground on a sand bar or gravel bar. If they were able to pry their craft free, the men escaped with nothing worse than a wetting: if not, there was the hard work of unloading supplies and wading ashore with them if the channel was not too deep, or of ferrying them in one of the Stick Indians' cottonwood canoes if the water was beyond their depth. They ran aground "fully a score of times," and Schwatka recorded that their "longest detention" was three hours and 50 minutes. They soon found also that it was desirable, wherever possible, to avoid slack water or eddies; these required a considerable effort with the oars to escape.

X

THE EXPLORERS WERE NOW PASSING A NUMBER OF TRIBUTARIES flowing in from the east that were already known to the miners, and on which some prospecting had been done. Schwatka renamed them all, but most of these names, like Perrier Pass, never came into general use. The Hotalinqu or Tes-Lin-Too of the miners he attempted to call the Newberry River; the Little Salmon he called

[62] *Ibid.*, p. 185, as is the quoted reference to the fire damage.
[63] *Ibid.*, p. 141.

153

the Daly; and the Big Salmon he called the D'Abbadie — a name that has survived on present-day maps as that of a small tributary of the North Big Salmon River. Only the name he gave to a tributary coming in from the west is still in use: he called it the Nordenskiold River, after Baron Adolph Nordenskiold, a Swedish Arctic explorer,[64] and described it, surprisingly and inaccurately, as "the peer" of the other three streams he had just named. A "conspicuous bald butte" near the mouth of the Nordenskiold he named Tantalus Butte, commenting that so tortuous was the course of the main river here, that this landmark "could be seen directly in front of our raft no less than seven times, on as many different stretches of the river. I was glad enough to see it disappear from sight."[65]

They passed the mouth of the Nordenskiold River on the afternoon of July 11, and were told by the Indians that ahead lay a dangerous reach of white water, through which the natives sometimes travelled in their own small rafts.

We started late on the morning of the 12th, and at 10 o'clock stopped our raft on the eastern bank in order to go ahead and inspect the rapids which we were about to shoot. . . . These rapids were very picturesque, as they rushed between fantastically formed trap rocks and high towers. . . . We essayed the extreme right-hand (eastern) passage, although it was quite narrow and its boiling current was covered with waves running two and three feet high, but being the straightest was the best for our long craft. . . . This extreme right-hand channel could, I believe, be ascended by a light-draft steamer provided with a steam windlass, a sharp bend in the river bank just before it is entered giving a short and secure hold for a cable rope;[66] and if I am not too sanguine in my conjectures, the cascades below the Grand Cañon mark the head of navigation on the Yukon River. . . . I named the picturesque little rapid after Dr. Henry Rink of Christiana [Copenhagen], a well-known authority on Greenland.[67]

Just below this rapid they sighted a moose, one of only two that they saw on the entire journey.

[64] Adolph Erik Nordenskiold, 1832-1901, led several expeditions to Spitsbergen and Greenland. His most notable achievement was the first successful navigation of the Northeast Passage across the top of Europe and Asia in 1878-79.

[65] Schwatka, *A Summer in Alaska*, p. 199.

[66] When steamer operations began on the upper Yukon between Whitehorse and Dawson City, the passage of these rapids on the upstream journey was assisted by a system of winching such as Schwatka envisioned, which was used until the service was discontinued in 1954.

[67] Schwatka, *A Summer in Alaska*, pp. 192-195.

That same evening — the 12th, we encamped near the first Indian village we met on the river, and even this was deserted. It is called by them Kit-ah-gon (meaning the place between high hills), and consists of one log house about eighteen by thirty feet, and a score of the brush houses usual in this country; that is, three main poles, one much longer than the rest, and serving as a ridge pole on which to pile evergreen brush to complete the house. This brush is sometimes replaced by the most thoroughly ventilated reindeer or moose skin, and in rare cases by an old piece of canvas. . . . In the spring Kit-ah-gon is deserted by its Indian inmates, who then ascend the river with loads so light that they may be carried on the back. By the time winter approaches they have worked so far away, accumulating the scanty stores of salmon, moose, black bear, and caribou on which they are to subsist, that they build a light raft from the driftwood strewn along the banks of the river, and float toward home. These rafts are almost their sole means of navigation from the Grand Cañon to Old Fort Selkirk, and the triangular brush houses almost their only abodes; and all this in a country teeming with wood fit for log houses, and affording plenty of birch bark from which can be made the finest of canoes.[68]

Much more impressive than the village was the setting, a "beautiful wide valley" which Schwatka named after "Graf Von Wilczek of Vienna." The river below the village was full of islands, often making it impossible to see both banks at the same time. These he called the Ingersoll Islands after one of his superior officers — a Colonel Ingersoll stationed in Washington, D.C.

Ever since leaving Lake Leberge, the travellers had begun to notice in the cut banks along the river, "a most conspicuous white stripe some two to three inches in width. After our attention had been attracted to this phenomenon for two or three days, we proceeded to investigate it. . . . A close inspection showed it to be volcanic ash, sufficiently consolidated to have the consistency of stiff earth, but nevertheless so friable that it could be reduced to powder by the thumb and fingers. It possibly represents the result of some exceptionally violent eruption in ancient times from one or more of the many volcanic cones, now probably extinct, with which the whole southern coast of Alaska is studded."[69] These ash deposits continued to be observed almost to the mouth of the Pelly River.

[68] *Ibid.*, pp. 199-200. This village was in the vicinity of the present settlement of Minto. In at least one of his confident statements regarding this place Schwatka was incorrect: there is very little birch in the Yukon valley above Fort Selkirk.

[69] *Ibid.*, p. 196.

At three o'clock that afternoon they reached the site of Campbell's Fort Selkirk, to find two chimneys still standing, and some blackened timbers. "Here," Schwatka commented, "we were on land familiar to the footsteps of white men who had made maps and charts, that rough and rude though they were, were still entitled to respect, and accordingly at this point I considered that my explorations had ceased, though my surveys continued to the mouth of the river."[70]

They remained three days at the fort, taking astronomical observations and investigating the river confluence.

I was very anxious [wrote Schwatka] to determine beyond all reasonable doubt the relative sizes of the two rivers whose waters unite just above old Fort Selkirk, as upon this determination rested the important question whether the Pelly or the Lewis [sic] River of the old Hudson Bay traders, who had roughly explored the former, ought to be called the Yukon proper; and in order to settle this point I was fully prepared and determined to make exact measurements, soundings, rate of current and any other data that might be necessary. This information, however, was unnecessary except in a rough form, as the preponderance of the old Lewis River was too evident to the most casual inspection to require any exactness to confirm it. The ratio of their respective width is about five to three, with about the ratio of five to four in depth . . . [with] the Lewis River being superior in both, and for this reason I abandoned the latter name, and it appears on the map as the Yukon to Crater Lake at the head.[71]

The party left Fort Selkirk July 15, and shortly came to the first inhabited Indian village that they encountered on the river, a settlement of brush huts belonging to the "Ayan (or Iyan) tribe." Their arrival was expected, and some two hundred "wild savages" waited on the beach to receive the white men. When the raft stopped, the natives entertained the visitors with dancing and singing, "their long, black hair floating wildly to and fro, and serving the practical purpose of keeping off the gnats and mosquitoes."[72] Schwatka noted that these Indians possessed graceful birch bark canoes in contrast to the clumsy cottonwood dugouts used on the upper river; that they had more elaborate grave houses than any he had yet encountered; and that they had "quite a sprinkling of old flint-lock

[70] *Ibid.*, p. 204.

[71] *Ibid.*, pp. 207-208.

[72] *Ibid.*, p. 225. Other quoted references to the Ayans in this paragraph are from p. 231 and p. 234.

Hudson's Bay Company muskets among them." He added dryly that "Many of the Ayans were persistent beggars, and next morning, the 16th of July, we got an early start before many of them were about, for as a tribe they did not seem to be very early risers."

They were now drifting through more mountainous country. "The river was still full of islands," Schwatka wrote, "many of which are covered with tall spruce, and look very picturesque in the almost cañon-like river bottom, the steep mountain sides being nearly devoid of heavy forests."[73] Some 30 miles below the fort, "a small but conspicuous mountain stream came in from the south, which I named for Professor Selwyn[74] of Ottawa, Canada." The travellers were soaked by "recurring and disagreeable thunder-showers," and found that morning fog-banks "were very common on this part of the river." So far on their journey they had seen very little game, but on this stretch they sighted a bear and "three white mountain goats."

Early in the afternoon of July 17, they came to the mouth of the White River, flowing into the Yukon from the southwest.

This stream resembles a river of liquid mud of an almost white hue, from which characteristic it is said to have derived its name from the old Hudson Bay traders. . . . The Indians say that the White River rises in glacier-bearing lands, and that it is very swift, and full of rapids along its whole course. So swift is it at its mouth, that as it pours its muddy waters into the rapid Yukon it carries them nearly across that clear blue stream; the waters of the two rivers mingling almost at once. . . . From the mouth of the White to Bering Sea, nearly 1,500 miles, the Yukon is so muddy as to be noticeable even when its water is taken up in the palm of the hand; and all fishing with hook and line ceases.[75]

Three hours later they were opposite the Stewart River, though they nearly missed the mouth as it was screened by islands. They camped that night on a gravel bar in the open air.

Their camp on July 18 was near a "noticeable but small stream coming in from the east" — McQuesten's Trundeck — which

[73] *Ibid.*, p. 235. Other references to this section of the river are from pp. 234-235.

[74] Professor Selwyn was Alfred R. C. Selwyn, the second director of the Geological Survey of Canada, who succeeded Sir William Logan in this office in 1869, and retired in 1895. He was the only Canadian recognized by Schwatka in his rash of name-bestowing on Canadian soil.

[75] Schwatka, *A Summer in Alaska*, pp. 240-241.

Schwatka claimed the traders called Deer Creek, because of the great herds of caribou that frequented it during the migratory period. As with some of his other suggested names, established usage was too well entrenched for his proposed change to endure, and today Reindeer Creek survives as a small tributary several miles upstream. Schwatka did comment on a prominent landmark at the rivermouth — a vivid scar resembling "a gigantic moose-skin stretched out to dry"[76] that had been scooped out by an old landslide on the face of a steep hill which the Indians called "Moose-skin Mountain." The travellers had no way of knowing that they were passing close to the Klondike gold fields, and that the scarred hillside would one day mark the end of the trail for thousands of stampeders from every corner of the world.

A few minutes before one o'clock [on July 19] we passed the abandoned trading station on the right bank of the river, which we surmised from certain maps and from subsequent information to be the one named Fort Reliance. It was a most dilapidated-looking frontier pile of shanties, consisting of one main house, probably the store, above ground, and three or four cellar-like houses, the ruined roofs of which were the only vestiges remaining above ground. The Indians said that Mr. McQuestion [sic], the trader, had left on account of severe sickness, but his own story, when we met him afterward on the lower river, was that he was sick of the Indians, the main tribe of which were peaceful enough, but contained several ugly tempered communistic medicine-men who had threatened his life in order to get rid of his competition in the drug business, which resulted greatly to their financial detriment.[77]

There were several Indian villages and camps on this section of the river. The weather was deteriorating, "alternating rain showers and drifting fog," which prevented the taking of astronomical observations to confirm the raft's position in relation to the "British boundary," that Homan's dead reckoning indicated they were approaching. Ever since passing the mouth of the Stewart, the travellers had in fact found that it was "absolutely impossible to identify any of the other streams from the descriptions and maps now in existence, even when aided by the imperfect information derived from the local tribes."[78] A "good sized" tributary coming in from

[76] *Ibid.*, p. 245.

[77] *Ibid.*, pp. 245-246.

[78] *Ibid.*, p. 249.

158

the west Schwatka named the Cone-Hill River, from a prominent conical hill in the centre of its broad valley. This was the Fortymile River, on which miners even then were prospecting, following the leads provided by Harper and McQuesten.

Not far below this stream they came to "a fairly constructed white man's cabin, which had once been used as a trading store, but was now deserted."[79] Schwatka later learned that this post was called Belle Isle, and had been abandoned after a year's occupation "as not paying." This station had been an early and short-lived experiment by an agent who attempted to use more modern and time-saving methods in dealing with the Indians, rather than the casual and leisurely techniques of the Hudson's Bay Company. It was quickly found out that the "rush method" of doing business did not suit the Indian temperament — hence the short life of the trading post. The site was later occupied by a United States military establishment, Fort Egbert, which became the settlement of Eagle.

XI

IN ALASKA, THERE WAS MORE TRAFFIC ON THE RIVER, AND THE names of the settlements and tributaries were so well established that even Schwatka made no attempt to change them. Shortly after crossing the boundary, the explorers overtook Joseph Ladue, now a trading partner of McQuesten and Harper, who promptly informed them that the raft "could not safely go much further,"[80] and tried to interest Schwatka in the use of "a fairly-made scow over twenty feet long." The scow, however, proved too small to hold all the men and their supplies and gear. Undiscouraged by his failure to do business, Ladue, who was expecting any day to meet the Alaska Commercial Company's river steamer *Yukon*, offered to accompany the raft downstream until the vessel was sighted. Schwatka also was very anxious to encounter the steamer, as his "civilized provisions" were very low, and in need of replenishment.

They caught up with the *Yukon* at Fort Yukon on July 27, and Schwatka was able to purchase sufficient supplies to last his party as far as Nuklakayet, at the mouth of the Tanana, where he was assured

[79] *Ibid.*, p. 259.
[80] *Ibid.*, p. 262, as is the other quotation in this paragraph relating to Ladue.

that he would find a better selection of goods. On board the steamer was her master, Captain Petersen, as well as McQuesten and an Eskimo crew. Petersen told Schwatka that there was a 12-ton river schooner or "barka" at Nuklakayet, which the *Yukon* on its return trip was to tow to the mouth of the river. The lieutenant was offered the use of this vessel for the remainder of his journey, Petersen assuring him that he would take the schooner in tow when he overtook it on his way to St. Michael's. He added that there were no sails except a jib, and that until he caught up with them the current of the Yukon River would still be their motive power. Schwatka was happy to accept the offer.

Schwatka had with him a copy of Raymond's map of the lower river which had been prepared by the latter in the course of his survey of 1869, and he showed it to Petersen, "who seemed astonished that so good a map was in existence."[81] Not surprisingly, the steamboat captain had not seen it before: Schwatka admitted that the War Department "does not publish and sell maps made under its direction." Petersen asked if a copy could be sent to him, and this Schwatka promised to do on his return to Washington, a promise he was unable to keep. The War Department was unbudging in its policy of not releasing its maps: a curious decision hardly justifiable even for military reasons, and one which certainly did not contribute to the development of the country. Petersen used Russian maps, "which are still the best of such as can be procured."

On July 29 the raft continued its downstream journey, the *Yukon* having already pushed off for Belle Isle, after the completion of the trading with the Fort Yukon Indians. The mouth of the Tanana was reached shortly after noon on August 6, and the landing at the Nuklakayet post was made at 6 p.m. "Mr. Harper, whom we found in charge, was the only white man present," Schwatka reported, "although Mr. McQuestion, and another trader who was down the river at the time (Mr. Mayo) make the station their headquarters."[82] Here they purchased more provisions and transferred their gear to the barka; here they laid the raft to rest, "perhaps to become kindling wood for the trader's stove." Though Schwatka had commented earlier, probably in a moment of extreme provocation, that "the raft is undoubtedly the oldest form of navigation extant, and

81 *Ibid.*, p. 279. Other quotations in this paragraph are from pp. 279-280.
82 *Ibid.*, p. 306.

undoubtedly the worst,"[83] he now took a kindlier and more sentimental view. "I had a friendliness for the uncouth vessel which had done such faithful service," he wrote, "and borne us safely through so many trials, surprising us with its good qualities. It had explored a larger portion of the great river than any more pretentious craft, and seemed to deserve a better fate."[84]

Schwatka and his men left Nuklakayet in their new vessel on August 8. On August 14 they passed Nulato, "quite an historic place along the river," and on August 22 they passed Anvik. The next night they experienced their first frost: two days later the *Yukon*, delayed by a blown cylinder head for which repairs had had to be improvised, caught up with them and took the barka in tow. On August 26 they arrived at Andreavsky on the delta, and on August 30 they ended their long journey at St. Michael's.

Severe gales were lashing the coast, and for a time there was doubt if any more south-bound ships would be calling at St. Michael's before the ice moved in. On September 8, however, the sloop *Leo* arrived, with a party aboard bound for San Francisco from an international meteorological station at Point Barrow, and room was found on her for Schwatka and his men. The *Leo* sailed on September 11, and as they worked their way south into more clement weather, the trials and discomforts of the journey faded from their memories. "The northwest winds sang a merry song through our sails," Schwatka exulted in a final, almost poetic, outburst, "as the meridians and parallels took on smaller numbers, and in a very few days ... anchored safely within the Golden Gate, our journey ended."[85]

XII

BETWEEN SCHWATKA'S JOURNEY OF 1883 AND THE NEXT EXPLORATION, that of the Yukon Expedition of 1887, the tempo of mining in the Yukon basin quickened considerably. In 1884 Cassiar Bar was discovered on the Yukon River, 27 miles below the mouth of the Teslin, and was soon yielding gold in the unprecedented amount of "as much as $30 a day to the hand." In 1885 Poplin returned once

[83] *Ibid.*, p. 149.
[84] *Ibid.*, pp. 309-310.
[85] *Ibid.*, p. 345.

again to the Stewart River, and this time he was well-rewarded. In the next two years the production from the various bars on this river was in excess of $100,000; 75 to 80 men were working there; and business became so brisk that McQuesten and Harper established a post at the mouth of the river to "accommodate" the miners. Late in 1886, however, a richer find punctured this ballon. Two men, Franklin and Madison, tried their luck on the Stewart and on the McQuesten without result, and testily dismissing these rivers with the statement that they "did not like the kind of trees that grew on the bars, and gold was never found where onions and wild leeks grew,"[86] they floated down to the Fortymile in the hopes of a better return. Here in September they made a rich strike of coarse gold, about 23 miles above the river's mouth, and as the news spread a modest stampede developed. The Cassiar Bar and the Stewart diggings were left almost deserted, even though two brothers named Day were busy recovering nearly $200 a week from one of the bars which Franklin and Madison had summarily rejected. In 1887 the yield from the Fortymile reached about $75,000, and there were nearly 300 men in the area.

While the miners unobtrusively followed their lonely trails, Schwatka was occupied in turning the spotlight of publicity on his exploits on the river. He resigned his commission in 1885, in order to devote himself to writing and lecturing, and to further exploration whenever he could find a sponsor. Several accounts of his travels were published, and he became a frequent speaker on the Chautauqua lecture circuits so popular at that time. His acclaim at home, however, was not accorded him by all of those who followed him on the river.

The most outspoken of his critics was George Dawson. That eminent geologist, in the course of his preliminary research for the Yukon Expedition, became of course familiar with Schwatka's accounts of his raft journey, and was at first impressed by this accomplishment. After travelling, however, over part of the same route as that followed by the American, any admiration that Dawson might have had for Schwatka's exploits had largely evaporated. In his own report he conceded to Schwatka "the credit of having made the first survey of the river, a survey which Mr. Ogilvie's work of 1887 proved to be a reasonably accurate one, in so far as its main

[86] Ogilvie, *Early Days*, p. 111.

162

features are concerned."[87] This, however, was almost the total extent of the complimentary remarks that he made concerning his predecessor.

To Schwatka's pretensions to be an "explorer" of the Yukon, Dawson gave short shrift. "Previous to 1883," he commented waspishly, "the river and some of its tributaries had become well-known to a number of miners and prospectors, and when Lieut. Schwatka, in the last-mentioned year, crossed the Chilkoot Pass and descended the Lewes, he merely followed in their footsteps."[88] He was not happy either with Schwatka's casual disregard of existing place names. "He has completely ignored," Dawson continued, "the names of many places already well-known to the miners, throughout the country, substituting others of his own invention, some of which even differ in the different versions of the map of his route which he has published. Strict justice might demand the exclusion of all these names on the definitive maps now published, but in view of the scientific eminence of some of the names which he has selected, it has been decided to retain as many as possible of these."

Dawson became particularly choleric when considering Schwatka's action in changing the name of the Lewes River. He conceded that it was a larger stream than the Pelly, as Schwatka asserted, but countered with the argument that "from what is now known of the Upper Pelly, that river is almost certainly the longer, its sources are furthest removed from the mouth of the Yukon and its course more directly in continuation of its main direction than is the case with the Lewes. Granting, however, that the Lewes excelled in all these particulars, it would still, I believe, be unjustifiable to alter an old established name for the sole purpose of giving to a river a single name from its mouth to its source. In any case it is incorrect to state that the Yukon (Lewes) rises in Lake Lindeman, or streams flowing into it, as is done by Schwatka, for by far the greater part of the water of the river enters by the Taku arm of Tagish Lake."[89]

For all his vehemence and considerable logic, however, this was one academic tempest that "Dr. George" was not able to settle in his favour. Though he restored the name of the Lewes River to his

[87] Dawson, *Report on an Exploration*, p. 142.

[88] *Ibid.*, pp. 141-142. The other quotation in this paragraph relating to place names is from p. 142.

[89] *Ibid.*, p. 12.

163

"definitive" maps, it was Schwatka's nomenclature that gradually came into popular use. In the early 1950's, the Board of Geographical Names in Ottawa officially recognized this fact, and discontinued the use of the name Lewes. Today, in spite of Dawson's strong feelings on the subject, the one name Yukon River is used to designate the whole of the great watercourse that flows from Marsh Lake to the sea.

Some of the criticism of Schwatka's exploration arose undoubtedly because of his own carping attitude towards his predecessors. He was, in Dawson's words, "not sparing in his condemnation" of the earlier mapmakers on the Yukon — he was, in fact, openly contemptuous of the work of most of them. Even Captain Raymond, whose map he generally praised, did not escape a printed castigation for overlooking one island on a particular stretch of the river. Yet his own work was not so free of inaccuracies that he could afford to adopt this lofty view. Dawson pointed out many of Schwatka's individual errors in the course of his own report: they were usually the result of having to make hasty judgments of country that was viewed only from the deck of the raft in midstream. Schwatka himself admitted that this expedition was a race against time, as it was essential, if they were to avoid wintering in the Yukon, "to make the entire length of the river within the short interval between the date of our starting and the probable date of departure of the last vessel from St. Michael's."[90] As a result of this tight schedule, "but little time was left for rambles through the country." Unfortunately, as a result of this haste some very slipshod geographical conclusions were pontificated by the explorer with a self-assurance that often proved unfounded.

Yet, in spite of the controversy and criticism, Schwatka's journey was a noteworthy achievement. One unique distinction of his passage is indisputable — he planted on the maps of the Yukon "the longest list of geographical names ever bestowed by a U.S. citizen in Canada."[91] The naming after him in the early 1960's of an artificial lake created by the construction of a power dam at Whitehorse is little enough recognition of the accomplishments of this arrogant but determined and unconventional man.

[90] Schwatka, *A Summer in Alaska*, p. 124, as is the other quotation in this paragraph.

[91] MacBride, "Schwatka's Northern Expeditions," *Whitehorse Star*.

CHAPTER SIX

Ottawa in the Northwest
The Yukon Expedition

Map Numbers 2 and 3, following page 58

I

IN 1887, THE PREDICTION WAS MADE THAT AN IMPORTANT DISCOVERY of gold in the Yukon basin was almost inevitable, and might occur at any time. The predictor was not a wild-eyed, ragged visionary with a gold pan, but one of the country's most eminent and respected geologists — George Mercer Dawson, the Assistant Director of the Geological Survey of Canada. His prophecy was no soaring flight of fancy, but a sober assessment based on personal observations, made during a season in the territory.

Almost all the large streams which have been prospected in the Yukon basin [he wrote] have been found to yield placer gold in greater or less quantity and the aggregate length of the rivers thus already proved to afford gold is very great, but little has been done toward the examination of their innumerable smaller feeders. Similar river-bar mining on the Stikine and Liard rivers preceded the discovery of the smaller creeks in which the richer deposits of "heavy" gold were obtained, and a few miles each of Dease, Thibert and McDame Creeks produced the greater portion of the $2,000,000 worth of gold credited to Cassiar in 1874 and 1875. Discoveries similar to these may be expected to occur at any time in the Yukon district, the generally auriferous area of which already proved is very much greater than that of Cassiar.[1]

Nine years later, on a small "feeder" of the Klondike, a strike just as Dawson described was finally made.

Indirectly, it was the expansion of Canada following Confedera-

---

[1] Dawson, *Report on an Exploration*, p. 23.

tion that brought Dawson to the Yukon. On July 1, 1867, when Nova Scotia, New Brunswick and the Province of Canada united under the terms of the British North America Act "to form and be one Dominion under the name of Canada," the process of building a nation on a continental scale had scarcely begun. Between the British crown colonies on the Pacific and the new union in the east, the Hudson's Bay Company still exercised its proprietary rights over the vast territory of Rupert's Land, which lay astride the lines of communication between one coast and the other. One of the first acts of the young government in Ottawa, as a step towards the realization of the vision of Confederation, was to start negotiations for the purchase of the Company's holdings, and the terms for cession — a payment of £300,000 by Canada and the retention by the Hudson's Bay Company of one-twentieth of the arable land in the ceded territory, as well as certain blocks of land around its posts — were agreed upon at a series of meetings held in London in 1868. The physical takeover, however, was delayed by the unexpected resistance of the Métis in the Red River colony under their fiery leader, Louis Riel, and it was not until July 15, 1870, that a settlement was finally reached. Manitoba, with boundaries enclosing only a small segment of the present province, was admitted to Confederation, and the remainder of the Hudson's Bay Company's holdings were acquired by Canada.

The government in Ottawa was not completely insensitive to its responsibilities in the unorganized territories. On the prairies, the influx of settlers necessitated land surveys on a massive scale, which the Dominion Lands Branch was organized to undertake in 1871. In the more remote areas the Geological Survey moved quickly to extend the exploratory traverses that its officers had begun in the Province of Canada: soon its reconnaissance parties were seen on the Fraser River and its tributaries, on the Peace and the Parsnip and in the Cariboo, in the valley of the Assiniboine and the Qu'Appelle, on the shores of Lake Athabasca, and on the islands of Queen Charlotte Sound. The inventory of the new lands was under way.

It was inevitable that in time the Yukon district should come under this scrutiny. The effects of the increased mining activity in that distant region were eventually felt in Ottawa, and already, in 1878, following the Cassiar finds, Joseph Hunter, a railway surveyor, had been sent to establish the location of the British Columbia-Alaska boundary on the Stikine River. After the opening of the

Chilkoot Pass to travellers in 1880, officials of the Department of the Interior[2] began to realize that some form of government control would eventually be necessary in the Canadian Yukon, and that as a prelude to any exercise of sovereignty, a scientific investigation of the area, and more detailed and accurate mapping, were obviously desirable. Thomas White, who became the Minister of the Interior in 1885, encouraged the organization of this project, and in 1887 three of the country's most highly-qualified civil servants led a well-equipped government party, known as the Yukon Expedition, into the northwest.

Dawson was the Expedition's senior officer, though only 35 years of age: a dwarf of a man with a humped back — the result of a childhood illness — he nonetheless left giant footsteps on the maps of his native land. Born in Pictou, Nova Scotia, on August 1, 1849, he was the eldest son of Sir John William Dawson, a brilliant educator, geologist, and naturalist, who was at that time provincial Superintendent of Education, and who in 1853 became the first principal of McGill University. Young Dawson, who inherited his father's academic interests, was educated by private tutors and later at Montreal High School and at McGill. He did not take his degree there, however, but continued his studies in Edinburgh and London, specializing in geology, and also receiving instruction in natural history, ethnology, and archeology. He graduated in 1872 as an associate of the Royal School of Mines, England, with the highest honours in his class. His first field work on his return to Canada was for the government of Nova Scotia, but in 1873 he was appointed geologist and botanist to the British North America Boundary Commission. Two years later he joined the Geological Survey of Canada as Chief Geologist, and became Assistant Director in 1883. He had already carried out investigations and research in the Queen Charlotte Islands, the Assiniboine country, on the Skeena and the Peace, and in the Alberta coal fields, when the opportunity to take charge of the Yukon Expedition was offered to him.

Richard George McConnell, Dawson's principal assistant, was also an officer of the Geological Survey. He was born on March 25, 1857, in Chatham, Quebec, and graduated with a Bachelor of Arts degree from McGill University in 1879, with first class honours in the

---

[2] The Department of the Interior was organized in 1873, with Sir John A. Macdonald as its first Minister. The work of the Dominion Lands Branch was absorbed by the new department's Survey Branch.

natural sciences. He joined the government service the following year. His early field investigations were undertaken in Quebec, but in 1881 he was sent to Alberta, on the first of a series of geological studies that he was to undertake in the west and northwest over the next 30 years. The appointment to the Expedition was the first of these assignments to take him into the Yukon basin, an area to which he would later return many times, and to which he would make many significant contributions.

William Ogilvie, D.L.S., the other member of the government triumvirate, was as distinguished in his chosen discipline of surveying as were his colleagues in the field of geology. He was born in Ottawa, Ontario, on April 7, 1846, and was educated there, being admitted to the practice of a Dominion Land Surveyor in 1869. He entered the civil service, and in 1872 married Mary Ann Sparks, a member of a pioneer Ottawa family. In 1875 he was sent west to assist in the subdivision of the prairie farmlands. He rose rapidly in the ranks of his profession: in 1880 he was one of three surveyors who were selected to introduce a block-outline system that speeded up the marking of townships, and in 1881 he started the survey of the 4th meridian northerly from its intersection with the 49th parallel. This line was later accepted without adjustment as part of the Saskatchewan-Alberta boundary.

By 1883 the work-load occasioned by the prairie land surveys was slackening. The Survey Branch was renamed the Technical Branch, and an opportunity was given to many of the men who had worked for it on the prairies to turn their hands to the challenge of exploratory surveys. Ogilvie was one of those who accepted the new task with enthusiasm: in 1883 he carried out a micrometer survey[3] of the Peace River as far as Dunvegan, and of the Athabasca from Athabasca Landing to its mouth. When the makeup of the proposed Expedition to the far northwest was being considered he was the logical man to carry out the mapping that was involved.

The purpose of the Yukon Expedition was defined by Dawson in the introduction to his report on the project as being that of "gaining information on the vast and hitherto almost unknown tract of

---

[3] The micrometer was an instrument for the measurement of approximate distances. Its operation involved the determining of the small angle subtended by fixed marks placed a known distance apart at the position previously occupied. It was the forerunner of the less cumbersome stadia system of measuring distances.

country which forms the extreme north-westerly portion of the North-west Territory ... referred to as the Yukon district, this name being rendered appropriate from the fact that the greater part of its area lies within the drainage-basin of the river of that name."[4] To carry out this objective, Dawson planned a three-pronged approach.

In consequence [he wrote] of information gained from persons having some knowledge of the region to be traversed, it was decided that Mr. Ogilvie should carry out an instrumentally measured traverse of the route from the head of Lynn Canal to the Lewes and along the line of the river to the 141st meridian, where he was to make arrangements for wintering, and in the spring and summer of 1888 continue his surveys north-eastward to the Mackenzie River and up that river to connect with previously surveyed lines on Athabasca Lake.

Having ascertained that there was a fair probability of his being able to carry a line of survey and exploration from the Cassiar district in northern British Columbia, by way of the Upper Liard and across the height of land to the Yukon basin, the writer decided on attempting that route, which, though known to be difficult, appeared to offer, in conjunction with Mr. Ogilvie's work, the best opportunity of adding to our knowledge of the country as a whole. Mr. McConnell was intrusted, in the first instance, with the instrumental measurement of the Stikine River, from the point to which surveys had previously been carried, as far as the head of navigation, and subsequently, with the exploration of the lower portion of the Liard River; the original intention being that he should return after reaching the Mackenzie, in the autumn of 1887, by the ordinary trade route of that river. Before we finally separated from Mr. McConnell, at the confluence of the Dease and the Liard, however, so many unexpected delays had occurred that it was considered advisable to instruct Mr. McConnell to endeavour to make arrangements for passing the winter of 1887-88 on the Mackenzie, and subsequently to descend the Mackenzie, cross the northern extremity of the Rocky Mountains to the Porcupine River, and by following that river and ascending the Lewes, to return to the Pacific coast at Lynn Canal. This arrangement further provided for the examination of a great additional region of which the geological structure was altogether unknown.[5]

The careful planning paid dividends. When the exploration was completed there was available a vast fund of new knowledge concerning the area, including maps more detailed and more accurate

[4] Dawson, *Report on an Exploration*, p. 1.

[5] *Ibid.*, pp. 2-3.

169

than any that had been available before. In this connection, Dawson reported with justifiable pride that

> ... Mr. Ogilvie's instrumentally measured line from the head of Lynn Canal to the intersection of the Pelly or Yukon[6] by the 141st Meridian, will form a sufficiently accurate base for further surveys. In addition to this we now have an instrumental survey of the Stikine from its mouth to the head of navigation (Telegraph Creek), which is connected to Dease Lake by a carefully paced traverse. This is continued by a detailed running or track-survey following the lines of the Dease, Upper Liard, and Pelly Rivers, and connecting with Mr. Ogilvie's line at the mouth of the Lewes. . . .
> Along the routes thus travelled numerous points have been fixed in latitude by sextant observations, and a sufficient number of chronometer longitudes have been obtained by which to lay the whole down within small limits of error. Special attention was paid to the sketching and fixing of mountain topography in sight from the line of travel, and the approximate altitudes of the more prominent peaks were ascertained.[7]

The conscientious and accurate work of the chart makers along the coasts was now being extended inland.

II

THE PARTY LEFT OTTAWA ON APRIL 22, 1887, AND JOURNEYED TO Victoria on the Canadian Pacific Railway, then in its second year of operation. They gained little, however, by the use of this faster mode of travel, as they did not reach Wrangell, at the mouth of the Stikine River, until May 18, because of what Dawson, with considerable restraint, referred to as "irregularities in the sailing dates of the Alaskan mail steamers." At Wrangell, Dawson and McConnell and their men thankfully disembarked, while Ogilvie continued on to Dyea and the Chilkoot Pass.

---

6 Campbell's use of the Pelly for the river below the confluence with the Lewes at Fort Selkirk had set a confusing precedent which the mapmakers of Dawson's time had not yet resolved. Whymper on a map published in his book called the river "Pelly" as far as the mouth of the Porcupine, and "Yukon or Kwichpak" below that point; Dall referred to the whole river below the Lewes as the "Yukon"; while Raymond used Whymper's nomenclature. McConnell in his report of his Yukon expedition compromised by referring to the "Pelly-Yukon," and this name has generally been used on the maps in this book.

7 Dawson, *Report on an Exploration*, pp. 6-7.

Their frustrations were not yet over. McConnell obtained Indians and canoes, and began his survey of the Stikine, while Dawson with his crew started upstream ahead of them, travelling in the first steamer of the season as far as Telegraph Creek, at the head of navigation on the river, and the location of the intended crossing of the Overland Telegraph line. A pack trail from this point to Dease Lake had recently been constructed by the provincial government, and Dawson had expected to be able to hire horses to transport his supplies over it. "Here again a delay of several days occurred," he reported resignedly, "as the animals had not yet been brought in from the range or shod for the season's work at the date of our arrival."[8] The head of Dease Lake was not reached until June 5, only to find that the greater part of it was still covered with ice. It was not until June 9 that the party was able to reach the location on the shore near Laketon where two men, sent on ahead with an Indian packer, were whip-sawing lumber for boats. In seven days three boats were constructed, and were then taken into Laketon to pick up provisions, a strong wind providentially breaking up the remainder of the ice on the day the boats were finished, the latest breakup recorded up to that time. Here McConnell caught up with them, bringing five Indians to assist Dawson in his upstream journey to Frances Lake and across the portage to the Pelly. Dawson already had three other men with him: J. McEvoy, B.AP.SC., a young geologist whom he had brought from Ottawa, and two labourers, L. Lewis and D. Johnson, hired in Victoria.

The combined parties started down the Dease River on the morning of June 19 and reached the "Lower Post"[9] on the Liard River at the mouth of the Dease on June 23, in a downpour of rain. This post

... the farthest outwork of "civilization" or trade in this direction, is situated at the edge of a terrace forty feet in height on the left bank of the Liard, about half a mile above the mouth of the Dease. It is of a very unpretentious character, consisting of a few low log buildings, in

[8] *Ibid.*, p. 4.

[9] This post was founded in 1872 by a private trader, Robert Sylvester, and was purchased by the Hudson's Bay Company in 1876. Sylvester called his establishment Liard Post, a name which was confused with Fort Liard, farther down the river. "Lower Post" (in relation to the Depot and Fort Liard) came into popular use to distinguish the two locations, but the change of name did not become official until 1940! Dawson always conscientiously used quotation marks when referring to this post, as when he was in the country the name was still unofficial.

the vicinity of which the woods have been entirely destroyed by fire.

The soil is poor near the post and the climate generally unfavourable, but potatoes and turnips have been grown here in small patches.

The Liard River is here said to open, as a rule, from the 1st to the 5th of May, though in 1887 this did not occur until the 18th of that month. In the autumn of 1886 it was frozen over on November 21st.

Mr. Egnell, in sole charge, received us on our arrival here with all distinction possible, displaying his Union Jack and firing a salute from his fowling piece. Before leaving we were indebted to him for many other courtesies, all of which are here gratefully acknowledged.[10]

Dawson had to remain at the post until June 25 before the weather was sufficiently clear for observations, "which were here necessary." The two parties, each reinforced by two more Indians hired locally, then parted company, McConnell starting downstream on the Liard, and Dawson, heading for Frances River and Frances Lake and Campbell's portage to the Pelly. "A straight line drawn from the mouth of the Dease to the lower end of Frances Lake," he wrote, "is ninety-four miles in length, but the distance between these points, following the flexures of the river, is one hundred and thirty-five miles. Almost every foot of this distance has to be made by poling or tracking against the rapid stream, and as our boats were heavily laden and not as well suited in build as they might have been for the work, the ascent to Frances Lake occupied twelve days, or an average distance of about eleven miles a day only."[11]

About six miles above the mouth of the Dease, they entered the Lower Canyon of the Liard, where they found it necessary to lighten the loads in their boats, and make four short portages, in order to get through. "The latitude observed at noon near the middle of the cañon was 60° 01′ 06″. Finding that we were so near the northern boundary of British Columbia (60°), we made a small cairn of stones on a prominent rocky point, in the centre of which a post was erected, on which the latitude was marked. The 60th parallel may be said to coincide almost exactly with the lower end of the cañon."[12]

In spite of the difficulty of travel against the current, and the need for frequent reconnaissance because of the maze of islands and the numerous, half-submerged gravel bars, Dawson overlooked little. He

[10] Dawson, *Report on an Exploration*, p. 89. There is still an Egnell Lake in the vicinity of Lower Post.

[11] *Ibid.*, p. 96.

[12] *Ibid.*, p. 96.

examined some coal seams in the river bank; he identified a river flowing from the southwest as the Rancheria; and he mentioned that in its vicinity, on the opposite side of the Liard, was a lake "reputed to be well stocked with fish" — probably a reference to Watson Lake, which was named Fish Lake on some early maps. "About seven miles below the mouth of the Frances," he noted "is an old Indian camping place, which is said to be frequented at certain seasons by the Tahl-Tan Indians [from the Stikine] for purposes of trade. It is reached by these people by some overland route which crosses the Cassiar Mountains to the north of the Dease River."[13] He was told that 50 miles above the mouth of the Frances gold had been found in 1875 on a tributary of the Liard that he identified as "Sayyea Creek," but the activity had been of brief duration. Four miners had died of scurvy in this area during the winter of 1874-75: Scurvy Creek on present-day topographic maps is a mute reminder of this tragedy.

The Frances River, like the Liard, was found to be "at a medium stage" — marks along the bank indicated that it had dropped about six feet since high water. On this river, Dawson encountered three "impediments to navigation," which he named Middle Canyon, False Canyon, and Upper Canyon; short portages were necessary to get through two of them. Middle Canyon was the most impressive. Dawson described it as being "about three miles in length, the river being hemmed in by broken, rocky cliffs of 200 to 300 feet in height for the greater part of this distance. . . . The total fall in the cañon is estimated at about thirty feet."[14]

Near the end of the reach above this canyon, Dawson noted that "two considerable streams enter on the west side, and on one or the other of these, at no great distance from the river, Simpson Lake of McLeod and Campbell is situated."[15] As the two Indians from Lower Post had already deserted, Dawson added that he was unable to obtain any information regarding this lake, except that it was "reported to be a good one for fish." One of the natives, before he left, had made on a sheet of canvas used as a boat cover an elaborate sketch map of the drainage pattern of the area, and with its aid it was possible to locate with fair certainty a stream supplied by

[13] *Ibid.*, pp. 97-98.
[14] *Ibid.*, p. 101.
[15] *Ibid.*, p. 102.

three or four small lakes which the Indians called the Too-Tshi-Too-A (the Tuchitua of present-day maps), which flows into the Frances just above the Upper Canyon. It was also possible to identify a fair-sized tributary on the east bank of the river, not far below the Upper Canyon, that "is supposed to be the Aga-Zi-Za of the Indians, and, if so, is represented as rising in a chain of small lakes. . . . The valley occupied by these lakes is a travelled route employed by the Indians."[16] On modern topographic maps this stream and the small lakes are nameless, but today the valley is followed by a road, built in 1961, that gives access to Canada Tungsten Mining Corporation's property at Tungsten, N.W.T.

Frances Lake was reached on July 8, and Dawson when he saw it promptly echoed Campbell's enthusiasm for the area, stating that "few lakes which I have seen surpass Frances Lake in natural beauty."

[It] closely resembles a large number of lakes in the mountainous regions of British Columbia, and has the long narrow parallel-sided outline characteristic of lakes which occupy old valley-excavations, the drainage of which has become interrupted in various ways. In this case, as in a number of others, there can be little doubt that the lake is held in by morainic accumulations. . . .[17]

The water of Frances Lake is clear and of a pale, brownish tint, and the lake is evidently very deep in its upper portions, though rather shallow where encumbered by the morainic accumulations already alluded to, and it does not appear to be subject to very great fluctuations. . . . Lake-trout, white-fish, pike, and suckers were found in the lake in considerable abundance.

The site of the old Hudson's Bay post is just above the narrow entrance to the east arm, on the edge of the bank, facing westward. Though Mr. Campbell had given me an accurate description of its position, it was so completely overgrown with bushes and small trees, that it was discovered with difficulty. The outline of the old stockade, with bastions at the corners, is still visible, though all traces of the structure itself has disappeared. This post has been abandoned since 1851. . . .

Taken as a whole, the growth of the forest and appearance of the country is remarkably pleasing, considering the high and northern position of the lake. The only characteristic difference of the woods here, as compared with those of the interior of British Columbia about the 54th parallel, is the great abundance and depth of the soft, mossy and lichenous floor which is everywhere found in them. The trees are also

[16] *Ibid.*, pp. 103-104.
[17] *Ibid.*, pp. 106-107.

often well bearded with moss, affording evidence of a continuously moist atmosphere."[18]

The highest peak in the range east of the east arm Dawson named Mt. Logan, for the late Sir W. E. Logan, the first Director of the Geological Survey. This name was later dropped in this location, to prevent confusion with a similarly named mountain in the St. Elias range.

There was more to do, however, than admire the scenery, though Dawson found time to gaze longingly north, up the valleys of the rivers that flowed into the upper ends of the two arms of the lake, where the country appeared "rugged and high," and the urge to explore further was almost irresistible. Instead, the travellers busied themselves with preparations for the portage to the Pelly.

It became our first object to endeavour to find the trail used many years previously by the Hudson's Bay Company, of which a general description had been furnished by Mr. Campbell. This necessitated a careful examination of the west shore of the west arm to its head, which enabled us to identify, with tolerable certainty, the stream which Campbell had named the Finlayson. It was supposed that the Indians might have employed the same route in the periodical journeys which they were known to make from the Pelly down the Frances to the little trading post at the mouth of the Dease; but though the remains of an old log *cache* of the Hudson's Bay Company were eventually found, together with the nails and iron work of a large boat which had evidently been burned on the beach near it, no sign of a trail could be discovered. It thus appeared very doubtful that we should be able to make our way across to the Pelly, with sufficient provisions and the necessary instruments for the continuation of our survey in the Yukon basin.

In order to exhaust the possibility of obtaining further assistance before making the attempt, I made a light trip in one of our boats round into the east arm ... but no Indians were found, in fact, we discovered traces of only a single camp which had been made during the same summer, most of the Indians signs being two or more years old.

All that now remained to be done was to make the best of our own resources. We, therefore, went carefully over all our stuff, separating out everything that was not absolutely essential, and making up the remainder in packs, together with as much food as could be carried."[19]

The excess gear and some provisions were cached in the bay immediately south of the mouth of the Finlayson. If the party were

[18] *Ibid.*, pp. 110-111.
[19] *Ibid.*, pp. 112-113.

able to cross the portage successfully, these supplies would be taken back to Dease Lake by the Indians, who would be paid off and sent home to the coast when the Pelly was reached. If the party was not able to find the route, and had to return, then there would be sufficient food in the cache to see them all back to Lower Post.

On July 17 and 18 they moved around to the north side of the delta, which they believed would be the best starting point. The supplies that they were taking to the Pelly they back-packed to the head of a canyon that made the three miles of the Finlayson immediately above its mouth impassable for river traffic. Here a portable canvas boat — which Dawson referred to as an Osgood — was assembled.

Into this a portion of our stuff was put, and two of our coast Indians were instructed to endeavour to track it up the shallow and winding stream, while the rest of the party found their way as best they could along the valley, with heavy packs. The walking was extremely fatiguing on account of the deep moss, alternating with brush and swamp, and as in addition the weather was very warm and the mosquitoes innumerable, our rate of progress was slow. On arriving at the forks of the stream we unfortunately took the wrong branch [McEvoy Creek] for several miles, leading to some loss of time, but we eventually reached a lake, which we recognized as Finlayson Lake, on July 24th. The canvas boat did not arrive until the evening of the next day, as great difficulty was met with in getting it up the shallow stream, which was badly blocked with fallen trees. In the meantime, observations for latitude and time were taken, and a raft was constructed on which the stuff might be floated to the head of the lake, which lay in the general direction of our route.

The lake proved to be nine miles and a-half in length, and near its head we again found the ruins of a Hudson's Bay *câche*, but no appearance of a trail. . . .

Soon after leaving the lake we fell upon small streams which evidently drained toward the west, and about noon on the 29th of July we had the satisfaction of reaching the banks of the Pelly River. From this place our five Coast Indians were sent back, with instructions to take back to Dease Lake, the articles left in the *câche* on Frances Lake, and this duty, we subsequently learned, they faithfully performed.[20]

The two geologists and two labourers were left with "nearly a month's provisions" for four, a camping outfit, survey instruments, a piece of canvas from which a canoe might be constructed — the Osgood boat had been abandoned at Finlayson Lake as too heavy to

[20] *Ibid.*, pp. 113-114.

176

transport farther — and tools and nails for building a wooden boat, if this type of craft were needed. For travel on the Pelly, with the current behind them and the possibility of "a dangerous rapid" ahead, they decided to use a canoe, and set to work to build one. Before starting downstream, they looked briefly for signs of the Hudson's Bay Company's establishment at Pelly Banks, but "saw no trace of the buildings which formerly existed, though the old site might, no doubt, have been determined by a little search, had we thought it worthwhile to devote the necessary time to it."[21]

III

THEY LAUNCHED THEIR CANOE ON THE PELLY ON AUGUST 1. AFTER the hard work of tracking and poling from the mouth of the Dease to Frances Lake, and the laborious carriage over the portage, the prospect of travelling for a time with the current to aid them must have been most welcome. The men were not entirely easy in their minds, however. Two miners at Dease Lake had given them "a most circumstantial account" of hostile Indians being on the rampage in the Yukon valley, and claimed that these Indians had retreated up the Pelly. Dawson had been unable to confirm or refute this report, though by the time the mouth of the Lewes was reached, it was realized that the story was apparently false.[22] It certainly, in Dawson's phrase, kept the party "in a state of watchfulness" for this portion of their travels.

Like Campbell, Dawson found the Pelly a pleasant stream on which to journey. In the course of his descent of it, he added a few place names to those which Campbell had bestowed, and in his detailed descriptions he recorded many details which Campbell missed, or had not the scientific training to observe. A short distance below the mouth of Campbell's Hoole River, for example, Dawson noted that "in one or two banks into which the river was cutting,

---

21 *Ibid.*, p. 118.

22 According to Diamond Jenness in his authoritative book *The Indians of Canada*, (Ottawa, The Queen's Printer, 7th ed., 1967), p. 369, "tradition states that about 1886 the original Pelly and Ross River Indians were destroyed by a band that crossed the Rocky Mountains from the vicinity of the Mackenzie — Hare Indians probably from the vicinity of Norman." It is possible, therefore, that there may have been some substance to the story that the miners told Dawson, though in 1887 he saw nothing to confirm it.

177

and where the surface was covered with a dense, mossy growth, frozen soil was observed. The depth to which it extended could not be ascertained, as it went below the water-level of the stream."[23] The presence of large areas of perennially frozen ground — now almost universally known as "permafrost" — was frequently noted by early northern explorers, but this was the first reference to this phenomenon in such a southerly latitude.[24]

Near the mouth of Ross River, Dawson commented on the existence of "a long, steep ridge, parallel to the course of the Pelly, and from 600 to 800 feet in height above it. The southern face of this ridge . . . is more than half, open grass land, and would afford excellent pasturage."[25] In this vicinity also a tributary that flowed into the Pelly from the south was named by Dawson the Lapie River, after the other member of the "2 inseparables" — Campbell had already honoured Kitza by naming another stream near by after him. The mountains plainly visible to the south, in which the Lapie and other north-flowing tributaries had their sources, Dawson called the Pelly Range.

Farther west, some 33 miles from Ross River, Dawson remarked on "a valley running to the north, which probably brings in a moderate sized stream. But this falls into a slough behind islands, and was not seen."[26] His assumption was correct: this valley is drained by a considerable watercourse, which today is known as Blind Creek. For a time in the 1960's the valley was an important temporary access route into Anvil Mining Corporation's huge lead-zinc mine in this locality, until a permanent bridge across the Pelly was completed a few miles farther downstream.

The high ridges to the north of the Pelly persisted almost to the mouth of the Glenlyon River, a tributary some 80 miles by water

---

23 Dawson, *Report of an Exploration*, p. 119.

24 The term permafrost was coined during World War II by Dr. S. W. Muller, a geologist at Stanford University. In the Pelly River valley and in the southern Yukon generally, the occurrences are patchy and sporadic — this area is part of the "discontinuous zone." Farther north, in the continuous zone, permafrost underlies the greater part of the mossy surface cover, and adds considerably to the cost and difficulties of road construction, mining, and building in this region.

25 Dawson, *Report on an Exploration*, p. 121. West Highland cattle were in fact kept at Ross River in the late 1950's and early '60's, and the grassy slopes that attracted Dawson's attention served as their summer range.

26 *Ibid.*, p. 122.

below the Ross. To the south, however, the Pelly Range terminated almost opposite Blind Creek. "Beyond the western termination of this range, for a distance of about twenty miles, no mountains were seen to the southward from the river-valley. From the fact that evidences of a more humid climate were found along the corresponding length of the river, it is highly probable that a somewhat important gap occurs in this direction, of sufficient width to admit the entrance of moisture-bearing winds."[27] This was another correct deduction: the "gap" was in fact that occupied by the Magundy-Little Salmon River system, and in a direct line along this valley, the Yukon River was less than 100 miles away. In later years this route was much used by bush pilots flying into the Pelly areas, particularly when the weather in the mountains was marginal. It is now also followed by the Campbell Highway.

Below the mouth of the Glenlyon, Dawson identified with reasonable certainty two tributaries which Campbell had named the Earn and the Tummel, after rivers in his native Perthshire. In this vicinity Dawson also named the Detour, a "peculiar flexure" of the Pelly in which it makes a sharp S-shaped bend to the north "cutting completely through [a] ridge which has previously bounded it on that side, [and] after a sinuous course of about fifteen miles to the north of the ridge, it turns again with equal abruptness to the southward, rounding the west point of the ridge, which here dies away."[28]

The river that Campbell called the MacMillan, the Pelly's largest tributary, was identified without difficulty. Near its mouth, the travellers saw several large rafts pulled up on the shore, in front of "a wide low gap opening to the north, by which the Indians evidently cross over to the valley of [the MacMillan]."[29] Close to this gap, two natives were encountered, a father and son, working their way upstream in a small dugout canoe. "They were the first human beings we had met with in the country," Dawson wrote, "since leaving the mouth of the Dease River, forty-three days previously, but as we were totally unable to communicate with each other except by signs, it was impossible to obtain any definite information from them."[30]

[27] *Ibid.*, pp. 122-123.

[28] *Ibid.*, p. 126.

[29] *Ibid.*, p. 126.

[30] *Ibid.*, p. 127.

The upper part of the MacMillan [Dawson continued] has never been explored, but its size would indicate that it may rise as far to the eastward as the Pelly, and probably, like it, in mountains representing the western ranges of the Rocky Mountains. We do not, however, know to what extent this river shares with the Stewart the drainage of the comparatively low country to the northward. I afterwards met a couple of miners (Messrs. Monroe and Langtry) who had ascended the Mac-Millan for several days in a boat, but not finding encouraging "prospects," had returned. They reported the existence of a large area of low land with good soil, and had met with no impediments to navigation as far as they had gone.[31]

About 13 miles below the MacMillan, Dawson and his men encountered the last obstruction on the river, Granite Canyon, which is today under consideration as a possible source of hydro power. "The cañon is about four miles in length," Dawson wrote of it, "with steep, rocky scarped banks, 200 to 250 feet in height. In the cañon are several little rapids, but the water is deep, and with the exception of some isolated rocks, the navigation would be quite safe for steamers, even at a low stage of water."[32] Below the canyon were many wide river terraces, with apparently fertile soil that supported a luxuriant growth of grass and poplar.

On August 11 the party reached the Lewes, and the ruins of Fort Selkirk. They had travelled, according to Dawson's calculations, 320 miles since launching their canoe at Pelly Banks, at an average rate of close to 30 miles a day, a welcome contrast to their eleven miles a day average on the Liard and the Frances. The rate of fall of the river Dawson estimated to be 4.4 feet per mile, mostly in the rapids and riffles, and he counted 218 islands.

All along the Pelly, Dawson was busy with his gold pan, with encouraging results.

Small "colours" of gold [he reported] may be found in almost any suitable locality along the river, and "heavy colours" in considerable number, were found by us as far up as the mouth of the Hoole River, in the bottom of a gravel-bed there resting on the basalt. The river has been prospected to some extent by a few miners, but no mining of importance has yet been done on it. Thomas Boswell, whom we met on the Lewes, informed me that he had found and worked for a short time, a bar which paid at the rate of $18 per diem. This was on a tributary which, from his description, is probably identified as the Ross River.

[31] *Ibid.*, p. 127.
[32] *Ibid.*, p. 130.

Two miners only, Messrs. Monroe and Langtry, were at work on [the Pelly] in 1887, and their operations were confined to the part below Granite Cañon, where they made, on a couple of bars, from $10 to $20 per diem to the hand. The headwaters of the MacMillan and Ross, and those of the Pelly itself yet remain unprospected, as well as the very numerous tributary streams of these rivers, in some of which "coarse" gold may yet be found.[33]

IV

AT FORT SELKIRK, DAWSON FOUND HIMSELF IN A QUANDARY THAT threatened for a time the successful completion of his work. Before the separation from Ogilvie the previous May, it had been arranged that the latter on his way downstream would cache sufficient supplies at Fort Selkirk for Dawson's ascent of the Lewes to Chilkoot Pass, but there was no sign at the post of either the provisions or of Ogilvie. A party of miners on their way out of the country, who reached the Lewes' mouth just as Dawson did, had not seen the survey party below Fort Selkirk. Obviously, therefore, Ogilvie was still somewhere on the Lewes, but how long he would be in reaching the rendezvous, or if he had been seriously delayed by some mishap, there was no way of knowing. Furthermore, the miners brought the news of the move of McQuesten's and Harper's post from the mouth of the Stewart to the Fortymile River, as the result of the previous year's discovery of gold there, and the stampede to the new workings. Dawson had hoped to be able to purchase supplies at this post if he was unable to contact Ogilvie, but the change in location affected this alternate plan considerably.

"From the place where we now were," he wrote unhappily, "we still had a journey of nearly 400 miles to the coast, with the swift waters of the Lewes to contend against for the greater part of the distance. If therefore it should have become necessary to go downstream 200 miles to Forty-mile Creek for provisions, so much would have been added to our up-stream journey, that it would become doubtful whether we should be able to afford time for geological work on the Lewes, and yet reach the coast before the smaller lakes near the mountains were frozen over."[34] Before a final decision was made, it would be essential first to replace the light canvas canoe,

[33] *Ibid.*, p. 133.
[34] *Ibid.*, pp. 5-6.

which was not suitable for upstream travel on the main river. Hoping that Ogilvie would appear in time to make the trip to Fortymile unnecesary, Dawson set the men to work building a more suitable boat, but two days after they began its construction, Ogilvie "very opportunely" arrived. Another forty-eight hours, and Dawson and his men would have been on their way downriver ahead of him.

As he started towards the Chilkoot Pass, Dawson was travelling in the reverse direction over the route that Schwatka had followed four years before. The army explorers had encountered no mining activity: now there was evidence of placer operations on many of the river bars. Schwatka mentioned only one encounter with miners: Dawson had several. "We were during this time," he wrote, "on the one travelled route of the country, and every few days fell in with small parties of miners, generally on their way out, up the river. A few men were still found working on bars, and six or eight passed down stream, with the purpose of wintering at or near Forty-Mile Creek."[35]

The rapid which Schwatka had named after Dr. Henry Rink, Dawson called "Rink or Five-Finger Rapid," the latter no doubt a name given to it by the miners, after the row of rocky islands that here obstruct the river like the fingers of a hand. Like Schwatka, Dawson believed that this "impediment" could be navigated by steamers, and he also felt that a second "riffle or minor rapid" below the Five Finger would not be an obstacle to river traffic. Today, Dr. Rink's name is given to this "riffle" of Dawson's, while the more imposing rapid that rushes through the rock islands is called Five Finger.

Above the rapids Dawson passed the mouths of the Nordenskiold, the Little Salmon, the Big Salmon, and the river he called the Tes-Lin-Too — "the Hootalinqu or Houtalinkwa" of the miners — as well as numerous smaller tributaries, one of which he noted was called the "Tatshun River." He described the mouths of these rivers in some detail, often taking issue with some of the statements that Schwatka had propounded concerning their characteristics. More than this, however, by querying miners that he met then or later — and Dawson seemed to have a gift for drawing out these taciturn and often suspicious men — he was able to fill in some of

[35] *Ibid.*, p. 140.

the gaps in the knowledge of the surrounding country that he himself did not have the time to explore.

From a miner named John McCormack, for example, one of a party of four who had spent part of the summer on the Big Salmon, he obtained "some particulars respecting it, together with a sketch of its course." McCormack described several tributaries, and three lakes near the river's headwaters, the "highest" of which he named Quiet Lake "of which he estimates the length at twenty-four miles. At the outlet of the lake is an Indian fishing place. The country to the south of these lakes is mountainous, granite being a common rock, and several streams run from these mountains into Quiet Lake."[36] Most river bars on the Big Salmon yielded fine gold, but not in paying quantities.

From another miner, T. Boswell, whom he met at the mouth of the Teslin-Too, Dawson learned further particulars of this river and the "great lake" from which it flowed. Boswell estimated that it was approximately 100 miles from the mouth of the river to the lake, and that the lake itself was also about 100 miles in length. He claimed that the principal river flowing into it was not found at its head, but in "an arm ten or twelve miles long, on the east side of the lake. This river, known to the Tagish Indians as Ni-Sutlin-Hi-Ni [Nisutlin River], must come from a north-easterly direction in the first instance, as it is represented as circling completely round the head of the Big Salmon River, and rising between that river and the Upper Pelly."[37] There were two "Indian salmon-fishing stations" on the Nisutlin, and from the head of what was described as the "east fork" a trail was reported to lead to the upper Liard and Lower Post. Another trail of "two long days packing" was said to lead from the upper end of Teslin Lake to the head of canoe navigation on the Taku River.

The miners on the Teslin River worked favourable-looking bars at various locations "and appear to have done fairly well."

On the Lewes River, Dawson encountered the first evidence of gold mining about six miles above the mouth of the Nordenskiold, and he reported that between the Big Salmon and the Teslin River "A number of Auriferous gravel-bars have been worked ... including

[36] *Ibid.*, p. 151.

[37] *Ibid.*, p. 154, as are other quotations in this paragraph. According to Dawson, the suffixes "Too" and "Hi-Ni" were both Tagish words for river.

183

Cassiar Bar, which so far has proved the richest on the river. Limited areas of the river-flats have also been worked over, where the alluvial cover is not too deep."[38] Dawson also reported that, at a location five and one-half miles above Rink Rapids, there was an exposure in the river bank which showed "at least three coaly beds, of which the lowest is about three feet thick. This and the other beds contain some good looking coal, of which a thickness of about a foot sometimes occurs, but the greater parts of the material is so sandy and impure as to be useless."[39] The value of these seams, Dawson added, was their importance "as indicating the existence of a coal-bearing horizon which may prove to contain thicker beds elsewhere and might become an important point in connection with the navigation of the river." Coal in commercial quantities was eventually discovered, and is still being mined, along this section of the river.

In time the explorers came to the large lake, which was "undoubtedly," according to Dawson, the one named after Mike Leberge. As Ogilvie's survey had followed the west shore, with only a few points established on the east side by triangulation, Dawson made a track-survey of the eastern shore to complete the mapping of the outline of the lake. Like Schwatka, he had trouble with the treacherous winds, "often so strong that miners have been detained in camp for many days. We lost almost the whole of one day, owing to wind, on our way up the lake."[40] Above Leberge the mouth of the Tahk-Heena River was passed, which Schwatka had already noted was part of the Chilkats' route from the coast to the interior. "[The route] is not used by the miners," wrote Dawson, "and now only to a small extent by the Indians themselves, on account of the long and difficult carriage from the sea to its head, but the lake at the head of the river once reached, the voyage down stream is reported to be easier than that by the main river, the rapids being less serious."[41] On Krause's map of the area, Dawson added, this lake was named "West Kussoā Lake,"[42] and the river flowing out of it was called the Yukon.

[38] *Ibid.*, p. 152.

[39] *Ibid.*, p. 147. The other quotation in this paragraph is from p. 148.

[40] *Ibid.*, p. 157.

[41] *Ibid.*, p. 160.

[42] On Dawson's map this lake was shown as Kusawah, which has become Kusawa on present-day topographic sheets. It also appeared on some early maps as Lake Arkell, after W. J. Arkell, publisher of *Frank Leslie's Illustrated*

Above the Tahk-Heena the current gradually became stronger and progress more difficult as Schwatka's Grand Canyon of the Yukon was approached. Like his Perrier Pass, however, this name had not found popular acceptance, and someone unknown, between Schwatka's passage and Dawson's, had substituted Miles Canyon for the more pretentious title — probably after General Nelson A. Miles, an American Civil War veteran who was at that time making quite a name for himself as an Indian fighter in the west. In similar fashion the rapids below the canyon had acquired the name White Horse, possibly inspired by the waves or "white horses" in the tumbling waters.

Approaching the canyon, Dawson was less interested in nomenclature than he was in the location of the upstream portages. The first of these was on the west bank, by the White Horse Rapid, the second was between the rapid and the foot of the canyon, and the third, five-eighths of a mile long, was in Miles Canyon. "This portage," Dawson wrote, "is on the east bank, and at the lower end, a very steep ascent has first to be overcome. Here a sort of extemporised windlass has been rigged up by the miners for the purpose of hauling up their boats. ... The river flows through the cañon with great velocity, but is unimpeded in its course, and it is therefore not very risky to run with a good boat. The White Horse Rapid is, however, much more dangerous, and though some of the miners have run through it — generally accidently — it should not be attempted."[43]

Once Dawson's party negotiated these carries, the journey to the lakes was quickly made.

V

FOR LAKE MARSH, DAWSON RETAINED ON HIS MAP THE NAME bestowed by Schwatka, and here he also completed the outline of the lake by making a track-survey along the east shore. Two prominent mountain peaks visible from the south end of his traverse he named Mt. White "in honour of the late Hon. Thos. White, to whose initiative the despatch of the expedition to which this report

---

Newspaper, which sent an exploring party into the area in 1890. (See Chapter Seven)

[43] Dawson, *Report on an Exploration*, p. 161.

refers was largely due,"[44] and Jubilee Mountain, "1887 being the year of [Queen Victoria's] jubilee." Between Lake Marsh and Tagish Lake was "a wide tranquil reach of river five miles in length. The current is here very slack, and the depth, according to Ogilvie, from six to twelve feet. The river is bordered by low terraces, which are particularly wide on the west side, and are covered with open woods, chiefly consisting of white spruce and cottonwood. . . . A mile above Marsh Lake, on the east bank of the river, are two roughly built houses belonging to the Tagish Indians. These are the only permanent houses seen along the whole course of the Lewes, and here the Tagish people, who roam over this part of the country, reside during the winter months."[45]

The lake which the miners, and Schwatka, referred to as Tako, Dawson called Tagish, feeling that in this case it was "permissible" to revert to the Indian name, which he interpreted as Ta-gish-ai, and which Krause rendered as Tagischa. The name Tako Arm, however, Dawson left unchanged, though Tako has since become Taku.

The Tako Arm [he wrote] really constitutes the main continuation and upper part of Tagish Lake. . . . This arm was not explored and with its connected waters yet remains to be properly delineated on the map. It runs in a south-eastward direction for a distance estimated at ten miles, beyond which it turns more nearly south, and its length and other features connected with it can only be given on the authority of Indian reports and sketches. A long way up this arm, possibly twenty miles or more, a considerable river enters from the east. This . . . is reported to be a tranquil stream of no great length, resembling that between Marsh and Tagish lakes. It flows out of the west side of another very long lake which lies nearly parallel to Tako Arm. . . . The name of this lake was given by one Tagish Indian as A-tlin, by another Ta-koo-shok and again Sik-i-ni-kwan, the last being said to be the Taku Indian name. The first-mentioned name is adopted on the map.[46]

Windy Arm of Tagish Lake, and the upper part of Bennett and its West Arm, Dawson described as having all the characteristics of true

---

[44] *Ibid.*, p. 164, footnote. White died in office in 1887, and did not see the results of the expedition that he was instrumental in organizing.

[45] *Ibid.*, p. 164. Many Whitehorse residents now have summer cabins on the Tagish River.

[46] *Ibid.*, p. 168. Though one might hesitate to describe the outlet at Atlin Lake as a "tranquil" stream, the remainder of this second-hand information appears to be accurate.

fiords. "The upper part of the main lake," he wrote of Bennett, "lies, as a narrow water-way, between beetling granite ranges which rise almost perpendicularly to heights of 3000 to 4000 feet above it. Many of the summits beyond the heads of these fiords, and in the vicinity, attain heights of 6000 to 7000 feet above the sea, and the region is in every sense an alpine one, though no dominating peaks of great altitude occur."[47] In a rare departure from the rather pedantic prose of his report, Dawson summarized this whole country as being "a singularly picturesque region, abounding in striking points of view and in landscapes pleasing in their variety, or grand and impressive in their combination of rugged mountain forms."[48] Only the Frances Lake area evoked from him a similar enthusiasm.

He did not leave the lakes, however, without making some changes in the existing place names. Schwatka's use of Bove Lake, for example, he rejected, feeling that this body of water was in fact part of Tagish Lake, but he did "attach" the name to Bove Island, at the entrance to Windy Arm. Lake Bennett and Nares Lake he retained in preference to the Boat Lake and Moose Lake of the miners, though not without some qualms of conscience. With some of the other usages on Schwatka's map he displayed much less restraint. "It will be observed," he wrote frostily, "on comparing Lieut. Schwatka's map with that now published, that he names the west arm of Bennett Lake (though nearly two miles wide at the mouth) 'Wheaton River.' To the river which enters near this arm from a valley parallel to the Watson valley, I propose to apply this name. In the same way, Windy Arm is put down as 'Bove Bay and possibly river,' and the great Tako Arm is shown as 'Tako River,' and described as a stream of inconsiderable dimensions. I can offer no reasonable explanation of these errors."[49]

On September 16, Dawson and his men approached the landing on the upper end of Bennett Lake with the thankful realization that their journey was nearly over, and that their long circuit had been accomplished before the freezeup trapped them in the country. They packed what remained of their gear and supplies to Lake Lindeman, and were then able to track their boat up the rapids without difficulty. At the far end of this lake, at the foot of the trail from Chilkoot

[47] *Ibid.*, p. 166.
[48] *Ibid.*, p. 165.
[49] *Ibid.*, p. 169.

Pass, a number of boats were drawn up on the shore, and considerable timber had been felled: the country was not as deserted now as it had been when Schwatka arrived there three years before and began the construction of his raft. As a party of miners had just preceded them, Dawson and his men had to wait two days for the arrival of more packers.

On September 19, with four Indians, they started their journey to tidewater. "The small lakes highest in the pass," Dawson wrote, "were, at the time we crossed, about two-thirds covered with new ice, which showed little signs of melting, even under the bright sun which prevailed. Hard frosts were evidently occurring here in the mountains every night at this season. . . . At the actual summit, the trail leads through a narrow, rocky gap, and the whole scene is one of the most complete desolation, the naked granite rocks rising steeply to partly snow-clad mountains on either side."[50]

The first night on the trail they stayed at Sheep Camp, an Indian stopping place on the southern slope of the pass where "arboreal vegetation of fair height is first encountered." The next day, September 20, they reached a trading post on Taiya Inlet, "and were hospitably received by Mr. J. Healey [sic], who has established himself at that point for purposes of trade with the Indians and miners." In a moving passage, Dawson wrote of their arrival:

We had at this time just completed our fourth month of arduous and incessant travel from Wrangell, at the mouth of the Stikine River, by the rivers, lakes and portages of the interior ... the total distance traversed being about 1322 miles. No serious accidents had befallen us by the way, and though, like the miners, we came back to the coast with a deplorably ragged and uncouth aspect, we had with us, intact, our collections, instruments, survey-records, and notes. It was not the least pleasing moment of the entire journey when, from a distance of some miles, we first caught sight of the sea shining like a plate of beaten bronze under the rays of the evening sun.[51]

VI

IT WAS A COMBINATION OF PROTRACTED NEGOTIATIONS FOR PACKERS and bad weather in Chilkoot Pass that had delayed Ogilvie's ren-

[50] *Ibid.*, pp. 174-175.
[51] *Ibid.*, p. 174.

dezvous with Dawson at Fort Selkirk. After leaving the other members of the Yukon Expedition at the mouth of the Stikine, the survey party reached Haines Mission on May 24, 1887. There the seven tons of "impedimentia" that had been brought from Victoria were redistributed into 120 packs, and the difficult task of rounding up enough Indians to carry this gear across the pass was commenced. Healy and the only other white man at the post, George Dickson, used their considerable influence with the natives to assist in making arrangements for the portage; and the support of Captain Newell, commander of the United States gunboat *Pinta*, which called at the Mission a few days after the surveyors' arrival, greatly assisted in the lengthy business of coming to terms.

Among the natives at Dyea was a squaw man named George Washington Carmack who "was then closely associated with the Tagish, or Stick Indians, as they were called. . . . Carmac [*sic*] spoke both languages [Tagish and Chilkoot] in a limited way, and had considerable influence with the Sticks. I employed him to help me over the pass and through his influence got a good deal of assistance from his Indian friends. Skookum Jim and Tagish Charlie were both there, and packed for me. Skookum well earned his sobriquet of 'Skookum' or 'strong', for he carried one hundred and fifty-six (156) pounds of bacon over the pass for me at a single carry. This might be considered a heavy load anywhere on any roads, but over the stony moraine of a glacier, as the first half of the distance is, and then up a steep pass, climbing more than three thousand feet in six or seven miles . . . certainly is a stiff test of strength and endurance."[52] These three men would eventually play a major role in the discovery of Klondike gold.

There was no escaping the exorbitant rates charged for packing, in spite of the best efforts of the traders and Captain Newell. Being a meticulous man, however, Ogilvie did his best to bring some organization to the formidable operation.

On the 6th of June [he wrote] 120 Indians, men, women and children, started for the summit. I sent two of my party with them to see the goods delivered at the place agreed upon. Each carrier when given a pack also got a ticket, on which was inscribed the contents of the pack, its weight, and the amount the individual was to get for carrying it. They were made to understand that they had to produce these tickets on delivering their loads, but were not told for what reason. As

[52] Ogilvie, *Early Days*, pp. 133-134.

each pack was delivered one of my men receipted the ticket and returned it. The Indians did not seem to understand the import of this; a few of them pretended to have lost their tickets; and as they could not get paid without them, my assistant, who had duplicates of every ticket, furnished them with receipted copies, after examining their packs.

While they were packing to the summit I was producing the survey, and I met them on their return at the foot of the cañon, about eight miles from the coast, where I paid them. They came to the camp in the early morning before I was up, and for about two hours there was quite a hubbub. When paying them I tried to get their names, but very few would give any Indian name, nearly all, after a little reflection, giving some common English name. My list contained little else than Jack, Tom, Joe, Charley, etc., some of which were duplicated three and four times. I then found why some of them had pretended to lose their tickets at the summit. Three or four who had thus presented themselves twice for payment, producing first the receipted ticket, afterwards the one they claimed to have lost, demanding payment for both. They were much taken aback when they found that their duplicity had been discovered.[53]

One of Ogilvie's party was William Moore, river captain and prospector, the man who had entered the country with Joe Ladue in 1883, and who had remained there. With his three sons he had made a fortune estimated at $90,000 by operating steam boats on the Stikine River during the Cassiar gold rush, only to have the money slip through his fingers with the decline of mining activity in that area. Now his enthusiasm for the trade prospects of the north had been rekindled. One of his sons had heard from an Indian "who could talk a good deal of Chinook Jargon" that "by way of the Skagway River was a longer route [to the interior] but not so high a pass to cross."[54] The old man — he was now 65 years of age — was anxious to investigate this pass for himself, and had been able without much difficulty to interest Ogilvie in the project. While the main party struggled up the Chilkoot Pass, Moore would reconnoitre this other possible route.

For a long time no native could be found who would accompany Moore as guide, as the Chilkoots seemed determined not to reveal any information concerning the "existence and condition" of the

53 William Ogilvie, *Information Respecting the Yukon District*, (Ottawa, Dept. of the Interior, Government Printing Office, 1897), p. 11.

54 Clarence L. Andrews, "Biographical Sketch of Capt. William Moore," *The Washington Historical Quarterly*, Vol. XXII, No. 1, (1931), p. 38.

pass, and the Tagish were too fearful of the Chilkoots to talk contrary to their wishes. It was only after some persuasion that an Indian, known only to the white men as Jim, agreed to go. He had been through this pass before, and fortunately proved "reliable and useful." Moore and Jim completed their traverse at the top of Chilkoot Pass. "The Captain," Ogilvie wrote, "was strongly of the opinion that the route is feasible for a wagon road and possibly for a railway," adding that "Every night during the two months [Moore] remained with us he would picture the tons of yellow dust yet to be found in the Yukon Valley. He decided then and there that Skagway would be the entry port to the golden fields of the Yukon, and the pass would reverberate with the rumble of railway trains, carrying supplies."[55] This alternate entrance way to the interior was named White Pass, after the Minister of the Interior.

Because of bad weather, and because the party had to pack some of their gear, including two Peterborough canoes, over the Chilkoot Pass themselves, it was the end of June before all Ogilvie's supplies were "laid on the beach at Bennett Lake," and July 11 before they were able to find and whip-saw the necessary lumber and build a boat sufficiently large to take all their supplies downriver to the boundary. The stores brought with them, including those for Dawson, exceeded the capacity of the canoes, which in any event were needed for the survey work. Ogilvie's main purpose was to locate accurately the 141st meridian, but it was necessary that he know his approximate position at all times, in order to determine when he was close to the boundary. This required that the survey be started at a point well-defined in latitude and longitude, and fortunately such a point was available on the near-by Chilkat River. Here in 1869 a distinguished American astronomer, Professor George Davidson, had built an observatory from which to view a total eclipse of the sun, and the location of this observatory had in the course of his work been established with precision.

"I assumed the position of an island referred to as fixed by him," Ogilvie reported, "and began my survey there, carrying it over the peninsula to Chilcoot Inlet at Haines Mission, from there across Chilcoot Inlet to the mouth of Dyea Inlet, up it and through the pass at its head to the summit, locating as I went the notable peaks around. . . . The survey was carried from the summit down to where

[55] Quoted in *Ibid.*, p. 39.

191

we built our boat, and when that was finished, loaded, and sent on the work was resumed and carried without interruption to the International Boundary Line."[56] For this work Ogilvie used a micrometer, the same instrument that he had employed on his traverse of the Peace River and the Athabasca in 1883: he claimed that the error seldom exceeded one part in a hundred, or three miles in a distance of nearly 700. "The system," he wrote, "while not accurate enough to think of determining the position of the boundary line by, was accurate enough to put in the topography along the river, and give its length from point to point."[57]

The descent to the boundary took approximately two months. On the lakes, because of the heavy swells, the party averaged only ten miles a day: on the rivers they managed twice that distance. On July 20 they reached Miles Canyon, which they passed through without incident, and shortly afterwards began the traverse of the west side of the lake "named after one Mike Labarge [sic], who was engaged by the Western Union Telegraph Company, exploring the river and adjacent country.... It does not appear that Labarge then, nor for some years after, saw the lake called by his name. The successful laying of the Atlantic cable in 1866 put a stop to this project, and the exploring parties sent out were recalled as soon as word could be got to them. It seems that Labarge had got up as far as the Pelly before he received his recall; he had heard something of a large lake some distance further up the river, and afterwards spoke of it to some traders and miners who called it after him."[58]

The delays in crossing the mountains, and the fear that for this reason he would be late for his projected meeting with Dawson, were very much on Ogilvie's mind as he methodically carried his survey downstream.

On the 11th of August I met a party of miners coming out who had passed Stewart River a few days before. They saw no sign of Dr. Dawson having been there. This was welcome news to me, as I expected he would have reached that point long before I arrived, because of the many delays I had met with on the coast range.... The same evening I met more miners on the way out, and the next day met three boats, each containing four men. In the crew of one of them was a son of

[56] Ogilvie, *Early Days*, pp. 52-53.

[57] *Ibid.*, p. 54.

[58] Ogilvie, *Information Respecting the Yukon*, p. 22.

Capt. Moore, from whom the captain got such information as induced him to turn back and accompany them out.

Next day, the 13th, I got to the mouth of the Pelly, and found that Dr. Dawson had arrived there on the 11th. The doctor also had experienced many delays.... I was pleased to find that he was in no immediate want of provisions, the fear of which had caused me a great deal of uneasiness on the way down the river.... The doctor was so much behind the time arranged to meet me that he determined to start for the coast at once. I therefore set about making a short report and plan of my survey to this point; and, as I was not likely to get another opportunity of writing at such length for a year, I applied myself to a correspondence designed to satisfy my friends and acquaintances for the ensuing twelve months. This necessitated three days' hard work.

On the morning of the 17th the doctor left for the outside world, leaving me with a feeling of loneliness that only those who have experienced it can realize.[59]

Ogilvie resumed his survey on August 19, and reached the mouth of the White on August 25. He was anxious to explore this river from its mouth to the boundary "to discover more especially the facilities it offered for the transport of supplies in the event of a survey of the International Boundary being undertaken,"[60] but he could make no headway with the canoes against the strong current in the braided, shallow channels. Later, Harper told him of a trip he had made up it with sleds in the winter of 1872, during which he had made what was probably the first sighting of the great interior massif of the St. Elias Range. About 65 miles from its mouth, he explained to Ogilvie, the river "deflects to the north-west running along the base of a high mountain ridge . . . across which many high mountain peaks could be seen."[61] One of these peaks he believed was Mount St. Elias, as it was higher than any of the others, but Ogilvie pointed out that "as Mt. St. Elias is about one hundred and eighty miles distant, his conclusion is not tenable. From his description of this mountain it must be more than twice the height of the highest peaks seen anywhere on the lower river, and consequently must be ten or twelve thousand feet above the sea." Ogilvie was correct in his assumption that this peak was not Mount St. Elias, but it is difficult to identify with certainty which peak it actually was. He was certainly conservative in estimating its probable height.

[59] *Ibid.*, p. 16.
[60] *Ibid.*, p. 16.
[61] *Ibid.*, p. 28, as is the other quotation referring to the mountains.

The mouth of the Stewart River was reached the next day. Here the surveyors met Alexander McDonald, a native of New Brunswick and an experienced miner, who had spent the season in the vicinity of that river and gave them some guarded information concerning it. He mentioned that he had seen a falls on one branch that he estimated to be between 100 and 200 feet in height, and he described a large lake 30 miles long and averaging a mile and a half in width: today these are known as Fraser Falls and Mayo Lake. Another river that he explored he identified as the Beaver River "as marked on the maps of that part of the country": he also reported that he had travelled downstream a short distance on a large river flowing north, which Ogilvie deduced was probably a tributary of the Peel.

Below the Stewart and the Sixtymile was the tributary of the Yukon that Schwatka had named the Deer River, and McQuesten the "Trundeck." Ogilvie gave a brief description of it, the first explorer of the region to do so:

It is a small river about forty yards wide at the mouth, and shallow; the water is clear and transparent, and of beautiful blue colour. The Indians catch great numbers of salmon here. They had been fishing shortly before my arrival, and the river, for some distance up, was full of salmon traps.

A miner had prospected up this river for an estimated distance of forty miles, in the season of 1887. I did not see him, but got some of his information at second hand. The water being so beautifully clear I thought it must come through a large lake not far up; but as far as he had gone no lakes were seen. He said the current was comparatively slack, with an occasional "ripple" or small rapid. Where he turned back the river is surrounded by high mountains, which were then covered with snow, which accounts for the purity and cleanliness of the water.

It appears that the Indians go up this stream a long distance to hunt, but I could learn nothing definite as to their statements concerning it.[62]

The survey party reached the mouth of the Fortymile River in September, and here Ogilvie met McQuesten and Harper for the first time. The two traders had just started to build a new post at this location, having been obliged to abandon their year-old station on the Stewart as a result of the stampede to the new diggings. The first full season's production on the Fortymile was estimated at $200,-000, with about 300 men working in the area: the steamers then on the river, however, could only bring in sufficient supplies to enable

[62] *Ibid.*, p. 30.

approximately 100 of these to winter in the country. Most of the remainder had already started to make their way outside when Ogilvie arrived, "some up the river by poling their boats, very hard, difficult work, and some down to St. Michael on the chance of catching a United States Revenue cutter home bound or the Alaska Commercial Company steamer to San Francisco."[63]

The approximate position of the international boundary was reached five days later. Here it was Ogilvie's task to build winter quarters and an open-roofed observatory, and over the next few months to obtain as many astronomical observations as the weather permitted in order to establish as closely as possible the location of the 141st meridian. The most accurate method of obtaining longitude employed at that time required the use of a telegraph line along which precise time signals could be transmitted, but as there were as yet no lines in the Yukon, this technique could not be utilized. Ogilvie was forced instead to use the method of measuring moon culminations, or moon transits "over the Meridian of the place."

These observations were not made without difficulty, the first of which involved the exact location of the observatory. As the tripod for the astronomical transit weighed over 400 pounds — even though it was a small portable model — Ogilvie had not brought it over the pass, devising instead "a set of brasses to be fastened on a stump of suitable size, and on these the telescope could be mounted in the same way as on the stand. These reduced the weight ... to less than eighty pounds."[64] To mount the brasses, however, a tree stump 22 inches in diameter at a height of five feet above the ground had to be found, and this required three days of searching to locate. Even then the stump when the tree was cut was smaller in diameter than was desirable, and it was necessary to reinforce it with blocks on the sides to get the proper support for the brasses. In addition, the tree was on a sidehill "which occasioned both inconvenience and inaccuracy, for it was found that the stump swayed up and downhill with a change of temperature, and seldom was absolutely stationary. Result, the transit had to be levelled every evening just before beginning work, but it continued to swing during work."

The extreme cold also did not make the operation any easier — Ogilvie commented that the temperature when observations were

63 Ogilvie, *Early Days*, p. 112.

64 *Ibid.*, p. 59. The other quotation in this paragraph is from p. 60.

taken varied from thirty to fifty below zero, and added feelingly: "Not only did the temperature add to the personal discomfort, and interfere with bodily freedom through excessive clothing, for one must be very warmly clothed indeed to remain standing still in an open-roofed observatory for two hours in such temperatures, but it also seriously interfered with the instruments used and impaired their delicacy. More especially was this the case with the chronometer. Chronometers are adjusted for temperatures within limits, but the temperatures here were much outside the limits generally accepted by makers. The one I had was a remarkably good one, but the temperatures it was subject to in this work was a strain for which it was never intended."[65]

In spite of these handicaps, reasonably good weather enabled Ogilvie to obtain 22 observations "in the November-December, December-January, and January-February lunations." When the observations were completed and reduced "the resultant position was marked by cutting a line through the woods north and south of the river for a distance. Then a survey was made up the Fortymile River and the boundary line marked on it."[66]

VII

OGILVIE'S INSTRUCTIONS WERE TO RETURN TO OTTAWA BY WAY OF the Mackenzie River when his task was finished, and report to the Minister of the Interior. At the beginning of March 1888, he started preparations for his journey, moving all the supplies and gear to Belle Isle, and letting it be known that he required guides, and would pay $2.50 a day for each dog team and driver that would assist in a winter carry of his stuff — including the two canoes — to the headwaters of the Porcupine River. He proposed to follow a route up the Tat-on-duc River (on modern maps the "Tatonduk"), a tributary of the Yukon that flows into it approximately 40 miles inside the Alaskan boundary, but which largely drains Canadian territory. After the usual uncertainty concerning the intentions of the Indians with regard to this offer, nine men and 36 dogs appeared in the surveyors' camp on March 16, and the journey was started the next

[65] *Ibid.*, pp. 57-58.
[66] *Ibid.*, p. 60.

day. Ogilvie left the country with some regret, as he had made many friends during his winter on the boundary. He very naturally experienced, however, "a thrill of satisfaction that I was now fairly started on the home stretch of my long journey, though over 2,500 miles yet lay between me and the nearest railway, nearly all of which had to be got over by foot or paddle."[67]

About 14 miles from its mouth, on the Canadian side of the boundary, the Tat-on-duc River forked, and the route to the Porcupine followed the branch that came from the northeast. Five miles farther up this fork was a camp of the Indians who were acting as Ogilvie's guides and carriers, and the party rested there for a day. It was Sunday, and Ogilvie noted with interest that the natives held a church service.

Some years ago [he commented], when Archdeacon McDonald ... was stationed at Fort McPherson, and afterwards at Rampart House, Charlie's band[68] used to resort to these posts for their trade, and that gentleman taught them to read, and instructed them in the principles of the Christian religion. It is pleasant to be able to testify that they have profited by this instruction, and still retain a loving memory of those times. They hold every Sunday a service among themselves, reading from their books the prayers and lessons for the day, and singing in their own language to some old tune a simple hymn. They never go on a journey of any length without these books, and always read a portion before they go to sleep. I do not pretend that these men are faultless, or that they do not need watching, but I do believe that most of them are sincere in their professions and strive to do what they think is right.[69]

The travellers encountered some canyons on the Tat-on-duc as they continued their journey: one they had to detour completely, as the guide reported that it contained a high waterfall which was impossible to ascend. Above the canyons was a short stretch of swamp from which there was "an effusion of sulphuretted hydrogen gas." The Indians told Ogilvie that nearby was a lake — which they would not approach — that was also kept agitated by gas, which

---

[67] William Ogilvie, "Exploratory Survey from the Pelly-Yukon to Mackenzie River. . . .", *Dept. of the Interior Annual Report, 1889*, Part VIII, Section 3, (Ottawa, Brown Chamberlain, 1890), p. 52.

[68] Charley's (or Charlie's) Village was an Indian settlement on the Yukon River in Alaska, close to the Canadian border. It was here that Schwatka on his raft journey met Ladue (See Chapter Five). McDonald, incidentally, was appointed Archdeacon by Bompas in 1875.

[69] Ogilvie, *Information Respecting the Yukon*, pp. 47-48.

had a fatal effect on any animals venturing near. McConnell commented later, when reviewing the report, that, in some localities, this gas issues from "petroliferous limestones," but added cautiously that in this instance the emissions might be due to volcanic action. In recent times there has been gas and oil exploration in this area, to date with inconclusive results.

Beyond the swamp the travellers entered a broad, open plateau, estimated to be roughly 3000 feet above sea level, from which, Ogilvie stated, was "one of the grandest views I have ever seen, and the profound stillness and vast solitude impress one as perhaps few other scenes in the world would."[70]

Leaving the river and continuing about a mile up the valley of a small stream coming from the east, we reach the top of a low ridge which forms the water-shed between the waters of the Tat-on-duc and those of a stream which the Indians assured me flows into the Peel. I had much difficulty in understanding this, as I could hardly believe that the water-shed was so near the Lewes, or Yukon; and it was not until they had drawn many maps of the district in the snow, and after much argument with them, that I gave credit to their statements. I then proposed to go down this stream to the Peel, and to reach the Mackenzie in that way, but at this they were horrified, assuring me as well as they could by word and sign that we would all be killed if we attempted it, as there were terrible cañons on it, which would destroy us and every thing we had; in fact, we would never be heard of again, and they might be blamed for our disappearance. Their statements . . . caused me to decide not to try it. This river has been named by Mr. J. Johnson, Geographer to the Department of the Interior, "Ogilvie River."[71]

This plateau area was as far as the Indian guides would go, though Ogilvie was able to persuade two of them to push ahead with one of his crew and make a track to the head of the Porcupine, a further 15 miles.

These people [Ogilvie explained] have a great dread of a tribe who, they suppose, dwelt at one time in the hills at the head of these streams and still exist somewhere in the vicinity, though exactly where they do not know. . . . They call this tribe Na-hone; I have generally heard the

[70] Ogilvie, "Exploratory Survey," p. 54.

[71] *Ibid.*, pp. 54-55. The Ogilvie is actually a westerly continuation of the Peel, forming that river's headwaters. Travel on its upper reaches is not easy, but not so perilous as the Indians made it out to be.

word pronounced Na-haune by the whites. It appears that they inhabited the head waters of the Liard and Pelly, and were much fiercer than the neighbouring Indians. Probably rumors of their aggressiveness have reached these simple and peaceful people, and created this dread, for they do not appear to have ever seen anything to justify their fears. ... They described them as cannibals, and living altogether outside, without shelter from the cold, and believed them to be such terrible creatures that they required no cover, but could lie down anywhere to rest, and did not need a fire to cook their food, but ate it raw. They seemed to ascribe to them supernatural powers.... To whatever it is due, this dread appears to be lively, so much so, that I believe only some pressing necessity, such as hunger, would induce them to remain in this locality for any length of time, and then only if they were in strong force.[72]

Ogilvie paid off the Indians on March 22, and they thankfully departed from this fearsome country. Left to their own devices, the surveyors dragged their much-abused canoes, and their supplies, into the watershed of the Porcupine, until they reached, early in April, a point which they considered to be the head of canoe navigation on that river system. As the labour of moving was "severe" they decided to camp here until after the breakup of the ice.

Game was plentiful: the men noted beaver, lynx, otter, marten, ptarmigan, moose, and "numberless" caribou that pawed over the snow in large areas as they grazed. Ogilvie's litany of spring echoed the observations that Dall had made on the lower Yukon a decade before:

The lowest temperature in the month of April was on the 4th —37° below zero, and for six days afterwards all the minimum temperatures were below 30° below zero. ... The highest temperature in April was on the the 30th —40° above zero. The highest temperature in May was on the 17th, 55°. The first time the snow showed signs of melting was 29th April. The first appearance of insect life was 30th April, when a small fly came out of the river in great numbers, flying about and crawling over the snow. The water in the river began to rise on 6th May. The first geese were heard flying overhead on 8th May; they were flying in a south-westerly direction, as though they had come from the Mackenzie. The common house fly made its appearance the same day. The first swans were heard 11th May. First mosquitoes seen 14th May. First cranes heard 15th May.[73]

[72] *Ibid.*, p. 56.
[73] *Ibid.*, p. 59.

On May 28 they were able to launch the canoes and begin their downstream travel, waiting occasionally for ice jams to move. Once the mouth of the Bell was reached they were in familiar terrain: they ascended this river to Lapierre House, arriving there on June 6. "The post here," Ogilvie wrote, "is kept up mainly for the meat it furnishes, the country around it abounding with game. The tongue of the deer or the moose is regarded as a delicacy, and the Indian generally brings it to the post, as he gets more for it than he would for an equal weight of other meat. The clerk in charge informed me that he had sent away that year thirteen hundred tongues to other posts, so that probably two thousand animals were killed in this vicinity."[74] Though Lapierre House was no longer a way-station for Fort Yukon, the supplies and returns to and from Rampart House were still transported through this establishment. The volume of freight, however, was now greatly reduced.

On June 8 Ogilvie continued up the Bell to the pass that separated that river from the Rat. There was still ice in the streams near the height of land, and the mistreated and battered canoes had to be man-handled across the Arctic divide. Ogilvie named this passage McDougall's Pass, "after the man [James McDougall of the Hudson's Bay Company] who first explored and surveyed it."[75] McDougall, while a clerk at Fort McPherson, investigated this route in 1872 to determine the feasibility of building a wagon road through it to improve communications between Fort McPherson and Lapierre House. The road was never built, but Ogilvie recorded that his survey traverse checked very closely in distance with that of McDougall. He was able to make a direct comparison, as many of McDougall's survey stakes were still standing, protected by pieces of sod, "as fresh-looking as if they had been planted but one year, instead of sixteen."

The Peel River was reached on June 19, and Fort McPherson on June 20. The "exploratory survey" was complete, but home was still a distant goal. It would not be until January 1889, that Ogilvie would complete his mission, and report as instructed to the office of the Minister of the Interior in Ottawa.

74 *Ibid.*, p. 63.
75 *Ibid.*, p. 64, as is the other quotation relating to McDougall's survey.

VIII

EXCEPT FOR THIS TRAVERSE TO THE MACKENZIE, OGILVIE'S SURVEY was confined largely to travelled routes: his accomplishment was to compile a more accurate map of the "sinuosities" of the Yukon River than anyone had produced before. McConnell's long journey on the Liard, the Mackenzie, and the Porcupine was, on the other hand, through largely unexplored country, even though these rivers had been for years trade routes of the Hudson's Bay Company. All his travelling in 1887 was in northern British Columbia and the Mackenzie River basin: it was not until July 1888, in the second year of his journey, that he set foot in the Yukon district. Following the Hudson's Bay Company's portage from the Peel to the Porcupine, he brought back the first geological notes and the first maps from this section of the country.

He arrived at Fort McPherson late in June, after Ogilvie had left but ahead of the supply steamer, and made a short trip up the Rat while waiting for it to arrive. He also arranged during this time to have the boat he had used on the Mackenzie taken across the portage by some Indians who were on their way to Lapierre House, as he had been told at the Fort that boats or canoes could not be obtained west of the mountains. Finally he felt that he could delay no longer. "On July 10th," he wrote in his report, "I decided not to waste any more time waiting for the steamer, as it was impossible to tell how long it might be delayed, and to trust to the chance of finding supplies at Rampart House."[76] Five more Indians were engaged, with the usual difficulty, to carry the outfit; the load for each of them on this carry being 40 pounds, in addition to blankets and supplies, and the pay the equivalent of 15 skins, or $7.50, paid in goods. The load was the same as in Murray's time, but the pay scale had probably increased.

Starting their journey, McConnell and his packers waded the same muskeg that Murray had encountered, and climbed the same two terraces: at the top of the second one the barometer registered 1200 feet above the elevation of the Fort, and the tree cover had been already left behind.

From the second slope [McConnell wrote] a wide plain reaches west-

[76] R. G. McConnell, "Extracts Relating to the Yukon District ... 1887-88," in Dawson, *Report on an Exploration*, p. 209.

wards towards the mountains. The walking here is exceedingly difficult, as the surface is covered with the rounded grassy sods which go in the country by the name of *Têtes des femmes.*[77] These project a foot or more above the clayey soil, and are the cause of constant stumbling, which becomes somewhat exasperating when one is weighted down with a pack. An attempt to walk on top of the mounds soon becomes excessively fatiguing, on account of the irregular length of the strides, and a slight miscalculation as to distance precipitates the unlucky traveller down into the muddy depths between. When down, the resolve is usually made, and adhered to for a while, to keep to the lower levels, but the effort required to step over the intervening hillocks presents obvious disadvantages of a different kind.[78]

They struggled across this plain for five hours, at the rate of about a mile and a half an hour, and then camped on the bank of a swift mountain stream. This led them the next day to the Rat River, where they paused while the Indians stalked and killed a mountain sheep which one of them spotted on a ledge on the side of the valley. Early on the third day, the party "crossed the watershed between the Mackenzie and the Yukon, and began our descent to the latter. The watershed has an elevation measured by the barometer of 2600 feet above the starting point on Peel River, or about 2650 above the sea, while the neighbouring mountains rise a thousand feet higher."[79] This was in substantial disagreement with Ogilvie's estimated elevation for the top of the pass of about 1200 feet, which appears to be much the more accurate elevation of the two: present-day topographic maps show the pass as being between 1000 and 1500 feet above sea level.

The night after crossing the pass, July 12, they camped in one of the canyons on the upper reaches of the Bell, and the next day continued their descent.

Three miles from camp the river washes up against the walls on the right hand side, and the trail, which has hitherto followed the right bank, crosses over to the left. The ford is a difficult one, as the stream is here deep and rapid, and its channel is paved with treacherous quartzite boulders. The greatest caution is necessary in crossing, as a stumble or false step would almost certainly be fatal to one encumbered with

[77] Now universally known in the tundra country as niggerheads, and certainly no easier to walk across than they were when McConnell first encountered them.

[78] McConnell, "Extracts Relating to the Yukon," pp. 209-210.

[79] *Ibid.,* p. 211.

a heavy pack. In fording these swift mountain torrents, it is customary to adopt a communistic plan. The party line up behind a long pole, and keeping a firm hold of it advance into the stream abreast. In this case the person above sustains the full brunt of the current, but is held up by those below, and a stumbler receives the support of those who have retained their footing.[80]

At Lapierre House, they found "the post deserted by all but Indians, the officers in charge having left some time before for Fort McPherson. . . . The boat which I had sent across the mountains by the McDougall Pass, I was glad to find had reached its destination in good order, and no time was lost in preparing for the descent of Bell River and the Porcupine."[81] McConnell's crew for this trip consisted of one man, a time-expired employee of the Hudson's Bay Company from Fort McPherson named Skey, whom McConnell was able to persuade "to come with me and go out by way of the Yukon." Like travellers before them, they found navigation on the Bell and the Porcupine below Lapierre House rather dull. As was "customary in these latitudes" the two men journeyed mostly at night, as they were in the six-week period following the summer solstice during which the sun remains above the horizon: they had, therefore, ample light, the weather was cooler, the mosquitoes less troublesome, and they avoided the strong headwinds which usually blew up the valley in the heat of the day.

On July 20, after four days on the river, the travellers reached Rampart House, near the international boundary. McConnell described this establishment as

... the most distant of the Hudson's Bay Company's posts ... established to replace Fort Yukon, after the site of the latter had been determined to be in Alaskan territory. This post was originally situated twelve miles farther down the river, but the position of the buildings in regard to the boundary being doubtful, these were burnt by the Hudson's Bay Company, and new buildings were erected at the present site. As a fur post it barely pays expenses, owing to the heavy cost incurred in the transportation of furs and goods, and is kept up mainly as a protection against the encroachment of traders from the west. . . .

I remained a few hours at Rampart House for the purpose of taking an observation for latitude, and making arrangements for the trip to Fort Yukon. An Indian was engaged to accompany us, and I was fortunately able to obtain a supply of dried meat from Mr. Firth, the

[80] *Ibid.*, pp. 211-212.
[81] *Ibid.*, pp. 213-214.

officer in charge of the post. A report had reached the fort that a steamer belonging to the Alaska Fur Company would pass Fort Yukon on its way to Forty-mile Creek, in a few days, and I decided, as we would now traverse Alaskan Territory, and had no object for delay, to hurry down to the forks as soon as possible and endeavour to obtain a passage up the Yukon as far as the Canadian boundary.[82]

These hopes were cruelly dashed. Travelling long hours, and fighting a head wind all the way, they reached Fort Yukon in three days. There, from a missionary, Mr. Canham, they received news that McConnell, with great restraint, called "far from cheering." The steamer they had hoped to meet had passed by the trading post the day before. In a country where steamer passages were usually weeks apart, they had missed their connection by less than twenty-four hours!

To reach the coast, McConnell now had two choices: either to continue on downstream to St. Michael's and book passage on a steamer to Victoria or San Francisco, a course of action which he found "almost irresistible," or to make his way upstream by the Yukon and the Lewes, and out of the country by way of the Chilkoot Pass. This alternative was almost entirely inside Canada, but it "promised to be a matter of no ordinary difficulty."

The short, square-sterned boat which I had hitherto used, was built to carry a load down stream and was altogether unsuitable to make an up-stream journey in, and an attempt to force it for hundreds of miles against a five or six mile current seemed well nigh hopeless, but no other was available. Our provisions were also running short, but Mr. Canahan [sic] kindly supplied our deficiencies in this respect to some extent, and we expected to be able to obtain fish from the Indians along the river. Trader John, the Indian who had piloted us down from Rampart House, and who had proved himself a capable and willing fellow, was induced, after some persuasion, to accompany us as far as Forty-mile Creek, and on the 25th of July, after a delay of four days, we succeeded in making a start.[83]

The beginning of the journey on the Yukon River more than lived up to McConnell's gloomy expectations, and his comments on it are reminiscent of those of Murray.

Notwithstanding the great width [he wrote] the velocity of the current is undiminished, and the up-stream navigation of this part, espe-

[82] *Ibid.*, pp. 224-225.
[83] *Ibid.*, p. 227.

cially in high water, is attended with greater difficulty than any other portion of the river. Beaches are seldom present, and tracking is impossible except for trifling distances at long intervals. The water along the cut-banks is too deep a few feet from the shore for poling, and to advance we were obliged to combine the use of an oar on the outside, a pole on the inside, while I steered and paddled behind. Even this complicated method of propulsion often became impracticable, and progression in some places was only attainable by clinging to the overhanging branches and pulling ourselves up foot by foot. . . . The width of the river is so great that difficult spots cannot be avoided as in other streams by crossing to the opposite bank, and the ascent must be made entirely on one side. The eastern side is usually preferred.

The length of [the] expanded island-filled stretch above the mouth of the Porcupine, was estimated at seventy miles. . . . We made the ascent in five days, but to do this we were obliged to work at our full capacity for fourteen or fifteen hours a day. With a proper boat, much better time could have been made.[84]

Near the head of the river-flats they visited the Indian camp of Chief Senatee of the Fort Yukon Indians, once an absolute and cruel ruler of his people, now an old man mellowed by the passage of time, and shorn of much of his authority. "He received us hospitably," McConnell commented drily, "and after an exchange of fish for tobacco had been made, commenced a long oration descriptive of his enduring love for the English (Hudson's Bay Company) and his regret that they had left the country, and his general dislike of the Yankees (Alaska Fur Company), but as time was precious the harangue was cut short by the presents of a couple of hand-fulls of tea, the probable object for which it was made, and we proceeded on our journey."[85]

As the river contracted, narrow beaches began to appear, which made it possible, to the travellers' great relief, to use the tracking-line in the place of oars and pole, and make much better time. On August 9, fourteen days after leaving the Fort, they reached Forty-mile River, "the headquarters of the miners on the Yukon." McConnell reported that the season of 1888 had to date been a poor one because of high water, and that the year's production at the time of his visit was believed to be "scarcely $15,000." A few days before his arrival nearly 150 men — about half the miners in the area — had stampeded downriver to the Beaver, a tributary stream which

[84] *Ibid.*, pp. 228-229.
[85] *Ibid.*, p. 229.

enters the Yukon from the north about 120 miles below the mouth of the Porcupine. "The amount of information required to stampede a mining camp is very small," McConnell commented, "and in the present case was almost ridiculous. A report was brought up by the men on the steamer that a miner had boarded the boat at the mouth of Beaver River, and after talking in a hurried manner to the captain, had suddenly departed, and in his haste had left his purse behind him. The miners reasoned that nothing but a rich find could cause such an excitement, and immediately loaded their boats and started on a wild goose chase down the river only to meet with disappointment at the end of their journey. A few received a passage up again on the steamer, but the greater number drifted on down towards St. Michael's, and left the mining country altogether."[86]

McConnell took advantage of the facilities offered by the camp to build a long, narrow, sharp-prowed boat, modelled on those generally used by the miners for upstream travel: this craft would make the remainder of their passage somewhat easier. Trader John, who had helped greatly in the ascent from Fort Yukon, had fulfilled his agreement and returned home to Rampart House: a miner named Buckley, desirous of seeing the last of the Yukon, was engaged in his place. They left the creek on August 14, though not before McConnell found time to do a little prospecting in the vicinity, noting that seams of "coarse serpentine asbestus [sic]" outcrop near the mouth of the river.[87] He also examined "a lode of argentiferous galena" (silver lead) located about two miles above the mouth of the Fortymile, a sample of which, taken outside by Ogilvie, yielded on assay over 38 ounces of silver to the ton. After his departure from the camp, McConnell continued to note the economic possibilities of the region, reporting that "copper-pyrites, in small quantities, was noticed at several points between Forty-Mile Creek and Fort Reliance,"[88] and that "all the way from the boundary to White River and beyond," there were many promising quartz veins and ledges. These were not yet of concern to the many miners

[86] *Ibid.*, pp. 232-233.

[87] This observation of McConnell's is of particular interest in view of the start of the production of asbestos in 1967 at the Clinton Creek mine of Cassiar Asbestos Corporation, located only eight miles from the mouth of the Fortymile River.

[88] McConnell, "Extracts Relating to the Yukon," p. 244. The other quotation in this paragraph is from p. 243.

passing up and down the river: for the moment their only interest was in the more easily worked placer deposits.

The mouth of the Stewart River was passed on the morning of August 19, and the White River shortly after. Once beyond Fort Selkirk, McConnell was following the route which Dawson had traversed the year before: he was able, therefore, to lay aside his notebooks, and concentrate on covering the remaining distance to the sea as quickly as possible. The three men reached tidewater at Taiya Inlet on September 15, 1888, in almost exactly a month of travel from Fortymile, which was fast time for the upstream journey. After eighteen months in the interior, the inlet must have been to McConnell, as it was to Dawson, a welcome and very moving sight.

IX

DAWSON'S REPORT ON THE YUKON EXPEDITION, INCLUDING MAPS AND seven appendices ranging in subject matter from "List of Plants Collected" to "Summary of Astronomical Observations," was first published in Volume 3, Part I of the *Annual Report of the Geological and Natural History Survey of Canada, 1887-1888,* which also contained a "progress report" on Ogilvie's survey, and a "preliminary report" on McConnell's exploration as far as the mouth of the Liard. In 1898, when the rush to the Klondike was at its height, Dawson's work was re-issued by popular demand, under the forbidding and jaw-breaking title *Report on an Exploration in the Yukon District, N.W.T., and Adjacent Northern Portion of British Columbia, 1887.* The original appendices were deleted from this edition, and that portion of McConnell's report which covered his exploration on the Liard and in the northern Yukon was appended instead. Additional information was also added to the mapsheets to bring them up-to-date. This publication is, beyond a doubt, the definitive work on the pre-gold rush Yukon.

Predominantly, of course, the report was an account of Dawson's exploration of the district, including the observations and notes so painstakingly gathered in the course of his travels. But more than this, the report was a compendium of most of the known facts concerning the Yukon. There was a section devoted to a general outline of the country and its principal geological and geographical features, as well as more detailed treatment of such subjects as flora and fauna, mining and minerals, glaciation and surface deposits, navigable waters and routes of travel, agriculture, the fur trade, climate, and some account of the journeys and accomplishments of earlier explorers and traders. Many of these men were still living, and Dawson corresponded with several of them, including Robert Campbell, "now of Manitoba."

It was in fact only in regard to his proposed studies of the Indians of the Yukon that Dawson had to admit to disappointment. He acknowledged ruefully that "Between the northern edge of the ethnological map of northern British Columbia prepared by Dr. Tolmie and myself in 1884, and the known portion of the area of Mr. W. H. Dall's similar map of Alaska and adjacent regions, a great gap has existed, which I had proposed to endeavour to fill in connection with the work of the Yukon Expedition. . . . This intention has been very imperfectly executed, owing especially to the fact that during a great part of our journey we met with neither Indians nor whites from whom information might have been obtained."[89]

Dawson garnered many further honours in the years following the Yukon Expedition: an honourary degree of Doctor of Laws from Queen's University in 1890; similar recognition from McGill in 1891; election as a Fellow of the Royal Society, England, in 1891; charter member of the Royal Society in Canada, and its president in 1893. In 1892 he was named one of the British Commissioners appointed to an international enquiry board investigating the disposition of the resources of the Bering Sea, and for his services in this capacity he was invested by Queen Victoria as a Companion of the Order of St. Michael and St. George. Professional recognition by his own government came in 1895 when he was appointed Director and Deputy Head of the Geological Survey of Canada, succeeding Dr. Selwyn in this position. A few weeks later he was elected a Fellow of the American Society for the Advancement of Science, and in 1897 he was the recipient of the prestigious gold medal of the Royal Geographical Society, London. It was a distinct shock to the scientific world, therefore, when the news came from Ottawa of his sudden death on March 2, 1901, of capillary bronchitis, after only one day away from his desk. He lived barely long enough to see his predic-

---

[89] George Dawson, "Notes on the Indian Tribes of the Yukon District and Adjacent Northern Portion of British Columbia," *Geological and Natural History Survey of British Columbia, 1887-88*, Vol. III, Part I, Appendix IIB, (Montreal, Government Printing Office, 1889), p. 191b.

tion of a major gold discovery in the Yukon came true: his loss was one that his young country and its embryonic civil service could ill afford.

McConnell, only 26 at the time of the Yukon Expedition, also enjoyed a distinguished, and lengthier, career in the public service, one that spanned forty years of field work and administrative responsibility. He did not return to the Yukon until after the Klondike discovery, but in the wake of the interest created by that find, he spent the summers from 1898 to 1905 back in the district, dividing his time between investigations of the new gold fields and further exploratory surveys.[90] In 1914 he was appointed Director of the Geological Survey and Deputy Minister of Mines, the Survey having become a branch of the newly-organized Department of Mines in 1907. He held this post with distinction until his retirement in 1921. He continued to work for several years as a consultant, including two summers in the field for the Ontario Department of Mines, near Sault Ste. Marie, though he was over 70 at the time. He died peacefully in Ottawa on April 1, 1942, when he was 86 years of age. Among other distinctions, he was a Fellow of the Royal Society of Canada, and a member of the Canadian Institute of Mining and Metallurgy. In 1896 he married Jean Botterell of Montreal, and they had one son and one daughter.

Ogilvie, alone of the three principals of the Expedition, was to spend a great part of the time remaining before the Klondike find in the Yukon, mostly in connection with further work on the boundary survey. By chance, he was staying at Fortymile when the discovery claim on Rabbit Creek was staked, and his integrity, and the respect

---

[90] In 1898 McConnell, with J. B. Tyrrell, prepared a preliminary memorandum on the gold deposits and gold mining in the Dawson vicinity; he began mapping the rock formations of the area in 1899, and published detailed reports on these investigations in 1903 and in 1905-06, which did much to spark the era of large-scale mining that eventually succeeded the pick and shovel workings. McConnell's other investigations in the Yukon took him into the Big Salmon-Teslin Lake country in 1898, after his visit to the Klondike; along a portion of the Tintina Valley and the lower reaches of the Stewart River in 1900; back to the Big Salmon in 1901, with special attention to the Livingstone Creek placers; up the MacMillan River in 1902; into the new Kluane Lake mining district in 1904, with a side-trip to report on the Whitehorse copper belt; and to the headwaters of the White River and to Windy Arm in 1905. His reports drew attention to many areas that possessed mineral potential, and they were a useful guide to the prospectors who began to fan out over the territory in the years that followed the Klondike finds.

in which he was held by the miners, were steadying influences in the hectic weeks that followed this fantastic event. For the first time, with his presence, there was a government representative in the district, an honest and sympathetic man with whom the miners could discuss their problems, and who had the ear of the minister and the deputy minister on his visits to Ottawa. He was the liaison between the men on the creek and the government. Dawson and McConnell realized the potential of the region: Ogilvie was one of the architects of the transition from an obscure outpost to, briefly, one of the great gold-camps of the world.

CHAPTER SEVEN

Surveyors and Explorers

Map Numbers 1, 2, 3, 4, 5 and 6, following page 58

I

WHEN OGILVIE REPORTED TO THE MINISTER OF THE INTERIOR IN Ottawa in 1889, he brought with him not only the results of his surveys but also pages of notes listing the problems and complaints of the miners, and the changes that they felt should be implemented in the district. Most of the discussions from which these notes were gleaned took place in Ogilvie's camp on the boundary during the winter of 1887-88, where many of the miners visited him, knowing that he was "in a measure" the government representative in the area. He recorded conscientiously the opinions of each of his callers, even though the views they held were often contradictory. "The best I could do," he commented, "was to hear as patiently as possible the views of all."[1]

The principal complaint of the men was the inadequacy of the mining regulations. In the Yukon these were formulated and administered by the Department of the Interior in far-off Ottawa, by men with no personal knowledge of conditions in the territory. Each miner was permitted to stake only one claim, which was limited in size to 100 square feet in area. All those who talked to Ogilvie were unanimous in declaring that in such a remote region, with a short season, high costs, and difficult working conditions to contend with, a claim of these restricted dimensions could not be mined economically, but they differed in their ideas as to what changes in the mining laws should be made. The men who had worked previously in American mining camps pointed out that the regulations in that

---

[1] Ogilvie, *Early Days*, p. 139.

211

country were much more accommodating: there "each community elected its own recorders, regulated the size of its claims, and did nearly everything else the majority of the miners thought wise, so long as they did not clash with the general mining law of the United States."[2] The American faction at Fortymile vociferously supported this system of local control for the Yukon creeks, but the Canadians generally, more conditioned to government authority, were not in favour of such a sweeping abrogation of sovereignty — they would settle for permission from the distant bureaucrats to stake large individual claims. Ogilvie himself favoured this point of view.

Another vexing problem, resulting from the discovery of coarse gold, was technical in nature and could not be solved by government intervention. "Up to the year 1887," Ogilvie explained, "all mining done in the territory was on the bars and banks of the streams, and most of this was known as skim diggings, that is, only the two to four feet of the surface was worked. This was because, in the great majority of cases, below that depth, water was encountered, which prevented profitable work. In the banks, too, frost was often met before the work extended far."[3] In mining coarse gold, on the other hand, paydirt was close to bedrock, and in these northern latitudes was almost invariably overlain by permafrost.

[This] frost was considered by many an insuperable barrier, and it was generally believed that bed-rock could not be reached by any practicable method. It was assumed that here, as elsewhere, the best pay would be found at the lowest depths, but how to get through twenty, thirty, and forty or more feet of frozen sand, clay, and gravel at reasonable expenditure of time and money was the question, and as it developed it was a *burning question*. All sorts of ideas were propounded and discussed, many impracticable from the paraphernalia required, and some impossible of execution; still, all helped the discussion along. As I had seen in the winter holes burned in the frozen crusts of the streets in Ottawa to reach defective gas and water pipes, and I had several times had to use the process myself for other purposes, I suggested this as I had seen it applied, substituting, of course, the wood of the country for the coke used in the city. . . . Whether my advocacy had much, or little, or anything to do with the inception of the method I cannot say, but it was tried, and a tremendous impetus was given to mining in the region. Bed-rock was reached, and a quality and quantity of gold was found that was not dreamed of before.[4]

[2] *Ibid.*, pp. 142-143.
[3] *Ibid.*, p. 138.
[4] *Ibid.*, p. 140.

This technique remained basic to mining in the Yukon until after the turn of the century and the beginning of gold recovery by the use of dredges. "A fire was built on the ground," explained a later writer, describing the operation in a government publication, "about six feet long by four feet in width. This fire was allowed to burn from eight to ten hours, and the ground which had thawed under it was then taken out. Another fire was started in the hole thus excavated, and by this means they gradually worked their way to bedrock. From two to three feet of dirt was taken out with each thaw. The gravel, and the bed-rock for about two feet below, contains gold. . . . A miner, after sinking his shaft through the overburden, then drifts by the same means along the bed rock containing the gold. It is not as a rule necessary for him to timber the drift, as the frozen ground holds up with perfect safety."[5]

This method of mining had also the effect of extending the season, as the underground work could be carried on during the winter — or during the milder part of it at least — and the excavated material treated by sluicing during the summer to extract the gold. Nonetheless, it was desperately hard work, and in an unproved prospect the returns were often meagre. McGrath, a surveyor who spent some time at Fortymile in 1890 on the way to his boundary camp, noted that "in the winter of 1889-1890 three men took out 23,000 buckets of dirt, which netted them $1,000 apiece for their three months of the hardest kind of mining work known."[6] All the rewards were not as lean as this, however: McGrath was shown a nugget worth $56, and during the summer of 1889 one was found which was worth $260. By the end of navigation in that same year McQuesten had shipped out on behalf of his customers about $40,000 worth of gold dust, which he estimated was slightly less than half of the total production for 1889.

Ogilvie, when he finally returned to Ottawa, spent considerable time conferring with the Minister of the Interior, and more particularly with A. M. Burgess, the Deputy Minister, who had deferred taking any government action in the territory until they received firsthand reports.

[5] *The Yukon Territory, Its History and Resources,* (Ottawa, Dept. of the Interior, Government Printing Bureau, 1909), p. 11.

[6] J. E. McGrath, "The Boundary South of Fort Yukon," Part II of "The Alaska Boundary Survey," *The National Geographic Magazine,* Vol. IV., (February 8, 1893), p. 185.

The condition of the country as I knew it [Ogilvie wrote] was gone over very thoroughly, and ... we discussed very fully what was deemed best to do in the interest of the Canadian part of the territory. Mr. Burgess was very frank in asking me to place my views fully before him, and I was asked to say freely and fully what I thought had best be done at that time. I told him that our mining regulations, as far as known, were unfavourably commented on in comparison with those of the United States. . . . I advised him that while Fortymile seemed to possess the essentials for a pretty stable camp, most of the diggings on it were on the American side of the boundary, that at the time there were not freighting facilities enough to support more than one small camp, and that until such times as there were more and better means of transport it would be unwise in us to interfere with the affairs of the region. . . . Generally, my advice was that, as the country was in a very unsettled state, and our mining laws, so far as known, unsatisfactory to the miners, even of our own nationality, any attempt to take charge of affairs on our side of the line would hinder prospecting by driving most of the prospectors to the American side, and they would stay there till something very rich was discovered in Canada, and that the chance of this would be put back by our action, if we entered with authority then.[7]

With these sentiments the authorities in Ottawa fully agreed. It was decided that for the present there would be no attempt to establish any form of government control; Ogilvie, however, was instructed to watch the course of events closely, and when he thought that the time had come to "take possession," he was to advise the Department to that effect. By this arrangement, the development of the district would not be set back by premature action, and yet through their representative in the country the government would maintain a watching brief on the situation in its remote territory.

II

OGILVIE'S BOUNDARY SURVEY OF 1887-88 HAD FILLED A PRESSING need, but many of the American miners felt that the location should be confirmed by their own authorities, and their petitions to this effect were not long in bringing results. In 1889 President Cleveland secured from Congress an appropriation of $20,000 to check

---

[7] Ogilvie, *Early Days*, pp. 142-144. During his traverse of the Tat-on-duc and Porcupine Rivers on his way out of the Yukon, Ogilvie named two of the prominent mountain peaks along his route after Dewdney and Burgess. These names are still found on present-day maps.

Ogilvie's survey on the Yukon, and to determine the location of the boundary on the Porcupine. The work was assigned to the United States Coast and Geodetic Survey, and the Canadian government offered full co-operation: Ogilvie was ordered to prepare a detailed report of his operations for the guidance of the Americans.

Two parties were organized in the spring of 1889. One, led by J. E. McGrath, was to camp on the Yukon River as close to the intersection of the 141st meridian as possible, and there repeat Ogilvie's observations. The other, under J. Henry Turner, would make independent observations of the Porcupine to locate the boundary there. Israel C. Russell of the United States Geological Survey was attached to the expedition "for the purpose of making such observations on the character and resources of the country as the nature of the journey would allow."[8]

The surveyors sailed from San Francisco in June 1889, and in early July reached St. Michael's, where they transferred to the river steamer *Yukon*. During their laborious upstream journey they had ample time to discover, as had their predecessors, that barren Arctic conditions did not prevail along the river during the brief summer season. "At fort Yukon," wrote McGrath in a paper prepared later for presentation to the members of the National Geographic Society, "which is little over a mile inside the arctic circle, the heat was almost insufferable, both in August and July; and the only warning given us of what we might expect a little later on was afforded at Nulato, where we saw a well being sunk which had already been driven through twenty-five feet of frozen ground."[9]

The young survey officers, when their purpose in travelling became known, were offered gratuitous advice at every trading station at which they stopped — a hazard to which the newcomer is still exposed today. "All the traders of St. Michael's were certain that the coming winter would be a severe one," McGrath noted, "because the one just past had been very mild. Rain had fallen on Forty-Mile Creek on January 1st, 1889, and according to all the laws of Alaska weather, the approaching winter would have to make up for the mildness of the preceding one."[10] Jack McQuesten, possibly with

---

8 Israel C. Russell, "A Journey up the Yukon River," *Journal of the American Geographical Society*, Vol. XXVII, No. 2, (1895), p. 143.

9 McGrath, "The Boundary South," p. 185.

10 *Ibid.*, p. 185, as are the other quotations in this paragraph relating to the weather.

tongue in cheek, told them cheerfully of "the winter of 1886, when the signal service thermometer at his station recorded −70°, and his face was frozen when going about 50 feet from his house to call some miners who lived in a cabin nearby to see how low the temperature was." Al Mayo "was certain that a later winter was still colder, but unfortunately he had no spirit thermometer that year, and so he had to judge entirely by his sensations." It was not surprising that the greenhorns, uncertain as to how much they were told was fact and how much was fancy, confessed to "much anxiety about what the future might have in store for us."

At Fort Yukon, marked now by only one ruined chimney, McGrath and his men disembarked, and the steamer started up the Porcupine with Turner and his party, accompanied by Russell. The journey began on August 3, but after only three days of travel, the steamer was stopped by low water 39 miles west of where the boundary was believed to be.

Captain Peterson refused to tarry [wrote Turner], since the river was still falling, as plainly indicated by wet lines along the banks and mud flats, and the danger of being stranded on a sand-bar until the following spring was too great a possibility to be overlooked. Supplies were consequently unloaded with all expedition possible, and the steamer returned to fort Yukon.

Had our time of arrival been delayed a week no difficulty would have been experienced in landing the party at the boundary, as the river rose rapidly in a few days. A whale-boat brought from San Francisco and a large, unwieldy lighter borrowed from the Alaska Commercial company were the sole means of transport at our command.[11]

The inexperienced surveyors with their unsuitable craft began the task of wrestling their stores upstream "in the face of a strong current, broken into rapids in many places." Predictably, their efforts hovered on the brink of disaster, but none the less the move was somehow accomplished. At first some Indians were hired to assist with the work, but one unfortunately was accidentally drowned. The others, after this mishap, refused to remain with the surveyors, becoming in fact quite hostile: only the intervention of Mr. Firth, the officer in charge of the Hudson's Bay Company's post at Rampart House, prevented serious trouble.

[11] J. Henry Turner, "The Boundary North of Fort Yukon," Part III of "The Alaskan Survey," *The National Geographic Magazine*, Vol. IV, (February 8, 1893), pp. 189-190.

Two of Turner's own men became casualties; one man broke an ankle, and one lost the tip of a finger while moving a heavy box. The final blow came when observations made at Rampart House revealed that the post was not, as had been generally believed, located on the boundary, but was inside Alaskan territory: the supplies had to be moved a further 33 miles upstream, or almost as far as they had already been transported. It must have been with an overwhelming sense of relief that Turner was finally able to record the arrival at their destination. "A well sheltered spot was finally selected," he wrote, "in a timbered valley at the mouth of the Sunaghun River, and preparations were begun to build a comfortable log house for winter quarters. The work was often interrupted by snow-storms of frequent occurrence, beginning in August. Ice began to form along the river banks in early September, and by the end of October a snowy mantle covered the country, and all the streams were locked fast in ice. The log cabin and all observatories were ready for occupation by October 1."[12] The station was named Camp Colonna.

McGrath's party, by contrast, arrived at their station in comfort, almost in luxury. The *Yukon*, after leaving Turner's crew on the Porcupine, returned quickly to the river mouth, with Russell as her only passenger, and McGrath and his men "took up their previous quarters on the steamer." The continuation of the upstream journey took them directly to the location on the 141st meridian that they were to occupy: the steamer then returned to Fort Yukon for the remainder of the supplies, which had been left behind to make the struggle against the current easier: "This delay," Russell commented, "enabled me to spend a number of pleasant days at Camp Davidson, as Mr. McGrath's station was named, and to explore some of the adjacent country."

Camp Davidson [he continued] had been previously occupied by a surveying party sent by the Canadian government, who built a commodious log house, in which they passed a winter. The house was still in good repair, and was at once cleared out and enlarged. An observatory of logs, built over the stump of a large tree which served for an instrument pier, was also found standing and was at once fitted up for use.

Over the large Russian stove, built of stones, in the cabin, hung a magnificent pair of caribou antlers, which told that game could be expected in the neighbouring forest. During my lonely climbs in the adjacent mountains, I found abundant signs of moose and bear, but was

12 *Ibid.*, pp. 190-191.

217

not fortunate enough to see large game. The trails of mountain sheep and mountain goats were abundant at elevations of about 3,000 feet. The river was known to abound in salmon at certain seasons, and grayling or Arctic trout were said to be plentiful. Taking all in all, Camp Davidson seemed to be an excellent place in which to pass an Arctic winter.

When the *Yukon* returned to Camp Davidson, I bade good-by to my friends ... and resumed my voyage up the river.[13]

On September 1, the steamer arrived at Fort Selkirk, the "highest point" on the river reached to that time, and the end of the voyage. Russell noted that Arthur Harper, who with "his Indian wife and several interesting children" had been a fellow-traveller, disembarked with a large stock of trade goods, intending to re-establish a trading post in the Fort Selkirk area.

The locality chosen was in a dense forest on the right bank of the river, opposite old Fort Selkirk. . . . A more unpromising place, to an inexperienced eye, for a store could scarcely be fancied. For fully a hundred miles before reaching it, we had not seen a human being not connected with the *Yukon*. Prolonged whistles from the boat, the usual signal for calling the natives, were not answered by a single canoe; and after continuing my journey up stream, I saw scarcely a score of Indians before reaching the coast. . . . In spite of these discouraging signs, however, the hardy Scotchman, who by the way, was one of the most genial and best informed men that I met in Central Alaska, went quietly on with his preparations for passing another winter as he had done many previous ones, in the solitude of the wilderness. The inducement that lures traders to such remote localities is, of course, the rich furs, at present, with the exception of gold, the sole export of the Yukon region.[14]

Russell made arrangements to continue upstream and over the Chilkoot Pass, travelling with four miners whom he encountered at Fort Selkirk. They were only as far as Tagish Lake when they woke one morning to find their blankets weighted down with snow, and the landscape white. These conditions persisted until they were well down the Pacific slope of Chilkoot Pass.

For the survey crews remaining in the Yukon the thermometer did

---

[13] Russell, "A Journey," p. 151. Incredibly, neither McGrath in his presentation to the National Geographic Society, nor Dr. T. G. Mendenhall who introduced him, acknowledged in any way the co-operation of the Canadian government, or mentioned the fact that the survey party occupied Ogilvie's former boundary camp.

[14] *Ibid.*, pp. 153-154.

not plummet that winter to the extremes that McQuesten had predicted might be reached — the lowest reading at either camp throughout their stay was −60.5° F. It was not the cold, but the depressing effects of the long, dark winter nights, that caused the greatest hardship. Camp Davidson was particularly hard hit, as the supply of coal-oil for their lamps was low. The use of artificial light in their quarters could, as a result, only be permitted for four hours a day, while in December and January darkness persisted for twenty. "We had many a dark hour to endure," McGrath wrote, "and those two months seemed almost endless."[15] At Turner's camp there was no coal-oil shortage, but because of their more northern location beyond the Arctic Circle, the party did not see the sun from November 16 to January 26. Turner reported that "as the first feeble rays struggled through the frost-laden windows the spirits of the men brightened, and, rushing forth from the cabin, they capered about like mad in an excess of joy."[16]

The winter of 1889-90 was a hungry one on the Porcupine, and the initial hostility of the natives to the surveyors was forgotten as the threat of starvation stalked the land.

Early in January [Turner wrote] the stock of provisions at Rampart house became exhausted. . . . Several hunting parties had gone out, to return empty-handed and to report that the deer had migrated southward. Many Indians were reduced to the necessity of subsisting upon moose-skin bags, deer-skin thongs, and old sled covers. Several old people died of sheer starvation, and the outlook grew gloomy. Timely assistance from the missionary, Mr. Wallis,[17] and a case of flour from camp Colonna tided them over the emergency until a few deer were secured by an expert hunter, who had been permitted the use of a Winchester rifle from our camp.[18]

It had been expected that the necessary observations could be obtained in one season, but abnormal cloudiness that prevailed during the first year made it necessary for both parties to remain in the country for the winter of 1890-91. Over the two winters McGrath finally obtained 13 observations, and Ogilvie was later

---

[15] McGrath, "The Boundary South," p. 187.

[16] Turner, "The Boundary North," p. 191.

[17] Rev. G. C. Wallis was a recruit to the Mackenzie River diocese of Bompas in 1886, and was sent to Rampart House to strengthen the work of the church in that area. (See also Chapter Eight.)

[18] Turner, "The Boundary North," pp. 191-192.

able to report with satisfaction, when results became known, that "the line as I had marked it was accepted until such time as better methods of observation could be utilized in the vicinity."[19] Turner too completed his work, the results of which were to chase the Hudson's Bay Company farther eastward, as they were still trespassers on American soil, though in this case, unintentionally. The surveyors left the territory in the summer of 1891, following the same route by which they had entered two years before. Before his departure from the Porcupine, however, Turner found time to make a dash to the Arctic coast in order to roughly trace the boundary to its northern limit, using dogs, sleds and guides borrowed from Rampart House.

They started out on March 27 in clear, calm weather "in happy anticipation of a swift and easy journey," but within twenty-four hours of leaving they were assaulted without warning by a screaming blizzard that held them stormbound for over a day. When the storm came Turner was a little behind the others because he was taking notes: he recounted that in the short time it took him to rejoin his companions in the shelter of a small hill "the end of my nose, one temple and the tip of the right ear were frozen solid, and a broad white streak fully an inch wide extended from eye to chin, bore evidence of the rapidity with which a man may freeze if the conditions be favorable. . . . For the remainder of that day, that night, and until noon of the following day the shrieking north wind swept over the trackless wastes in all the fury of a Dakota blizzard. Traveling was quite out of the question; men and dogs huddled together in a promiscuous heap, striving to secure protection from the bitter blast."[20]

The storm died away as quickly as it began, and by late the next day, from the summit of a pass, the men saw spread out before them "and extending eastward to the furthest horizon . . . a plain covered with a dense growth of spruce, birch and cottonwood — a veritable oasis in the midst of utter desolation. . . . Fifty miles away to the northward a range of low mountains was discerned, trending to the eastward, and forming the northern boundary of the plain."[21]

---

[19] Ogilvie, *Early Days*, pp. 60-61. In 1909 a resurvey of the boundary was carried out by the Joint Boundary Commission using the "star transit and electric telegraph method." Ogilvie's line was found to be only a few yards "from where it ought to be." *Ibid.*, p. 61.

[20] Turner, "The Boundary North," p. 196.

[21] *Ibid.*, p. 196, as is the quotation relating to the encounter with the Eskimos.

The little party was three days reaching this distant range, as they threaded their way through the "innumerable lakes" on the Old Crow flats. On the first day of this crossing "a tribe of Nigalek Eskimos were encountered. They were fine looking savages, and seemed surprised to meet white men so far away from the trading posts." Turner had already noted that Eskimos occasionally came to Rampart House "in order to exchange walrus lines for wolverine skins, which are afterwards traded to passing whalers for whisky or old-fashioned breech-loading Winchesters."[22]

Beyond the plains they crossed a second and higher pass, at an elevation of 3,000 feet, and began the abrupt descent of the Arctic slope.

The route led through a valley hemmed in by most forbidding-looking mountains, running up in jagged spurs to a height of 6,000 or 8,000 feet. Three rivers in this valley run into one, which has its outlet near the eastern extremity of the basin. A large area was covered with ice, the result of overflow. . . . This river was followed to the Arctic ocean, passing often between towering mountains or through gloomy canyons, where the wind howled dismally.

On the eighteenth day, April 8, the ocean was reached. A stiff breeze was blowing from the southeast, and the mercury registered −30°. A fire of driftwood was made and shelter was secured under the lee of a snow bank. The drifting snow shrouded the horizon until late in the afternoon, when the wind ceased and a long line of hummocky ice was revealed skirting the gloomy shore.[23]

Their objective was accomplished, and they lost no time in starting the return journey to Camp Colonna. There was little on this inhospitable coast to encourage them to linger: the fact that a vast reservoir of crude oil lay buried close to where they stood would hardly have interested them at that time, even if they had known it was there.

III

IN 1891, THE SAME YEAR THAT THE COAST AND GEODETIC SURVEY crews departed by the Yukon's mouth, Frederick Schwatka entered the country again from the south. He had already been back in

22 *Ibid.*, p. 194.
23 *Ibid.*, p. 197.

Alaska once since his rafting journey, when in 1886 he led an expedition supported by *The New York Times* that carried out "geographical research" in the vicinity of the St. Elias range, and made an attempt to climb Mt. St. Elias, at that time the highest known peak in the Alaskan littoral. The climbers failed to reach the summit, but from the levels they did obtain, they had tantalizing glimpses to the north of a vast jumble of unexplored mountain peaks, "amongst which," one of them wrote, "I think it is doubtful if anyone will ever penetrate for any long distance, owing to the difficulties of transport."[24] Now, financed by another newspaper syndicate, Schwatka hoped to cross these "impenetrable" mountains from the Canadian side, by following the White River to its source deep within the range.

A request was sent by the syndicate to the Director of the United States Geological Survey asking if one of his officers could be detailed to accompany the expedition, and the assignment was given to an experienced field geologist, Charles Willard Hayes. Schwatka's "popular" description of the exploration presumably appeared in the pages of the newspapers that sponsored him. Hayes, on his return to Washington presented, at a meeting of the National Geographic Society on February 5, 1892, a paper recounting "the main facts of scientific interest observed throughout the journey."[25] This account of the expedition was later published in the Society's magazine of May 15, 1892, and is the form in which the record is most readily available today.

Schwatka had intended to come into the territory over the Chilkoot Pass, retracing his own earlier footsteps, but during a stopover in Juneau, "at the request of the citizens, backed up by their substantial assistance, it was decided to go in by way of Taku river, with a view to determining whether a trail for pack animals could be constructed over that route."[26] An experienced miner named Mark Russell, who had covered some of the ground before, agreed to accompany the expedition. Six Indians were hired as boatmen and packers, and "a large two-ton dugout canoe" was supplied by the people of Juneau to serve as transport on Taku Inlet and on

[24] H. W. Seton-Karr, "Explorations in Alaska and North-west British Columbia," *Proceedings of the Royal Geographical Society*, (February 1891), p. 65.

[25] C. W. Hayes, "An Expedition Through the Yukon District," *The National Geographic Magazine*, Vol. IV, (May 15, 1892), p. 118.

[26] *Ibid.*, p. 118.

the river. The journey began on May 25, 1891, and seven days later the party reached "the head of canoe navigation, eight miles above the South fork [the Inklin River] and about 80 from Juneau."[27]

Ahead of them was an overland carry of 85 miles to Teslin Lake, by way of the Nah-Kina (Nakina) River to the height of land, and down a smaller river, today known as the Hayes, to the lake. "Our outfit was made up into twelve packs of about one hundred pounds each for the portage. . . . As there were but six packers, each was obliged to make two trips; so that our progress was extremely slow."[28] All the gear was not delivered to the lake until June 16, when the Indians were paid off and returned to Juneau. The three white men assembled two portable canoes that were part of their stores, and paddled down Teslin Lake to the Teslin River, and down it to the Lewes, which they reached on June 28. Four days later they landed at Harper's newly-established trading post at Fort Selkirk.

Schwatka's plan was to cross the St. Elias Mountains by way of a pass which the White River Indians called Scolai, the name that they gave to Nicolai, the chief of the Copper River Indians in Alaska, with whom they occasionally traded. It had been Schwatka's intention to reach the pass by paddling up the White River, but at the trading post he was persuaded that the easiest way to reach the head of the river was by an overland route, and the idea of ascending the White was abandoned. Word of this decision was passed to the Indians on the Pelly, and soon about forty of them were camped at the post, awaiting developments. The ritual of haggling for packers began.

Only a few of them [wrote Hayes], were able-bodied men, and it was extremely difficult to persuade these to go with us; and when they had promised it was only to back out the next day. After laboring with them for over a week it seemed that the attempt to secure the necessary packers was hopeless, and we were preparing to go down to the mouth of the White river and try the ascent by boat, when the tide was turned by the opportune arrival of a prospector, Frank Bowker. He had come up the river from Forty-mile creek, intending to spend the summer prospecting in White River basin. With him were two natives from further down the river, muscular and willing fellows, very different from the wretched specimens from Pelly river. Bowker's arrival, as he

[27] *Ibid.*, p. 120.
[28] *Ibid.*, p. 121.

came with authority from Mr. Harper, who has great influence over the natives, put new backbone into our enterprise. Five packers were soon secured, who promised to go with us to the country of Scolai, beyond the mountains. Dogs were obtained to carry the remainder of the outfit, from twenty-five to forty pounds being packed upon each in panniers of birch bark or moose skin.[29]

On July 9 the party of four white men (Bowker had agreed to accompany them as far as the White), eight Indians, and 11 dogs left Harper's post and headed for the beckoning St. Elias Mountains. The area that lay ahead of them was, Hayes stated, "geographically a blank. So far as can be learned it had never been penetrated by a white man, and the lakes, rivers and mountains which appear on many maps are the products of the geographer's imagination."[30]

They climbed quickly out of the river valley, and entered the plateau country that lay south and west of the trading post. It was a terrain of jumbled whale-back hills, characterized by weathered rock and castellated outcrops on their treeless upper slopes, and intersected by several timbered river valleys. The expedition passed around the headwaters of the stream that Schwatka had called the Selwyn, skirting as they did so a tributary now known as Hayes Creek. They then crossed the Klutassin (Klotassin) and the Nisling Rivers, indigenous names which Hayes retained on the sketch map of the route that he compiled. On the Nisling they encountered a group of six native families "making a fish trap in anticipation of the arrival of the salmon, which was anxiously looked for. These Indians are closely related to those living on the Pelly. . . . They have no permanent dwellings, but several substantial log caches were seen, which they use for storing their winter's supply of dried fish and moose meat. The country seems to be fairly well supplied with game, goats on the highest rocky summits, moose and bear in the river valleys, and reindeer or barren-grounds caribou on the plateau above the timberline."[31]

From the high ground beyond the Nisling the explorers had their first glimpse of the White River valley "with the river pursuing its extremely tortuous course among innumerable low islands and

[29] *Ibid.*, p. 122.

[30] *Ibid.*, p. 120.

[31] *Ibid.*, pp. 122-123.

bars."[32] To their surprise the valley floor seemed to be almost completely covered with snow, though they were to discover at closer range that the white mantle was in fact a very heavy concentration of volcanic ash "into which one sinks from four to twelve inches in walking. A scanty growth of dwarf alder and blueberry bushes has gained a precarious foothold in some places, and a few stunted spruce trees grow in protected spots along the streams."[33] This deposit, rather than glacial action, was obviously the principal cause of the turbidity of the river.

As they approached closer to the imposing barrier of the mountains, the men encountered three glacier-fed streams that originated within the range, for which Hayes also retained the native names — the Donjek, the largest of the three and a major tributary of the White, the Kluantu, and the Klutlan. All these rivers were unfordable, but they crossed the Donjek and the Kluantu on rafts which they obtained from a second group of Indians who were camping on the Kluantu's banks. To cross the Klutlan, however, they "were compelled to go around its head and cross upon the glacier from which it flows. Although this was not attended by any special danger it caused great dismay among the Indians, who regard a glacier with superstitious terror."[34]

Twelve miles beyond this crossing they came to a small stream which the Indians told them was the Klet-san-dek (Kletsan or Copper Creek), the reputed point of origin of most of the copper used on the Canadian side of the mountains.

Native copper [wrote Hayes] has long been known to exist in the Copper River basin, but exactly where or in what quantity has never been ascertained through actual examination by a competent observer. Its occurrence in White River basin also has been suspected from the presence of native copper among the Yukon Indians, although they were known to trade with those living on Copper river from whom they might have obtained the metal. The Pelly Indians whom we obtained at Selkirk for packers promised to show us the source from which in the past they had secured copper for making arrow-heads and more recently for making bullets, which are still used to some extent when lead cannot be obtained. While still at Selkirk they told us of great masses of copper on the Klet-san-dek. . . . As we approached this locality, however, the

---

[32] *Ibid.*, p. 134.
[33] *Ibid.*, p. 147.
[34] *Ibid.*, p. 123.

masses of copper rapidly decreased in size, first to pieces as big as a man and then to bowlders of such size that they could be lifted by prying with a stout stick, and finally what they actually showed us consisted of small nuggets, the largest only a few ounces in weight.[35]

The Kletsan flowed out of a narrow gorge high above the valley floor, and the explorers spent a short time prospecting it for the source of the copper, but without success, as the snow line lay only a short distance up the creek. Hayes noted, however, that the rock formations in the locality bore a superficial resemblance to the copper-bearing series of the Lake Superior region.

This creek was as far as any of the Fort Selkirk natives had ever been from home, and they refused to go farther, assuring the white men that the pass was crossed only in winter using snow shoes. Bowker, who had already come further than he intended, announced that he was turning back with the Indians. Schwatka, Hayes, and Russell found themselves in a quandary, as their provisions were low. "It was something over two hundred miles back to Selkirk," Hayes explained, "and although through an unknown country, a considerably shorter distance to an Indian village on the other side of the mountains. Trusting in our ability to reach the latter inside of two weeks ... we decided to push forward. Discarding everything not absolutely essential, our packs still amounted to 75 or 80 pounds apiece, so that progress was necessarily slow."[36]

In three days they reached White River, flowing out of a deep, narrow valley, at the head of which they hoped that they would find the pass. In spite of the Indians' stories of the perils they would face, the three men were over the divide almost before they realized it, even though they had to cross one tongue of Russell Glacier — the source of the White — which they had been assured would take at least four days to traverse. In a short time they were off the ice and camped on a stream flowing into the Pacific, which they identified as the Nizzenah, or eastern branch of the Copper River. They struggled down a narrow canyon choked with a dense growth of alder and spruce, taking four or five hours to travel a mile. Finally in desperation they stopped to build a boat, using "a very dull axe and our pocket knives" — after which they made better time. On August 12, just 14 days after separating from the Indians and

[35] *Ibid.*, p. 143.
[36] *Ibid.*, p. 123.

Bowker at Copper Creek, the explorers reached the native village of Taral, on the Copper River, "exactly on scheduled time, with three pounds of flour and a handful of tea remaining of the provisions with which we left Selkirk."[37] Nicolai was at Taral, and the chief gave the white men "a most hospitable welcome."

The pioneer portion of the expedition was completed. Not only would the rest of their journey be in the company of the chief, who was about to leave on his annual visit to the coast, but the explorers were back in country that had already been surveyed by Lieut. H. T. Allen of the U.S. Army, who in 1885 carried out an investigation of the Copper River from its mouth to its headwaters, and left the country by the Tanana River and the Yukon. Hayes was reasonably satisfied with what had been accomplished. "Under the conditions of travel," he commented, "only a hasty reconnaissance of the region traversed was possible, but so little has been known of it geologically or otherwise that such observations as were made possess a value out of proportion to their completeness."[38]

In spite of the physical difficulties of travel, a careful sketch map of the route was drawn.

At the head of Taku inlet a "track survey" was begun and carried continuously to the mouth of Teslin river, where it connected with the line surveyed by Mr. Ogilvie in 1886. The instruments used were a prismatic compass for determining direction, and a sextant for latitude. Distances were obtained during the boat journey on the Taku, lake Ahklen [Teslin], and Teslin river by time and eye measurements, and on the portage between Taku river and the lake by pacing. Altitudes were determined from the mean of four aneroids with synchronous readings of a base barometer at Juneau. . . . The route was plotted in the note book and relief indicated by sketch contours; all prominent points within sight along the line of travel being approximately located by compass bearings. . . .

Between Yukon river and the St. Elias mountains. . . . a track survey was made similar to the one already described. Excepting about fifty miles traversed by water, the whole distance of 330 miles from Selkirk on the Yukon to the junction of Chittenah and Nizzenah rivers[39] was carefully paced; and the two ends of the line being located by astronomic observations, the former by Ogilvie and the latter by Allen, the location of intermediate points cannot be far out of the way.[40]

[37] *Ibid.*, p. 125.

[38] *Ibid.*, p. 118.

[39] The confluence of these two streams marked the start of the Copper River.

[40] Hayes, "An Expedition," pp. 119-120.

Technical information on the country, with emphasis on geology, supplemented the map and constituted a large part of the report. Hayes was particularly interested in the glaciation of the region, and in the origin of the large deposits of volcanic ash.

Hayes went on to a distinguished professional career, becoming ultimately the Director of the United States Geological Survey. For Schwatka, though, this was the last exploration. Within a year of completing this journey he died suddenly in hospital at Portland, Oregon, from the effects of an overdose of laudanum that he was taking for the relief of chronic stomach trouble. He was only 42 at the time of his death, and he had certainly crowded an unconventional and diversified career into his relatively short span.

IV

WHILE SCHWATKA AND HIS PARTY WERE PLODDING ON FOOT TOWARDS Scolai Pass, the first packhorses were entering the country from the opposite direction, by way of the Chilkat Pass route. Edward James Glave was the leading spirit behind this endeavour, but it is the name of his companion, Jack Dalton, that is today most remembered in connection with the project.

The two men met for the first time in 1890, the year before their venture with the packhorses. They were of very different backgrounds and temperaments. Glave was a young explorer-journalist, born in England in 1862, and an associate for a time in Africa of the explorer Henry M. Stanley. He came to the United States in 1889 on a lecture tour after three years of exploration in the Congo. Dalton, in contrast, was born in the Cherokee Strip in Oklahoma in 1855, and had worked as a logger and cowboy in many parts of the west, before coming to Alaska for the first time in 1886. He signed on as a "cook and man of all work" with *The New York Times* expedition under Schwatka: liking what he saw, he returned to the area whenever he could obtain employment with one of the many scientific or exploration parties that were working along the coast.

Glave's lecture tour was a success: it lead in 1890 to an invitation from *Frank Leslie's Illustrated Newspaper* of New York to join an expedition into "the interior of Alaska," and to write reports for the paper during the journey, an offer which he was happy to accept. Dalton was a member of the same expedition. The two men became travelling companions, and from this relationship there developed mutual respect. "He was a most desirable partner," Glave wrote of Dalton, when they finally parted two years later, "having excellent judgment, cool and deliberate in time of danger, and possessed of great tact in dealing with the Indians. He thoroughly understood horses, was as good as any Indian in a cottonwood dugout or skin canoe, and as a camp cook I never met his equal."[41]

The Frank Leslie Exploring Expedition consisted of six men, under the leadership of E. H. Wells. In the early summer of 1890, the whole party trekked into the Kusawa Lake country previously explored by Krause, and travelled part way down the lake by raft. At a bend in this long, narrow body of water, the men split up. Wells and three of the others continued the traverse of the lake, intent on reaching the Yukon by way of the Takhini River, while Glave and Dalton turned their steps towards the Alsek River, a branch of which they hoped they might be able to descend to the sea.

They left Kusawa with only such provisions and gear as they were able to carry on their backs, since there were no packers to assist them. "It is anything but desirable," wrote Glave in one of his reports, "that conditions such as these should accompany works of travel, and our attempt to cover so much ground with such small resources seemed foolhardy; but there is a keen fascination in travelling through unknown lands; to be the first white man to erase from the map the hypothetical and fill up the blank area with the mountains, lakes, and rivers which belong to it. It is a great consolation to have some such comforting reflection, and with such an incentive, discomfort can be suffered and hardship and privation endured."[42] By way of a lake which Glave named Frederick "in loving remembrance of my brother, who died a few years ago," they came in a short time to Lake Klukshu, south of Dezadeash.

This sheet of water [Glave wrote] is about one-quarter of a mile wide and five miles in length, and lies north and south, walled on the west

---

[41] E. J. Glave, "Pioneer Packhorses in Alaska," *The Century Illustrated Monthly Magazine*, Vol. XLIV, (September and October 1892), p. 672.

[42] E. J. Glave, "Our Alaska Expedition," *Frank Leslie's Illustrated Newspaper*, (November 15, 1890), p. 226.

and east by wooded hills. There is a settlement of Gunana[43] [Stick] Indians on the western shore; the houses, however, are only inhabited during a few months of the year when the Indians are fishing, but there are undoubted evidences of former occupation by great numbers of people; whole forests of trees have been felled, the oldest marks being most numerous. . . .

We remained on this lake but one day, and then again got on the trail for the south, marching sometimes along the banks of the stream, at other times along the mountain sides and over the brows of foothills, and again through marshy swamps, forcing our way past a network of brittle undergrowth and scrubby brush which clothes the mountain sides. Magnificent scenery all around, lofty mountains on either side hem in the valley of the Alseck.[44]

Glave believed that Lake Klukshu was the "principal" source of the "Alseck" River: it is in fact the source of the east fork of that river system, which today is known as the Tatshenshini for the greater part of its length. The west fork, when he came to it, Glave called the Kaskar Wurlch, his interpretation of its Indian name. Today it is the lower reaches of this fork that are called the Alsek, though one of its branches still retains the name of Kaskawulsh. The 60 miles of river between the confluence of the two forks and the sea has also consistently been called the Alsek, by natives and explorers alike, and today the name of this stretch remains unchanged.

The trail which the two men followed from Klukshu brought them after a journey of roughly 35 miles to another settlement, which Glave reported was called Neska-Ta-Heen, and described as being "the headquarters of the Gunana or Stick Indians. It is composed of a dozen houses, large and small, which in this country means accommodation for a great quantity of people, as several whole families reside in one house. At the time of our visit, all the inhabitants were downriver some sixty miles at their fishing camp on the Alseck."[45]

As far as Neska-Ta-Heen, water travel had been out of the question. Now, though the river was still wild, its volume had increased considerably, and they saw occasional dugout canoes. Deciding that

---

[43] Gunana was a Tlingit word for "strange or different nation," that is, Indians who were not members of the Tlingit tribes. Glave equates this term with the Sticks, but actually the term was broader in application than this specific reference.

[44] Glave, "Our Alaska Expedition," November 22, 1890, p. 286.

[45] *Ibid.*, November 29, 1890, p. 310.

any means of travel was to be preferred to walking with packs, they made arrangements to hire a canoe and guide for their own use, obtaining after some difficult bargaining and for "an exorbitant sum" the services of a medicine-man whom they referred to as Shank. He proceeded to prove his knowledge of the river ahead by recounting a cheerful list of accidents and drownings that had already occurred, a list not calculated "to exercise a soothing tendency on our minds." Fortunately, Shank proved to be an excellent river man.

Having packed our belongings so as to get the little craft into good trim, we embarked and shot out into the stream and were whirled along the raging torrent. The stream, rushing through several channels cut in the rock-strewn valley, at times is hemmed in narrower limits by the nearer approach of the rocky mountain walls which form its banks. Its forces then combine in one deep torrent which tears along at a bewildering rate, roaring as if enraged at its restricted bounds. Our little dugout, dextrously handled, plunged along on the disordered surface, her sharp bow dashing through the waves, drenching us all with spray but shipping little water.

This stream is the wildest I have ever seen; there is scarcely a one-hundred-yard stretch of fair water anywhere along its course. Running with an eight- to ten-knot current, and aggravated by rocky points, sharp bends and immense boulders, the stream is also rendered dangerous by the innumerable rapids and eddies which disturb its surface.[46]

As their descent of the Alsek (Tatshenshini) continued, the explorers found themselves "brought in actual contact with the giant ice-fields of Alaska," and noted a wide pass at right angles to their course filled with an immense glacier (Melburn) ending in a terminal moraine. "All this part of the country," wrote Glave, "is suggestive of violence; these colossal heaps of rock rudely hurled from the mountain heights, the roaring and thundering of the internal forces of the glacier and moraine, whole forests laid low by the fury of the tempests; the wild, angry torrent of the Alseck River, roaring as it sweeps past the desolate scenes — a combination framed by nature to be inimical to life."[47] In places the glacier fronts stood directly on the river banks, and the danger of calving ice blocks was added to the normal hazards of navigation. In spite of all perils, however, the little canoe suffered no mishap. They reached Dry Bay at the river's

[46] *Ibid.*, December 20, 1890, p. 370.
[47] *Ibid.*, December 27, 1890, p. 396.

mouth in safety, and walked the beach to the nearest trading post on Yakutat Bay.

It was the difficulties of travel during this journey that convinced the two men that the use of packhorses would be a feasible and practicable way of moving about in this country, and they decided that they would return the following year and give this method of transportation a trial. "Defective transport," wrote Glave, expressing sentiments still familiar to northerners, "was the sole reason for the undeveloped and unexplored state of the land. The Indian carrier was the only means of transportation; he controlled the situation, and commanded most exorbitant pay. Moreover, his arrogance, inconsistency, cunning, and general unreliability are ever on the alert to thwart the white man."[48] It was desirable, in Glave's opinion, to keep any party venturing into the interior small in numbers, and he decided that Dalton would be his only companion.

We equipped ourselves at Seattle with four short, chunky horses weighing about nine hundred pounds each, supplied ourselves with the requisite pack-saddles and harness, stores and ammunition, then embarked on board a coast steamer, and sailed north from Puget Sound, through the thousand miles of inland seas, to Alaska. We disembarked at Pyramid Harbour, which is by far the most convenient point, from which to start for the interior. No horses had even been taken into the country, and old miners, traders, and prospectors openly pitied our ignorance in imagining the possibility of taking pack-animals over the coast-range. The Indians ridiculed the idea of such an experiment; they told us of the deep, swift streams flowing across our path, the rocky paths so steep that the Indian hunter could climb in safety only by creeping on his hands and knees. Finding that their discouraging reports failed to influence us, the Chilkat Indians, foreseeing that our venture, if successful, would greatly injure their interests by establishing a dangerous competition against their present monopoly, held meetings on the subject, and rumor reached us that our further advance would be resisted. However, when we were ready, we saddled up, buckled on our pistol-belts, and proceeded on our journey without any attempt at hindrance save by verbal demonstration.[49]

There was still snow in the mountain passes when the two men disembarked, but at the Chilkat village of Klokwan (Klukwan), 25 miles from the sea, they found a good meadow for their horses. Towards the end of May 1891, conditions had improved sufficiently

[48] Glave, "Pioneer Packhorses," p. 671.
[49] *Ibid.*, pp. 672-673.

to permit a further advance, following at first the "stony valley" of the Kleeheenee (Klehini) River, and then turning almost due north into the Chilkat Pass. "The steep hillsides of the higher levels," wrote Glave, "we found covered with a dense growth of brittle shrub and coarse grass, and, on the extreme heights, snow-fields and moss-covered rock. . . . We reached the summit, 4750 feet elevation, by slow and careful ascent, without any serious mishap. On the extreme heights of the divide a giant table-land extends for several miles in all directions. The air was cold, and the view cheerless, all lower lands were out of sight, and a distant circle of snowy peaks penciled out the horizon with glistening ruggedness."[50]

It took two days to traverse the pass. Beyond it, they "struck away to the westward, into a great valley, reaching as far as the eye could see, and walled on each side by a lofty line of mountains, thickly wooded to the snow-line."[51] Two more days of travel, and they reached a bluff overlooking Neska-Ta-Heen, to which they made their way after announcing their arrival by firing several rifle shots.

Our arrival [wrote Glave] created excitement among the natives; our horses, of course, were of far more interest than ourselves. They had never seen such animals before, and, for the want of a better name, called them "harklane ketl" (big dogs). This village looked as we had left it twelve months before; there was the same stifling atmosphere, and the natives themselves were wearing the same unwashed garments stiffened with fat and dirt. They received us good-naturedly, and the old chief Warsaine portioned off a corner of his hut for us and our supplies, and the chief's wife consented to be photographed. . . .[52]

Neska-ta-heen is a most important rendezvous. During the winter the natives of the interior roam over all the land in small parties, hunting and trapping, but return here with their spoils of black and brown bear, black, cross, gray, white, and red fox, wolverine, land-otter, mink, lynx, beaver, etc., and exchange them for blankets, guns, powder, and to-bacco, which the Chilkat Indians bring to them from the coast. The latter have always enjoyed a monopoly of this trade, and the natives of the interior have been prevented by them from going to the coast.

From this point valleys of comparatively open country stretch away to the four quarters of the compass: to the east lies the way we had just traveled over; the valley of the Alseck River runs south to the Pacific Ocean; to the west there is a way to the back of Mt. St. Elias; and lakes Dassar-Dee-Ash [Dezadeash] and I-Shi-Ik [Aishihik] lie to

[50] *Ibid.*, p. 677.

[51] *Ibid.*, p. 678.

[52] *Ibid.*, pp. 679-680.

the north. Future research must tell what treasures lie concealed in these unknown regions.

From the coast to Neska-ta-heen we had taken the Indian trail as a basis, following it when good, and, as far as possible, avoiding its bad features. After that experience, we concluded that we could take a fully loaded pack-train from the sea to this village in seven days. Our successful experiment wrests from the Chilkat Indians the control of the road to the interior; the bolted gate hitherto guarded by them, to the exclusion of enterprise and progress, has swung back at the approach of the pack-horse.[53]

In later years, this trail would also become the basis of part of the Haines Road, built as a war-time link between the coast and the Alaska Highway, and now a popular tourist route.

V

AS FAR AS NESKA-TA-HEEN, GLAVE AND DALTON HAD BEEN ACCOM-panied by two Chilkat guides and an interpreter, who were paid two dollars a day and their board. The value of their services to the explorers was dubious: the Chilkats followed the most difficult trails, hoping that the horses would be a failure, and they sought out the longest possible routes, hoping to prolong the journey because of the per diem basis of their pay. By the time they got to Neska-Ta-Heen, however, the Chilkats had had enough of this rather vigorous mode of travel, which they seemed unable to discourage, and returned to the coast.

Glave and Dalton wished to continue their journey farther into the interior, but could not get guides from the Sticks, only the usual stories of frightful perils ahead.

They dared not go to the White River [wrote Glave] which we wished to reach; the Indians of that region being always on the warpath. In former days the latter had made raids on this settlement and killed off the natives; in fact the present small population of about a hundred at Neska-ta-heen was attributed to fights with the Yookay Donner people dwelling on the banks of the White River. They pictured to us a frightful list of hideous obstacles to overcome — hostile natives, bottomless swamps, cañons, glaciers, and swollen torrents. Should we continue our course, we might possibly reach this far-away land and then be killed by the hostile Indians, and it was so far that

[53] *Ibid.*, p. 682.

we could not get back over the divide before winter set in, and we and our horses would perish. They begged us to change our plans and to make a journey through some safer part of the land, and to avail ourselves of their considerate guidance at two dollars a day and board.[54]

As well as this, it was a time of plenty at Neska-Ta-Heen, and no one was inclined to leave: Glave mentioned that "in summer . . . an abundance of salmon stems the Alseck current and passes the very doors of the Indian huts; the land abounds in wild berries; and the native hunter, who knows the haunt of every beast, can rely on finding game. But other bands of the Goonennar [sic], or Stick nation, living around the northern lakes I-she-ik and Hoot-chy-eye [Hutshi], have no such plenteous supply; so when winter is gone they take the trail and move to this southern settlement, and there recuperate on the fattened fish."[55]

Glave and Dalton left finally without guides, relying on compass and sextant, and a crude sketch map scribbled by the Indians, to find the way. Their route now lay along a broad valley trending to the northwest.

Everywhere we found convenient camping-places, with good water and plenty of food for our horses, which, although incessantly worried by mosquitoes and other flies, remained in good condition. We nursed the little band of horses with the greatest care, attended at once to any soreness or lameness, and loaded very lightly any animal at all unwell. We used them simply for packing our belongings; each of us took charge of two of them, which were led tied one behind the other. Through this wild land the management of four horses proved ample employment for us, combined with our other duties, which consisted of striking camp in the morning, loading up the pack-bags, and saddling up, searching out the trail, cutting roads through timber lands, and at night pitching tent, unharnessing, stacking away supplies, cooking, and maintaining a constant lookout for our horses.[56]

The explorers soon found that the map and instruments were not enough to find their way, and that without a guide they were continually losing the trail, which in many places was very ill-defined. Dalton even went back to Neska-Ta-Heen to attempt to persuade someone to change his mind and accompany them, but without much success. He did bring a big, strapping six-footer back with him

54 *Ibid.*, p. 682.
55 *Ibid.*, p. 869.
56 *Ibid.*, p. 870.

to the camp where Glave was waiting, but the fellow began the recital of a string of woes as soon as he saw the horses, and when the travellers woke up next morning their guide, not unexpectedly, was gone. "Once more we saddled up our little band of horses," wrote Glave, "and plodded along alone, feeling decidedly disheartened. But two days after this, good fortune came to our aid: two Indians from Lake Hootchy-Eye came into camp. They had been down south to trade off their winter furs with the coast Indians and were returning home with weighty packs of blankets, powder, and shot. . . . In consideration of their showing the way and helping to cut roads through the timber-lands, we agreed to carry their heavy packs on our horses."[57]

This mutually beneficial arrangement speeded up travel for both the white men and for their new companions, Nanchay and his son Tsook, who were anxious to rejoin their family, as the hunting season had begun. Before long they came to the Kaskar Wurlch, (Kaskawulsh) the Alsek's west fork, about a quarter of a mile wide. Dalton swam the horses across, while Glave and the Indians ferried the outfit over on a raft.

For the next three days we tramped over valleys of rocks, threaded a way amidst a labyrinth of pools and lakes and swamps, crossed fertile grasslands, and finally ascended to a table-land, and tramped along a ridge of thickly wooded foot-hills, through which we had to cut a trail. This part of the land is known to the Indians as Shak-wak, being an immense valley running northwest from Lake Kusu-ah [i.e. Kusawa or Arkell] almost to the eastern arm of the Copper River. This low-lying area has within its limits ranges of hills, forests, swamps, lakes, and streams, and throughout its whole extent traveling is tedious and difficult. . . . Here and there an old fox-trap could be seen, and a few rude huts of tamarack boughs used as winter camps by hunters and trappers, and stumps of timber ten or twelve feet high cut when the snow was deep. Every time we reached exposed positions our Indians would set fire to trees, but no answering column of smoke replied to the signal; we were the sole occupants of this vast region.[58]

They finally caught up with Nanchay's family in a temporary hunting-camp consisting of brush shelters, storage platforms, and drying racks. "They were all busy collecting and preparing a supply for the long winter months ahead; already their roofed platform

[57] *Ibid.*, p. 873.
[58] *Ibid.*, p. 875.

sagged and creaked and threatened to topple over with its weight of caribou, moose, mountain sheep, rabbits, squirrels, and fish.... While at this camp the natives kept us well supplied with game, and delicious moose-steaks, mutton cutlets, and sun-dried rabbits reinforced our usual insipid fare."[59]

Not all these interior Indians, Glave learned, traded at Neska-Ta-Heen; some went north to the Yukon River to barter with the white traders there. From where they were, this was a journey of six or seven days, but it was too late in the season to attempt this with horses: for the same reason, it was not possible to visit the northern lakes, Hootchy-Eye and I-she-ik. In tales reminiscent of those heard by Hayes, the Indians in Nanchay's camp "gave most encouraging accounts" of copper to be found to the northwest. "They assured us," Glave reported, "that boulders of solid copper were piled at the bases of the mountains, from which they chopped off all they needed. Of course their information was highly colored for our edification, though they had several little nuggets with them which they carried for repairing purposes.... They told us they had several lumps in [their] village, each as much as a man could carry."[60] Attempts by Glave and Dalton to persuade someone to guide them to "this interesting region" were fruitless: they were told the usual tales of difficult terrain and great distances, though Nanchay did promise that if the white men came back the next year, he would take them to where the copper was.

In a few days, the Indians divided into two parties and moved on to new hunting grounds. Nanchay was going north to hunt for moose, and he made an impressive exodus at the head of a motley band of "women, boys, and girls, all carrying heavy loads of blankets, old cooking-tins, fish-nets and poles, parcels and baskets of dried fish, bundles of hides, and a goodly sprinkling of babies lashed securely on the packs. Nanchay himself carried a very light load, and was the only man in the procession...."[61] The remainder of the Indians were going to a large lake they called Tloo Arny (Kluane), to hunt sheep on the mountains. Glave and Dalton accompanied them, carrying their packs on the horses in exchange for their services as guides.

[59] *Ibid.*, p. 876.
[60] *Ibid.*, pp. 877-878.
[61] *Ibid.*, p. 878.

237

Lake Tloo Arny [wrote Glave] is a most important waterway; at its southern extremity it is seven miles wide, and stretches like a sea away to the northwest as far as the eye can reach. The Indians say that at its northern end a river drains into the Yukon; if such is the case, transportation can be carried on from this point by water. . . . Streams draining the land around have grooved out ways from all points of the compass. The mountains around are rich in cinnabar, and the cañons hewn out in the rocky uplands show signs of gold and silver; but though there is plenty of good quartz, still we found no free metal. The general formation was granite, slate, and quartz, which is a good combination for mineral prospects.[62]

While the Indians took to the hillsides for their sheep hunt, Glave and Dalton camped on the lake shore. Hidden in the bush they found a dugout canoe, which they decided to use for a short journey of exploration, leaving the horses securely hobbled in a grassy meadow. It was nearly a fatal decision: Kluane, they found, was a treacherous body of water. Its surface was "perfectly calm" when they launched the canoe, yet almost before they knew it they were fighting for their lives. The water "became gradually ruffled" as a stiff "northerly breeze" sprang up, and water began to "tumble in over our slight bulwarks. Despite my greatest efforts at baling, the water was gaining on us, the little craft was slowly settling, the breeze had grown to a squall, and high waves rolled on all sides."[63] To save themselves, Glave and Dalton were forced to jump into the water and cling to the upturned canoe, hoping that they would be swept on to the rocky beach before their strength gave out.

After a long and dogged struggle "a big sea with a hissing crest swept us ashore, where, paralysed with cold and battered almost senseless, we lay in a heap piled on the rocks with a splintered canoe."[64] They had lost many irreplaceable items — rifles, ammunition, cooking utensils, gold pans and miners' picks, Dalton's watch and chain, compass and sextant. Fortunately their blankets, camera and notebooks were sealed in a waterproof sack, which was picked up on the shore after the storm abated, and the greater part of their supplies had been left with the horses.

The season was now well-advanced, and they decided that the time had come to heed the advice they had already received several times,

62 *Ibid.*, p. 878.

63 *Ibid.*, pp. 878-879.

64 *Ibid.*, p. 879.

and return to the coast. They followed the same route as that of their inward journey, riding the horses nearly all the way. At Neska-Ta-Heen there was sixteen degrees of frost, and in the pass they encountered three snow-storms, and drifts already four feet deep. But the country they were leaving was a richer one than they had expected to find in these latitudes, and it had impressed both men deeply. Glave wrote in summary that

... colossal heights mantled in never-melting snow tower thousands of feet in the air, but within the shadow of these mighty uplands, in the sheltered hollows beneath, lie immense valleys carpeted in richest grasses, and gracefully tinted with wild flowers. Here in the summer a genial clime is found, where strawberries and other wild fruits ripen to luxuriance, where there are four and a half months of summer and seven and a half of winter. In June and July the sun is lost below the horizon only for a few hours, and the temperature, though chilly at night, has an average of sixty-five degrees in the daytime.[65]

Glave never saw these fertile valleys again. By the following year he was back in Africa, and he was killed there in 1895, at the age of 33, on another expedition to the Congo. Dalton did return, first to Juneau, and then to Haines Mission, where in 1894 he leased land for a trading post and a hotel. By 1896 he had established the pack trail to the Yukon River that was given his name — part of it following the route of the 1891 journey. The rush for the Klondike would not find him unprepared, and even though the mainstream of the rush would pass him by, he would emerge from it a moderately wealthy man.

VI

WHILE THE PACKHORSES OF GLAVE AND DALTON WERE CLIMBING the Chilkat Pass, a much more casual traveller was also entering the Yukon district. He was Warburton Pike, sportsman, explorer, prospector and writer, another footloose young Englishman who, like Frederick Whymper, sought an outlet for his restless nature in the unfettered Canadian northwest. Born in Dorsetshire in 1861, he attended Oxford University for a time but, unhappy and dissatisfied with the academic life, he suddenly quit his studies to emigrate to Canada. In the northern bush country he found the release that he

[65] *Ibid.*, pp. 880-881.

had been seeking: he quickly became a skilled woodsman, and learned to travel unmarked wilderness trails, delighting in the challenge and the risks. His first journey of note was into the Northwest Territories in search of muskox, which he described in a book, *The Barren Grounds of Northern Canada*, that appeared in 1892. When this publishing venture proved successful, he was able to start making arrangements for another journey that he had long been planning, a trip down the Yukon River by canoe. Long familiar with the work of the Yukon Expedition and Dawson's report, he proposed to follow in "Dr. George's" footsteps and enter the country by way of the Stikine rather than by the Chilkoot Pass, winter on Frances Lake, then descend the Pelly to the mouth of the Lewes and paddle down the Pelly-Yukon to the sea.

His 18-foot canoe he had specially built in Vancouver to his own specifications, his design being a compromise between the characteristics of the type intended for use in open water, and those of the type adapted to river travel. As companions he had with him an English friend, whom he identified only as Reed, who was on his way to the Cassiar for a big game hunt, and Gladman, a Canadian, who had already made two trips north with government survey parties. They carried only "indispensable" supplies: "flour and bacon enough to last for three or four months, tea and tobacco in large quantities, a good supply of ammunition for rifles and shotguns, nets, hooks, and lines, dog harness, a large canvas lodge similar to the tepee of the Crees and Blackfeet, a Kodak camera, blankets, and kitchen-box containing kettles, frying-pans, and all such simple necessaries for camp cooking."[66] For the first part of their journey they would live off the land, though once on the lower Yukon they expected to purchase their needs at the trading posts. Fishing and hunting, therefore, would occupy much of their time: their survival would be dependent on their success with net and line and gun.

The journey started with the formal launching of the canoe at Fort Wrangell late in July 1892, a rather festive occasion prolonged by the generous hospitality of the few miners still in the town. On August 16 the travellers crossed from the Pacific drainage basin into that of the Mackenzie, and shortly afterwards reached Laketon, on Dease Lake, once a centre of mining activity, but now a ghost town.

---

[66] Warburton Pike, *Through the Sub-Arctic Forest*, (New York, Arno Press, reprint for the Abercrombie and Fitch Library, 1967), p. 12. The original publication was in 1896.

"At the present there are not more than twenty miners in the whole district," Pike wrote, "and I doubt if many of these are working paying claims — hanging on year after year in the hope of better times coming on the discovery of a new strike. A few Chinamen make up the mining population, being of persevering nature, satisfied with small returns for their labour, and extremely reticent as to the amount of gold they have taken out."[67]

Paddling down the Dease River, they reached the Hudson's Bay Company's post at Sylvester's Landing on August 19, and Lower Post on September 1, after a meeting along the way with Henry Thibert, who was still prospecting in the country that, for a time, had made him rich. At one or the other of these posts Pike had hoped that he would be able to hire a boat and crew to transport his supplies to Frances Lake, but they could not obtain local Indians at either station. Most of the natives, they were informed by the Hudson's Bay Company's officers, were untrustworthy and lazy, and expected the same wages that they had been paid during the peak of the Cassiar gold rush. Without a boat and crew Pike decided to remain in the vicinity of Lower Post for the present, and haul the stores and canoe to Frances Lake by dog team during the winter.

Most of the winter was occupied in moose hunting and moving the supplies. Neither Reed nor Gladman continued beyond Lower Post: Reed because he was still desirous of carrying out his projected hunting trip in the Cassiar region, and Gladman because he was already committed to joining another survey party in Victoria the following spring. To replace them Pike was fortunate in obtaining the services of a reliable Indian named Secatz to act as guide and interpreter as far as the Pelly, and three Manitoba half-breeds, Smith and two brothers, Archie and Alix Flett, employees of the Hudson's Bay Company who were making their way out of the country, as the Company had decided to sell its now unprofitable Cassiar operation. These experienced trail runners made quick work of transporting the gear to Frances Lake, though when it came to moving the canoe Pike would trust no one but himself to handle the dog team and sled that carried it. By April 24, 1893, all the supplies were at the outlet of Frances Lake, and two small hand sleds were built for the comparatively easy haul to the north end of the

[67] *Ibid.*, pp. 57-58.

lake across the ice. The only open water was around the mouths of some of the tributary streams.

Dawson in his report had expressed doubts in retrospect that the Finlayson Lake - Pelly Banks portage was the best route to the Pelly. "I now feel convinced," he wrote, "that if we had had Indian guides, we might in all probability have shortened the land carriage and possibly have found a travelled Indian trail, by following up the waters tributary to the west arm of Frances Lake."[68] Pike also felt that this route might well provide easier access, "gaining the advantage of falling on the Pelly at a much higher point than that reached by the old portage, and having at the same time a totally unexplored country to travel through."[69] Accordingly the little party continued with their loaded sleds past the mouth of the Finlayson and its jutting delta to the far end of the west arm. Here, at the mouth of a large river that flows into the Frances — the Yusezyu of present-day maps — they fortunately found two families of Pelly Indians who were hunting for beaver. After the usual haggling, and the ritual attempts at discouragement by a recital of the alleged perils that lay ahead, the natives agreed to assist the white men in finding the crossing to the Pelly. Their guide, an Indian named Narchilla, led them for a considerable distance upstream on the Yusezyu, and then struck off in a northwesterly direction along a tributary stream which led, Narchilla assured them, to the Pelly watershed. The travellers were still using their hand sleds, though, wrote Pike, "the hours of frost were getting shorter and the ice was becoming more rotten each day. Men and sleighs were continually breaking through, to the great detriment of our tea and other perishable articles, but the weather was warm and wood plentiful, so the men were nothing the worse for an occasional mishap."[70]

The first rain of the season, on May 9, threatened to flush away the small amount of snow remaining and reduce the party to backpacking, but it was followed by a frost that formed an icy crust, enabling the men to drag the sleds as far as a large swamp which lay astride the height of land, beyond which the snow had completely disappeared. At this point, both Narchilla and Secatz, having discharged their obligations, turned back, after first pointing out a still

[68] Dawson, *Report on an Exploration*, p. 114.

[69] Pike, *Through the Sub-Arctic Forest*, p. 135.

[70] *Ibid.*, pp. 141-142.

ice-bound creek that, they said, flowed into Pelly Lakes. On May 16 Pike and his men cached the canoe and the bulk of their supplies, and started out on foot down this stream, which they called Ptarmigan Creek, from the large numbers of these birds in the swamp at its headwaters. Arriving at the lake, they camped there until Ptarmigan Creek was free of ice, setting up a fishery, and carrying out a reconnaissance of their immediate vicinity. After the breakup, Pike and two of the men went back for the canoe and the remainder of the gear: returning on the spring flood they experienced a wild ride, a succession of "sudden alarms and narrow shaves" that tested the canoe and canoemen to the utmost. It must have been with mingled relief and satisfaction that they ran the last rapid and shot out into the quiet water of the lake.

Pike used the canoe to make a more detailed examination of the whole area. Pelly Lakes, he found, consisted in fact of a chain of three long, narrow lakes, one of them, into which Ptarmigan Creek emptied, being fairly large, about eight miles long. All the lakes appeared to be widenings of the Pelly River, which it was generally believed entered from the east and discharged to the west. Pike was particularly anxious to locate the source of the Pelly, but when he reached the eastern end of the chain, he was disappointed to discover that the stream which flowed into it was "much smaller . . . than it was supposed to be from the account of it given to Campbell by Indians at the time of the existence of the Pelly Banks Post."[71]

The men began an ascent of this stream in their canoe, but because of the numerous rapids and canyons they soon had to abandon their craft and continue the journey by following the river on foot, trending in a generally easterly direction. The supposed source, when they reached it in a cul-de-sac at the head of a swampy canyon, was unimpressive. "We had expected," Pike confessed, "to find the Pelly a larger stream heading from a more northerly direction, and had even some hopes of crossing the divide at its head and making an attempt to reach the Mackenzie by some stream flowing to the eastward."[72]

Any ideas of further exploration in this locality were, however, dampened by the accidental damaging of Pike's Winchester rifle, on which they relied for the killing of large game. He repaired it as best he could without tools, but it was no longer a reliable shooting piece,

[71] *Ibid.*, p. 153.
[72] *Ibid.*, p. 167.

now averaging three misfires for every shot, a serious drawback in a country in which its use was essential for survival. The travellers were left with little choice but that of returning to the Pelly Lakes and continuing their downstream journey. They reached the Ptarmigan Creek campsite about the middle of June, and turned their faces westerly.

On the banks of the river that flowed out of the lakes, there were deserted Indian camps, at which huge stages for drying fish, and traps carefully stowed away for future use, gave evidence of a large salmon run in its season.

After following down the stream for about 8 miles [wrote Pike] in a general southwest direction, although with many turns on the course of the stream, we were suddenly surprised, on rounding a bend, by running into a broad river heading a little to the eastward of north with a strong current swollen by the melting snows — fully three times the size of the stream that we had been following with the mistaken idea that we were exploring the source of the Pelly, whereas we had in reality only succeeded in reaching the head of a comparatively small tributary.[73]

This discovery that the main course of the Pelly River was not through Pelly Lakes, as previous maps had indicated, opened up interesting possibilities for further exploration. Here was a river "unknown to any white man, and unmarked in any map, heading away towards the distant range of snow-capped mountains which were just visible from our camp."[74] Unfortunately, game at that moment was scarce and the provisions were low; the damaged rifle was an uncertain provider; and, most serious deterrent of all, the flooded condition of the river, with the water running over its banks and choked with driftwood, made upstream travel almost out of the question. Reluctantly, Pike gave the order to continue on their downstream course.

They were still in unexplored country until they reached the

[73] *Ibid.*, pp. 179-180. The river east of Pelly Lakes which Pike explored is today known as the Woodside River. Gull Lake, north of the Woodside, was also discovered and named by Pike in the course of this exploration, and the name survives on modern maps. So do Ptarmigan Creek, on his route to the Pelly, and Narchilla Brook in the same area, named for his guide. Pike's investigations in this region are, in fact, well-commemorated by the cartographer — more so than is the work of several better-connected and more serious-minded expeditions.

[74] *Ibid.*, p. 180.

mouth of Campbell Creek, "named by Dr. Dawson": for the remainder of their journey on the Pelly they had as a guide Dawson's description of the river, and his excellent maps. The water continued to rise until June 25, and then began to drop "quickly and continually." For three days it rained in torrents, and then hot, sunny weather began, which lasted almost until the river-mouth was reached. Even the travellers' rather serious food situation — their supplies were reduced to a few pounds of flour which they were carefully husbanding — was alleviated when Pike finally shot a moose above Campbell Creek. "For three days we relapsed into the habits of the Indians," he wrote, "and held one of those meat orgies so dear to the hearts of men who hunt their livelihood in the northern forests, and only to be really enjoyed after a lengthy period of hard times."[75]

They reached Fort Selkirk on July 8, and at Harper's trading post found themselves in "comparative luxury": they even caught up on the news from outside relayed by a party of miners on their way downriver after crossing the Chilkoot Pass. When the journey was finally resumed, Pike found that the easy travel on the relatively placid Yukon was a pallid contrast to that on the streams which they had already traversed. "The men were of the same way of thinking," he added, "and as soon as the first glamour of the high living was over, they came to the conclusion that paddling down the long stretches of river was too easy work, and everybody would have welcomed a rapid or even a portage as a change from the monotony of the long, uneventful days that now ensued."[76] At the mouth of the Sixtymile they stopped briefly at Ladue's new post, and were promptly advised to stock up on supplies and head up the creek, as the new diggings on it gave promise of being extremely rich. "The trader was incredulous," commented Pike, "when I told him that we were not mining, and were only running down the Yukon as the shortest way out of the country. He finally came to the conclusion that we were either Government officials or gamblers — apparently the only professions left open to the traveller on the Yukon who is neither miner, trader nor missionary."[77]

On July 11 they arrived at Fortymile, where they quickly attracted considerable attention, and were kept busy answering questions con-

[75] *Ibid.*, pp. 188-189.
[76] *Ibid.*, pp. 208-209.
[77] *Ibid.*, pp. 216-217.

245

cerning the mineral prospects of the country through which they had travelled. Pike had expected to find here letters of credit for him with the Alaska Commercial Company, but they had not arrived. This was something of a set-back, as the free and easy extension of credit by the Company to transients on the lower river had been too often abused following the increase in traffic, and formal credit arrangements were now necessary to obtain goods at the posts below Fortymile. Pike hesitated to push on without these documents, and he delayed a short time to wait for the arrival of the steamer *Arctic* from St. Michael's. The letters of credit, however, were not on board, and he had no choice but to leave without them if he was to reach the coast before winter. McQuesten, according to his usual practice, advanced supplies to Pike without hesitation, but the traders down-river refused to accommodate him. For the remainder of the journey, the men had to rely on their "skill as hunters and traders to keep the pot boiling, and to limit . . . purchases to the merest necessities."[78] It was only when the voyage was over that Pike learned that this inconvenience had been completely unnecessary. The letters of credit had reached Fortymile before he arrived — the local post office had mislaid them!

The lack of funds hastened the travellers' progress, and stifled any tendency to linger long at any one spot. They continued down the river at a brisk pace until they arrived at the mission station at Incogmut: here they joined forces with a visiting band of Indians and portaged with them to the Kuskokwim, as they had been assured that it would be easier to make connections with a south-bound steamer from Bristol Bay than it would be from St. Michael's. Arriving on the coast, they found that this information was correct: they were able, by putting up their canoe as security, to obtain passage to Unalaska on a coastal steamer, and once there they did not have to wait long for a steamer connection to the south. The journey was over, and though it had been undertaken for adventure and sport rather than in the spirit of scientific enquiry, nonetheless it did contribute to the growing knowledge of the geography of the Yukon basin.

[78] *Ibid.*, p. 243.

CHAPTER EIGHT

Prelude to Bonanza

Map Numbers 1, 3 and 7, following page 58

I

AT THE TIME THAT PIKE VISITED FORTYMILE, THE COLLECTION OF cabins that had sprouted haphazardly around McQuesten's trading post had become the largest settlement on the Yukon River. Slow but steady growth had followed the original staking. Fresh discoveries on some of the tributary creeks had made more ground available, and the new techniques employed to penetrate the permafrost had extended the working season. Almost inevitably these developments brought more men into the area. To keep pace with the burgeoning demand for goods and services, the Alaska Commercial Company in 1889 launched a new steamer, the *Arctic*, and this powerful vessel, nearly twice the length of any steamer then operating on the river, made her maiden voyage to Fortymile later that year. In 1889 also the first saloons were opened: soon ten were in operation, and became the social centres of the town. There was little organized amusement: once in a while a "squaw dance," a rather joyless ritual in which stolid Indian women acted as the miners' partners; an occasional visit by a travelling repertory company or vaudeville act; a debating society; a library staffed by volunteers.

None of these well-meaning measures, however, could counteract the isolation of the settlement. The short, ice-free summer was succeeded by the long cold winter, when the steamers were frozen in and no goods were unloaded at the docks. Mail was infrequent, with, according to a report made later by the North-West Mounted Police, "only one mail in the year that could be relied on, that which is brought in by the Commercial Company's steamer. . . . In the ordinary course of the present mail service, or rather want of mail service, a letter written in eastern Canada later than May would not arrive at Forty Mile until the following May, and no answer would be received for another year."[1] Occasionally this slow process was speeded up: letters were sometimes delivered by individual miners "who happen to think of them" before leaving Juneau or Taiya. But most of these men had enough to carry without taking on this additional responsibility.

The town was untidily laid out: Ogilvie, when he came to survey it, wrote that "it is the worst jumble I ever saw."[2] The cabins were built of native timber, either spruce or poplar, and the logs were limited in size to a dimension and length that could be handled by the builders, usually two men. Ogilvie described typical construction techniques in some detail:

The roof consisted of small poles laid from the ridge-pole to the wall on either side; on this series of beams, as they might be termed, was put a layer of the moss found so abundantly in the country, of a depth of about a foot; on this was placed about an equal thickness of the clay of the place. This made a close warm roof, and in summer-time, unless the rain fell unusually heavy, it was dry too.

After the size of the building had been decided on, a space somewhat larger in extent was cleared of the surface moss, leaves, and sticks; on this the first two logs were laid parallel to each other, the ends saddled to receive the notched ends of the next pair of logs to be laid on the saddles prepared for them. The ends of the last pair were then saddled as with the first pair, and so on, till the height of the walls was reached. . . . In the walls, as they rose, were left openings for the door and window, or windows, which were dressed to measure, and squared after the walls were finished. The door was made of slabs; it might be split from suitable logs, or, if possible, whip-sawed from the same. Very often the door was mounted on wooden pin-hinges, made on the spot, as household hardware was not much dealt in in the earlier years of the territorial settlements. Glass was often scarce, and other means of admitting light through the windows had to be substituted. Sometimes untanned deerhide, from which the hair had been removed, was used; this was translucent to a limited degree, but not by any means transparent. Sometimes a bit of white cotton canvas was used, and sometimes empty

[1] Inspector Charles Constantine, "Report of Inspector Constantine, 10th October, 1894," in *Report of the Commissioner of the North-West Mounted Police Force, 1894*, (Ottawa, The Queen's Printer, 1895), p. 77.

[2] Ogilvie, *Information Respecting the Yukon*, p. 52.

white glass bottles or pickle jars were placed on end on the window-sill, and the interstices between them stuffed with moss. . . .

The walls, door, and windows finished, the space between the logs, and every other space visible, was chinked, or stuffed, with moss, driven tight with suitably shaped sticks.[3]

In the short, intense growing season, the clay roofs quickly produced an abundant crop of weeds, and some of the cabin owners took advantage of this fertility to grow vegetables on them, particularly radishes and turnips.

The stools, beds and tables were home-made, generally of small poles and of blocks cut from tree trunks. Tableware was basic — tin cups, tin plates, cheap but sturdily made spoons, knives and forks. Cooking was mostly done in frying pans, called spiders, or in Dutch ovens. Stoves in the early days of the settlement were almost unknown; the cooking chores were performed often in very slap-dash fashion, on rock fire-places built into one wall of the living quarters. "It was not an uncommon thing," commented Ogilvie, "for a cabin, say sixteen feet by eighteen, to house four or more men. My winter quarters at the boundary for seven men was twenty-two feet square inside, and was thought palatial in dimension; it certainly was in comfort, being well heated by a rock stove three feet wide, three high, and eight long; the rear end, three feet square, continued in a chimney to the roof. . . . I never spent a more comfortable winter in my life than in that house."[4]

In the absence of government authority during the settlement's beginnings, the men maintained their own law and order by bringing north with them from the California diggings the device of the miners' meeting. This was an assembly of the occupants of a camp summoned to decide on mining laws or to settle disputes, though in the Canadian Yukon this transplanted institution served only the latter purpose, as all mining was regulated by the Department of the Interior. "In the first days of mining in the territory," wrote Ogilvie in a reminiscent vein, "when the mining groups were scattered, with

---

[3] Ogilvie, *Early Days*, pp. 297-299. When building on permafrost, incidentally, the practice of removing the "surface moss, leaves, and sticks" was a serious mistake, though it was the accepted technique when building under frost-free conditions. The destruction of the natural insulation caused the ground to thaw and settle, which in turn caused sags and heaves in the cabin, and continuous problems for its occupants.

[4] *Ibid.*, pp. 300-301.

but a few members in each, [the meetings] were simple, fairly just, inexpensive, quick in results, and promptly executed. Can we claim all this for our more elaborate judicial machinery?"[5] The assembly could be called by either party to a dispute, simply by posting a prominently displayed notice.

When the meeting was summoned, all who could spare the time repaired to it, for all knew that some day they might be in trouble too, and if they did not manifest some interest in camp doings, it might be a cool time for them when their trouble came. After the meeting was organized by electing a chairman and secretary, which last was generally the camp recorder, each disputant was asked to state his case, and then evidence was heard. When all was in, it was discussed openly and a vote taken, the majority carrying the judgment, which was promptly executed. At some of the meetings all this formality was not observed, but where the meeting contained experienced men it generally was.[6]

The first miners' meetings in the Canadian territories were held in 1887 at McQuesten's post at the mouth of the Stewart River during its brief existence. Two men were sentenced to be exiled from this camp, one for the attempted poisoning of his partners, and the other for stealing butter from the trader's store at a time when that commodity was in very short supply — a very grave offence in a frontier community. On the verdict being given, each of the men "was furnished with a sled, provisions enough to get out if he could, and was ordered to move at least one hundred and fifty miles from that camp, and assured that if ever he was seen within that distance of it, any one then present would be justified in shooting him on sight."[7] Though this might well have been a death sentence, both these exiles eventually succeeded in reaching the coast, the would-be poisoner causing considerable alarm in Haines Mission by spreading a wild story of an Indian uprising on the Stewart River to account for his unseasonable arrival on the salt-chuck. This fanciful tale greeted Ogilvie on his first arrival at the mission, and caused him a great deal of unnecessary anxiety when he ventured into the interior.

The miners' meeting moved to Fortymile with the stampeders. As the town grew, however, the decisions of the assemblies became more capricious, and more coloured by local prejudices and nationalistic

5 *Ibid.*, pp. 245-246.
6 *Ibid.*, pp. 246-247.
7 *Ibid.*, p. 50.

feelings than by the justice of the case. After saloons appeared in the settlement, most of the meetings were held on these premises, with the inevitable unsavoury hangers-on taking an active part in the proceedings, and often constituting the greater part of those present. The meetings became too prone to assess fines for trivial reasons, to be spent immediately for drinks. A French Canadian, loser by a close decision in a case that was of dubious legality to start with, complained bitterly to Ogilvie that, as well as being fined, he had to pay twenty dollars for the use of the hall and buy drinks for everyone in it. It was not to be wondered at that a reaction to these high-handed proceedings would eventually set in, and that complaints regarding the system would in time be heard by the government authorities in distant Ottawa. Fortymile's free and easy days of self-regulation were to be of comparatively brief duration.

II

ON AUGUST 4, 1892, BISHOP BOMPAS, ONE OF THE MEN WHO WERE to have much to do with the eventual exercise of government control in the Yukon, arrived at Fortymile. He had now completed 26 years of Christian service in the northwest, but the veteran missionary, far from giving any thought to retirement, was undertaking still another task, this time "beyond the mountains." Yet another Anglican diocese had been created in the west — that of Selkirk, later to be called Yukon — and Bompas, by his own wishes, had just a year before been ordained its first bishop. He proposed to establish at Fortymile the administrative centre for his new episcopate.

This move to a smaller and more remote diocese was for Bompas the final step in a chain of events that had begun with the first division of Rupert's Land in 1874, and his appointment to Athabaska. This new diocese, it had soon become apparent, was still too large for an effective ministry among the scattered native bands, and Bompas had soon started appealing to the ecclesiastical authorities for more clergy, and for a smaller territory that could be itinerated more easily and efficiently. In 1884, largely because of these persistent representations, Athabaska had been further subdivided, with the southern portion retaining the old name, and a new diocese of Mackenzie River — including the Yukon — being established north of the 60th parallel. Bompas had once again retained for himself this more isolated area, happy that now "he would be able to accomplish more definite work, and carry on his beloved translations."[8] This hope proved to be wishful thinking.

Mackenzie River had quickly proved to be no improvement administratively over Athabaska, particularly in view of the increasing number of miners in the Yukon, and the difficulty of access between the two portions of the diocese.

The missionaries now labouring in the [Yukon] district [he wrote] are very isolated, and much need the support of episcopal oversight, which it is hoped may be no longer denied them. From the Mackenzie River it appears impossible to superintend the district. A visit thither from the east side of the Rocky Mountains would involve a journey of 5,000 miles or more, and an absence of two years. The Rocky Mountains form a natural barrier between the Mackenzie River and the larger country farther west.[9]

In 1890 the formation of the diocese of Selkirk was sanctioned, with Bompas as its bishop: he formally took office in 1891, and crossed the mountains to assume his new responsibilities. Before coming to Fortymile he spent several months at Rampart House, serving as a temporary replacement for Rev. G. C. Wallis, who had been stationed there since 1896, and who had returned to England on furlough to be married.

In the early spring of 1892 the bishop received word that his wife, who because of ill health had been forced to return to her home in 1887, would be arriving back in the Yukon on the first steamer from St. Michael's, and that with her would probably be workers for the new mission field: Wallis and his bride; Rev. and Mrs. T. H. Canham, who had served with the Eskimos in the Mackenzie delta for many years, and who more recently had been on loan to the diocese of Alaska; and a recruit, Benjamin Totty, who was coming to Canada to study for deacon's orders under Bompas' instruction. The bishop, therefore, left Rampart House immediately after the break-up and descended the Porcupine to Fort Yukon to meet the *Arctic*, the ship on which he expected that his wife and the others would be travelling. To his joy and relief, they were all on board. "We were between laughing and crying when he saw me," wrote Mrs. Bompas later in a letter to a friend, "The steamer stopped and he was soon

[8] Cody, *An Apostle of the North*, p. 229.

[9] *Ibid.*, pp. 253-254.

on board and I on deck, which, happily, we had to ourselves. He looks older, and his hair very grey, but I suspect has altered less during the five years since we parted than I have, and he says he is fairly well."[10]

The Wallises, who were to be stationed again at Rampart House, left the steamer for the trip up the Porcupine, while the others continued on to Fortymile — the Canhams to go farther upstream to Selkirk, and Totty to remain with Bishop and Mrs. Bompas. One of the first tasks at the new headquarters was to make the mission buildings habitable again.

The house here was scarcely finished [Mrs. Bompas wrote in another letter] when Mr. Ellington[11] left on account of failing health, and Archdeacon Macdonald put one of the native catechists in charge, who allowed a number of Indians to have a free run of the house, and the state of filth and disorder when we took possession was really terrible. However, with much hard work and patience, a good cleaning has been effected, many repairs carried out, partitions made in the rooms, besides tables and benches, and hanging up the school bell. I have taken up my quarters for the present in a good-sized loft, which is divided into three rooms by means of curtains. I have my own furniture around me, which came quite safely, my chairs and little tables and carpet and mats, all the dear home treasures of pictures and photographs, with my bookshelves which are quite full, so you may think of me as very snug and comfortable, although with only sloping rafters. . . . The quiet life and mountain air suit my health. There is no bustle or excitement here, but yet I have so much to do that I never feel dull.[12]

The loft with its "treasures" was a pitifully small oasis of graciousness in a harsh environment. At times, though rather casually, Mrs. Bompas wrote also of the more unpleasant aspects of her domestic life. In winter, she noted, she played her harmonium at services

[10] A. S. Archer, *A Heroine of the North: Memoirs of Charlotte Selina Bompas,* (London, The MacMillan Company, 1929), p. 129.

[11] Rev. John William Ellington, the son of a clergyman, was ordained as deacon by Bompas at Fort Simpson in 1886, and in 1887 was sent to Fortymile, where a new mission station was being built. Unfortunately for the eager and serious-minded young man, his ministry coincided with the turbulent founding days of the Fortymile camp, and Ellington proved to be temperamentally incapable of dealing with the miners. He became the butt of many crude and boisterous practical jokes, as on one occasion when he was tricked into reading the burial service over an empty coffin, to the raucous delight of the "mourners." He eventually suffered a nervous breakdown, and had to be sent back to England. He never recovered his health.

[12] Archer, *A Heroine of the North,* pp. 132-133.

"when the keys are not too hard frozen";[13] in the church "the lamps would hardly burn from the frozen oil." "Can you imagine," she asked in one letter, "the cold of the handle of a kettle on the fire being so intense that one cannot touch it, while the kettle itself is boiling. The temperature has now moderated and we can breathe more comfortably, although you will not think 46° (below zero) very mild."

One of the bishop's priorities at Fortymile was the establishment of a diocesan school, at which in the beginning he shared the teaching duties with his wife, though later this work was taken over by an Irish girl, Susan Mellett, sent to the mission in response to a plea for help from Bompas. This school, and the one Mr. Canham established at Selkirk, together with an older school at Rampart House, were the first educational institutions in the territory. Their enrolment was not large, as few of the Indian families were prepared to leave their children behind at the mission stations, where they did not learn the skills required on the trapline, and their help was not available in camp. As a result, many of the pupils were orphans, or children abandoned by their parents — the schools, therefore, also played a welfare role.

Bompas' years of self-exile among the Indians had made him ill-at-ease in his contacts with the miners: on their part they found the motivation that drove this stern old man almost incomprehensible. The bishop and his wife, however, in time won the grudging respect of the town, and even a modicum of active support. "We have just now about twenty miners who attend our Sunday afternoon English service," the bishop wrote shortly after his arrival, "and afterwards we lend them some books to read; but I have not a very good selection for them. They ask mostly for history or travel, but this I do not possess. I have some magazines, and they have taken *Leisure Hour* more than any other book."[14] On Christmas day, 1892, a splendid gold nugget was presented to Mrs. Bompas "as a mark of respect and esteem from the miners of Fortymile, irrespective of creeds and religions, and further, that it be distinctly understood to be a personal present to the first white lady who has wintered among us."[15]

[13] *Ibid.*, p. 136. The other short quotations in this paragraph are from p. 139 and p. 146 respectively.

[14] Cody, *An Apostle of the North*, p. 268.

[15] *Ibid.*, pp. 268-269.

The greatest concern of the bishop and his wife was the demoralizing effect on the adult Indians of the miners' way of life, particularly during the coldest of the winter months, when not much mining was carried on. "We have every reason to fear," wrote Mrs. Bompas, "that their goings on will be very sad and distressing, and to the ruin of our poor Indians."[16] Bompas did what he could to counteract this influence. Whenever a band of natives appeared in town, he busied himself attending to their wants, and giving them religious instruction, "if only for a few days." He tried to dissuade them from lingering in the settlement once their business there — usually the sale of caribou or moose meat — was finished. Now, however, they often had money, and the younger Indians in particular were prone to take their example from the white men "in irreligion and debauchery." The miners' own decree prohibiting the sale of liquor to Indians was not unfailingly observed.

Bompas longed for government control to curb the lawless element in camp, and he made representations to the authorities in Ottawa to this effect. One of his letters was written to the Superintendent General of Indian Affairs in May 1893:

I think it right to inform you of the danger to which the Indians of the neighbourhood are now exposed for want of any police restraint upon the free and open manufacture and sale of intoxicating liquor among them.

About 210 miners have passed the present winter in this vicinity, in British Territory. The Indians have learned from them to make whiskey for themselves, but there has been drunkenness of whites and Indians together with much danger of the use of fire arms.[17]

Like many communications to government, this letter brought no immediate reply. But as the difficulties inherent in expansion continued, others in the community came to agree with the bishop — though not for the same reasons — that a showing of the flag in the Yukon basin was now essential. In time their letters also reached Ottawa, and the desks of the men who were concerned with the administration of the far northwest. This mail was no popular clamour for reform, but the writers were men of influence, and they could not be long ignored by the government of the day.

---

[16] Archer, *A Heroine of the North*, p. 132.

[17] Gartrell, "The Work of the Churches," pp. 34-35.

ONE OF THOSE WHO WROTE TO OTTAWA WAS A CITIZEN OF FORTY-
mile named John J. Healy. A former law officer in Montana who
had become a trader, he was the operator of the post at Dyea when
Dawson passed through that country on his way out of the Yukon
in 1887. From his grandstand seat at the head of Lynn Canal Healy
watched with cool calculation the increasing traffic over the Chilkoot Pass, and when he felt that the moment was right, he followed
his customers down the river to Fortymile. He was soon convinced
of the trade potential of this developing area, and of the possibility
of competing with the entrenched Alaska Commercial Company by
establishing his own posts, and his own line of river steamers to
supply them. Returning to the United States, he persuaded a number of Chicago businessmen — including the Cudahy meat-packing
family—that his scheme was practicable. These men in 1892 formed
the North American Transportation and Trading Company, with
Healy as manager. A steamer about the same size as the *Arctic*, and
named the *Porteous B. Weare* after the new Company's president,
was fabricated on the American west coast, and assembled at St.
Michael's. The maiden voyage to Fortymile, with Healy aboard,
began in the fall of 1892, but the steamer only got as far as Nulato
before being stopped by ice. The journey was completed in 1893:
immediately on arrival Healy began the construction of a large warehouse and a store, and living-quarters for his staff, himself and his
wife. He selected a location on a river bench about a mile downstream from Fortymile, calling this site Cudahy, in honour of his
financial backers.

Healy was no glad-hander. He did not operate by McQuesten's
casual methods of extending almost unlimited credit; instead he
presented his accounts monthly, and demanded prompt payment.
This enabled him to sell at lower prices than his rival, and was good
for business, but it did not bring him the respect or the gratitude of
the community. The miners — individualists all — were willing to
take advantage of the savings, but they resented being called to
account within a specified time. When, therefore, Healy eventually
became embroiled in a miners' meeting, as the result of a complaint
laid by a serving girl employed by his wife, the result was inevitable.
Though the case was a flimsy one and much of the evidence per-
jured, the meeting decided in favour of the girl and assessed Healy

a considerable sum of money. Not a man to knuckle under, he paid under protest, and dispatched to Ottawa an angry letter demanding an end to the capricious frontier system of maintaining law and order in the Yukon. Though Healy was not a Canadian, the letter was to an old acquaintance of his Montana law enforcement days, who was now Superintendent Samuel B. Steele, a power in the North-West Mounted Police. This communication, therefore, was read with more than casual respect.

Finally, in September 1893, Ogilvie, back in the country but "busy with boundary matters" in the Juneau area, decided from reports reaching him that the time had come to advise the Minister of the Interior, in accordance with his previous instructions, to make a move "in the matter of establishing authority over the Yukon in the goldfields."[18] By now the "more and better means of transport" were on hand to supply the increasing numbers of men that were remaining in the country, and the fears of four years ago that government surveillance would stifle development and drive it into Alaska were no longer valid. There was, indeed, a chance of a move in the opposite direction. The many Americans working in the Canadian diggings still chafed at even the minimal restrictions to which they were subjected under the Yukon mining laws, and they lost no opportunity of contrasting their sorry lot at Fortymile with the freedom to direct their own affairs enjoyed by their compatriots across the international boundary line. An active American takeover in the Canadian Yukon, Ogilvie feared, could well be the final step resulting from this pro-American attitude, and might very possibly follow a spectacular strike. Beyond a doubt, the time was ripe for the government to show the flag, and exercise its sovereignty in the Yukon.

In the face of these varied reasons advanced by such distinguished advocates, the authorities had little choice but to make a move. The North-West Mounted Police were instructed to send an officer into the territory on a fact-finding mission, which would include a report on the current situation in the district, and an assessment of its future needs. For this assignment the force selected their most experienced trouble shooter, Inspector Charles Constantine, at that time Commanding Officer of the police post at Moosomin, N.W.T. Constantine, born in England in 1849, the son of an Anglican clergy-

[18] Ogilvie, *Early Days*, p. 144.

man, was brought to Canada by his family when he was five. In 1870, the year after the first Riel rebellion, he came west with the Red River Expedition, and was commissioned a lieutenant at the age of 21. When the Expedition was disbanded in 1880 he remained in the west, becoming for a time the chief of police of the stripling province of Manitoba. When the second Riel rebellion broke out in 1885, he re-enlisted in the 91st Winnipeg Light Infantry, and served as adjutant throughout the campaign that followed. His work brought him into frequent contact with the Dominion's newly-organized peace-keeping force, the North-West Mounted Police, and he was much impressed by the calibre of its officers and men, and the variety and scope of its tasks. When hostilities ended with the suppression of the uprising, Constantine applied for a commission in the force — a procedure "unusual" today — and was gazetted to inspector's rank. He quickly established a reputation as a strict but fair, if sometimes unorthodox, disciplinarian, bluntly outspoken, respected by his superiors, and regarded with considerable awe by the men who served under him.

He reported to Ottawa for a briefing on May 20, 1894, and left the capital on May 26, arriving at Victoria on June 17. There he was joined by Staff-Sergeant Charles Brown, whom he had requested be allowed to accompany him, and whose "energy and knowledge of boatwork" he was to officially recognize as being "invaluable." Because of the erratic steamer schedule, the two men were delayed five days in the west coast port before they were able to sail for Juneau, and there they had another three-day wait for a connection to "Dai-yah." Constantine utilized this second delay to stock up on supplies, as well as on the tools, nails and other items that would be needed to build a boat. The opportunistic citizens were quick to take advantage of the inspector's enforced presence to extol the virtues of the Taku River route as an easy entry to the country, as they had to Hayes and Schwatka.

The policemen reached the head of Lynn Canal on June 29, and "at once set about to arrange our final start into the interior."[19] Here the redoubtable inspector more than met his match, as the native packers were unimpressed by the scarlet uniforms. "The Indians here seem to be able to take in but one idea," Constantine commented

[19] Constantine, "Report . . . 10th October, 1894," p. 70. The other quotations in this paragraph are from pp. 70-71.

angrily, "and that is how much they can get out of you, and being at their mercy as to packing I had, as a rule, to submit to their extortion." They crossed the pass between July 1 and July 3, "with seven packs, weighing 800 pounds, at 15¢ per pound." Fortymile was reached on August 7, "after twenty days actual travelling, having lost, through weather, building of boat, etc., sixteen days."

Constantine remained four weeks at the settlement, systematically questioning, probing, observing, and obtaining as much first-hand information of local conditions and needs as he could. He returned to Victoria by way of the lower river, leaving Brown in the Yukon for the winter. Back at Moosomin, he immediately started work on his report, completing it in October. It was a terse document, written in Constantine's characteristic short, abrupt paragraphs. Though understandably its organization showed some evidence of the haste with which it was prepared, its coverage of the district was thorough and complete.

A considerable portion of the report was purely descriptive — it was, after all, being written for administrators four thousand miles away from the area. Constantine began by recounting the highlights of the trip into the country, with descriptions of the various routes, which he listed as "the Chilkoot pass, the Chilkat pass, the White pass, and up the Taku Inlet and river."[20] The Taku route he described in some detail, quoting extensively from Hayes' account of his trip through it with Schwatka, and concluding by quoting Dawson as saying of it that "by this route all the bad water on the Lewes-Pelly-Yukon would be avoided. It might well be worth a thorough exploration and survey."

Once he reached Fortymile, Constantine's notes became detailed, and he ranged over a multitude of subjects.

The village or camp [he wrote] consists of about 150 log cabins, of an average size of 20 x 24 feet. There are about half a dozen fair sized houses, two or three being two stories high. McQuestion [sic] and Company have built a large warehouse. All the buildings are log. . . .
The flat on which the camp is built contains about 700 or 800 acres, and is divided from the mainland by a ravine [overflow channel], which, during the period of high water, is a fair sized river. The place was flooded this spring to a depth of about four feet. . . .
St. John's mission [of Bishop Bompas] is on an island of about 5 or 6 acres and on it are erected the buildings occupied by the bishop as a

20 Ibid., p. 71. The quotation by Dawson is from p. 72 of this report.

dwelling house, and the school buildings. The large school room is used as a church on Sundays. The Indian village is on this island.

The mission buildings are the first that you come to on the way down the river.

Fort Cudahy is about a mile lower down the river to the north, and north of Forty Mile Creek. The land here is higher but not so wide. The flat ends, at the north, at an abrupt rock which rises almost perpendicularly from the river to a height of about 800 feet. . . . There are twelve cabins on this flat besides the store and store houses of the North American Transportation and Trading Company.

Rugged hills form the background, these are covered with small timber. The river (Yukon) opposite Fort Cudahy is nearly 800 yards wide at low water. The current runs between four and five miles an hour.[21]

The population during the winter before his visit had been, according to the inspector, about 260, with 500 expected during the winter ahead. Constantine added that up to July 1 of the current year "535 souls had passed Dia-Yah [Taiya] for the Yukon district. . . . A few went back from or after leaving Dia-Yah frightened with the outlook, two or three from the Cañon, or White Horse. Some went out by the mouth of the river after being at Forty Mile a day or two."[22] The cost of living did not encourage lingering: at the trading posts, Constantine commented, "prices are high, if not in some cases exorbitant."[23]

The men were predominantly Americans or Canadians, "about equally divided." There were also several French Canadians, some Englishmen, a number of Scandinavians, and a handful from even more remote homelands — Constantine listed one Arab, three Armenians, one Greek, and one "Chilian" as working on the various creeks, adding that "all appear to get on well together." Yet racial prejudice was not unknown. A rather unsavoury incident had occurred shortly before the two policemen crossed Chilkoot Pass, when a party of Japanese and Chinese that landed at Taiya with the intention of mining on the Yukon was refused admission to the interior by the decision of a miners' meeting. "A party representing the miners," wrote Constantine in recounting the episode, "went back [from the pass] until they met these strangers and told them

[21] *Ibid.*, pp. 83-84.
[22] *Ibid.*, p. 80.
[23] *Ibid.*, p. 76. To northerners this comment has a familiar ring!

that they would not be allowed to go into the country and that if they valued their lives they would not make the attempt. The foreigners took the hint and returned. This shows the feelings as regards the Chinese in this section of the country."[24]

The inspector took a more liberal view of the inhabitants of Fortymile than did Bishop Bompas and his wife, whose outlook was inseparable from concern for the "poor Indians."

For a mining camp [Constantine wrote] the place is very quiet. In the fall when the miners come in there is a general carouse accompanied with the firing of pistols and guns.

A woman is treated with more respect here by the miners than she would be in an eastern town by those who are supposed to be far above them, morally and socially. During the four weeks I was there I saw but one drunken miner. On the other hand the men have not yet come in, in any numbers, from the diggings.

Gambling appears to be the principal amusement during the long winter, and many lose all the proceeds of the summer's work in a night or two. There are no regular gambling houses, it being done in the different cabins as chance may bring them together, and in the saloons. The miners are very jealous of what they consider their rights, and from what I could see and learn, any enforcement of the different laws will have to be backed up with a strong force at least for a time.[25]

Elsewhere in the report, Constantine mentioned that "Law and order in the country has been enforced by a committee of miners, and with the exception of one shooting and cutting case last winter, it has been quiet and orderly, as much so as in other parts of the North-west Territories.

"In the case of shooting and cutting mentioned the parties implicated were both drunk. The miners took the matter up and gave the principals to understand that they would be ordered out of the country if any further trouble took place between them, and the one who did the shooting that if the man he shot died, they would hang him. Since then things have been quiet."[26]

The inspector, predictably, was unimpressed by the local Indians, dismissing them curtly as a "lazy, shiftless lot [who] are contented to hang around the mining camps. They suffer much from chest trou-

24 *Ibid.*, p. 80.
25 *Ibid.*, p. 81.
26 *Ibid.*, pp. 80-81.

ble, and die young."[27] On August 13 Bishop Bompas arranged a meeting for him with some of the natives, and acted as interpreter. Constantine warned those present that they would find themselves in serious trouble if they persisted in drinking whiskey and making hoochinoo. The Indians, on their part, complained of their treatment at the hands of the traders, expressing the wish that the English — i.e. the Hudson's Bay Company — would "come and trade with us, because the goods are better, and they deal more fairly with us." Another of their grievances concerned the killing of their dogs by the white men in the settlement, but this complaint Constantine dismissed bluntly by telling his listeners that "if they took more care of their dogs, there would not be so much trouble about them; that white men knew the value of these dogs in the country but had to protect their property, and that the owners of the dogs should help to do so, so far as they were able, by tying them up, but from what had come under my notice on the way down, did not do so, but had shared with the dogs what they had stolen from the boats."

In his notes on mining, Constantine painstakingly catalogued with descriptive comments the various diggings that comprised the Fortymile field, most of them being, as far as was known, on the American side of the boundary line.

Forty Mile Creek is worked out; Franklin Gulch is about half worked; Nugget Gulch has not been much worked; Davis Creek about half worked; Clinton Creek has not turned out of much value; O'Brien Creek has not been much worked, as it was only this summer that it was discovered; Napoleon Creek has only been worked this season and has shown up well so far; Cañon Creek has been worked by a few men two seasons and has paid $12 or $14 per day; Madison Creek is new, worked only one season; Sixty-Mile Creek is 120 miles south of Cudahy.... Gold Creek [a tributary of Sixtymile] is good, this is the second season. Miller's Creek is also being worked and has proved the best creek in the country so far. Glazier [sic] Creek has only been opened this season, and so far the returns have been good. Last summer two men worked this creek and made $21 a day each. They are still working there. . . .

Bar diggings are not permanent, as the bars are continually shifting, especially Stewart River. Any work that is done in winter has to be done by the aid of fire. In the gulches during the past two years considerable

<hr>

[27] *Ibid.*, p. 78. The quotations referring to the meeting are from p. 79. The problem of keeping dogs under control is still a lively one in northern communities.

of this sort of work has been done by those who have remained in the gulches during the winter.

The Stewart is all bar diggings up to the present, and so far has proved to be the best paying. The Pelly is doubtful at present. Hootalinka [*sic*] has done fairly well and much is expected from it in the future. Both on the Stewart and Pelly many men have been working this summer.

The Big and Little Salmon have also paid well to the few who have been working. These are all bar diggings.

One reason why more men are not at work on these rivers is the difficulty of getting in provisions.

The miners as a rule have faith in the future of the country, not that gold is in any one place in large quantities, but appears to be all through it, and that it only requires exploring and opening up.[28]

The inspector estimated that production in the previous year — 1893 — was "about $300,000 from all sources," adding that "only one large nugget has been found, and that in Franklin Gulch. Its weight was 30 oz. and intrinsic value $510." In addition he noted that an estimated $40,000 - $50,000 worth of furs would be shipped from Fortymile that year — a reminder that mining was not the only source of income in the area.

For the miners, the size of mining claims — unchanged since Ogilvie's representations on the subject — and the exact location of the boundary in the Fortymile - Sixtymile area, continued to be touchy problems that required quick solutions. The developers of much of the new ground often did not know in which country their claims were located, or by what set of mining laws they were operating. "The boundary in the gold-bearing belt," wrote Constantine unequivocally, "should be fixed without delay."[29]

There were other community needs. One obvious one was the necessity of a speed-up in the mail service, and the replacement of the existing haphazard system by the award of government mail contracts. Constantine proposed a schedule that would result in four mails in and five out during the year, which he estimated could be operated for $5,000 or $6,000 a year. Schools were also essential if the country was to be opened up. "Many of the respectable miners," the inspector commented, "would bring in their families if schools were established or if they would be within a reasonable time. At

[28] *Ibid.*, pp. 74-75, as is the quoted reference to the nugget in the next paragraph.

[29] *Ibid.*, p. 75.

present there are about eight white children of school age."[30] The mission schools were a commendable effort, but their instruction was adapted to the teaching of natives and not the miners' children. A school more attuned to these needs would obviously be a factor in developing the country, and the inspector noted that as an inducement "the North American Trading and Transportation Company through Mrs. Healy said they would board a female teacher free for a time."

Some of the other government services that Constantine felt were required were more restrictive, and he knew that these would not be popular. One was the "distasteful" necessity of collecting customs dues. The inspector after his stay at the settlement brought out with him "cheques, drafts and orders amounting to $3,248.82" in collections, and he estimated that Brown, who would remain in Fortymile for the winter to wind up this part of the business, would bring out another $2,000 to $3,000 in the spring. In addition, "the American customs were giving all the trouble they could to the North American Trading and Transportation Company on account of their buying many of their goods in Canada."[31] To check these and other abuses, and to collect the now considerable annual revenue that was the government's due, Constantine recommended that a Collector of Customs should be stationed at Fortymile.

There was the need too of "a strong hand" in controlling the liquor traffic, which in 1894 was expected to reach a volume of about 3,000 gallons. Most of it came over the Chilkoot Pass and was brought down the river in scows: an impatient whiskey peddlar was in fact popularly supposed to have been the first man to have run Miles Canyon and the Whitehorse Rapids with a fully-loaded boat. "So far as my information goes," Constantine reported, "the miners would like to see a high license and a stop put to the sale of liquor to Indians. Prohibition would be very hard to enforce, if not almost impossible, owing to the nature of the country, with its facilities for hiding liquor and illicit stills in the many ravines and gulches, which Indians only could find and travel to."[32] Ogilvie echoed this opinion with a brief comment of his own: "Liquor could not be kept

[30] *Ibid.*, p. 78, as is the other quotation in this paragraph.
[31] *Ibid.*, p. 84.
[32] *Ibid.*, p. 76.

out of the country," he wrote, "if the whole North-West Mounted Police were scattered around the river."[33]

The concluding sections of the report dealt with the composition and logistics of a police detachment in the district, "if it is decided to send them into that country" — though it was obvious that in his own mind the inspector had already decided that a force was an absolute necessity if many of his recommendations were to be implemented. For its makeup he proposed "two officers, one surgeon, three sergeants (one to act as sergeant-major), three corporals, and thirty-five or forty constables."[34] These men would require extra clothing and blankets, and should bring their own rations, including as a safeguard a year's reserve supply in case of a food shortage due to an accident to one of the trading companies' river boats. The detachment would have to enter by St. Michael's and travel upriver by steamer — Constantine boggled at the thought of the struggle that would be involved in bringing a party of this size, and their baggage and supplies, across the Chilkoot Pass. The majority of the men would be stationed of course at Fortymile, but in the summer, outposts on the upper river would be desirable, as well as a small sternwheeler for river patrols.

To his report Constantine attached a copy of his diary, "rough maps and a plan" of Fortymile and Cudahy, and a meteorological return for the years 1892 and 1893. He signed the document on October 10, 1894, and, doubtless with mixed feelings, saw it dispatched to "The Honourable W. B. Ives, President of the Privy Council, Ottawa." For the rest of the winter he resumed his ordinary duties at Moosomin: he had not, however, seen the last of the Fortymile.

IV

ONE MAN WHOM CONSTANTINE WAS UNABLE TO INTERVIEW AT Fortymile was the settlement's most prominent citizen, Jack McQuesten. That shrewd trader, realizing even before the coming of the investigating policemen that increased government surveillance in the Canadian Yukon was sooner or later inevitable, was busy establishing

[33] Ogilvie, *Information Respecting the Yukon*, p. 53.
[34] Constantine, "Report . . . 10th October, 1894," p. 81.

the nucleus of a new mining camp 240 miles downstream, on the American side of the boundary line. The previous year he had sent two Russian half-breeds to prospect for him in the vicinity of Fort Yukon, searching for the now almost legendary "preacher's creek" that Archdeacon McDonald had mentioned so casually many years before. Late that same fall, on Birch Creek, an Alaskan tributary of the Yukon, the Russians found gold in paying quantities, and the legend was vindicated. In 1894, as soon as the main river was free of ice, McQuesten hastened to the scene, taking with him all the provisions and supplies that could be spared from his warehouse at Fortymile, and built a steamer landing and a small shed on the Yukon River, convenient to the new find. This done, he continued outside on his annual buying trip to Seattle. When he returned in September he found, according to Ogilvie, "about 75 miners waiting for the boat. They had laid off a townsite, and had about thirty cabins under construction. In that and the following season, nine paying creeks were discovered. . . . The entire cleanup in 1895 was about four hundred thousand dollars."[35]

The rival to Fortymile was called Circle City, as it was thought to be on the Arctic Circle. One of its early inhabitants, a dog musher named Arthur Walden, a preacher's son, wrote that

. . . a more appropriate name still would have been the City of Silence. People have an idea of a 'roaring mining camp', but in this town in the summer nothing but pack-trains plodded through the soft muck of the streets; there was no paving; no wagons, no factories, no church bells, not even the laughter of women and children. There was little or no wind in this part of the country. The screech of a steamboat's whistle in the summer, sometimes weeks apart and the occasional howl of the dogs were only part of the great silence. In winter time the silence was still greater. Even the scrape of a fiddle playing for the squaw dances was bottled up, and everything was hushed by the snow. . . .[36]

Circle City was unique in some ways, and for more than one reason. Here was a town made up of men from all parts of the world, intelligent men all. I knew an Oxford man, a younger son, married to a squaw who had blondined her hair: he could quote Greek poetry by the hour when he was liquored up. Another man, who had been raised in the wilds of the Rocky Mountains, never drank and didn't have a squaw, and had taught himself to read and write. In Circle City the saying went, 'If you look for a fool you find only *one*.'

[35] Ogilvie, *Early Days*, p. 113.

[36] Arthur T. Walden, *A Dog-Puncher on the Yukon*, (Boston and New York, Houghton Mifflin Company, 1931), p. 42.

Here was a town of some three or four hundred inhabitants which had no taxes, courthouse, or jail; no post-office, church, schools, hotels, or dog pound; no rules, regulations, or written law; no sheriff, dentist, doctor, lawyer, or priest. . . . Here life, property, and honor were safe, justice was swift and sure, and punishments were made to fit the case. . . .

Only gold dust was used as barter at the stores: this had to be weighed out for every purpose, and it was considered a matter of courtesy to turn your back while the man was weighing it. If things cost less than a dollar, you simply took more of them, making up the amount.[37]

This accelerating activity caused a considerable increase in the amount of freight coming up the river from St. Michael's. By 1895 both the Alaska Commercial Company and the North American Transportation and Trading Company had large, ugly sheet iron warehouses at Circle City. That same year the Alaska Commercial Company put into service two new steamboats, the *Alice* and the *Bella*, while the faithful *Arctic*, commanded by the veteran riverman William Moore, set a record still unequalled on the river by travelling over 14,000 miles in a little over two months, making one trip from Anvik to Fortymile and back to St. Michael's, and four runs from St. Michael's to Fortymile and return. The opposition countered by also launching a new vessel, the *John J. Healy*, a sister ship to the *Porteous B. Weare*. These steamers even ventured occasionally on to the upper river: Ogilvie noted that the *Arctic* went once to Selkirk, the *Alice* to the mouth of the Sixtymile River, and the *Bella* to the mouth of the White.

The Chilkoot Pass was now primarily an entrance way only, as most of the men who climbed it were headed for the Fortymile or the Circle City diggings, and if their luck was bad or they could not find employment, they floated on downriver to St. Michael's and the hope of a passage on a steamer to Victoria or San Francisco. For the affluent arrivals entering the country — generally traders or gamblers — there was now a packtrain service from Dyea to Sheep Camp, from which point the Indians, revelling in undreamed-of prosperity, were now charging one cent per pound per mile to pack to the headwaters of the Yukon.

Some unusual freight was beginning to appear. Horses, now in demand for packing between the settlements and the creeks, were being shipped into the country in considerable numbers, and a rather

[37] *Ibid.*, pp. 44-46.

drastic technique had been evolved for manhandling them over the steep slopes of the pass. "[They] were fastened in a rope sling," reported Walden, a witness of the operation, "and led up the trail on a long rope, with a hundred men or more to each horse, until the horses lost their footing, when they were hauled up to the summit lying on their sides. They were then led through the sharp cut blindfolded, backed over the edge, and slid down the other slopes on their backs to Crater Lake, some four hundred feet below."[38] Once on the lakes, the survivors of this rough treatment were transported in scows to Fortymile or Circle City. Their working life usually was mercifully brief. The mosquitoes often drove them mad in summer — Walden noted grimly that they were usually covered with a sheet of canvas for at least some protection, and that their nostrils had to be frequently cleaned out to prevent them from choking. The luckless animals that lived through the onslaughts of the insects were so debilitated that few were still alive after exposure to the bitter cold and lack of feed in winter. Once the Dalton Trail was opened, many of the animals were brought in by this route, and the rough manhandling over the Chilkoot was no longer necessary.

In 1895, both Ogilvie and Constantine returned to Fortymile: Ogilvie to extend the international boundary as far as the Sixtymile diggings, as recommended in the inspector's report; and Constantine as Officer Commanding a police detachment, and as a representative of the government generally, being "Magistrate, Gold Commissioner, Land Agent, and Collector of Customs,"[39] as well as a policeman. The authorities in Ottawa had accepted with uncharacteristic promptness his assessment of the need for controls in Yukon, and the North-West Mounted Police had been dispatched to enforce them.

The force that disembarked from the *Porteous B. Weare* on June 24 consisted of two officers, accompanied by their wives, one assistant-surgeon, and 16 non-commissioned officers and men — a smaller, detachment than Constantine had recommended as being necessary, but nonetheless the first tangible evidence of the sovereignty of Canada in the Yukon basin. The immediate task was the erection of permanent quarters. A site was selected at Cudahy, and the back-breaking labour of clearing and building was started. One by one,

---

[38] *Ibid.*, p. 6.

[39] Ogilvie, *Early Days*, p. 265.

268

the components of the rather ambitious establishment were completed, all built of logs: "first the guard-room, 30 x 22; next the barracks, 70 x 22; then the store-house, including offices, 48 x 22; then the officers' quarters, one 35 x 22, one 33 x 22; next the hospital, 33 x 22; and lastly, quarters for the staff-sergeants and assistant-surgeon, each 16 x 16, eight buildings in all."[40] The layout was that of the traditional hollow square, with the spaces between the buildings protected by a stockade and two bastions. Constantine was justifiably proud of the progress made in the construction. "Considering that the ground was cleared of trees and bush," he wrote at the end of the year in his annual report, "stripped of moss and ditched, the logs cut about 30 miles up the river, rafted and floated down, sawn square, carried fully one-third of a mile by the unaided exertions of the men, buildings completed, and all comfortably housed within three months of arrival, it speaks well for the energy and aptitude of the men of the North-West Mounted Police sent to this extreme corner of the Dominion."

The completion of the post, which was named Fort Constantine, did not mean the end of hard work for the Inspector's men. Winter was closing in, and wood was the only fuel available for heating and cooking. To purchase, the cost was high — $8.00 a cord in eight-foot lengths, a price too rich for the not overly generous police budget. The detachment, therefore, obtained their own. "Two days a week there is a general wood fatigue," Constantine reported, "every man except mess cook, carpenter, and hospital orderly, who is also cook for the sergeants, turns out. Officers with their servants cut and haul for their own quarters. The men for the barracks and general offices. We shall require wood for at least seven months, averaging 1½ cords per day for that period, being a total of 315 cords, all of which has to be cut and hauled by main strength in severe weather. The miners have a simple method of determining when it is too cold to work, by hanging a bottle containing mercury outside the house, when it freezes it is time to remain inside."[41] This occurred at 40° below zero.

---

[40] Inspector Charles Constantine, "Report of Inspector Constantine, 20th January, 1896," in *Report of the Commissioner of the North-West Mounted Police Force, 1895,* (Ottawa, The Queen's Printer, 1896), p. 8, as is the other quotation in this paragraph.

[41] *Ibid.,* p. 10. Mercury (or quicksilver) as an indicator of the temperature was the first stage in an elaborate system of gauging the cold that was supposed

For this labour the police received 50¢ a day, the cost of one drink of whiskey in a Fortymile saloon: in contrast the wages on the creeks, though seasonal, ranged from $6.00 to $10.00 per day. To partially compensate for this glaring pay differential, and to "stimulate and content" the men, Constantine proposed to Ottawa that the rate of pay for work parties be increased to $1.00 a day, and for "skilled artisans" to $1.50; a suggestion doubtless welcomed by his young constables, who to date were finding more bullwork than adventure in this far northern assignment.

The police work itself was certainly not onerous — probably a fortunate thing in view of the energy that had to be expended on mere existence in the inhospitable climate. "No crime of any seriousness had been committed,"[42] Constantine wrote, and for the year his official report listed one man ordered to leave camp as a potential trouble maker; one case of selling liquor to Indians; one assault, "but the party had left for lower down the river before the information was laid"; and a rumoured blood feud that was supposed to have resulted in two or three deaths among the Indians on the Pelly. Constantine added in this connection that "it is my intention, as soon as travelling can be done, to go up and enquire into these cases." This was an unmistakable reminder to his superiors that the

---

to have been devised by McQuesten when spirit thermometers were not available. This system involved the use of items readily procurable in the district — usually quicksilver, coal oil, Jamaica ginger (an extract), and a patent medicine known as Perry Davis' Painkiller. A teaspoon of each of these ingredients was placed in a separate glass bottle or vial arranged on a rack in front of the cabin, and the effect of cold temperatures watched with interest. The quicksilver, it was claimed, would freeze at —40°F; the coal-oil at —50°; the ginger extract at —60°; while the Painkiller turned white at —60°, crystallized at —70°, and froze solid at —75°. As an historian, even if not as a taxpayer, it was interesting to read in the *Yukon News* of August 16, 1973, that a researcher at the National Research Council recently tested the liquids used in this "sourdough thermometer," and scientifically confirmed the accuracy of the miners' observations. This is one myth that emerges unshattered from technological scrutiny. Also, Perry Davis' Painkiller, according to the Council, is still available in Canadian drug stores, though exactly where is not specified. This is to be regretted, for what a medicine this pain killer must be!

It should be added that quicksilver forms an amalgam with gold, and this property is utilized by the miners to separate fine gold from the heavy black sand remaining in the pan after the lighter material is removed.

[42] *Ibid.*, p. 12. Other quotations in this paragraph are from p. 13.

small sternwheeler that he had requested for patrol work on the river had not yet been received.

Ogilvie arrived at the settlement on August 1, by a rather circuitous route, and under unhappy circumstances. Late in the previous year, after Constantine's report had been digested in Ottawa, he had been instructed to wind up his work in the Juneau area and undertake a reconnaissance of the Taku River-Teslin Lake access route that the inspector had so strongly advocated after his exposure to the citizens of Juneau. After a wretched journey, Ogilvie had returned from his investigation on March 1, 1895, declaring flatly that "a most rigid search revealed no practical wagon road."[43] Tragic news awaited him. His "dear second son" had died on January 20, after a lingering illness: heart-sick, Ogilvie hurried back to Ottawa as quickly as possible.

In the capital, once the shock receded, he took part in discussions during which the decision to send the police to Fortymile was made, and expressed the opinion that the force proposed in Constantine's report was larger than was at present necessary for law enforcement in the district. Burgess, the Deputy Minister with whom Ogilvie had conferred previously, proposed that, in addition to the police detachment, an Agent-General be appointed for the Yukon, "a sort of everything in one, to represent the Government in the Territory, and administer the laws, and carry out the Government directions."[44] This position was offered to Ogilvie, but because of his son's death, he declined, requesting that he be allowed to spend some time with his remaining two boys, and these duties were assigned to Constantine. There were other tasks to be performed in the Yukon, however, and Mr. Daly, the new Minister of the Interior, must have been a persuasive man. Against his wishes, Ogilvie found himself agreeing to return to the district "for a season," to carry out the urgent task of extending the boundary survey and ending the touchy situation on the creeks, and to perform "any other work that I deemed proper."

Taking his eldest son with him, he re-entered the country over the Chilkoot Pass, after picking up a crew in Victoria "from my old hands on the Boundary Commission work." He used the new "horse-packing service" to get his supplies to Sheep Camp, and his old

[43] Ogilvie, *Early Days*, p. 149.

[44] *Ibid.*, p. 150. The other quotation in this paragraph is from p. 152.

friends Skookum Jim and Tagish Charlie helped him make the carry across to Lake Lindeman. On the way downriver he investigated some land applications at Selkirk, and recommended that the government "sell the applicants the land they ask for. They have all occupied and cultivated part of it for several years, raising in their gardens such roots and vegetables as the climate will permit."[45] At Cudahy, he conferred with Constantine, and looked briefly into the land situation there and at Fortymile, noting that because of the increasing adoption by the miners of the technique of burning and drifting, more of the men were now staying year-round on the creeks, "so that there is not that demand for town residences during the winter that existed formerly, and consequently town lots are at somewhat of a discount." He also examined, at Constantine's request, the coal seams that were known to occur near the settlement. The inspector was already concerned with finding a substitute for the dwindling supply of wood.

These chores completed, Ogilvie continued down the Yukon to the boundary, where he proposed, as a first step in his survey, to check his previous observations and those made by the Americans. He found that his old observatory had been burned and his quarters wrecked: the first task of his party, therefore, was to repair the damage before the coming of winter. When this work was well in hand, he began to plan a hunt to secure fresh meat for the camp, but this need solved itself when the vanguard of a caribou herd appeared as if on cue on the far bank of the river.

As quickly as possible we crossed the river in our canoe, and in less than a minute after landing had killed six, and in less than half an hour had secured twelve. . . . They were migrating southwards at the time, and remained in thousands around our camp for more than a week. Our houses were objects of great curiosity to them, and numbers of them would swim over and approach the buildings cautiously, whistling and snorting as they did so. They often came so close and were so noisy that they became a nuisance, and we would go out and chase them away. At any time one looked out they were to been seen swimming across the river, and as they were crossing for about ten days, thousands of them must have passed this place.[46]

During the November-December lunations Ogilvie obtained six

[45] Ogilvie, *Information Respecting the Yukon*, p. 48, as is the quotation relating to the townsite lots at Fortymile.
[46] Ogilvie, *Early Days*, pp. 154-155.

observations, which when reduced differed from the mean of his 1887-88 results by 0.13 seconds, well within acceptable limits of accuracy. He hoped to measure further culminations during the January-February lunations, which would further confirm the boundary line location. As soon after that as the days were long enough to make field work worthwhile, he would start its extension towards the Fortymile.

There was other activity in the district. E. W. Nelson, a biologist with the United States Department of Agriculture, in the course of a four-year study of the fauna of Alaska, crossed into Canadian territory in 1895. In the course of his investigations, he came upon a previously unknown species of mountain sheep, "a superb snow-white animal," the first specimens of which were obtained for him by McQuesten in the vicinity of Fort Reliance. Nelson named the new species *Ovis Dalli*, or Dall sheep in honour of the Overland Telegraph Company's explorer-naturalist. He also studied the habits and range of moose, black bear, and caribou in the district, being the first in the area to differentiate between woodland and barren land caribou. He even noted the presence of the cheeky whiskey jack, "a kind of jay with a dull smoky-brown coat and bright inquisitive eyes, [which] will furnish amusement to many a gold-hunter in his lonely camp."[47]

At Fortymile in 1895, Bishop Bompas received another recruit, Mr. W. J. Bowen, who had interrupted his studies at a "preparatory institute" maintained by the Canadian Missionary Society in Clapham, England to hasten to the mission field. His arrival was particularly welcome. Bompas had already lost one worker when Wallis, after less than a year at Rampart House, had to return to England as the result of the illness of his wife. In the resultant shuffle Canham had been sent to replace him and Totty — who had married the daughter of one of the traders in 1894 — had gone to Selkirk, leaving the bishop alone at Fortymile. His old anxiety over his difficulties in communicating with white men had been nagging him, and Bowen relieved him of this worry by agreeing to serve as a missionary to the miners.

First, however, he was sent to the Fort Reliance Indians in their fish camp at the mouth of the Trondiuck. This traditional gathering

[47] E. W. Nelson, "Notes on Wild Fowl and Game Animals of Alaska," *The National Geographic Magazine*, Vol. IX, (April 1898), p. 130.

place had been visited occasionally by the missionaries ever since they had been in the area, and Canham, who knew it well, felt that if it had not been so close to Fortymile, "it would long ago have been chosen for a Mission station." "Great hauls of beautiful large salmon are taken in traps and nets each summer," he wrote in a missionary magazine, "which accounts for so many Indians being found here. The fact that the salmon were so plentiful at this point, decided a miner to establish himself there for the purpose of putting up salmon in barrels, to sell to the miners who were working Forty Mile Creek. He was very successful, and made much more than he would have done at mining. Of course he charged very high for his fish. This, by the way, is only one of the many instances of how the poor Indians are being robbed, not only of their land and the wealth of their land, but also of their very subsistence."[48]

In the last boat of the season Father William Henry Judge, a Jesuit priest, arrived at Fortymile to establish a Roman Catholic mission. Judge had been a missionary with his order on the lower Yukon since 1890, working by choice in the more isolated stations, his last post being Nulato: now he had been selected to serve in the new camp. "Father Superior wished to start a mission there long ago," Judge noted, as he prepared for his move, "but he could not spare the men. This year the Catholics among the miners begged so hard for a priest, that he could hardly refuse them."[49]

Almost as soon as he was settled at Fortymile, Judge, an inveterate letter writer, was describing his new surroundings to his family in Baltimore. "It is life in the Far West," he told his youngest brother, "and I think a little different from the ordinary 'Far West' of the novels; although we have Indians, bears, wolves, moose, deer, etc., all around us; and, as a rule, log-cabins for houses. . . . I have two cabins, or rather, one with two sections, each about fourteen feet square. One serves for chapel and the other for house. The latter is divided by a partition into two rooms, one of which is bedroom, kitchen, and dining-room, and the other, sitting-room and reception-room."[50]

[48] Rev. T. H. Canham, "The Diocese of Selkirk: Its Work and Workers," *The Church Missionary Intelligencer*, Vol. 23, (January 1898), p. 130.

[49] Rev. Charles J. Judge, *An American Missionary, Rev. William H. Judge, S.J.*, (Maryknoll, N.Y., Catholic Foreign Missionary Society of America, 1907), p. 129.

[50] *Ibid.*, pp. 163-164.

To his sister, a nun who had served for some time in the American west, he wrote: "You may have a better idea than the others, what a western mining-camp is like; but I suspect that an Alaskan mining-camp is different from what you have seen. There are only about one hundred and fifty people living here now; but there are about five hundred in the neighborhood, who have to come here for their provisions. There are two trading companies with large stores, a hardware store, a barber-shop, and a number of saloons. The English government has a post with twenty soldiers or police, customs collectors, etc. The officers have their families with them and are very nice people. They all belong to the Church of England, but are very kind to me, and have invited me to dinner several times."[51]

On this almost idyllic domestic note the year ended, with no inkling of the shattering events ahead.

V

BY 1896 FORTYMILE WAS BEGINNING TO ACQUIRE A FACADE OF permanence. The demand for goods and services was increasing. Enterprising small business men were competing successfully in specialized fields against the two large trading companies, and the services of a barber and two doctors were available to the townspeople and to the men on the creeks. An old man with a small garden was making a good living growing potatoes and turnips for sale to the miners. During the summer, a herd of 40 live beef cattle was driven overland through the Chilkat Pass to the vicinity of Selkirk, and then brought down the river in scows to the settlement. Encouraged by these amenities and the stabilizing presence of the police, more of the married miners were bringing in their wives, and carpets, lace curtains, and even oil paintings were being introduced into the interiors of some of the rough log cabins. Shaken by such fripperies in their midst, the hard-core habitués of the saloons could only mourn over their whiskeys the passing of the camp's unfettered pioneer era.

The year began little differently from its immediate predecessors.

---

[51] *Ibid.*, p. 165. Judge's knowledge of the fine points of local government jurisdiction was as shaky as his recognition of the location of the international boundary line — but his ideas on these subjects were shared by the majority of the men in camp!

The sun, which had not been visible since December 8, appeared again from behind the mountains on January 4, and almost immediately Father Judge set out to visit the miners who were scattered along the creeks. He had a light sleigh and only one dog, as the cost of these animals — $50.00 to $75.00 apiece — put the acquiring of more beyond his means. He journeyed, unless it was unavoidable, only when the mercury was thawed, that is when the temperature was higher than −40°F. As was the custom when travelling on the creeks, he stayed overnight at whatever cabin he happened to be nearest, the hospitality of the trail being offered and accepted without question. "All received me well," he wrote, "Protestants as well as Catholics, and I often had an opportunity of explaining Catholic doctrine to those who had never heard a true statement of our faith."[52]

On a lonely stretch of his circuit, with the temperature well below zero, he learned again the lesson that northern travel is never routine. Crossing a stream, he broke through an overflow on top of the ice, and "had to walk in the water, almost up to my knees, for about two hundred yards; and, as I was not prepared to find water, my boots were not suitable and my feet got wet."[53] The mishaps almost had serious consequences. There was an empty cabin ahead, but Judge was not sure how far; the ice that had formed on the sleigh slowed his rate of travel; the short daylight period was ending, and he was afraid that he might wander off the trail in the dark. For two long, agonizing hours he plodded on, and was almost ready to give up when he came to the cabin. It had no floor, window, or door, but to his great relief it had a stove. In this, after several tries, he finally succeeded in starting a fire, and immediately began first aid.

As soon as I started to thaw the ice off my boots [he wrote], I felt a pain shoot through my right foot, so I knew that it must be frozen. At once I went out and filled a box, that I had found in the cabin, with snow, then took off my boot and found that all the front part of my foot was frozen as hard as stone. . . . I could not make a mark on it with my thumb nail. So, I had to go away from the fire and rub the foot with that awfully cold snow, which is more like ground glass than anything else, until I got the blood back to the surface, which took at least half an hour. After that I held my foot to the red-hot stove for about an hour before it was completely thawed out. With such treatment, no harm

52 *Ibid.*, p. 161.
53 *Ibid.*, p. 167.

follows from the freezing; but if you go into a warm room, or put the frozen part to the fire before rubbing with snow till it becomes red, it will decay at once and you cannot save it. It is the first time I have been frozen; but I have doctored others, and I knew what was necessary, and so, thank God, I escaped.[54]

Three days after this mishap, a cold spell gripped the creeks: for ten days the quicksilver "thermometers" in front of the cabins remained frozen, and travel and mining work were both suspended. "I stopped with an Irishman and his wife," Judge commented, "and was very comfortable. I said Mass every day and had six or seven present every time, for there were other Catholics living nearby; and six received Holy Communion."[55] Early in February, the weather modified sufficiently to enable Judge to complete his round of the creeks, and return to Fortymile before the temperature dropped again.

Ogilvie, in his camp on the boundary, obtained four more culminations, making ten in all, and when these were reduced and the mean obtained, the position of the line was found to be "practically where it was." On February 22, the days by then being of reasonable length and the sun increasing in warmth, he began cutting line from the Yukon River south towards the gold fields, an operation that required that a tent camp be moved with the crew. Much of the country they were traversing was above timber line, and the surveyors lost several days of work, Ogilvie reported, because of "fierce winds."

As there were no important creeks between the Yukon and Forty Mile Rivers I did not cut the line out continuously, but left it so that anyone wishing to can place himself on or very near to the line. The distance from the Yukon to Forty Mile River is a little over twenty-five miles. . . . I reached Forty Mile River with this survey on the 13th March. From this point southwards there are many streams cut by the line, all of which are more or less gold-bearing and all have been more or less prospected. This necessitated my cutting the line out continuously from Forty Mile River onwards, which increased our work very much. The valleys traversed are generally upwards of 1,000 feet deep and often very steep, so that the work was exceedingly laborious.

Transporting our outfit from camp to camp was often a very hard task as the hills were so steep everything had to be packed up them, which in the soft deep snow was anything but easy. I reached a point

[54] *Ibid.*, pp. 168-169.
[55] *Ibid.*, p. 169.

within two miles of Sixty Mile River on the 14th April, and as I had passed all the creeks of any note, and many of them were already running water and our way lay down them, I thought it well to quit work on the line and return to Forty Mile and Cudahy, and attend to the local surveys there. The weather was fine and warm, and so much water ran in the creeks by which we had to return that we could only travel a few hours in the early morning and forenoon.[56]

During this survey, from one of his stations on the boundary, Ogilvie observed a previously unknown mountain peak which he named Mount Campbell, after one of the "pioneers of the country ... the late Mr. Robert Campbell of the H.B. Co." The peak Ogilvie described as being "about 60 miles due east of here and is noteworthy in that it stands on top of an extensive well-defined range, rising like a lofty pillar about 1,000 feet above the ridge. . . . I do not think its summit is much if anything less than 10,000 feet above the sea. No one noticed it before for the reason that it is only about 600 feet wide, is always black, and very distant from points where it can be seen around here."[57]

Ogilvie had expected, when he got back to Fortymile, to be working on the "local surveys" only until the departure of the first steamer, as his promised "season" in the north had nearly run its course. Instead a letter was waiting for him, brought in before navigation opened, that dashed his immediate hopes of returning to his family. "The Canadian government," he explained, "had entered into negotiations with the United States Government for a joint commission to lay down the International Boundary Line with authority, and finally, from the Pacific to the Arctic. I was to be the Canadian Commissioner, and was directed to await further advice on the matter. I was also informed that assistants would likely soon join me with all the necessary outfit."[58] Swallowing his disappointment, Ogilvie made arrangements for a passage for his son on the steamer. He

[56] Ogilvie, *Information Respecting the Yukon*, p. 51. Today tourists driving over the road from Dawson City northerly known as the Boundary or Sixtymile Road can view the spectacular scenery in comfort and appreciate Ogilvie's transport difficulties. This road also gives access to the Fortymile River country in Alaska.

[57] *Ibid.*, p. 54. Today this peak, from its distinctive shape, is known as Tombstone Mountain, and a campaign by Clifford Wilson, former editor of the Hudson's Bay Company's *Beaver*, to have the former name restored is not making much headway.

[58] Ogilvie, *Early Days*, p. 158.

then turned his attention to the work on hand, for which he would now have more than ample time.

Several chores were awaiting his attention. First he undertook a complete survey of the layout of both Fortymile and Cudahy, locating all cabins and boundaries, a far from easy task, and then considered the other applications that had been accumulating for several years.

I made a survey of the island for the Anglican mission [he reported], and of another island for a man named Gibson. This is in the delta of Forty Mile Creek, and he intends to make a market garden for the growth of such vegetables as the country will produce. Many here have small gardens, and are fairly successful with ordinary vegetables. I have advised many to correspond with the experimental farm at Ottawa, with a view to learning the best sort of vegetables for growth in this climate. There is an application in, and the purchase money and the cost of survey paid, for 80 acres just west of Cudahy town site, which I will survey in a few days. There is also an application in for 40 acres containing a hay swamp on the east side of the river, about 2 miles below here, which I will survey before starting out. . . . I would respectfully call the attention of the department to the fact that the services of a surveyor are urgently needed in here and will be for some years to come, and I would suggest that one be appointed to look after and take charge of all the land interests in this district. He will find plenty to do, and any work outside of departmental which he might be asked to do (and there is much of it, and will be more in the way of engineering) would help materially to pay his salary which would of course in here have to be liberal.[59]

It was a quiet summer. Ogilvie waited in vain for further instructions from Ottawa. Father Judge left on the first steamer for the lower Yukon to "attend to supplies for the coming year," after which he expected to return upriver to Circle City to establish a mission there. Bishop Bompas saw his wife off to England, summoned by the serious illness of her sister, and welcomed recruits — Rev. and Mrs. H. A. Naylor from Montreal, and Mr. F. F. Flewelling of Wycliffe College, Toronto. Canham and his wife left the Yukon on a well-earned furlough, creating a vacancy at Rampart House. Once again Bompas had to shuffle the assignments of his staff. Bowen was sent to the Porcupine, as he was the only one of the diocesan clergy who spoke Tukudh, while Naylor replaced him in the work amongst the miners at Fortymile, and Totty took over the Indian

[59] Ogilvie, *Information Respecting the Yukon*, p. 52.

279

mission there. Flewelling left with the bishop for Selkirk, where Bompas was hoping to establish a new headquarters at which the Indians could visit him without being exposed to the temptations of the white man's way of life.

Later in the summer, Bishop Rowe of the Episcopalian Church in Alaska appealed for the loan of Bowen to go to Circle City and start a Protestant mission at that locality. Bompas agreed that this move should be made, probably during the following winter, particularly in view of the fact that Rampart House was by now practically a ghost town, at which it was no longer worth the expense of maintaining a missionary. The Hudson's Bay Company had closed down the trading post there in 1894, and most of the Indians by degrees had made their way back to Fort Yukon. Bowen tried to dissuade the few remaining families from moving by buying furs from them himself, and reselling them later to the Alaska Commercial Company, but even this unorthodox scheme failed in its purpose. Before 1896 ended, Bowen watched the last of the Indians still living at Rampart House move away.

At Cudahy, Constantine busied his young constables in making improvements to the post, and in the seemingly endless labour of obtaining wood, which by fall was being cut and rafted from as far as 60 miles up the Yukon River. As in the previous year there was little crime: in his "Report on the Yukon Detachment" dated 20 November, 1896, the inspector noted that "the most serious [offence] was giving liquor to Indians, a warrant was issued but the accused could not be found. It is supposed that he has gone to Circle City, Alaska. The other cases were, one of wife-beating and a few petty larcenies committed on the creeks. The Indian trouble at Pelly referred to in my report of last year has gone no further."[60] A miners' meeting was convened at Miller Creek as the result of a dispute over wages between the owner of a claim and his labourers, and by the decision of the meeting the owner was dispossessed. Constantine, when the news of this action reached him, set aside the verdict and sent police to the creek to enforce his jurisdiction. "The trouble ended," he reported bluntly, "by the Canadian law being carried

---

[60] Inspector Charles Constantine, "Report on the Yukon Detachment, 20th November, 1896," in *Report of the Commissioner of the North-West Mounted Police Force, 1896*, (Ottawa, The Queen's Printer, 1897), p. 234, as is the quoted reference relating to the miners' meeting.

out." This action effectively undermined the last shreds of authority still clinging to the district's earlier form of frontier law.

The inspector found himself spending much time chained to his desk, enduring, not always with patience, the inevitable frustrations of a conscientious government administrator in a remote posting. He had not yet received the patrol launch that he had repeatedly requested; civil courts were badly needed; the miners were demanding the construction of roads to the creeks "as some return on the large amount of money paid in by them"; the government had taken no steps to deal with the liquor question, though there were now "several" saloons in Fortymile and one in Cudahy. Constantine was particularly concerned by the fact that a great deal of whiskey was being traded to the natives "for furs, walrus ivory bone, and their young girls"[61] by whalers wintering on Herschel Island and at the mouth of the Mackenzie. In addition, many of the crewmen who were able to escape the vigilance of their officers were deserting to make their way overland to the gold fields, and though most of these were heading for the comparative freedom of Circle City, they were causing considerable trouble at Rampart House by demanding food and clothing, "which if not given they will take by force." Constantine suggested that "the presence of an armed government vessel would do much good service in putting an end to the traffic."

In spite, however, of the administrative problems, the year was not without some progress. The new summer mail contract, which had been awarded to old-timer William Moore, now a lively 73 years of age, helped to combat the isolation. The contractor, Constantine reported, was required to make three round trips in a season between Juneau and Fortymile. The first of these mails arrived on June 18; the second, carried by the captain's son Ben, on July 27; and the third on September 11. The inspector had also been asked to prepare an estimate of the cost of winter mails; but the figure was high, between $1,500 to $2,000 a round trip, and he was not very optimistic that the government would implement this proposal.

Some improvements were finally made in the mining regulations. The prolonged petitioning for the increase in the length of a claim to 500 feet was finally heeded, though staking was still limited to one claim for any individual, with the exception that the man who staked the discovery in a new field was allowed a second adjoining claim.

[61] *Ibid.*, p. 238, as are other quoted references in this paragraph.

The permitted minimum age for staking was lowered from 21 to 18, and the method of setting out and marking posts was simplified — leading Ogilvie to comment rather cynically that the new regulations were not observed much better than the old. And a little of the work load was at long last removed from Constantine's shoulders, when W. D. Davis arrived during the summer as Collector of Customs. Davis claimed that when his position was being discussed in Ottawa, the suggestion was seriously advanced that he be paid what he made in collections instead of a salary. If this statement was true, and the proposed arrangement had been accepted Davis would certainly have been a wealthy man by 1900!

There was no spectacular increase in the gold production on the creeks: it was expected that the value of the year's output would be in the $250,000 to $300,000 range, about the same as before. Little new ground was developed during the year: the greater part of the mining activity was confined to Miller and Glacier Creeks, with about 350 men at the two locations, most of them working for wages. "They are the richest creeks yet found on the Yukon," Ogilvie reported, "and are both tributaries of Sixty Mile River. . . . There are nearly 100 claims, all of which pay well. One on Miller Creek I understand will yield 75 to 80 thousand dollars this season, and the owner will net, it is said, between 40 and 50 thousand dollars. He took out, it is reported, nearly half that sum last year off the same claim, and expects to do equally well next year. This is much the richest claim yet found, but all on those creeks do well."[62] A few other areas were also being worked: in his report Constantine identified these as being "all but one mile of Bed-rock, Moose and the first fork of Moose Creek, one mile of the 3 heads of Smith Creek, and of the several heads of Canyon Creek, about one mile of the Poker and Davis branches of Walker Creek, one and a half miles of Walker Creek."[63]

In a field with all the known ground staked and occupied, there was little inducement for the newcomers who were floating down the river in ever increasing numbers to linger at the settlement, and most of them continued on to Circle City. Many of the old-timers in the camp also pulled up stakes and followed the drifters into Alaska, discouraged by the barren outlook, and the restrictions — real or

[62] Ogilvie, *Information Respecting the Yukon*, p. 51.
[63] Constantine, "Report on the Yukon Detachment," p. 235.

imaginary — on their personal freedom. They departed, wrote Ogilvie, "with anything but friendly feelings for the district, criticizing the place, the officials, and especially the mining regulations, which extracted a recording fee of $15.00, and limited the dimensions of placer claims to 500 feet in length and the width of the valley bottom, as against a recording fee in Alaska of 2 to 3 dollars — whatever the community of miners at the place made it — and a claim 13 hundred and 20 feet square. Many of them, even Canadians and Britishers, called their change of residence going back to 'God's country'."[64] These men would shortly have reason to reverse these sentiments.

Even the completion of the long-requested boundary survey did not bring complete satisfaction, though it did end the uncertainty as to the location of the claims that adjoined it. As it turned out, some of the richest ground, which the miners had generally assumed to be in Alaska, was found after the line was run to be in Canadian territory. The police lost little time in sending notices to the owners concerned advising them of the change in jurisdiction, and reminding them that they were now subject to Canadian mining regulations and fees. A few of the men objected "on the grounds that there was no joint survey, and a possibility of error in the work." Constantine quickly demolished that argument. "I went up to Miller and Glacier Creeks," he reported succinctly, "and all dues were paid without any trouble, except that of a hard trip, and as all trips in this country are of that nature, it was part of the bargain."[65]

There were other clouds on the horizon. It had been a hot, dry summer with little rain: the creeks as a result had turned early into mere trickles, bringing the year's mining operations to a premature halt. Potentially more serious, though at the moment more remote, was the possibility of hunger before spring. Because of the low water, the navigation had been exceptionally short, with only two steamers reaching Fortymile during the period of open water, and two more caught in the ice at Circle City before they were able to reach the settlement. To make matters worse the caribou, so plentiful the year before, had not appeared in the district by December. It was feared that they had changed the route of their migration, and that this

[64] Ogilvie, *Early Days*, p. 207. It is worth noting that Canadian miners going into Alaska had to become American citizens to work there, though there was no restriction on Americans mining in Canada.

[65] Constantine, "Report on the Yukon Detachment," p. 234.

bountiful source of fresh meat would not be available throughout the long months of winter. Even dog feed was in short supply, the result of the failure of the salmon run, which was also a consequence of the low water. "Dog feed is so scarce," wrote Constantine, "that several freighters have been compelled to go to Circle City to winter their dogs. We have no feed and can procure none for our own dogs. To date they have been subsisting on spoiled bacon, but in future they will have to live on what scraps they can pick up."[66]

In spite of these gloomy portents, however, there was little to indicate as the season ended that it was to be Fortymile's last year as a viable mining camp, and that before another spring most of its cabins would be empty, and the creeks almost deserted. It would be a more potent force than the prospect of a hungry winter that would move the miners out. As August waned and the first frosts touched the poplars, stories of a spectacular find not far upriver began to percolate through the diggings, and a first trickle of departures to the scene of the rumoured strike soon swelled to a stampede. The rich find that Dawson had expected would some day be made in the territory was apparently a reality, and every able-bodied man in the established camps was leaving everything he had already accomplished behind him, and heading for the mouth of an obscure salmon stream with an unpronounceable native name.

VI

THE NEW FIND WAS MADE BY THE YUKON'S MOST CASUAL PROSpector, George Washington Carmack, Ogilvie's old acquaintance from his days of packing over the Chilkoot Pass, but it was sparked by the country's most stubborn, a fanatic miner named Bob Henderson. Born on Big Island, off the coast of Nova Scotia, Henderson was a lonely, taciturn man whose only passion was the search for gold; in Ogilvie's words "not so much to become rich as to find adventure, for those who knew him best do not believe he would work the richest claim on earth if he had to stay on it till it was worked out."[67] To further his quest he became a seaman, and had been "pretty well over the globe" when his wanderings brought him

[66] *Ibid.*, pp. 237-238.
[67] Ogilvie, *Early Days*, p. 119.

to the mines of Colorado, where he remained for 14 years. Now, with two companions, he was on the move again, lured north by the will-of-the-wisp chase that had motivated him all his life. The three men climbed the Chilkoot Pass and made a disappointing venture up the Pelly. Continuing downstream, they arrived in July 1894, at the mouth of the Sixtymile River.

Here, the year before, Harper had established a trading post, which he had named Ogilvie, "in pursuance of a resolution made by him and McQuesten ... to name any future trading posts they might establish on Canadian territory after officials, notably those who had visited the country, and as I was the first they met, they began with myself."[68] In charge Harper had placed Joe Ladue, whose bubbling enthusiasm was still unquenched by his many years of wandering up and down the country. Ladue greeted the new-comers with a glowing report — largely a product of his fertile ima-gination — of the prospects on the Indian River, a substantial tribu-tary of the Yukon which joined it 20 miles below the mouth of the Sixtymile. It was practically virgin ground, the trader told them, and this fact in itself was enough to interest Henderson. His companions did not share his enthusiasm — they had had enough of fine words and empty promises, and turned back, leaving the Nova Scotian to prospect the new area alone. He preferred it that way. It was typical of the man, Ogilvie wrote, that "when others were tramping over Fortymile and Birch Creek regions, Bob was in another quarter."[69]

For two years Henderson, grubstaked by Ladue, examined with care and patience the Indian River and its tributaries, staying in the hills summer and winter until the need for further supplies would force him to return, empty-handed, to the post, where he would replenish his simple needs. He fought insects and heat, frostbite and loneliness, but his panning showed only "colours," and the prospect holes that he laboriously fired and thawed to bedrock were little more productive. On one occasion he spent 16 days building a dam to impound water for sluicing, and worked feverishly for another three days after he released the water, yet recovered only thirteen dollars. On another of his solitary forays he slipped off a log and skewered himself through the calf of one leg on the jagged butt of a branch, a painful injury which immobilized him for 14 days in his

[68] *Ibid.*, pp. 67-68.
[69] *Ibid.*, p. 120.

lonely camp, and which continued to bother him for the rest of his life. But it never occurred to him to quit.

In the winter of 1895-96, on a tributary of the Indian River that he had named Quartz Creek, he made preparations for a cleanup on a scale more elaborate than any he had previously attempted, and when the breakup brought water for sluicing, he recovered $620 in gold. Encouraged, he made another quick swing up the Indian, without results, and returned to Quartz Creek. This time he climbed to its headwaters and, crossing the dome that formed the height of land, he descended into a creek that he called Gold Bottom, which he had not explored before. Here in a gully near its source he once more panned the gravel, as he had done a hundred times before — but this time the glint of gold was visible in the bottom of the pan. Further prospecting proved that this ground was definitely worth development, but first he must replenish his supplies. Back at Ogilvie, in the best tradition of the mining fraternity, Henderson told Ladue the news, knowing that it would soon be broadcast.

The work went well, but about the middle of July 1896, his food ran low again, and another journey to Ladue's post became necessary. Henderson followed his usual route by way of Quartz Creek and the Indian River, but on the Indian the water was very low, because of the abnormal dry spell. His little moosehide boat frequently grounded, and he soon realized that he would be unable to return upstream with a load. There was an alternate way of getting back to the property, however. If Gold Bottom Creek was, as he believed, a tributary of the Trondiuck,[70] then it should be possible to return to it by travelling up that river, which flowed into the Yukon below the mouth of the Indian. The only problem might be to identify correctly the lower reaches of Gold Bottom, but Henderson was confident of his ability to recognize the creek when he saw it. He loaded his supplies and, drifting with the current, he passed the mouth of the Indian and headed for the Trondiuck and the confrontation that was to change the course of history in the Yukon district.

Carmack was camped at the river mouth, and there the two men met for the first time: the stubborn ex-Maritimer to whom prospect-

[70] Ogilvie translated Trondiuck as "hammer-water," derived, he claimed, from the hammering into the river bed of the stakes that formed part of the fish-traps which the Indians every year erected at the mouth of the river. This is only one of several versions of the origin of the name which the world was to know as Klondike.

ing was the breath of life, and who felt that the success that had so long eluded him might finally be within his grasp; and the indolent squaw man who, Indian-like, prospected in desultory fashion when the spirit moved him.[71] Carmack had come to the Trondiuck primarily for the fishing, and perhaps to cut a few saw logs for sale to the mill that was now established at Fortymile. It was for him a sort of family outing, as were many of his ventures, since he was accompanied by his native wife Kate and his daughter, and by the inseparables, Skookum Jim and Tagish Charlie. The idea of looking for gold in this location did not even occur to him until after the meeting with Henderson.

Later, when the significance of the conversation that took place between the two men was fully realized, and the bitter controversy as to what was actually said arose, Ogilvie, who was still in the country, interviewed several times everyone involved in the meeting, "and reduced the purport of our talks to writing." It is beyond dispute that Henderson told Carmack of his find on Gold Bottom, as he had told Ladue and any others whom he had met, and invited Carmack to come and stake on it. "Carmac [sic] promised to take it in," Ogilvie reported, "and take his Indian associates with him, but to this Henderson strongly objected, saying he did not want his creek staked by a lot of natives, more especially natives from the upper river. Carmac seemed to be offended by the objection so they parted."[72]

Henderson located Gold Bottom Creek without difficulty, and resumed work on his claim. Carmack and the Indians kept on for a time with their fishing, though they still toyed from time to time with the idea of getting out some logs, chiefly for the purpose of obtaining a little money with which to buy provisions that would relieve the monotony of their straight fish diet. Finally Carmack sent Skookum Jim up the Trondiuck Valley to search for suitable trees. Jim located good timber "in various places" on Rabbit Creek — later more appropriately named Bonanza — a small stream that flowed into the

[71] In one of his periods of activity, Carmack pioneered coal mining in the Yukon. Constantine, on his way into the country over the Chilkoot Pass in 1894, noted that "about five miles above the Five Fingers, Cormac [sic], of Fort Pelly, has driven a tunnel in the bank of the river, nearly 60 feet above the water. This he has timbered, and I am informed has mined some fair coal which does well for blacksmiths' use." Constantine, "Report . . . 10 October, 1894," p. 74.

[72] Ogilvie, *Early Days*, p. 125.

Trondiuck less than a mile above its mouth. "In order to learn whether or not [the logs] could be floated down to the Yukon," Ogilvie wrote after his interviews, "he had to make a close examination of the creek bed. In doing this he found some colours of gold at various places in the gravel and particularly at where claim sixty-six below discovery was afterwards located he found what he considered very fair prospects."[73] Jim hurried back to camp full of enthusiasm for his find, and anxious to investigate further. Carmack, however, had meanwhile changed his mind about logging, which might involve some hard work, and at the moment he was not interested in prospecting either. Jim had no choice for the present but to bottle up his eagerness: among the natives, Carmack's word was law.

About 20 days after this first encounter with Henderson, however, Carmack changed his mind again, and decided to investigate for himself the prospects on Gold Bottom.

Jim, Charlie and George started up Bonanza on the quest [Ogilvie noted] with a gold pan, spade, axe, and such other tools as were necessary for a prolonged stay from camp, and such provisions as their means afforded, and according to the Indians the supply was not extensive or diversified, being mostly fish. Travelling up the valley of Bonanza through the thick underbrush at that season was tiring and fatiguing, and the mosquito-laden atmosphere added torment to fatigue. A short distance below where they afterwards made discovery, both Jim and Charlie told me they, while panning during a rest, found a ten-cent pan. . . . It was decided that if the Gold Bottom trials failed they would devote further attention to this place. The Indians both told me they asked George if they would tell Bob of this find, and that George directed them to say nothing about it till they came back, if they did, and investigated further, then if they found anything good they might tell.

Travelling was so tiresome and tedious in the valley that, when they came to the confluence with the creek now called Eldorado, they took to the divide between it and Bonanza, and followed the crest of this divide around the head of Bonanza Creek, where, finding the marks made by Henderson, they descended to him. Arrived there they were nearly bare of provisions, and completely out of tobacco, a serious predicament for Jim and Charlie. Henderson, either through shortage himself or dislike of the Indians, or both, would not let them have anything, though Jim and Charlie both assured me they offered to pay well for all they could get, which Jim was both able and willing to do. As they did not find any prospect approaching in value the ten-cent pan on Bonanza, they remained a very short time at Henderson's camp, and

[73] *Ibid.*, p. 127.

made their way back to the head of the creek which first gave fame to the Klondike — Bonanza.[74]

This second meeting between Henderson and Carmack was evidently as acrimonious as the first, and it was to have an even more bitter aftermath. Henderson later maintained that Carmack before he left agreed to send word back if any worthwhile prospects were discovered on the return journey. This promise, if it was made, was certainly never kept.

Heading back down the valley they had climbed, Carmack and the natives made slow progress. They were weak from hunger, as their food supplies were almost gone. Jim, the one among them best able to travel, was sent on ahead finally to hunt for a moose, while the others continued to follow lethargically along the creek bed. When they were all close to complete exhaustion Jim was successful in making a kill. He then, according to Ogilvie, "called on the others, whom he had left some distance away, to come to him. While waiting for them to come he looked in the sand of the creek where he had gone to get a drink, taking with him a bit of the moose. He found gold, he said, in greater quantities than he had ever seen it before. When the others joined him the moose meat was cooked, and they had a feed. Then he showed them the gold in the sand. They remained two days at this place panning, and testing the gravel up and down the creek in the vicinity. After satisfying themselves that they had the best spot, [they] decided to stake and record there."[75]

On August 16, as they prepared to stake, a rift appeared in their relationship. Skookum Jim claimed that the discovery claim was his by right, and that under the new regulations he was entitled to stake also one of the adjoining claims. Carmack, faced by the dazzling prospect of sudden wealth, disagreed. He reserved for himself the right to discovery and the adjoining claim on the specious grounds that Jim as an Indian would not be allowed to record them. It was the moment of truth, and the squaw man had a change of heart

[74] *Ibid.*, pp. 127-129.

[75] *Ibid.*, p. 129. Carmack was later to claim that he was the one who made the find, but Ogilvie does not seem to have believed his story. There are, incidentally, several other versions of the discovery, and the exact sequence of events will probably never be known with certainty. Ogilvie's story was at least carefully researched, and written shortly after the find — it is probable, therefore that it is reasonably close to the truth.

regarding the status of his native friends! Jim on his part did not accept this edict with his usual meekness, and it was night before they reached a compromise. Carmack would stake and record the discovery claim, but would assign a half interest in it to Skookum Jim.

So it was that on the morning of August 17, 1896, on a creek that had been a part of McQuesten and Harper's hunting terrain in their Fort Reliance days, "Carmac staked discovery claim five hundred feet in length up and down the creek valley, and No. 1 below discovery of the same length; both the full width of the valley bottom, or from base to base of the hill on either side, as the regulations then read. No. 2 below was staked for Tagish Charlie, and No. 1 above for Skookum Jim."[76]

At this moment in the history of the north the pre-Klondike era ended, and nothing in the Yukon district was ever quite the same again.

[76] *Ibid.*, p. 130.

Epilogue

Prelude to Bonanza

THE CATACLYSMIC CHANGES THAT WOULD AFFECT THE LIVES OF almost everyone in the country as the result of Carmack's find began when he arrived at Fortymile to record his claims. At first he was not taken seriously, as his reputation as a rather desultory miner was well-established in the settlement, and his association with Indians had stirred up considerable local prejudice against him. When, however, to confound his doubters, he poured out on a bar-room counter the nuggets he had collected from the gravel on Rabbit Creek, the disbelief vanished, and almost overnight the rush from Fortymile to the new ground began. "The town was almost deserted;" Ogilvie reported, "men who had been in a chronic state of drunkenness for weeks were pitched into boats as ballast and taken up to stake themselves a claim, and claims were staked by men for their friends who were not in the country at the time."[1] By November 20, according to Constantine, 338 claims had been recorded in the Klondike, and 150 more were being processed, which "in all cases gave better prospects than any other heretofore. Many old miners state that this creek is fully as rich as any found in California in the early days."[2]

By June 1897, Dawson City, the new settlement at the mouth of the Klondike named in honour of Dr. George Dawson, had a population in excess of 4,000 people, and over 500 buildings crowded the hastily-laid-out site. Circle City was as empty as Fortymile, yet even

[1] Ogilvie, *Information Respecting the Yukon*, p. 58.
[2] Constantine, "Report on the Yukon Detachment," p. 234.

the first arrivals from there, who had reached Dawson in January, were too late to stake any of the ground on Bonanza Creek or its tributaries, and had to be content for the moment with looking for fractions that in the confusion had been overlooked, or with searching for prospects farther afield. Long before the stampeders from outside began landing in thousands on Dawson's waterfront, there was no known placer ground open, and fortunes were already being lost and won. As in any mining rush, some of those first on the scene gave up too quickly and let wealth slip through their fingers, while others were soon on the way to acquiring riches on a scale that they had never dreamed of.

None deserved better of the country than Jack McQuesten and his partners. For Arthur Harper in particular, the Klondike gold rush should have been an occasion of triumph and reward, but after his years on the creeks the discovery came too late. In July 1897, he left the territory ill and penniless, his passage outside paid as a charity by the Alaska Commercial Company, which he had served so well and yet so reluctantly for so many years. "Harper," wrote his good friend Ogilvie, "though well aware of the country's potential worth, could not afford to begin the development of it himself, but his letters to friends on the outside helped to arouse curiosity and create interest. Thus the man who first thought of trying it as a mining field, was compelled by circumstances to devote himself to something else. He lived in the region for twenty-four years, and after testing nearly every mining field except the Klondike . . . had to leave Dawson in 1897, almost exhausted with tuberculosis, and died from it at Yuma, Arizona the following November, just as the Klondike was opening its golden gate to him. . . . We cannot help feeling that fate was unkind to one who had come so near the achievement of wealth through hard work, yet died just past his prime, sixty-two, at a time when everything seemed most favourable for the realization of the hopes he had entertained throughout all the trying years of his waiting, watching, and struggling."[3]

To an associate of the lean years in the Yukon, Joe Ladue, the Klondike brought the financial rewards that were denied to Harper, but not the time or leisure to enjoy them. Surprised perhaps to find that one of the prospects that he had urged on others was at last bearing fruit, Ladue lost no time in joining the rush to the new dig-

[3] Ogilvie, *Early Days*, p. 101.

gings, attracted not by gold but by the commercial possibilities of the place. While others toiled on the creeks he hastily erected a ramshackle saloon and a sawmill, and staked a townsite on level ground at the mouth of the Klondike, on which he was soon selling building lots at astronomical prices. He did not long enjoy, however, the returns from these astute and profitable business ventures: like Harper, he also became a victim of consumption and died only a few years after the Klondike find. "He was a most enthusiastic advocate of the Yukon and its possibilities," Ogilvie commented, "which sometimes led him into awkward situations.... [But] it takes such enthusiasm to sustain a man in such a country, and happy is he who is ultimately rewarded by having his visions realized."[4]

Alone among the pioneer traders it was their leading spirit, Jack McQuesten, who derived from the Klondike both wealth and the enjoyment of it. He lingered on in Circle City as long as possible after the exodus began, and then, reluctantly, he quit his now deserted fiefdom and followed the last of his customers upstream to Dawson City and the new creeks. He arrived, like the others from the Alaska side, too late to stake open ground, but he acquired a share in an existing claim — many miners were already selling out or were looking for partners to help finance their operations — and this in due time returned modest dividends. But mining had never been his primary interest, nor did it become so now. Instead, he supervised the construction on the banks of the Yukon of yet another sheet iron warehouse for the Alaska Commercial Company — the last that he was to build in the country, and by far the largest. When the rush subsided and the settlement began to empty, McQuesten was a wealthy man. He was able to build a luxurious house in California, and live out his days with his Indian wife in well-earned comfort under warm southern sunshine.

The Alaska Commercial Company, whose foundations McQuesten so ably laid on the upper Yukon, survived the business vicissitudes of the post-Klondike years and the cycles of war, depression, and regrowth that followed. The international scope of its operations, with stores at Dawson City, Mayo, and Whitehorse in the Yukon, as well as numerous stores and trading posts in Alaska, was recognized by a name change to the Northern Commercial Company. Today the international flavour has dwindled, though the

4 *Ibid.*, p. 119.

name remains: the firm no longer has any retail outlets in Canada, having sold its last remaining store in the Yukon in 1969. Its Caterpillar machinery agency in Whitehorse, however, is a long-standing and still flourishing business, and in Alaska its operations in the large cities and remote hamlets continue on an impressive scale.

The original stakers of the Klondike, unlike many of the discoverers of new mining fields, became financially independent as a result of their find. Carmack returned to his ground late in August, with provisions for a few weeks, and he and the Indians began to work their claims. In eight days, with a very ramshackle, makeshift outfit, they recovered $1,200, which Carmack claimed could have been obtained in two days with a proper mining set-up. They did not continue this haphazard operation long themselves, but in the trading and jockeying for claims that followed the original rush, they leased their property for shares, and for the rest of their lives they lived, each in his own way, on the comfortable income that this arrangement brought them.

Tagish Charlie and Skookum Jim returned to the country of their birth in the lakes at the head of the Yukon River, and in time became inhabitants of the new village of Caribou Crossing, a station on the White Pass and Yukon Railway, which was later called Carcross. Tagish Charlie became a hotel owner there and a man of substance in the community — also on occasion a heavy drinker. This in the end proved his undoing: during a too enthusiastic Christmas holiday celebration he fell off the White Pass Railway bridge, and was drowned. Skookum Jim built himself a large house but seldom lived in it, as most of the time he was in the hills in search of another Bonanza claim. His ambition was to make a sensational strike in his own right, free of the shadow of George Washington Carmack; but in spite of the fact that he made some fantastic journeys during which he lived entirely off the country, far from any base of supplies, a second find eluded him. Even his magnificent physique could not withstand indefinitely the physical abuse of such demanding travel. He died in 1916, and was buried in the same cemetery at Carcross in which Tagish Charlie had been interred only a few weeks before.

Carmack outlived both his companions. Ironically, the man who for years had lived and worked and travelled only with Indians, and whose dislike of Bob Henderson stemmed largely from the latter's disparaging remarks concerning Skookum Jim and Tagish Charlie, now completely reversed his attitude. The one-time squawman abandoned his Indian wife Kate — she returned to her own people at Carcross, supported by a small pension — and married a white woman in Dawson who kept a brothel, or "cigar store" as such establishments were euphemistically referred to in the town. In this potentially ill-starred union Carmack found great happiness. He moved with his wife to Vancouver, far from his past associations, and settled contentedly into the role of respected citizen. He invested wisely, largely in real estate, and when he died in 1922 he left his wife in comfortable circumstances. For the once-scorned mining dilettante, the wheel had turned full circle.

To one man, however, the feverish activity in the new field brought only the bitterness of gall. Though Bob Henderson more than anyone else was responsible for the fact that prospectors had found the area at all, no word of the events taking place so near at hand came from either Carmack or the Indians, and Henderson continued to patiently work his ground on Gold Bottom Creek, while the frantic staking rush on the Klondike passed him by. When news of the stampede finally chanced to reach him, there was no ground open on either Bonanza or Eldorado, and even the lower reaches of Gold Bottom had been staked and renamed Hunker Creek, and the right of discovery on it had been granted to another miner, Andrew Hunker. Henderson had never had the time or the funds to make the trip to Fortymile to record his find: as a result the full benefits of even his own comparatively modest discovery, the culmination of his two years of pioneering exploration, were denied to him. He left the country in disgust, but could not abandon long his compulsive, lonely search for gold, and he soon returned. To the end of his days he roamed the Yukon bush, searching, like Skookum Jim, for another Bonanza. Eventually, the Canadian government awarded him a pension of $200 a month in recognition of the part he played in the discovery of the Klondike gold fields, but the thought of abandoning his quest never occurred to him. Stimulated probably by the adrenalin of his bitterness, he outlasted all his Yukon contemporaries. He died of cancer in 1933 in the midst of planning one more sortie, this time to the Pelly River. His second Bonanza, like Skookum Jim's, remained undiscovered: for him, as for most of his breed, the search was the only reward.

The little handful of men who in 1896 were at Fortymile for disinterested reasons — Bompas, Judge, Constantine, Ogilvie — were as much affected by the events of the stampede as were the traders and miners. For Bishop Bompas, the hordes of gold seekers descending to the Klondike were a threat to the morals of the Indians living there: as well, they reawoke all the anxiety and uncertainty that plagued the old man in his relationships with white men. The task of Christian ministry in this new field, he realized sadly, was one he must delegate to others. He sent Flewelling, therefore, to look after the Klondike Indians, who were persuaded to settle at Moosehide, a village which was at least a few miles away from the distractions of the booming new settlement. Bowen was sent to Dawson to minister to the miners, continuing the work that he had begun at Fortymile, and would have carried on at Circle City if that community had not suddenly emptied. To Bowen the bishop also entrusted £250 that he had received as a grant towards the construction of a church at Fortymile from another missionary organization, the Society for the Promotion of Christian Knowledge. "The stay of the miners at Dawson," Bompas wrote in a letter to the secretary of the Society to account for the change of location of the building, "is likely to be permanent for ten years at least, and in case the whites should leave, there has always been a band of Indians at Klondike for whom the church would be available."[5] Bowen used the gift to build a small log church, which was called St. Paul's, and which was replaced a few years later by a larger and more imposing frame structure that is still in use. At one stage, Bompas himself had to act as rector of this church for a short period, but for him it was a worrisome assignment. To the man who had lived most of his long years in the north among the Indians, the boisterous, carousing miners were as alien as visitors from another planet.

In 1901 Bompas and his wife finally moved from the almost empty shell of Fortymile to Caribou Crossing, where the bishop occupied himself with his translation work, with letter writing, with teaching at the Indian school, and with attending to the needs of the local Indians. In 1905 he relinquished his episcopate, and was delighted when one of the most able of the younger clergy in the diocese, Rev. Isaac O. Stringer, was named as his successor. In June 1906, as he worked at his desk preparing a sermon he suffered a sudden stroke, and before anyone could reach him the veteran missionary was dead. Mrs. Bompas after his death returned to England for a short time, and then settled in Westmount, Quebec, with two nieces. At the age

[5] Cody, *An Apostle of the North*, p. 283.

of 83 she broke her hip, but was able to walk without crutches within a year. She lived until January 1917, when death claimed her shortly before her eighty-seventh birthday. Her active interest in missionary affairs and in the Yukon in particular continued unabated as long as she lived, and she was always much in demand as a speaker at missionary gatherings and church meetings.

For Father Judge, in contrast, the gold rush offered a joyful challenge, which he hastened to accept. In the fall of 1896 he left the lower Yukon for Circle City, to begin the work he had been instructed to undertake there. Before settling down at his new location, however, he unloaded his supplies and continued upriver by steamer to Fortymile to collect some personal effects and "churchgoods" that he had left there on his departure for Alaska in the spring. It was his intention to return immediately to Circle City on the same steamer: instead the vessel was trapped at Fortymile by an abnormally early run of ice, leaving Judge no choice but that of remaining there until overland travel was practicable. He never did complete his journey, however; instead he too became involved in the changes that Carmack's strike had set in motion. "It was very providential," he wrote early in 1897 to one of his brothers, "for, after I left here in the summer, gold was found on a creek fifty miles up the river, and later discoveries show the region to be one of the richest and most extensive gold-fields ever known.... They have started on the Yukon, at the mouth of the principal creek, a town to be called Dawson City, and lots there 50 x 100 feet are selling as high as a thousand dollars already."[6] Judge secured three acres on high ground at the north end of the townsite on which to build a church and hospital, and requested that the Sisters of St. Ann be sent to take charge of the latter.

For the hospital there was soon a desperate need. The first winter on the Klondike brought food shortages, and scurvy: later, when river navigation opened, typhoid fever was also introduced, and quickly reached almost epidemic proportions. The hospital, named St. Mary's by Judge, opened on August 20, before it was completed, and before the sisters had arrived to staff it. All the details of overseeing its operation, and attending to the spiritual needs of the ill and the dying, fell on the shoulders of the little priest. It was a

---

[6] Judge, *An American Missionary*, p. 179.

demanding regime, with hardly any time for sleep, and none for relaxation.

In 1898 Judge's workload became even heavier. The sisters arrived, but so did a flood of gold seekers that reached alarming proportions, and a steadily increasing number of sick and destitute men presented themselves at the door from which no man "of any creed, or no creed at all," was ever turned away. Judge, though now in theory only the hospital's chaplain, made no effort to spare himself, though by the end of the summer his own health, never robust, began to deteriorate. At Christmas time the citizens of Dawson packed one of the town's largest theatres for a benefit performance to raise funds for the hospital and honour its founder. The tribute was only just in time. On January 7, 1899, Judge was stricken with pneumonia, and on January 16, with shocking suddenness, he died, though only 49 years old. "His buoyant and cheerful spirit," read one of the many resolutions of sympathy, "struggled manfully under a load of debt and grave responsibility incurred for others; but the task was too great, and his death cannot but be regarded as a voluntary martyrdom in the cause of charity."[7]

Constantine's contribution to Dawson City was more mundane perhaps, but equally useful. He was one of the first to appreciate that a great influx into the country would inevitably follow the spreading of the news of Carmack's find, and as a policeman he realized all too well what some of the more undesirable consequences of this invasion might well be. He immediately began the task of convincing the authorities that a larger police detachment was essential if law and order were to be maintained and the anarchy that had prevailed in some of the rougher American mining camps was to be avoided. At first it was an uphill and exasperating struggle, moving him to comment angrily on one occasion that if the detachment in the Yukon was not increased, the few men already there should be taken out. Fortunately for the district he persevered, and the bureaucratic machinery in Ottawa moved in time. When Constantine left the country early in 1898 he held the rank of superintendent, and the force in the Yukon had grown to ten officers and 254 non-commissioned officers and men, whose presence ensured that the people of Dawson, even when the city was bursting at the seams, were able to walk their streets unarmed and unafraid. On his depar-

[7] *Ibid.*, p. 281.

ture, Constantine was presented with a hand-painted scroll expressing the appreciation of the miners and traders for his services to the district, and a poke containing $2,000 worth of nuggets — the only gold that this incorruptible man took out of the country with him.

The remainder of his career was also in the north — there was to be no sinecure backwater appointment in which he would peacefully serve out his time, however much he might have earned it. Instead, in 1903 he was placed in charge of a patrol that travelled from Fort Saskatchewan to Fort McPherson to establish the first Mounted Police post beyond the Arctic Circle. In 1905 he assumed command of a new division organized in the Athabasca-Mackenzie region, with headquarters at Lesser Slave Lake, and almost immediately became involved in a pointless and futile attempt by the federal government to use a detachment of police, equipped only with axes and shovels, to build a pack road from Fort St. John to the Yukon, through some of the most remote and rugged terrain in North America. For three years the project continued, exacting a senseless toll of exhausted men and dead horses, before it was discontinued with the trail construction incomplete. One of the victims was Constantine himself. His health finally undermined by his strenuous northern assignments, he received a medical discharge from the force, and died in San Francisco in 1916. Like Father Judge, he was ultimately the victim of his own dedication and talents.

Ogilvie, very much against his will, was still in the Yukon at the end of the summer of 1896, still waiting for word concerning the boundary commission. As a result, he was able, on September 6, 1896, to send from Fort Cudahy a dispatch to his department that must have caused a stir.

I am very much pleased to be able to inform you [he wrote] that a most important discovery of gold has been made on a creek called Bonanza Creek, an affluent of the river known here as the Klondyke. It is marked on the maps extant as Deer River, and joins the river a few miles above the site of Fort Reliance.

The discovery was made by G. W. Cormack [*sic*], who worked with me in 1887 on the coast range. The indications are that it is very rich, indeed the richest yet found, and as far as work has been carried on it realizes expectations. It is only two weeks since it was known, and already about 200 claims have been staked on it, and the creek is not yet exhausted; it, and its branches are considered good for 300 or 400 claims. Besides, there are two other creeks above it, which it is confidently expected will yield good pay; and if they do so, we shall have

800 to 1000 claims on this river, which will require over 2000 men for their proper working.[8]

He finally received word on the last steamer of the season that the boundary commission negotiations had fallen through, and was instructed to return to Ottawa "with all possible dispatch." Unfortunately, the same early ice run and unseasonable snowstorms that had detained Father Judge at Fortymile also prevented Ogilvie from leaving it. Once navigation ended, travel by dog team was the only way out of the country, and Ogilvie did not feel that the expense and delay involved in a journey of this sort would be justified.

Dogs [he explained] ... are scarce and dear, ranging from thirty or forty dollars to one hundred and twenty-five dollars apiece. Dog food, like all other food, is scarce by reason of the poor salmon run in the river last season — practically none were caught near here — and the result is the dog-owners here have to use bacon for food, which, at twenty-five to forty cts. per pound, is expensive.

I would require a team of eight dogs to take my outfit and my man Fawcett with our provisions and the dogs' food as far as Taiya. There, the dogs would have to be abandoned or killed, as they are worthless on the coast except to parties coming in here early in the season. Starting from here say December 1st, it would be February before I reached Ottawa, and during thirty-five or forty days of this time we would be exposed to much cold and hardship and some hazard from storms.

The journey has been made, and I would not hesitate to undertake it were things more reasonable here and dog food plentiful, but it would take at least $1,000 to equip me with transport and outfit, which sum, I think, I can expend more in the interests of the country by remaining here and making a survey of the Klondak [sic] of the miners.[9]

So it was that in January 1897, instead of journeying outside, Ogilvie travelled to Dawson City "to lay out the townsite and survey several other blocks applied for there," and to become part of the history of the gold rush, first as the surveyor who prevented chaos on Bonanza Creek, and later, from 1898 to 1902, as commissioner of the newly-created Yukon Territory. He died in 1912 in retirement in Winnipeg, just after making one last visit to the Yukon as a private individual, and completing the manuscript of his book of reminiscences of the north.

[8] Ogilvie, *Information Respecting the Yukon*, pp. 55-56.
[9] *Ibid.*, p. 57. Ogilvie's problems in getting out of the country make thought-provoking reading in this day of jet-age travel.

Today, Fortymile is a handful of decaying cabins, and Dawson City is struggling valiantly to stay alive. The men who some 75 years ago were present at the death of the one settlement and the birth of the other are themselves dead, and the memory of them is dim in the land to which they contributed so much and in which they never lost faith. Their names sprinkle the mapsheets of north-central Yukon: the Ogilvie Mountains and Ogilvie River; McQuesten Lake and the McQuesten River and its branches; Ladue Lake and the Keno Ladue River; Mayo[10] Lake and River, and the settlement of Mayo Landing at its mouth; Mount Harper; the settlement of Carmacks; Henderson Creek and Henderson Dome. This mute evidence of their presence is almost the only tangible memorial of these pioneers of the placer creeks.

It was the search for gold, and the earlier search for furs, that began to unlock for outsiders the secrets of Canada's extreme northwest. The process is continuing today, though with different methods and changed objectives, but in the excitement of new discoveries and fresh developments the contribution of the pre-Klondike miners, traders, and explorers should not be overlooked. By their difficult and sometimes incredible journeys they sketched in broad strokes the first outlines of the land. Whatever has been accomplished since, in the development of the Yukon, rests upon the foundation that they built.

---

[10] Al Mayo left the Canadian Yukon in 1894 to establish a trading post of his own at a new settlement, Rampart, on the lower Yukon River in Alaska, and the Klondike strike did not lure him back to his former stamping grounds. He disposed of his post in 1899 to the Alaska Commercial Company, but continued to operate for many years a sawmill and a hotel in the same vicinity, until he finally sold out and left the north for an unknown destination.

Acknowledgements

Prelude to Bonanza

THE RESEARCH AND THE WRITING OF THIS BOOK SPANNED A NINE-year period, on a part-time basis. Its beginnings, several years before the founding of the Yukon archives, were on a very casual basis, and almost entirely dependent on the help of others. Fortunately, several people became interested in the project. They produced information when it was requested; they loaned books for extended periods; and in many instances they supplied rare and precious source material that was not then available in the Yukon, or which was difficult to consult because of the necessity of spending, in the course of my regular work, long periods of time away from Whitehorse and the regional library.

My first tentative enquiry, seeking details of the life of Robert Campbell, was sent to the Hudson's Bay Company in August 1965. A prompt and generous reply from Mrs. Shirlee Smith, then the Company's librarian in Winnipeg, and later their archivist, was most encouraging to a neophyte researcher: it led to further enquiries to her over a period of several years, all courteously and promptly answered. Alice M. Johnson of the Company's London Archives also contributed useful extracts from correspondence that assisted in evaluating the personal relationships of its Yukon officers. Roy Minter of the White Pass and Yukon Route loaned me his own copy of Campbell's journal, a privately-printed edition that was the first of the original writings of the period that I was able to obtain in its entirety, instead of in the form of quoted excerpts. Mrs. D. M. Sutherland, librarian of the Geological Survey of Canada in Ottawa, also loaned books and supplied a mouth-watering list of other material that she had that was too valuable to be allowed out of the library, but which served as a useful guide for other searches. From Ottawa also, Inspector W. R. Pilkey, then liaison officer for the Royal Canadian Mounted Police, and since retired with the rank of assistant commissioner, contributed from the Force's rich store of information photostat copies of Inspector Constantine's annual reports of 1894, 1895, and 1896, containing a terse account of the coming of law and order to the Fortymile camp.

In Whitehorse, Bea and George McLeod made freely available a treasured possession, the Klondike Edition (April 1898) of *The National Geographic Magazine*, and also loaned, for as long as I required it, a rare copy of William Ogilvie's *Early Days in the Yukon*. Lew Green, territorial geologist, unearthed in his office several copies of the 1898 re-issue of George Dawson's invaluable report on the Yukon Expedition, which for some reason were not on his inventory, and one of them became mine. Later Lew also contributed to my library a copy of Frederick Schwatka's *On Alaska's Great River*, and an old St. Paul's Church bulletin from Dawson City, which contained an interesting article on Bishop Bompas by his wife. Garth Graham, director of the Yukon Library Services, gave much helpful advice and assistance, as did Flo Whyard, at that time editor of *The Whitehorse Star*, then Canadian editor of *Alaska Magazine*, and now an elected member of the Yukon Legislative Assembly. Thanks to Art Deer for the author's photograph.

Farther afield, the Adelphi Book Shop, R. D. Hilton Smith's late haven for book lovers in Victoria, proved, through its fascinating monthly catalogues, to be a real treasure for the seeker after knowledge of the Pacific northwest. From the Adelphi's listings I was able to purchase over a period of time the nucleus of a personal library on the early Yukon: two long essays on the activities of the Russians in North America, reprinted from the *British Columbia Historical Quarterly*; a copy of W. H. Dall's *Alaska and Its Resources*; a biography of Bishop Bompas by H. A. Cody; a biography of Father William H. Judge, by his brother; the Yukon journal of Robert Kennicott, reprinted in a book by James A. James of Northwestern University; *Flag Over the North*, L. D. Kitchener's history of the Northern Commercial Company; and Arthur Walden's *A Dog Puncher on the Yukon*. Though I made these buys without ever entering the shop, it was with real regret that I received in 1974 the notice that the Adelphi was closing its doors with the retirement of its owner.

From all this help, and from my own searches and selections, came the first draft of the book, finished late in 1971. Jim Smith, Commissioner of the Yukon Territory, sent a copy of the manuscript to his friend Willard Ireland, provincial librarian and archivist for British Columbia, for a critical review. In May 1972, a most encouraging letter arrived from Mr. Ireland. It lifted me over a period of discouragement: I was suffering from overexposure to my own work, and viewing the results of my efforts with a decidedly jaundiced eye. The support from such an authority as Mr. Ireland could not have come at a more needed time, and for it I will always be grateful.

In September 1973, I showed the manuscript to Gray Campbell, president of Gray's Publishing Ltd., who had been lured into spending a working vacation in the Yukon, during delightful autumn weather. Gray liked what he read. He took the manuscript back to Sidney with him, exposed it to two readers, Cecil Clark and Maralyn Horsdal, still liked it, and agreed to publish on the completion of the final draft. It was a heady moment for this first-time author.

I returned to the work with new enthusiasm. A grant from the Canada Council, made through their very useful Horizons program, made it possible to visit the archives in Victoria, and to discover there, with the help of the capable and obliging staff, most of the information that I needed to fill the gaps that I knew existed in the first draft, as well as other material applicable to my subject that I was not aware existed. On returning to Whitehorse I consulted also our own Yukon archives — which did not open until 1972 — and experienced the enthusiasm and knowledge of Brian Speirs, the territorial archivist, and that of Diane Johnston and Jean Cook, his staff.

It was during this stage that I discovered that there is more to preparing a manuscript for publication than collecting material and writing a text. Spelling, to which I usually take a casual approach, had suddenly to be both correct and consistent. There was agonizing over the choice of words in dubious situations. There were footnotes to prepare. There was the grind of proofreading. Happily for me, for these pedestrian tasks also help was forthcoming, and again in abundant measure.

Jinx Ross, an old Yukon friend, undertook to proofread the manuscript before it was typed, a brave venture in the face of untidy pages, pock-marked with inserts and erasures. Another old friend, Marg Waddington, drew on years of experience in deciphering hand-written drafts, and produced a clean typescript in record time. John Callan of Victoria, a skilled practitioner of the dying art of freehand lettering, prepared the maps, though I selected the areas to be covered. Mechanical limitations imposed by space and scale, and a desire that the maps be printed in the upright position on the page to make them easier to consult while reading, made some compro-mise necessary in their layout, but every place mentioned in the text will be found on one or another of them.The map used in the end sheets is a portion of one of the three sheets which accompanied Dawson's report and was supplied through the courtesy of Dr. Peter Harker, head of the Geographical Information Division of the Geo-logical Survey of Canada.

In Sidney, Maralyn Horsdal continued her input. An honours major in geography, who had worked on The National Atlas of Canada in Ottawa, she was given a free rein in reviewing and edit-ing the changes in the final draft. For me, this was a period of fearful thralldom. Maralyn exercised a gimlet eye and a ruthless scalpel, while I struggled to attain the standards on which she insisted. For this help, however, and that of the others, I offer my thanks. Much of whatever erudition this book possesses is due to the vigilance of these overseers. Nonetheless, the responsibility for the text is indubi-tably mine.

I admit to some arbitrariness in its preparation. I decided, for example, that because of the considerable variations found in the original sources, the spelling of place-names in the text would generally be that adopted on the mapsheets of the National Topo-graphic Series, even in those instances in which the version of the present-day cartographers seems to have been rarely used by any of the early writers. So "Fortymile" appears in the text, but "Forty Mile," "Forty-mile," or "Forty-Mile" was preferred by its con-temporaries. There was even more variation in the place-names of native origin. A small landing at the head of Lynn Canal, for example, which is now "Dyea" on the maps, was variously "Taiyah," "Dayah," and "Dai-yah." These names in print were of course phonetic versions of the sound of the place, and differed wildly with the ear of the writer.

The problem of the spelling of Russian place-names was solved by an equally capricious decision. One of the sources used in the preparation of my book was an English translation of the travels of Zagoskin in Russian America published by the University of Toronto Press, and among its appendices was a "Glossary of Geographic Place-names," and an "Index of Names of Persons," prepared by the editor, Henry N. Michael of Temple University. Here was a reference ready to hand that could not be overlooked, and I borrowed from it freely. The spellings of these two lists have as a rule been used in the pages of this book.

In all quotations, of course, the spelling used by the original author has been preserved.

The sources of the quotations that are part of the text — and there are many of them — have been conscientiously listed in the footnotes, though the story I hope is readable and understandable without the distraction of consulting them. For the compulsive delver, however, these notes do contain a few nuggets of inconsequential information that nevertheless add to the flavour of the period: the recipe for making hooch, for example, or a tale of mosquitoes that help each other, or a description of the sourdough thermometer and its cold-resistant ingredients. Ingenuity, and a vein of humour, have always been desirable attributes of life in the north.

One last acknowledgement remains to be made. Traditionally, but sincerely, I wish to thank my wife Glenna for her patience and forbearance during the fitful incubation period of this book. Writing is a solitary pursuit, and financial returns, if any, are very much a future thing. Without the loyal support of my wife during the lonely periods of my work, this project would not have been possible. Any success it may have will be her just reward.

Bibliography

Prelude to Bonanza

ANDERSON, BERN. *The Life and Voyages of Captain George Vancouver, Surveyor of the Sea.* Toronto: University of Toronto Press, paperback, 1960.

ANDERSON, JAMES. Unpublished letters, as noted, in the archives of the Hudson's Bay Company and in the Provincial Archives of British Columbia.

ANDREWS, CLARENCE L. "Biographical Sketch of Capt. William Moore." *The Washington Historical Quarterly*, Vol. XXI, Nos. 3 and 4, 1930, Vol. XXII, No. 1, 1931.

ARCHER, A. S. *A Heroine of the North: Memoirs of Charlotte Selina Bompas.* London: The MacMillan Company, 1929.

BEARDSLEE, L. A. *Reports of Captain L. A. Beardslee, U.S. Navy, Relative to Affairs in Alaska.* Washington, D.C.: Government Printing Office, 1882.

BOMPAS, CHARLOTTE S. "Bishop Bompas. (A Short Sketch of His Work)." *St. Paul's Parish Magazine.* Dawson City, Y.T.: Vol. I, No. 5, March 1902.

BOND, COURTNEY C.J. *Surveyors of Canada 1867-1967.* Ottawa: The Canadian Institute of Surveying, 1966.

BRYCE, REV. GEORGE. "A. K. Isbister, in Memoriam." *Transaction No. 8.* Winnipeg: Manitoba Historical and Scientific Society, Season 1883-84.

CAMPBELL, ROBERT. *Two Journals of Robert Campbell (Chief Factor, Hudson's Bay Company), 1808 to 1853.* Seattle: Limited edition, privately printed by John W. Todd, Jr., 1951.

CANHAM, REV. T. H. "The Diocese of Selkirk: Its Work and Workers." *The Church Missionary Intelligencer*, Vol. 23, January 1898.

CODY, H. A. *An Apostle of the North*. New York: E. P. Dutton and Company, 1908.

CONSTANTINE, INSPECTOR CHARLES. "Report of Inspector Constantine, 10th October, 1894," in *Report of the Commissioner of the North-West Mounted Police Force, 1894*. Ottawa: The Queen's Printer, 1895.

――――. "Report of Inspector Constantine, 20th January, 1896," in *Report of the Commissioner of the North-West Mounted Police Force, 1895*. Ottawa: The Queen's Printer, 1896.

――――. "Report on the Yukon Detachment, 20th November, 1896," in *Report of the Commissioner of the North-West Mounted Police Force, 1896*. Ottawa: The Queen's Printer, 1897.

COOK, JAMES and JAMES KING. *A Voyage to the Pacific Ocean*. 3 vols. London: G. Nicol and T. Cadell, 1784. (See Paul W. Dale, *Seventy North to Fifty South*.)

CRUIKSHANK, JULIE. *Through the Eyes of Strangers: A Preliminary Survey of Land Use History in the Yukon During the Late Nineteenth Century*. Report to the Territorial Government and the Yukon Archives, February 1974.

DALE, PAUL W. *Seventy North to Fifty South*. Englewood Cliffs, N.J.: Prentice-Hall, Inc., 1969. This book, "a modern annotation of Cook's final journal," contains many quotations from the account of the voyage to the Pacific by James Cook and James King, and was the only source for this material that was available to me when this chapter was written.

DALL, W. H. *Alaska and its Resources*. Boston: Lee and Shepherd, 1870.

――――. "A Yukon Pioneer." *The National Geographic Magazine*, Vol. IX, April 1898.

DAWSON, GEORGE M. *Report on an Exploration in the Yukon District, N.W.T. and Adjacent Northern Portion of British Columbia. 1887*. Ottawa: The Queen's Printer. Re-issued 1898, with "Extracts Relating to the Yukon District, N.W.T. . . . 1887-88," by R. G. McConnell.

――――. "Notes on the Indian Tribes of the Yukon District and the adjacent Northern Portion of British Columbia." *Geological and Natural History Survey of British Columbia, 1887-88*, Vol. III, Part I, Appendix IIB. Montreal: Government Printing Office, 1889.

―――. "Notes on the Occurrence of Mammoth Remains in the Yukon District of Canada and in Alaska." *The Quarterly Journal of the Geological Society of London*, Vol. L., February 1894.

"Five Pioneer Women of the Anglican Church in the Yukon." Yukon Diocesan Board, Women's Auxiliary, Anglican Church of Canada, Whitehorse, 1964.

"From the Youcon to London." *Church Missionary Gleaner*, Vol. I, 1874.

GARTRELL, GEORGE E. "The Work of the Churches in the Yukon During the Era of the Klondike Gold Rush." London, Canada: unpublished M.A. thesis, University of Western Ontario, April 1970.

GLAVE, E. J. "Our Alaska Expedition." *Frank Leslie's Illustrated Newspaper*, New York: April 12, 26; June 21, 28; July 5, 12, 19; August 9, 16; September 6; November 15, 22, 29; December 6, 13, 20, 27; all 1890; and January 3, 10, 1891.

―――. "Pioneer Packhorses in America." *The Century Illustrated Monthly Magazine*, Vol. XLIV, Nos. 5 and 6, September and October 1892.

HAYES, CHARLES WILLARD. "An Expedition Through the Yukon District." *The National Geographic Magazine*, Vol. IV, May 15, 1892.

HEMSTOCK, C. ANNE and GERALDINE A. COOK. *Yukon Bibliography, Update 1963-70*. Edmonton: Boreal Institute for Northern Studies, University of Alberta, January 1973.

HENDERSON, DANIEL. *From the Volga to the Yukon*. New York: Hastings House, 1944.

INNIS, HAROLD A. *The Fur Trade in Canada*. Toronto: University of Toronto Press, 1962.

ISBISTER, A. K. "Some Account of the Peel River, N. America." *Journal of the Royal Geographical Society*, Vol. XV, 1845, Part II.

JAMES, A. J. *The First Scientific Exploration of Russian America, and the Purchase of Alaska*. Evanston, Ill.: Northwestern University, 1942. (See also "Kennicott")

JENNESS, DIAMOND. *The Indians of Canada*. Ottawa: The Queen's Printer, 7th ed., 1967.

JUDGE, REV. CHARLES J. *An American Missionary, Rev. William H. Judge, S.J.* Maryknoll, N.Y.: Catholic Foreign Missionary Society of America, 1907.

KENNICOTT, ROBERT. "The Journal of Robert Kennicott, May 19, 1859 - January 20, 1862." In James, A. J. *The First Scientific Exploration of Russian America, and the Purchase of Alaska*. Evanston, Ill.: Northwestern University, 1942.

KITCHENER, L. D. *Flag Over the North*. Seattle, Wash.: Superior Publishing Company, 1954.

KRAUSE, AUREL. *The Tlingit Indians*. Tr. Erna Gunther. Seattle: University of Washington Press, paperback, 1970. The original edition of this work, entitled *Die Tlinkit-Indianer*, was published in Jena, Germany, in 1885.

LOTZ, J. P. *Yukon Bibliography*. Ottawa: Department of Northern Affairs and National Resources, May 1964.

MACBRIDE, WILLIAM D. "The Story of the Dalton Trail." *The Whitehorse Star*, February 14, 1966.

————. "Lieutenant Schwatka's Northern Expeditions." *The Whitehorse Star*, January 20, 1966.

MACDOUGALL, DIANE N. "Sourdough Thermometer." *The Yukon News*, August 16, 1973.

MACKAY, DOUGLAS. *The Honourable Company*. Toronto: McClelland & Stewart Limited, paperback, 1966.

MACKENZIE, ALEXANDER. "Journal of a Voyage Through the North-West Continent of America," in *Voyages From Montreal ... to the Frozen and Pacific Ocean*. New York: C. F. Hopkins, 1802.

MCCONNELL, R. G. "Extracts Relating to the Yukon District ... 1887-88," in Dawson, *Report on an Exploration in the Yukon District, N.W.T. ... 1887*. Ottawa: The Queen's Printer, re-issue of 1898.

MCGRATH, J. E. "The Boundary South of Fort Yukon," Part II of "The Alaskan Boundary Survey." *The National Geographic Magazine*, Vol. IV, February 8, 1893.

MCQUESTEN, LEROY N. *Recollections of Leroy N. McQuesten, Life in the Yukon 1871-1885*. Pamphlet, privately printed for Yukon Order of Pioneers, June 1952.

MURRAY, A. H. *Journal of the Yukon 1847-48*. Ed. L. J. Burpee. Ottawa: Government Printing Bureau, 1910.

NELSON, E.W. "Notes on Wild Fowl and Game Animals of Alaska." *The National Geographic Magazine*, Vol. IX, April 1898.

OGILVIE, WILLIAM. "Exploratory Survey from the Pelly-Yukon to Mackenzie River by Way of Tat-on-duc, Porcupine, Bell, Trout and Peel Rivers." *Dept. of the Interior Annual Report, 1889*, Part VIII, Section 3. Ottawa: Brown Chamberlin, 1890.

————. *Information Respecting the Yukon District*. Ottawa: Dept. of the Interior, Government Printing Office, 1897.

————. *Early Days on the Yukon & the Story of its Gold Finds*. Ottawa: Thorburn & Abbott, 1913.

PENLINGTON, NORMAN. *The Alaska Boundary Dispute: A Critical Reappraisal.* Toronto: McGraw-Hill Ryerson Limited, 1972.

PIKE, WARBURTON. *Through the Sub-Arctic Forest.* New York: Arno Press, reprint for the Abercrombie and Fitch Library, 1967. The original publication was in 1896.

RICKMAN, JOHN. *Journal of Captain Cook's Last Voyage to the Pacific Ocean.* Amsterdam: N. Israel, facsimile reprint, 1967.

RUSSELL, ISRAEL C. "A Journey up the Yukon River." *Journal of the American Geographical Society,* Vol. XXVII, No. 2, 1895.

SCHWATKA, FREDERICK. "The Expedition of the New York Times (1886)." *Century Magazine,* Vol. 41, 1889.

————. *A Summer in Alaska.* St. Louis, Mo.: J. W. Henry, 1894.

SETON-KARR, H. W. "Explorations in Alaska and North-west British Columbia." *Proceedings of the Royal Geographical Society,* February 1891.

SHERWOOD, MORGAN B. "Ardent Spirits: Hooch and the Osprey Affair at Sitka." *Journal of the West,* Vol. IV, No. 3, July 1965.

SHIPLEY, NAN. "Anne and Alexander Murray." *The Beaver,* Winter 1967.

SMITH, R. D. HILTON. *Northwestern Approaches; The First Century of Books.* Victoria, B.C.: The Adelphi Book Shop Ltd., 1969.

STEFANSSON, VILHJALMUR. "The Strange Fate of Thomas Simpson," in *Unsolved Mysteries of the Arctic.* New York: Collier Books, paperback, 1962.

TERO, RICHARD D. "E. J. Glave and the Alsek River." *The Alaska Journal,* Vol. 3, No. 3, Summer 1973.

"Tidings from the Yukon." *The Church Missionary Intelligencer,* May 1867.

TOMPKINS, STUART R. "After Bering: Mapping the North Pacific." *British Columbia Historical Quarterly,* Vol. XIX, Nos. 1 and 2, January-April 1955.

———— and MAX L. MOORHEAD. "Russia's Approach to America." *The British Columbia Historical Quarterly,* Vol. XIII, Nos. 2, 3, and 4, April, July-October 1949.

TURNER, J. HENRY. "The Boundary North of Fort Yukon," Part III of "The Alaskan Boundary Survey." *The National Geographic Magazine,* Vol. IV, February 8, 1893.

WALDEN, ARTHUR T. *A Dog-Puncher on the Yukon.* Boston and New York: Houghton Mifflin Company, 1931.

WAXELL, SVEN. *The Russian Expedition to America.* New York: Cromwell-Collier, paperback, 1962.

WHYMPER, FREDERICK. *Travels in America and on the Yukon*. New York: Harper & Brothers, 1869.

———. "Russian America or 'Alaska,' the Natives of the Youkon River and adjacent Country." *Transactions of the Ethnological Society of London*, Vol. 7, 1869.

WILSON, CLIFFORD. *Campbell of the Yukon*. Toronto: MacMillan of Canada, 1970.

WINSLOW- SPAGGE, LOIS. *Life and Letters of George Mercer Dawson 1849-1901*. Private printing, March 1962.

The Yukon Territory, its History and Resources. Ottawa: The Department of the Interior, Government Printing Bureau, 1909.

ZAGOSKIN, L. A. *Lieutenant Zagoskin's Travels in Russian America 1842-44*. Ed. Henry N. Michael for Arctic Institute of North America. Toronto: University of Toronto Press, 1967.

Index

McQuesten (McQuestion) LeRoy
Napoleon (Jack) 124-127
establishes his first trading post
on Yukon River, 130-133 activi-
ties in Yukon and Alaska, 137,
138, 139, 158, 160, 162, 194
meets with Ogilvie, 213, 215,
219, 246, 247, 250, 256, 265-266
establishes Circle City, 273, 285,
290, 292, 293
Miles Canyon 185, 192, 260, 264
Mikhailovsky Redoubt 17, 18, 20
(*See also* St. Michael's)
Miller (Miller's) Creek 262, 280,
282, 283
Mr. P. (Pambrun) 60, 63
Moore, William 138, 190, 191, 193,
267, 281
Moose-Skin Mountain 158
Moosomin, N.W.T. 257, 259, 265
Mount Michie 149
Mt. St. Elias 2, 222
Mud Lake 148
Murray, Alexander Hunter 50-58
establishes Fort Yukon, 59, 66
studies Indians, 68, 119, 201, 204
Murray, Anne (and Children) 52,
53, 57, 68

Nahani (Nahany, Na-Hone, etc.)
Indians 34, 198
Nah-Kina (Nakina) River 223
Narchilla 242
Nares Lake 147, 148, 187
Natche Kutchin Indians (Gens de
Large) 110
National Geographic Society 215,
222
Naylor, Rev. H. A. 279
Nelson, E. W. 273
Neska-Ta-Heen 230, 231, 233, 234,
235, 237, 239
New Racket 139
Nicolai, Chief (*See* Scolai, Chief)
Nisling River 224
Ni-Sutlin-Hi-Ni (Nisutlin River) 183
Nordenskiold River 154, 182, 183
North American Transportation and
Trading Company 256, 260,
264, 267
Northern Commercial Company 293
(*See also* Alaska Commercial
Company)

Northwest Company 16, 28, 43
North-West Mounted Police 247,
257, 258, 265, 268, 269
Northwest Passage 5, 6, 7
North-West Territories 124, 125,
169, 240, 261
Norton Sound 8, 9, 16, 17, 18, 42,
66, 96, 116
Norway House 44, 75, 76
Nowikakat 105, 106
Nuklukahyet 104, 159, 160, 161
Nulato (Fort) 19, 20, 23, 24, 96,
97, 99, 100, 101, 102, 103, 104,
110 111, 112, 113, 114, 161, 215,
256
Nulato River 18, 21, 58, 274

Ogilvie (trading post) 286
Ogilvie River 198
Ogilvie, William 125, 131, 163, 168-
170 participation in Yukon Expedition, 181, 182, 184, 186,
188-196 traverse of Yukon River
and establishment of boundary,
196-200 exploratory survey by
way of Tat-on-duc River, 201,
202, 206, 207, 209, 211-214
discusses problems of miners, 215,
248-251 description of Fortymile,
257, 263, 264, 266, 267, 269,
271-272 confirms location of
boundary on Yukon River, 277-
279 boundary surveys on Fortymile and Sixtymile, 283, 284,
285, 287-289 describes Carmack-
Henderson meeting, 291, 292,
293, 295, 299-300 goes to Dawson
City
Old Crow River 53
Osprey, H.M.S. 121, 134
Ottawa 166, 168, 196, 200, 208, 209,
211, 251, 255, 257, 258, 268, 270,
271, 279, 282, 298, 300
Overland Telegraph Company 93,
94, 95, 96, 102, 105, 110, 112,
171

Pavloff, Ivan 100, 101
Peace River 29, 91, 124, 125, 166,
167, 168, 192
Pease, Charles 94, 96, 97